Rights at Risk

Rights at Risk

THE LIMITS OF LIBERTY
IN MODERN AMERICA

David K. Shipler

Alfred A. Knopf · New York · 2012

THIS IS A BORZOI BOOK
PUBLISHED BY ALFRED A. KNOPF

Knopf, Borzoi Books, and the colophon are registered trademarks
of Random House, Inc.

Grateful acknowledgment is made to John E. Reid & Associates for permission
to reprint excerpts from various online Investigator Tips at http://www.reid.com/.
Reprinted by permission of John E. Reid & Associates.

Grateful acknowledgment is made to Vladimir Bukovsky for permission to reprint
excerpts from "Torture's Long Shadow," *Washington Post*, Outlook, Dec. 18, 2005.
Reprinted by permission of Vladimir Bukovsky.

Library of Congress Cataloging-in-Publication Data
Shipler, David K., date.
Rights at risk : the limits of liberty in modern America / David K. Shipler.
p.   cm.
Includes bibliographical references and index.
ISBN 978-0-307-59486-0
1. Civil rights—United States—History. 2. Liberty—United States. I. Title.
KF4749.S525 2012
342.7308'5—dc23   2011034754

Jacket photograph by tk
Jacket design by tk

Manufactured in the United States of America
First Edition

For Madison, Ethan, Benjamin, Kalpana, Dylan,
and those of their generation yet to come

In a free society, some are guilty, but all are responsible.

—*Abraham Joshua Heschel*

CONTENTS

THE BILL OF RIGHTS

FIRST AMENDMENT

Congress shall make no law respecting an establishment of religion, or prohibiting the free exercise thereof; or abridging the freedom of speech, or of the press; or the right of the people peaceably to assemble, and to petition the Government for a redress of grievances.

SECOND AMENDMENT

A well regulated Militia, being necessary to the security of a free State, the right of the people to keep and bear Arms, shall not be infringed.

THIRD AMENDMENT

No Soldier shall, in time of peace be quartered in any house, without the consent of the Owner, nor in time of war, but in a manner to be prescribed by law.

FOURTH AMENDMENT

The right of the people to be secure in their persons, houses, papers, and effects, against unreasonable searches and seizures, shall not be violated, and no Warrants shall issue, but upon probable cause, supported by Oath or affirmation, and particularly describing the place to be searched, and the persons or things to be seized.

FIFTH AMENDMENT

No person shall be held to answer for a capital, or otherwise infamous crime, unless on a presentment or indictment of a Grand Jury, except in cases arising in the land or naval forces, or in the Militia, when in actual service in time of War or public danger; nor shall any person be subject for the same offence to be twice put in jeopardy of life or limb; nor shall be compelled in any criminal case to be a witness against himself, nor be deprived of life, liberty, or property, without due process of law; nor shall private property be taken for public use, without just compensation.

SIXTH AMENDMENT

In all criminal prosecutions, the accused shall enjoy the right to a speedy and public trial, by an impartial jury of the State and district wherein the crime shall have been committed, which district shall have been previously ascertained by law, and to be informed of the nature and cause of the accusation; to be confronted with the witnesses against him; to have compulsory process for obtaining witnesses in his favor, and to have the Assistance of Counsel for his defence.

SEVENTH AMENDMENT

In Suits at common law, where the value in controversy shall exceed twenty dollars, the right of trial by jury shall be preserved, and no fact tried by a jury, shall be otherwise re-examined in any Court of the United States, than according to the rules of the common law.

EIGHTH AMENDMENT

Excessive bail shall not be required, nor excessive fines imposed, nor cruel and unusual punishments inflicted.

NINTH AMENDMENT

The enumeration in the Constitution, of certain rights, shall not be construed to deny or disparage others retained by the people.

TENTH AMENDMENT

The powers not delegated to the United States by the Constitution, nor prohibited by it to the States, are reserved to the States respectively, or to the people.

PREFACE

The people in these pages stand where the Bill of Rights meets everyday America, from the courtroom to the classroom. They benefit when the Constitution is upheld and suffer when it is evaded. Most of their names will not be familiar, because these citizens and aspiring citizens are typically violated invisibly, well below the radar of public attention. For many of them, losing their rights may be tragically momentous, but few of their cases are landmarks. They shape the constitutional culture imperceptibly, accumulating only gradually into trends and patterns. My task here is to throw light on those shifting patterns of liberty.

This book may lead readers to their own verdicts on the guilt or innocence not only of criminal defendants but also of those who interrogate and prosecute them, and even represent them. Wherever a person's freedom is balanced on a fine edge, the state itself may be culpable or virtuous. In the ranks of the guilty and the innocent there stand not only immigrants but also officials who deport them, not only political protesters but also police who arrest them, not only dissenting schoolchildren but also principals who suspend them for their speech.

I have tried here to portray the law in human terms and to see the human stories in the context of the law. I am not an attorney, so I owe much to the generosity of defense lawyers, prosecutors, and judges who taught me what they could about the Constitution, the courts, and the law. They answered myriad questions, provided volumes of documents, and made themselves available for multiple consultations. Those who deserve thanks beyond what I could offer in the text are named here.

David Tatel, a friend and federal appeals court judge, put me in touch with well-informed judges and lawyers, educated me on the law and the

Constitution, and made helpful suggestions on drafts of chapters. A. J. Kramer, the federal public defender in Washington, D.C., gave me an office and weeks of access to his team of skilled attorneys, who discussed cases, took me to hearings and trials, and helped me see firsthand the elements of the Bill of Rights most seriously at risk. Kramer provided feedback and fact-checking on parts of the manuscript.

The assistant public defenders Tony Axam, David Bos, Beverly Dyer, Neil Jaffee, Jonathan Jeffress, Tony Miles, Shawn Moore, Michelle Peterson, Mary Petras, Lara Quint, Gregory Spencer, Robert Tucker, and Carlos Vanegas were immensely generous in guiding me through the complexities of criminal law. Other helpful defense attorneys included Whitney Boise, James Brosnahan, Frank Dunham, Richard Foxall, Steve Kalar, Larry Kupers, Bob Luskin, Jerome Matthews, James McCollum, Andrew Patel, Gregory L. Poe, Barry Portman, Jay Rorty, Elden Rosenthal, Bryan Stevenson, Marc Sussman, and Kristen Winemiller. William B. Wiegand, an assistant U.S. attorney, expertly answered legal questions about asset forfeiture and other issues, making me the beneficiary of his precise thinking and extensive knowledge. Most prosecutors and some judges preferred anonymity, so my gratitude to them has to remain private.

Anthony Lewis and David Cole offered initial orientation on key issues. Ann Beeson, Jameel Jaffer, Joe Onek, Judge Scott Vowell, and James Woodford helped with contacts, cases, and insights, as did many others who are cited in the book. Alan Hirsch, an expert on confessions, read several chapters and offered useful critiques.

I was assisted and advised on immigration issues by Adem Carroll, Mary Holper, Sin Yen Ling, Bryan Lonegan, Rachel Meeropol, Tram Nguyen, Debi Sanders, Paromita Shah, Nicole Siegel, and Jesse Wing, among others. Adem Carroll kept me abreast of developments and helped arrange interviews with immigrants in New York and overseas. Debi Sanders invited me to accompany her group of pro bono lawyers on prison visits. In multiple conversations, Mary Holper and Paromita Shah explained the law's intricacies and read a draft of the immigration chapter, providing comments and corrections. Lisa Faeth spent many hours offering documents, notes, and explanations about the case of her friend Waheeda Tehseen.

My analyses and viewpoints are my own, however. None of those who provided insights and contacts should be seen as endorsing what I have written, with which they may or may not agree.

I made extensive use of government documents obtained by the American Civil Liberties Union (ACLU) under the Freedom of Information Act and various lawsuits; the documents were valuable in assembling an account of police surveillance of protest groups before the 2004 Republican convention in New York. The ACLU, the Cato Institute, the Constitution Project, and the First Amendment Center were important sources on cases under litigation. My friend David Burnham gave me data on immigration enforcement through TRAC, the Transactional Records Access Clearinghouse, which analyzes digital information from government agencies. John Conroy's investigations published in the *Chicago Reader* were indispensable in recounting cases of torture by the Chicago police. Among the books I found most useful in understanding the development of case law on various issues were David M. O'Brien's *Constitutional Law and Politics* and Geoffrey R. Stone's *Perilous Times*. Jane Mayer's incisive reporting in her book *The Dark Side* provided details on torture by the United States.

I owe gratitude to others for a few titles and for one phrase. I first heard the line "the power to listen," which appears in Chapter Seven, from a young Rwandan woman who had seen her father slaughtered and then spent many years gathering the strength to facilitate trauma-healing workshops. She described herself as finally attaining the power to listen. The title of the Introduction, "The Insolence of Office," comes from Shakespeare, *Hamlet,* act 3, scene 1. The title of Chapter Five, "Below the Law," was written by my daughter, Laura Shipler Chico, to name a case in her book, *Assisting Survivors of Human Trafficking: Multicultural Case Studies*.

All people in this book are real. I deplore the creation of composite characters, so there are none here. All who were willing are identified. The notes at the end of the book that go significantly beyond simple sourcing in their explanations of the law or their descriptions of the cases are indicated by underlined superscripts in the text.

Esther Newberg, my agent, and Jonathan Segal, my editor, have been enthusiastic and loyal supporters during the many years of research and writing. Lydia Buechler at Knopf has expertly overseen the meticulous copyediting. My son Michael Shipler and my wife, Debby Shipler, read the manuscript perceptively and improved it with their critical and candid suggestions.

The epigraph at the beginning of this book was written by Abraham Joshua Heschel as an indictment of the entrenched system of racial segregation against which he marched with Martin Luther King Jr. Yet the words rise majestically above the particular, calling everyone to duty.

Rights at Risk

The Insolence of Office

> Society in every state is a blessing, but Government, even in its best state, is but a necessary evil; in its worst state, an intolerable one.
>
> —Thomas Paine, *Common Sense*, 1776

ON JULY 11, 1787, as the Constitutional Convention debated how to determine apportionment in the House of Representatives, James Madison spiced up a dense discussion with several pointed warnings about governmental authority. The question was whether to trust the House itself or to impose the constitutional requirement of an impartial census every decade. "All men having power ought to be distrusted to a certain degree," Madison declared. He spoke of "the political depravity of men, and the necessity of checking one vice and interest by opposing to them another vice & interest."[1]*

In the end, the census was chosen to deny House members control over the composition of their own body. It was one of many precautions that have come down to us in the Constitution's separation of powers and in the Bill of Rights, whose provisions were designed to restrain government from trampling on people's liberties.

Yet people remain vulnerable. They do not play on a level field against a potent executive branch. Their constitutional rights are routinely overwhelmed, largely out of sight in criminal courts, where few citizens go to watch; in police interrogation rooms, where the public is not allowed; in the closed offices of prosecutors and immigration bureaucrats; and in schools whose authorities show the next generations of Americans that elements of the Bill of Rights can be suspended, evaded, or ignored. This does not happen everywhere all the time, but often enough to damage the constitutional culture. On their way to jail, to deportation from the country, or to expul-

---

* Underlined note numbers indicate that significant information beyond sourcing can be found in the corresponding notes at the end of this book.

3

sion from school, those who confront the muscle of the state frequently see their rights bruised, their liberties wounded. This book is about some of those people. Therefore, it is about all of us.

When compared with other high-income countries, the United States does poorly in limiting governmental powers—only ninth in a field of eleven selected by the World Justice Project for its Rule of Law Index—behind Sweden, the Netherlands, Australia, Austria, Japan, Canada, Spain, and France. Among seven countries of Western Europe and North America, the United States is ranked last.[2]

This seems surprising, since the framers were intensely wary as they created a federal government. With the excesses of British colonialism fresh in their minds, they hobbled the new regime with checks and balances among three branches and circumscribed it with the venerable right of habeas corpus, which allows anyone arrested the right to summon his jailer to court to justify the imprisonment. That was enough to forestall arbitrary rule, the convention delegates believed, and they wrote the Constitution on the assumption that government would have no power that was not expressly given by the people.

That was not enough for the states, which demanded more specific guarantees as the price of ratification. Protections were then provided in the first ten amendments, the Bill of Rights, which spelled out liberties that government could not invade. These were not purely American inventions. The framers were reviving traditional principles in English law that they had seen abandoned by the British crown, so they drew from the Magna Carta of 1215, the 1689 English Bill of Rights, and the unwritten body of rules and precepts known as English common law.[3]

The end result displayed three salient characteristics. First, it was concise and broadly worded, avoiding the long-winded specifics typical of other constitutions. When there are intricate details, a right not listed may be taken as a right denied. Instead, the framers found strength in brevity, which keeps the Constitution alive by allowing each generation room to reconsider limits on governmental behavior, to reinterpret the meanings of "unreasonable searches," "cruel and unusual punishments," "probable cause," and other key concepts. As Chief Justice John Marshall declared in 1819, the Constitution was "intended to endure for ages to come, and consequently to be adapted to the various crises of human affairs."[4]

Second, unlike the constitutions of many other nations, ours does not bestow rights but recognizes rights that we already possess. Any doubt on this point is snuffed out by the Ninth Amendment, which states explicitly that the enumeration of rights does not "deny or disparage others retained by the people." Key sections dictate what government may not do: "Congress shall make no law," begins the First Amendment. "The right of the people . . . shall not be violated," states the Fourth. "No person shall be held," begins the Fifth, continuing in a string of negatives. The negatives, the proscriptions against government, are the most potent protections.

Third, all the obstacles to overweening authority are built into the brick and mortar of the Constitution so that individual liberty does not depend on the goodwill of particular officials. Madison and others, understanding the universality of human foibles, made sure that protections were lodged deeply within the system itself. They erected interlocking barriers to autocracy, one right relying on the others so that none thrives without reinforcement by the rest. As a result, critical provisions of the Bill of Rights, stitched together to get the Constitution ratified, function more coherently than their fractious political origins might have predicted. Government cannot be held accountable without the guarantee of freedom of speech and the press in the First Amendment. Justice cannot be served unless upheld by the Fifth Amendment's requirement that no one "be deprived of life, liberty, or property, without due process of law," which cannot be effected without the ingredients of that "due process" that are specified in the Sixth Amendment: the rights to counsel, to public and speedy trial by jury, to confront and summon witnesses.

The American experience has been a long struggle to live up to the Constitution. Periodically reversed, the effort was set back most recently after al-Qaeda hijackers flew airliners into the World Trade Center and the Pentagon on September 11, 2001. The latest deviations from constitutional principles could be counted as the sixth time in its history that the country had lost its way, detours that began in the earliest years.

First, a virtual naval war with France brought the Alien and Sedition Acts of 1798, under which foreigners could be arrested and deported without due process and citizens could be jailed for speaking and writing against the government. Then came the suppression of speech during the Civil War and Lincoln's suspension of habeas corpus. World War I brought the 1917 Espionage Act and the 1918 Sedition Act, facilitating the prosecution of thousands of labor leaders, socialists, and anarchists who demonstrated for workers' rights or dared to oppose entry into the war. World War II saw the internment of 120,000 ethnic Japanese, 80,000 of them American citizens, and the passage of the 1940 Smith Act to prosecute communists and fascists. The fifth departure, during the Cold War, was marked by the witch hunt of supposed communists and the secret surveillance of antiwar, civil rights, and other dissenting groups. The clandestine monitoring ran well into the 1970s.[5]

The spasm of fear that coursed through government after 9/11, when officials worried acutely about other imminent attacks, sent the United States well beyond the rule of law. "Don't let this happen again," President George W. Bush told Attorney General John Ashcroft, and so the FBI was instructed to follow every phone call and e-mailed tip, no matter how thin. In the manner of the 1919 Palmer Raids that had seized thousands of supposed anarchists after a series of bombings (one on the porch of Attorney General A. Mitchell Palmer), the 2001 Ashcroft Sweeps rounded up at least 1,182 Muslim residents of the United States. They were jailed on suspected immigration violations, sometimes brutalized by guards, and released or deported only after months of FBI and CIA investigation. None was linked to terrorism. Another 6,000 Muslims who had ignored deportation orders were targeted for arrest and removal, and male citizens from twenty-five predominantly Muslim countries were ordered to register in person at immigration offices. Those found to be out of status were immediately taken into custody. This drove many illegal aliens, Pakistanis in particular, to flee north seeking asylum in Canada.

Several end runs were made around the Constitution. Two key tools were used to dodge the Fourth Amendment, which recognizes the "right of the people to be secure" against searches unless there is probable cause to believe that evidence of a crime will be discovered. The first evasion came with little debate, when a panicked Congress passed the Patriot Act, a collection of amendments to various long-standing privacy statutes. The major revisions loosened the 1978 Foreign Intelligence Surveillance Act (FISA), which had imposed limitations on domestic surveillance after the abuses during the Cold War.

When enacted, FISA allowed a secret court to issue clandestine orders for wiretapping, bugging, and covert searches of homes and offices only for "the purpose" of intelligence gathering, usually to catch spies or to spy on foreign governments. Under the Patriot Act's revision in 2001, "the purpose" was changed to "a significant purpose," which diluted the intelligence prerequisite and enabled the monitoring in ordinary criminal investigations, which were supposed to be governed by the Fourth Amendment's warrant requirements. This opened the door to secret surveillance whenever an American or other U.S. resident was suspected of contacts with a foreign power or an international terrorist organization. No probable cause of criminal activity had to be demonstrated, so fishing expeditions and extensive domestic spying were legalized, and the evidence was used in criminal prosecutions unrelated to terrorism. The Fourth Amendment, already damaged by permissive court rulings on vehicle searches and other everyday police work, began to look more like a quaint curiosity than a centerpiece of liberty.

The second tool of evasion was employed entirely in secret, for a time. Without consulting Congress or the Foreign Intelligence Surveillance Court, Bush unilaterally ordered the National Security Agency to scoop up vast amounts of electronic data, from phone conversations to e-mails, and filter them for key words and phrases to track contacts among suspected terrorists. Agency officials conceded that journalists, humanitarian workers, and others were also monitored as "eyes on the ground" for whatever they might report about the countries where they worked. Interceptions were formally permitted only where at least one party was outside the United States, but purely domestic communications were also being intercepted, according to telecommunications company employees and government officials. Despite a burst of outrage when the program's existence was first disclosed by James Risen and Erich Lichtblau in *The New York Times,* Congress later legalized it by amending the law to provide general, minimal oversight by FISA judges while severely restricting their authority to rule against the data collection. Since the targets never knew who they were (except for one—a Muslim charity whose identity was accidentally disclosed), they could never go to court to challenge the basis of a surveillance order. This transfer of power to the executive branch has remained part of the damaging legacy of 9/11.

Bush also evaded the provisions of the Fifth and Sixth Amendments by deciding, without legislative or judicial approval, to designate two Americans and one legal foreign resident in the United States "enemy combatants" who could be held indefinitely in military custody inside the country, without lawyers, charges, or trials. They were questioned and coerced as the administration tried to block their access to the courts. As the courts began to grant their attorneys' petitions for writs of habeas corpus, the government capitulated, transferring them one by one from military custody. Two were prosecuted in the civilian justice system, and one—a dual Saudi-American citizen—renounced his U.S. citizenship in exchange for being released to live in Saudi Arabia.[6]

The government attempted similar measures against terrorism suspects imprisoned at the U.S. naval base in Guantánamo Bay, Cuba, labeling them enemy combatants and then unilaterally creating military tribunals that would have heard their cases under biased conditions—by giving the prisoners minimal rights to summon witnesses, present evidence, or suppress statements that had been extracted by torture at one of the CIA's "black sites" in various foreign countries. The scheme ran afoul of the Supreme Court, which first recognized the prisoners' right of access to the civilian courts through habeas corpus and then required that some reliable fact-finding process determine whether they were rightfully held. The legislative branch finally acted, but again to legalize unconstitutional proceedings. The Republican-led Congress enacted into law military commissions that could try cases of foreign "enemy combatants" seized anywhere, including inside the United States. Unlike civilian courts or courts-martial, however, the military commissions could admit into evidence statements extracted by abuse and material seized in violation of the Fourth Amendment, whether done in Iraq or Indiana. The rules were tightened after Barack Obama became president, when the Democratic-led Congress amended the commissions act to exclude evidence from illegal searches or coerced interrogations, except that statements made under duress during combat or immediately after capture could be admitted.[7]

Enhancing prisoners' rights to put on a defense gave the military commissions a better chance of assessing the truth of the government's allegations. Yet they were still military commissions, which meant that they operated wholly within the executive branch, with no role by the judiciary except on appeal, when a federal court in the D.C. Circuit could reexamine a case and reverse a commission verdict. This, too, has left excessive power in executive hands.

These dramatic constitutional violations are not unique to counterterrorism. They have less extreme parallels in the ordinary workings of the criminal justice process and in the administrative detention apparatus of the immigration system. Prisoners have been tortured not only by the CIA but also by the Chicago Police Department. Confessions have been falsified not only by suspected terrorists in military hands but also by suspected murderers in civilian custody. Not only were inmates in Guantánamo Bay initially denied attorneys, but so are legal immigrants who cannot afford lawyers to defend them against deportation, and impoverished Americans in certain parts of the country are assigned inadequate counsel in state courts. The executive branch avoids trials not only for many enemy combatants but also in nearly all criminal prosecutions, where defendants are induced and threatened into guilty pleas, at both federal and state levels. Not only in counterterrorism has the executive accumulated extensive powers. Laws on sentencing, probation, and the forfeiture of property have shifted enormous authority to police and prosecutors, at the expense of the judiciary as well as the accused.

This is the second volume of a journey through America's landscape of civil liberties. The first, *The Rights of the People,* concentrated on the Fourth Amendment's guarantee against unreasonable search—the right weakened most severely by the "wars" being waged on drugs, on street crime, and on terrorism. It also surveyed the country's historical departures from constitutional principles leading to the post-9/11 violations in pursuit of suspected terrorists.

This book now travels through adjacent territory, exploring the impact of government's intrusive shortcuts across rights that are critical in promoting accuracy in the criminal justice system, restricting executive power over individuals, and preserving the freewheeling debate essential in a constitutional democracy. When the state trespasses on this ground, it tampers with the country's safety in unexpected ways. While the society takes risks when rights are observed—that a suspect will not talk, that a search cannot be done, that unconstitutionally obtained evidence will be excluded from trial—other risks arise from noncompliance: A sloppy investigation jails the innocent while the guilty remains at large. The police waste precious resources on useless intelligence gathering and frivolous arrests. The criminal courts act less as impartial adjudicators than as conveyor belts from street to prison, in a system that some disillusioned participants have nicknamed McJustice.

Contrary to a popular impression that police work is impeded by individual rights—to silence, to an attorney—the discipline imposed by these liberties actually makes investigators smart, helping to solve crimes reliably by requiring professionalism and precision in collecting valid evidence. The first duty of the criminal justice system is to discover the truth, after all. This seems obvious, yet it sometimes gets forgotten in the tussles over interrogating prisoners, inducing them to confess, and compromising their right to have lawyers who will force police and prosecutors to prove the case against them. The Fifth and Sixth Amendments empower defendants to scrutinize and contest the charges. Without that fairness, actual guilt or innocence cannot be determined correctly, and punishment, if warranted, cannot be justly administered.

Curtailing the rights of the accused, then, as many security-minded Americans would like, undermines security interests by making the fact-finding mission less effective. Once the rights lose their vitality, police work grows lazy and prone to error.

The discerning reader may notice that most of the victims in these pages are black, Hispanic, Muslim, or members of other minorities—most, but not all. Many are criminals, terrorists, or misfits—many, but not all. They are often guilty—often, but not always. They get little sympathy from the larger, law-abiding citizenry. But they should, for if a retarded man is abused during police interrogation, if a poor woman is denied a competent lawyer, if a dissenting student is punished for the slogan on her T-shirt, the rights they lose are lost to everyone.

Most Americans cannot imagine themselves in such circumstances, and so they have trouble identifying with people who are there. Few in the right-wing Tea Party movement who railed against big government mentioned its intrusions on civil liberties. The invasion of constitutional rights after 9/11 merited no question from reporters during the presidential debates, and candidates generally don't bring it up on the campaign trail. Voters seem mostly indifferent.

This is unhealthy. In the American constitutional system as a rule, rights are not defended in court until they are violated, and they are not violated until government targets someone as suspicious, dangerous, or disruptive. How the system treats those under suspicion is a moral issue and a legal question, but if those aren't reasons enough for close attention by mainstream Americans, then self-interest ought to be. The fact is, the rights of the upstanding citizen are no different from the crook's. When the courts interpret the Constitution and place limits on the police, the precedents accumulate into a body of case law that applies to the honorable as well as the criminal. When the courts use their power of judicial review to strike down laws that violate constitutional rights, everyone's rights are protected. In an odd twist, therefore, the virtuous and the conformist rely on the nefarious and the radical to mount challenges when authorities step on rights that belong to them all. Ernesto A. Miranda, as a telling example, kidnapped and raped a mentally defective teenager, yet his victory in the Supreme Court over coerced interrogation has made police departments more humane throughout the land. The Constitution binds us together. Liberty is not divisible, and neither is its violation.

The legal and personal stories addressed here are parts of that whole, woven together by a theme of long-standing concern in American history: government's authority to infiltrate personal liberty. A common denominator in containing state power is the freedom to seek and speak the truth, both in the courtroom and in the public square, where the din of ideas keeps society open, supple, and responsive. There is no neat division between robust speech and robust criminal defense, for the Bill of Rights safeguards adversarial argument both in matters of high policy and in the everyday process of criminal justice. The Constitution protects both the right to silence and the right to speech.

This book begins at the right to silence and moves along a continuum to freedom of speech. A keystone in the integrity of criminal procedure, the right against self-incrimination, holds that no person "shall be compelled in any criminal case to be a witness against himself," in the words of the Fifth Amendment. As in every legal right, the origin of this one lies in its violation, in this case an ancient history scarred by torture. The machinery of torment provoked the guarantee in the Magna Carta of 1215: "In future, no official shall place a man on trial upon his own unsupported statement, without producing credible witnesses to the truth of it." The pledge has not always been fulfilled.

The first two chapters consider violations by the United States. Chapter One, "Torture and Torment," compares abuses inflicted on black prisoners by Chicago police and on Muslim prisoners by the Central Intelligence Agency. It traces the origin of the Miranda warning ("You have the right to remain silent . . .") and follows the routes of forced confessions from foreign prisons into American courtrooms. Chapter Two, "Confessing Falsely," describes legally approved interrogation techniques that have elicited phony confessions from innocent Americans inside the United States.

The third chapter, "The Assistance of Counsel," examines the reality beneath the Sixth Amendment's exalted requirement that every criminal defendant have the right to an attorney, a right insufficiently protected in certain parts of the country. The amendment's other provisions—the rights to a speedy jury trial, to know "the nature and cause of the accusation," and to call and cross-examine witnesses—have all been ignored in some of the most notorious counterterrorism actions since September 11, 2001. Those violations, which have corrupted the fact-finding process with special drama, also occur somewhat less severely in the everyday prosecution of street crime.

In other aspects of the criminal justice system, enhanced executive powers have unbalanced the ingenious checks and balances envisioned by the framers. People can be locked up largely at the will of officials whose business of investigating, charging, and fashioning punishments is dominated by the executive branch, where policies and practices of law enforcement agents and government prosecutors hold overwhelming influence. The legislative and judicial branches have yielded substantial authority.

This has been true not just in counterterrorism, where the Bush administration sought unchecked power for the president and his departments, but also in ordinary criminal procedure and immigration enforcement. Chapter Four, "The Tilted Playing Field," assesses the decisive leverage granted to the prosecutor through coercive plea bargains and sentencing guidelines that avoid jury trials and limit judges' discretion. The chapter also portrays the extraordinary power of the executive to jail men and women who are on probation, even without proving a violation beyond a reasonable doubt, and to seize cash and other assets without any evidence of a crime.

Chapter Five, "Below the Law," describes the life-altering penalty of deportation imposed on legal immigrants convicted of crimes, even minor offenses years earlier that brought little or no jail time. Imprisoned as they await their "removal," they are entirely in the hands of the executive branch, whose immigration agents arrest them, whose immigration agency keeps them behind bars, and whose administrative judges decide their fates. Unlike criminal defendants, those in the immigration system are held under civil law that leaves them beyond the reach of many constitutional protections.

The final chapters report on an American paradox: the raucous debate alongside the state's incursions into the right of free speech even as the First Amendment shield is often breached in times of war. Chapter Six, "Silence and Its Opposite," covers verbal and symbolic expression by immigrants, accused terrorists, and ordinary citizens who run afoul of police and prosecutors, illustrating how law enforcement sometimes violates the Supreme Court's First Amendment rulings. It is not always easy to implant high court opinions on speech rights into the lowly grass roots of America. Chapter Seven, "A Redress of Grievances," reports on street demonstrations by dissenting groups that are intrusively monitored and sometimes thwarted by authorities. Chapter Eight, "Inside the Schoolhouse Gate," focuses on high schools and colleges, where First Amendment rights are often violated and education in the principle of free speech is often absent. The chapter is essentially about the future, for as young citizens grow up seeing their civil liberties restricted or ignored, their adult citizenship may be impaired. "When we are planning for posterity," wrote Thomas Paine, "we ought to remember that virtue is not hereditary."[8]

The American experiment has succeeded so far because of the capacity for self-correction, that vital quality of a decent society. We correct by bringing problems into the light. We correct by electing new leaders and legislators.

We correct by striking down unjust laws, by protecting minority interests against majority abuse, by empowering the powerless, by ensuring that the humble may stand tall before the awesome authority of the state. These are not just wishful ideals; they are principles of the Constitution, whose mechanism of self-correction is a lasting gift, if we keep it faithfully.

CHAPTER ONE

Torture and Torment

I plead guilty to having rated the question of guilt and innocence higher than that of utility and harmfulness. Finally, I
plead guilty to having placed the idea of man above the idea
of mankind.

—Rubashov, in *Darkness at Noon*

BODY AND MIND

ANDREW WILSON and Khalid Sheikh Mohammed had two things in
common: they were killers, and they were tortured by Americans using
near suffocation—Wilson by Chicago police officers in 1982, Mohammed
by CIA officers twenty-one years later.

Wilson had shot two Chicago cops during a traffic stop. Mohammed
had masterminded the attacks of September 11, 2001. In the Chicago police
station at Ninety-first Street and Cottage Grove Avenue, a plastic bag was
placed over Wilson's head; he could barely breathe. At a secret CIA prison,
possibly in Poland, Mohammed was "waterboarded"—strapped to a gurney
with his head tilted down, while water was poured into a cloth covering his
nose and mouth to create the sensation of drowning; he struggled in panic,
writhing against the restraints and injuring his wrists and ankles.[1]

Other techniques were applied in a coercive combination, and experts
know that it is the combination, not just the individual methods, that works
its will. Chicago detectives gave Wilson electric shocks to his gums, lips,
nose, and genitals. They burned him, first with a cigarette and then by
stretching him, handcuffed, across a hot radiator. CIA interrogators shackled Mohammed to the ceiling by his arms so that he couldn't sleep for days.
For a month they kept him naked, exposing him to female personnel as a
tactic of degradation.

Wilson was kicked, slapped, punched, and bloodied by several officers
to the point where guards refused to accept him in the lockup, forcing
his police escorts to take him to the hospital. Mohammed was underfed,
beaten, chilled in cold cells, stifled in hot cells, and slammed into walls to

the point where CIA headquarters interrupted the "questioning." He would not be allowed to die, Mohammed was told by an American, but would be taken to the "verge of death and back again."[2]

The United States has lost its way a few times during its history, most recently in the era of modern terrorism. As the abuse in Chicago shows, however, the post-9/11 violations are not unprecedented. They are variations on old themes, always in the name of protecting the nation or the neighborhood against some threat, internal or external. These measures, these shortcuts across the Constitution, form a spectrum of paradoxes, bringing more danger than safety. They are designed to produce investigative accuracy and security, against both common crime and terrorist plots, but they often do the opposite. They generate error, jeopardize the country's morality, undermine its rule of law, and put everyone at risk. Torture, one of many shortcuts, stands at the extreme end of that spectrum.

The interrogations of Andrew Wilson and Khalid Sheikh Mohammed had different objectives: the contrast between the past and the future. Wilson was questioned about what he had already done, Mohammed about what his cohorts were planning to do. The rules were not the same for gathering evidence inside the United States and gathering intelligence outside, for prosecuting a criminal case and for preventing the next act of terrorism. Yet the questioners actually used similar techniques, and nothing new in the annals of torture.

They created not only physical suffering but psychological torment. "Coercion can be mental as well as physical," the Supreme Court had noted back in 1960. "The blood of the accused is not the only hallmark of an unconstitutional inquisition."[3] Humiliation, disorientation, and helplessness descended on both men until they talked. Wilson admitted to the murders, which his lawyers later conceded he had committed. Mohammed expressed pride in arranging for 9/11 and added considerable information about al-Qaeda.

To end the torture, however, Mohammed mixed fact and fiction together. On the factual side, he reportedly named multiple names, leading agents to capture Riduan Isamuddin, a.k.a. Hambali, head of the South Asian movement Jemaah Islamiyah, which had killed over two hundred people in a Bali nightclub bombing and (according to President George W. Bush) planned to fly a hijacked airliner into the Library Tower in Los Angeles.[4] Former Vice President Dick Cheney insisted repeatedly that the "enhanced interrogation techniques" had generated valuable intelligence, which he urged be declassified to prove his point.

Yet Mohammed's tales of his own grandeur began to sow skepticism among CIA officials. They came to doubt his boasts of laying plans to assassinate former presidents Carter and Clinton and Pope John Paul II, for example, and his claims to have personally beheaded Daniel Pearl, a *Wall Street Journal* reporter, in Pakistan. Agents understood Mohammed as an organizer who killed only by remote control, never staining his hands with the blood of his victims. "Although few outside of the CIA knew it, Mohammed had recanted substantial portions of his initial confessions," writes Jane Mayer in *The Dark Side*.[5]

Later, when the torture had ended, he bragged to the International Committee of the Red Cross that he had filled his sessions with fantasies. "During the harshest period of my interrogation," he said, "I gave a lot of false information in order to satisfy what I believed the interrogators wished to hear in order to make the ill-treatment stop. I later told interrogators that their methods were stupid and counterproductive. I'm sure that the false information I was forced to invent in order to make the ill-treatment stop wasted a lot of their time and led to several false red-alerts being placed in the United States."[6] But CIA officials also claimed that after being water-boarded 183 times, he provided useful and accurate information on al-Qaeda, leading to at least five arrests (including that of an Ohio truck driver planning fancifully to bring down the Brooklyn Bridge with blowtorches).[7] In his memoir, Bush wrote that he had personally approved waterboarding, and former officials in his administration claimed—without offering any evidence—that "enhanced interrogation" had extracted the pseudonym of a courier (supposedly a protégé of Mohammed) who was then followed to Osama bin Laden's hideout in Pakistan, where an American squad killed him in 2011. Rough questioning of a Guantánamo prisoner "provided a crucial description of the courier," *The New York Times* was told by officials, but waterboarding didn't get the information. In fact, officials said that Mohammed had given misleading information about the man.[8]

There are layers of lessons in the cases of Wilson and Mohammed, the African-American with the Chicago police and the Pakistani Muslim with the CIA. First, torture generates truth, and torture generates lies, and it is nearly impossible to tell the difference. In the repugnant debate following 9/11 over whether torture is ever acceptable, proponents argue that it can loosen tongues and provide critical information to defuse the ticking bomb—a hypothetical scenario not yet witnessed, as far as we know, anywhere at any time.

Second, "our most deeply held values," cited by President Barack Obama after ending the CIA's torture regime, turn out to be shallow, held by only half of Americans, who split down the middle on torture, 49 percent pro to 47 percent con, in a sample polled by the Pew Research Center. And this came not in a fury of fear but in 2009, after a long, quiet, eight-year hiatus from domestic terrorism. Completing the statement "Torture to gain important information from suspected terrorists is justified _____," 15 percent said "often," 34 percent said "sometimes," 22 percent said "rarely," and merely 25 percent said "never."[9] Two out of three Republicans approved of torture, compared with just over one-third of Democrats. A high school teacher near Seattle, Katie Piper, said in 2010 that for most of her advanced-placement government students, the legitimacy of torture, once a closed question, had become "open," a topic for consideration.

When supporters claim that torture works, opponents reply that it doesn't, the utilitarian argument. This conversation, once unthinkable in America, has been dragged down from an ethical plane to a low dispute about pragmatism, where the answer to the tough guys has to be equally tough-minded and self-interested: Coercion creates false confessions and false intelligence, sending the wrong people to prison and deploying soldiers and agents on phony leads. Softer, rapport-building sessions are more effective.

Opponents might just declare torture immoral and leave it there, but they don't have the luxury of principle. They might offer their own hypothetical scenario, posed by Michael Sandel: "Suppose the only way to induce the terrorist suspect to talk is to torture his young daughter (who has no knowledge of her father's nefarious activities). Would it be morally permissible to do so?" Shifting the abuse from the presumably guilty suspect to the innocent child "offers a truer test of the utilitarian principle."[10] It would be interesting to hear Cheney's response.

An example of the pitfalls of pragmatism emerged in the interrogation of an al-Qaeda operative, Abu Zubaydah, who apparently told all that he knew before the abuse began. Another case produced an imaginary tale that gave Bush officials a rationale for the Iraq war, Jane Mayer writes, when Egyptians torturing a captive got him to fabricate a story about three al-Qaeda operatives "going to Iraq to learn about nuclear weapons."[11]

Professional interrogators have joined this debate, arguing persuasively that it's more effective to treat captives with dignity—something they don't expect. Brutality is a sign of an investigator's incompetence, writes Colonel Stuart Herrington, a retired army intelligence officer who questioned prisoners from wars in Vietnam, Panama, and the Persian Gulf. "In the course of these sensitive missions," he says, "my teams and I collected mountains of excellent, verified information, despite the fact that we never laid a hostile hand on a prisoner." Instead, "one has to 'go to school' on each captive. Who is he? Can I communicate with him in his language? What are his core beliefs? His loves? Hates? Fears? Where do his loyalties lie? Does he have a family, an inflated ego, perhaps some other core vulnerability?" And so on. But it takes patience and time, and interrogators at the U.S. prison at Guantánamo Bay naval base in Cuba, whom he advised, told him they were under pressure to get information by the end of the day.[12] Eventually, once the reports are declassified, we'll know the truths and falsehoods that were extracted by torture; we'll never know what other truths might have been learned through humane interrogation.

The third lesson is this: our national boundaries are not quite the fortress against torture that we would like to think. We cannot do it abroad and expect that it will never seep into the homeland. The hand-cranked generator used to shock Wilson and more than one hundred other black suspects from the early 1970s into the 1990s resembled the army field phone employed on prisoners in Vietnam, where the method was called the Bell Telephone Hour, and was nicknamed the Vietnam special or the Vietnam treatment in Chicago's Detective Area 2. The white police commander there, Jon Burge, who was eventually fired for torturing, had joined the department after serving in the army's Ninth Military Police Company in Vietnam in 1968 and 1969.[13]

A reverse contamination also occurred, according to a senior legal officer in the air force, who told me that military guards had complained about reservists carrying to Iraq the violent, humiliating methods they used in their jobs as civilian "correction officers" in U.S. prisons. The most notorious example was Specialist Charles Graner Jr., sentenced to ten years as the ringleader at Abu Ghraib, the prison in Iraq where American soldiers, with approval from superiors, staged and photographed degrading abuse—the naked prisoners in a pyramid, the hooded prisoner with wires attached, the prisoner collared like a dog, the thumbs-up grin next to a dead prisoner's body—images now memorialized as icons of America's brutality. Graner had been a prison guard in Pennsylvania, where he was accused of slipping a razor blade into an inmate's mashed potatoes, bloodying his mouth, and of beating prisoners.[14]

The effects of the Iraq war on American policing have not yet come to light. We do not know if police practices inside the United States have been tainted by work that officers may have done as guards and interrogators in Afghanistan, Iraq, and Guantánamo Bay. If it is happening, judging by the Chicago case, it will take many years, many complaints, and many court motions and prisoner lawsuits to work its way out of the deep shadows cast by police loyalty and prosecutor acquiescence. Abuse in closed interrogation rooms is hard to prove.

It's safe to say, nonetheless, that most American police departments do not apply electrodes to most suspects. They do not generally put plastic bags over their heads, burn them on radiators, or even beat them—at least not to leave visible marks, which were the Chicago cops' undoing. But there are many other ways of coercing confessions, and there are many confessions that are given to stop the coercion. Some are true, some are false. So here, as in other areas of the Bill of Rights, we are looking at a spectrum, with waterboarding in Afghanistan and plastic hoods in Chicago at one end, and other methods spread broadly along the continuum.

CHICAGO

Andrew Wilson, on parole for armed robbery, was wanted on two warrants. He and his brother Jackie had just committed a burglary when a patrol profiling suspicious-looking vehicles pulled them over. Andrew, getting out of the passenger seat, grabbed one officer's gun, struggled, shot him dead, then turned to the other and killed him as well. They then drove off in what witnesses described as a brown two-door Chevrolet Impala with a bent front grille.

The shootings brought to four the number of officers killed in the district in just a month, sending the police department on a frenzied manhunt that Jesse Jackson likened to a "military occupation." Hordes of cops invaded apartments and swept innocent black men from streets. "It was a reign of terror," the *Chicago Reader* quoted a detective as saying. "I don't know what Kristallnacht was like, but this was probably close." The gang unit's "idea is you go out and pick up two thousand pounds of nigger and eventually you'll get the right one."[15]

The Wilson brothers escaped the dragnet, but like most crooks who get caught, they were not very smart. When Jackie made the mistake of asking an old acquaintance to paint his Impala and fix its grillwork, the repairman recognized the car from the police description and called the cops. Andrew was the first arrested, by Jon Burge personally.

As in many instances of coerced confessions, this one came from a mentally defective man who had an IQ of seventy-three and never learned to read, even later after years of effort in prison. Yet torture has a way of focusing memory, and Wilson's account of police brutality remained mostly consistent, with only minor variations. As he told it, two other cops, not Burge, administered the initial abuse, which he resisted at first. He did not yield to the kicks and slaps and beatings, which left bruises and cuts on his right eyelid and elsewhere on his face. Nor did he give in to the plastic bag over his head or the cigarette burn on his arm. (Another victim described biting a hole in the bag so he could breathe.) When Burge entered, Wilson remembered, he told his officers that "if it had been him, he would not have messed up [Wilson's] face." Indeed.

Moved to a nearby room and shackled to the wall, Wilson refused Burge's order to confess. Then came the "Vietnam treatment." A grocery bag was brought in by two other officers, who took out a black box with a crank on the side and two wires ending in alligator clips. One was snapped onto his nostril, the other to his ear, which was left with telltale marks. A turn of the crank delivered a charge. Still no confession.

He was moved to yet another room, he recalled, and Burge took over, cranking electricity into his earlobes, then into his fingers as Wilson ground his teeth and screamed. "Burge then took out a device that looked like a curling iron," reported a court-appointed special prosecutor. With his prisoner "on his knees stretched across the radiator . . . Burge began rubbing the device between Wilson's legs, and Wilson could feel a tingling sensation. The shock from this device was stronger than from the crank device." (Cattle prods were used on other prisoners.) If Wilson confessed, Burge assured him, all this would cease. Wilson finally agreed.

But torture is more complex than a cold method of extracting information; it boils with revenge and sadism. After Wilson admitted to the murders, two officers "continued to abuse him" as they transported him to the jail and then to the hospital. One cop smashed him in the back of the head with a gun, opening a gash that required stitches, the special prosecutor confirmed, and one or both told him to refuse medical treatment "if he knew what was good for him."

Wilson moved to suppress his confession at trial, lost, and was sentenced to death. Thanks to the cops' zealous carelessness in leaving cuts, bruises, and burns that were documented by two doctors and a nurse, however, his story had the traction of credibility. It led the Illinois Supreme Court to find coercion and send the case back for retrial, minus the confession. Enough other evidence existed to convince the new jurors of his guilt, but they couldn't agree on execution, so he received a life sentence.

From behind bars, Wilson continued his quest to expose the torture. He filed a civil suit and persuaded a jury that a de facto police policy of abuse existed; the city paid $1 million in damages.[16] It was a rare victory for a convict, especially a hardened cop killer, yet it never quelled his emotions, which overtook him until he died in prison in 2007. He could not discuss his torture without tears. "He still cried when he talked about it," said his lawyer, John Stainthorp, "and it still made him furious that he cried. Obviously for Andrew it was important to be strong. One thing about torture is that it makes you weak, and it makes you know that you are weak."[17]

Weakness and disintegration cannot reliably bring truth. When a man's esteem collapses into hollow ruins, belief in a falsehood may gradually occupy the vacuum, as Arthur Koestler leads readers to witness in *Darkness at Noon*. His composite character Rubashov is yielding to manipulation by his interrogator, Gletkin: "He had believed that he had drunk the cup of humiliation to the dregs. Now he was to find that powerlessness had as many grades as power; that defeat could become as vertiginous as victory, and that its depths were bottomless. And, step by step, Gletkin forced him down the ladder."[18]

That was in Moscow, in the 1930s. In Chicago, in the 1980s, Andrew Wilson proved himself stronger than he felt, and the American system of justice, haltingly, nourished his small seed of power until it overwhelmed even the police. His persistence led to other suits by other victims, which brought lesser settlements and, more important, a bounty of sworn affidavits and investigations by journalists and officials.

The resulting descriptions of the victims' experiences in the police interrogation rooms added up to an unusually detailed picture of a torture system, exposed by prisoners' complaints, relentless reporting by John Conroy of the *Chicago Reader*, a belated finding of torture by the police department's Office of Professional Standards,[19] and a four-year investigation by a special state's attorney (prosecutor) appointed by the Cook County Circuit Court. The special prosecutor concluded in 2006 that the abuse of three suspects could be proven beyond a reasonable doubt and that victims in "many other cases" were telling the truth. The three-year statute of limitations had run out, however, so no indictments could be brought against any officers for torture.

At least one civil suit provided a hook for charging one officer. In 2008, Jon Burge was indicted by a federal grand jury for committing perjury and obstruction of justice by denying under oath that he or officers under his command had ever used any of a long list of abusive methods, from "verbal coercion" to "physical beatings" to "electric shock." The indictment asserted that he had, and Burge was arrested at his retirement home in Florida.[20] He was convicted by a jury in 2010 and sentenced to four and a half years in prison—too little to satisfy some of his victims.

The plaintiff in the civil case, Madison Hobley, had been seen by two witnesses at a service station pumping a gallon of gasoline into a can an hour before his apartment burst into flames, killing his wife, his year-old son, and five other residents. The fire was ruled arson. In Area 2, he claimed, officers denied him a lawyer, handcuffed him to a wall, hit and kicked him, and covered his head with a plastic typewriter cover. He blacked out and, when he came to, was given a lie detector test, which he was told he'd failed. Hobley then confessed orally, according to an officer who had allegedly kicked him in the shins, but the confession was never written or recorded, and Hobley consistently denied admitting anything. He was found guilty nonetheless and sentenced to death, and his purported confession was confirmed by every court up the line. He finally gained a pardon as part of Governor George Ryan's effort to cleanse death row of questionable convictions.

As in Wilson's case, though, Hobley might have been found guilty even without his supposed confession, given the other evidence available. Besides being immoral and impractical, torture is sometimes superfluous.

So it was with another Chicago defendant, Phillip Adkins, whose confession was omitted from trial with no ill effects for the prosecution. He was convicted anyway of attempted murder and armed robbery for taking hostage and pistol-whipping an off-duty cop, who happened to be a customer at a gas station during a holdup. Arresting officers had driven him to an isolated area near railroad tracks, Adkins said, then hit him again and again in the stomach and groin with fists and a flashlight until he was weaving in and out of consciousness, lost control of his bowels, and defecated and urinated on himself. A cop bought a pair of khaki shorts, had him change clothes, and disposed of his soiled jeans and underpants. At the station house, he gave a confession—and a complaint about brutality—to an assistant state's attorney. He was admitted to intensive care, and the hospital records showing trauma and possible kidney damage made his account credible to the special prosecutor two decades later. He was sentenced to eighteen years and paroled after eight.

In other instances, though, the coerced confession was the only thing that the detectives bothered to get, a substitute for solid investigation. Children were not immune. After a 1991 gang shooting, Marcus Wiggins, thirteen, was picked up, taken to a station-house interrogation room, and told to put his hands on the table, he testified. Electrodes from a box were attached to his hands. "My hands started burning, feeling like it was being burned," he said. "I was—I was shaking and my—and my jaws got tight and my eyes felt they went blank. . . . I felt like I was spinning. . . . It felt like my jaws was like—they was—I can't say the word. It felt like my jaws was sucking in. . . . I felt like I was going to die."[21] Charges were dropped, and the city settled his lawsuit for nearly $100,000.

Similarly, the Chicago police beat Alfonzo Pinex until he confessed to a gang-related murder, but they had little else as reliable evidence against him. Detectives had collected statements from other alleged participants in the crime, two of whom were ultimately convicted. When the policemen played the tapes for Pinex, though, he stonewalled, said they were lying, and asked for his lawyer. The cops replied with a fist in his right eye, he claimed, followed by punches in the ribs, a knee in the left eye, and so much beating that he defecated in his pants. In the midst of the maelstrom, he yelled that he'd say anything they demanded and finally signed a police report full of lies, including a fabrication that he'd been advised of his *Miranda* rights to silence and an attorney.

When his lawyer arrived, she found him crying and hysterical. He told her of the torture, she moved to suppress his confession, and the judge agreed on the grounds that he'd been denied his request for counsel, without ruling on the alleged beating. Then two key witnesses refused to testify, leaving the prosecution with no case and no choice but to drop the charge.

A remarkable sentence appears at the end of the statement signed jointly by Pinex, a detective, and an assistant state's attorney: "Pinex said that he had been treated well by the police and that no threats or promises had been made in return for this statement."[22] It was the boilerplate shield against accusations of brutality, which gave police superiors, prosecutors, and judges an excuse to look the other way for most of two decades.

Like the CIA's practice of torturing terrorism suspects, the police torture of criminal suspects was enabled by widespread complicity. Chicago officials may not have ordered the abuse, but neither did they bring it to a halt. The police superintendent, Richard Brzeczek, failed to pursue a reliable complaint about Wilson's injuries from the doctor at the prison health services, merely forwarding the letter to his investigative office but never following up with his own men.[23] He sent it also to Cook County's chief prosecutor, the state's attorney Richard M. Daley, who later became Chicago's mayor, asking for guidance on how to investigate without jeopardizing Wilson's prosecution. Daley never replied and never acted.[24]

"Despite the fact that Brzeczek believed that officers in the Violent Crimes unit of Detective Area 2 had tortured Andrew Wilson, he kept that belief to himself for over twenty years," the special prosecutor concluded. "He also kept Burge in command at Area 2 and issued a letter of commendation to all of the detectives at Area 2."[25]

What's more, a number of Daley's subordinates, assistant state's attorneys, were told of the torture by victim after victim; many suspects testified that they had complained as prosecutors entered interrogation rooms to take confessions. The Cook County bench is now peppered with those former prosecutors and others who were involved. A lawyers' petition in 2006 asking that civil suits be moved out of the county contained this count: Three judges were former Chicago police detectives, two of whom had worked with Burge. Three other judges had defended the city in lawsuits over police brutality. Sixteen judges had been assistant state's attorneys involved in torture cases, either having taken confessions, prosecuted those who'd given them, or testified for officers at police board hearings.[26]

After Burge was finally fired, the police union tried to enter a float honoring him in the St. Patrick's Day parade.

HUMANE TORTURE BY THE CIA

The Chicago tortures were rationalized by community safety. The CIA tortures after September 11 were rationalized by national security. Invoking safety and security to justify torture is like injecting religion into warfare: the higher purpose excuses the lower impulse.

Despotic regimes play this mind game on their own soil as a method of control. Democracies can do it abroad while staying relatively civil at home, as the British demonstrated in Malaya, the French in Algeria, and the Americans in Vietnam. They imagine the international frontier as a wall sealing the homeland from the necessary roughness beyond.

That may be so in certain cases but something of an illusion in others, as the United States has recently discovered. In our latest misconception, we thought we could lock the toxic mixture of security and torture safely outside. We have now relearned the fact that borders are never airtight. The cry of national security has stirred fears and impaired liberty inside America's boundaries beginning with the eighteenth century's Alien and Sedition Acts, continuing through the early twentieth century's Espionage and Sedition Acts, the Japanese internment during World War II, the secret surveillance of dissident citizens during the Cold War, and echoing into the current era shaped by 9/11.

Most torture carried out during the presidency of George W. Bush was not committed in the United States. We could argue about it from a safe distance as it occurred in Guantánamo and Abu Ghraib and invisible CIA prisons in unknown countries. It was a passionate moral issue, certainly, but not one that appeared to penetrate American justice, which seemed insulated from American misdeeds overseas. That has not proved entirely correct, for torture opened a way of thinking.

Under the Bush administration's legal rationale, "Americans in any town of this country could constitutionally be hung from the ceiling naked, sleep deprived, waterboarded, and all the rest—if the alleged national security justification was compelling," wrote Philip Zelikow, a State Department lawyer who tried to stop it.[27] If torture is acceptable in a military prison to prevent a terrorist attack, why not in a federal lockup to stop a presidential assassination, or in a county jail to head off a school shooting, a child's kidnapping?

So far it cannot be done in a county jail, not constitutionally anyway. Yet brutal interrogations outside have tainted the American system inside.

After Obama came into office with a pledge to close Guantánamo and resolve the prisoners' cases, his lawyers struggled to pull inmates from the netherworld of lawless confinement and abuse into some form of a fair, truth-finding process. Bush had originally designated them enemy combatants, unilaterally deciding that they could be left in Guantánamo indefinitely with no charges brought or allegations tested in trial. Had that policy held, the interrogation methods might have been legally irrelevant, aimed at gathering intelligence rather than building prosecutions. But those transferred to the criminal justice system would suddenly have rights, and torture would become an exasperating legal problem.

Evidence coerced cannot be introduced in trial, a simple protection under interpretations of the Fifth Amendment. In theory, that rendered inadmissible the confessions and much information extracted by the Bush administration, leaving Obama prosecutors with a mess of useless, unreliable dossiers. Judges don't always see coercion where defendants do, making it far from certain that every piece of information pried from prisoners would be excluded. But since these were not prosecutions the government was willing to lose, only those based on evidence gathered properly, without abuse, could be safely tried in criminal court.

Even cases built on more than coerced confessions relied on supposedly "clean" evidence that had sometimes been uncovered by leads from witnesses who had talked under torture. There was a close call for prosecutors of Ahmed Khalfan Ghailani, tried in 2010 for conspiring to bomb the

American embassies in Tanzania and Kenya in 1998. Finding that Ghailani had been coerced into naming a man who had sold him the explosives, the judge ruled that even though the seller was willing to testify, he could not do so, since his identity was the product of abusive questioning. Without that evidence, the jury barely found grounds for guilt, and Ghailani was convicted on just one of more than two hundred counts. So the "enhanced interrogation" worked its way into the crevices of a prosecution and contaminated the otherwise admissible proof needed to convict. (He was sentenced to life nonetheless.)

Unwittingly, American officials had modeled their torture methods on Chinese techniques designed precisely to generate false confessions for propaganda purposes. The CIA, which had little interrogation experience, derived its program from the samples of torture used in SERE, the Survival, Evasion, Resistance, and Escape course that trained U.S. military pilots, Special Forces troops, and others in what to expect if captured. The ranking Bush administration officials who approved the CIA approach reportedly did not know, and did not trouble themselves to learn, that the SERE methods were created to mimic the abuses encountered by American prisoners of the Chinese during the Korean War. Some GIs had succumbed, giving phony statements of guilt and remorse, produced not by "brainwashing," according to government reports at the time, but by less sophisticated brutalities—forced standing, cold cells, sleep disruption, and food limitations—tactics adopted a half century later by the CIA. "The Communists do not look upon these assaults as 'torture,'" said a study in 1956.[28]

In 2002, the Americans did not look upon these assaults and others as "torture" under the federal law as generously construed by compliant attorneys in the Bush Justice Department's Office of Legal Counsel. Since the office is responsible for interpreting the law to guide government agencies, the memos of interpretation carried weight as a shield against the prosecution of American interrogators, a kind of immunity in advance—although the documents suggest that the CIA tortured first, then later asked for legal approval, which was obligingly provided.

The lawyers' lengthy rationalizations, contained in a series of memos made public by the Obama administration,[29] recorded with detached precision the limits of the permitted "techniques" as described by the CIA: Sleep deprivation could last no more than eleven days, later reduced to 180 hours, and would be halted if it caused hallucinations. The prisoner could be shackled either seated on a stool or standing with wrists attached to the ceiling, the chains just long enough to keep the hands "between the level of his heart and his chin." Should he doze off and hang by his arms, "he will lose his balance and awaken." The temperature would have to be at least sixty-eight degrees for him to be kept naked, except for an adult diaper, which would be changed, frequently and considerately, to avoid rash. Nudity could not involve sexual degradation, the lawyers wrote, yet they gave no sign of recognizing the degradation implicit in their approval for female officers to see detainees unclothed.

"Walling" had to be done with a towel or collar around the neck to prevent whiplash, a method suggested by the Israelis, Mayer was told by a CIA official. The towel was used to pull the prisoner forward, then smash his shoulder blades against a wall that was supposed to be false, designed to create a loud sound rather than injury. Interviewed by the International Committee of the Red Cross, Khalid Sheikh Mohammed said that he was first thrown against a concrete wall, then put into a box. When he was let out, a piece of plywood had been erected in front of the concrete—the false wall, apparently, to satisfy the rules.

Bland liquid nourishment, usually Ensure, could be given at a minimum of 1,000 calories daily, which exceeded many weight-loss programs, one memo noted. The limited diet would be supplemented if the prisoner's weight dropped by more than 10 percent.

In "water dousing," the water that was poured or splashed on the prisoner had to be potable, the room had to be above sixty-four degrees, a mat or poncho had to be placed between the prisoner and the floor to avoid loss of body heat, and the water temperature determined the "total duration of exposure," which could not exceed two-thirds the time that submersion at that temperature would cause hypothermia.

A "facial slap or insult slap" required the fingers to be slightly spread while "the hand makes contact with the area directly between the tip of the individual's chin and the bottom of the corresponding earlobe." An "abdominal slap" was administered with the back of an open hand. "The interrogator must have no rings or other jewelry on his hand."

Three different stress positions were specified. Time limits were imposed for stuffing a prisoner into a cramped box, depending on the size: two hours for small, eight hours for large. He could be informed that a stinging insect would accompany him inside, as long as nothing more harmful than a caterpillar was actually inserted, and he wasn't told that the bug would cause severe pain or death. The technique was never used, according to a footnote.

Waterboarding, which was imposed on three of the captives, had to be done with a saline solution to avoid diluting the sodium in a prisoner's blood if he swallowed a large amount. Water could be poured onto the cloth for only twenty to forty seconds, then three or four breaths would be allowed, then another twenty to forty seconds, and so on for up to twenty minutes at a time in a two-hour session. There could be two such sessions in each twenty-four-hour period and five such days within each thirty-day period. A physician would have to be standing by to intervene if necessary. Mohammed said that a device attached to his finger was checked frequently—probably measuring his blood oxygen level.

Indeed, the constant presence of doctors and psychologists was presented by the Justice Department memos as evidence of civilized precaution, when in fact it violated medical oaths and professional ethics by giving cover to brutality. The CIA had invented a novel paradox: a form of clinically humane torture.

The word "torture" is vivid and vague. It conjures up assaults that were not approved and presumably not used: no fingernails pulled, no electrodes applied, no rack or thumbscrew or dismemberment. Yet if its core meaning is upheld, it surely encompasses the more sophisticated modern methods of teaching helplessness through suffering. None of this was "torture" under federal law, according to the lawyers who manufactured a definition so extreme that the routine abuse being directed against terrorism suspects would be legal.

The law wasn't exacting, and lawyers who were looking for wiggle room found some. Torture was defined by the federal statute as "an act committed by a person acting under the color of law specifically intended to inflict *severe* physical or mental pain or suffering (other than pain or suffering incidental to lawful sanctions) upon another person within his custody or physical control" (emphasis added). The law went on to define severe mental pain or suffering as "the *prolonged* mental harm [emphasis added] caused by" various actions including "the threat of imminent death" and "procedures calculated to disrupt profoundly the senses or personality."[30] Perhaps Congress meant to exclude some unpleasant behavior, but it is not specified.

The two fudge words in the statute were "severe" and "prolonged," which gave the pro-abuse lawyers the flexibility to play with the meaning of "torture." To rise to the level of "severe," they wrote in their memo, pain would have to be as intense as that "accompanying serious physical injury, such as organ failure, impairment of bodily function, or even death." To be

considered "prolonged," psychological harm must be "of significant duration, e.g., lasting for months or even years. . . . The criminal statute penal-
izes only the most egregious conduct," according to the August 1, 2002,
memo by John Yoo and Jay S. Bybee (who later became a federal judge).
Both standards were made up; they had no basis in law or precedent.

The CIA methods wouldn't cause "severe physical suffering," because
the times during which they were applied were so short, the memos said.
And while waterboarding was "likely to create panic in the form of an acute
instinctual fear arising from the physiological sensation of drowning," this
was "distress," not "suffering," the lawyers concluded. "Physical distress
may amount to 'severe physical suffering' only if it is severe both in intensity and duration."

The word "Orwellian" has been overused to describe the Bush administration's euphemisms and circumlocutions, but it has no adequate synonym
to characterize the Yoo and Bybee memo, especially this statement: "The
waterboard could not be said to inflict severe suffering. The waterboard is
simply a controlled acute episode, lacking the connotation of a protracted
period of time generally given to suffering."

In an interview, Yoo blamed the "very narrow statute," which his office
merely interpreted. "The law tells you what the boundaries of legal conduct
are," he explained patiently. "It's up to the policymakers to choose where in
those boundaries" policy should be located, a lawyerly way of washing his
hands. He favored the "class of conduct that is not torture, but is called
cruel and degrading treatment," and he clearly shaped his legal interpretation to permit it. "I think in this conflict, because of its unconventional
nature, we cannot as a society rule those kinds of things out of bounds,
especially when there's no statute, there's no congressional view that these
things are illegal."

In a disquieting style of sweet reason, Yoo spoke about brutal issues
with clinical calmness. He gave no indication of knowing that days of sleep
deprivation and perpetual interrogation, called "conveyor" in Russian, were
used to manufacture the phony confessions of the Stalinist show trials of
the 1930s.[31] He gave no hint of knowing that waterboarding had been introduced into the arsenal of torture by the Spanish Inquisition, prosecuted
in war-crimes trials of Japanese following World War II, used by the Chinese against Americans, and employed by the Pol Pot regime in Cambodia.
A similar method had been inflicted on black prisoners forced to labor
in Southern mines and factories during the early twentieth century.[32] He
seemed unaware that his own Justice Department, two decades before,

had won convictions of a Texas sheriff and three deputies for waterboarding prisoners.[33]

Given the propensities of Yoo and other Bush lawyers, it was left to the Democratic-dominated Congress to try to close that imagined loophole, in February 2008, by amending the laws to prohibit waterboarding explicitly. But the bill didn't pass.[34] Under the memos' legal reasoning, therefore, confessions extracted by waterboarding could have been admitted into evidence by military judges conducting trials of noncitizens, even those arrested and interrogated inside the United States, who had been designated "unlawful enemy combatants."[35]

That risk to people inside the country was not well understood in the debate surrounding torture. While the discussion focused on detainees in Guantánamo Bay and elsewhere outside the United States, the interlocking pieces of the law and its interpretations allowed the president to label anyone anywhere, whether in Afghanistan or Alabama, as an enemy combatant and then, if an alien, to bring him before a military commission whose rules would allow confessions extracted by the CIA's abusive methods, because they were not defined as "torture."

This was made possible by the combination of the lawyers' memos and the Military Commissions Act of 2006, which excluded confessions and witnesses' statements elicited by "torture," but added that those "in which the degree of coercion is disputed" could be ruled admissible if the interrogation occurred before December 2005. A military judge needed to find only that "the totality of the circumstances renders the statement reliable . . . and the interests of justice would best be served by admission of the statement into evidence."

Interrogations conducted after 2005, when restrictions were imposed by the Detainee Treatment Act, were admissible only if they avoided "cruel, inhuman, or degrading treatment," the rule drawn verbatim from the Convention Against Torture.[36] Yet here, too, the Justice Department lawyers thought that the CIA techniques complied with that standard. The permissive interpretations were withdrawn toward the end of the Bush administration, but if they had prevailed, evidence obtained by torture—which was defined as neither "torture" nor "cruel, inhuman, or degrading"—could have been heard by military commissions trying enemy combatants seized and abused inside the United States.[37] The powers were not employed, but a legal gateway was opened for torture to infiltrate the country. It was nearly closed in 2009 by a revised Military Commissions Act that excluded statements extracted by such methods but still admitted information obtained by coercion during capture or combat.

Torture entered the United States most directly following the arrest on May 8, 2002, of an American named Jose Padilla, who was picked up at Chicago's O'Hare Airport after returning from Zurich. He had become a suspect during the interrogation of Abu Zubaydah, a personnel clerk in an al-Qaeda training camp,[38] who named Padilla as a plotter to disperse radioactivity by setting off a "dirty bomb."[39]

Padilla had converted to Islam in prison, where he had done time for murder as a juvenile and then for gun possession as an adult in Florida. Upon release he lived in Egypt and visited Saudi Arabia, Pakistan, and Afghanistan, where he allegedly took instruction in an al-Qaeda camp the year before 9/11.

When he tried to come home, he was seized in Chicago, moved to New York, held in a civilian jail as a material witness, and assigned a lawyer. One month later, without notice to his attorney, Padilla was spirited out of prison to the navy brig in Charleston, South Carolina, under a one-page order by President Bush designating him an enemy combatant, "based on the information available to me from all sources," according to the censored version of the document.[40] The "sources" were later identified as Zubaydah and at least one other captive whose information was made dubious by the interrogation methods. Yet the authorities never provided specific evidence to justify Bush's move to imprison him indefinitely without charge or trial. Padilla went one year and eight months in military custody without being allowed to see a lawyer, and for three years and eight months he was kept in isolation before finally being transferred to the civilian court system, a shift essentially forced by court decisions in other enemy-combatant cases.[41]

In the Charleston brig, his attorney told the court, military interrogators warned Padilla that they would send him abroad or to Guantánamo Bay. Guards manipulated him into a sense of powerlessness by unpredictably providing and then withdrawing a mirror, a pillow, and a sheet; by keeping him in glaring lights, then in darkness; by locking him in a cold cell without a shower for weeks; by allowing him to exercise only at night.

"He was threatened with being cut with a knife and having alcohol poured on the wounds," according to his lawyer's brief. "He was also threatened with imminent execution. He was hooded and forced to stand in stress positions for long durations of time. He was forced to endure exceedingly long interrogation sessions, without adequate sleep, wherein he would be confronted with false information, scenarios, and documents to further disorient him. Often he had to endure multiple interrogators who would scream, shake, and otherwise assault Mr. Padilla. Additionally, Mr. Padilla was given drugs against his will, believed to be some form of lysergic acid diethylamide (LSD) or phencyclidine (PCP), to act as a sort of truth serum during his interrogations."[42] (If it happened, the drugging violated even the Justice Department's permissive guidelines.)

This abuse produced various statements about supposed schemes alongside the alleged dirty-bomb plot, most notably a plan to "undertake a mission to blow up apartment buildings in the United States using natural gas," a Senate committee was told by Deputy Attorney General James Comey. Padilla was said to have admitted to (or boasted of) conspiring with Khalid Sheikh Mohammed and other al-Qaeda leaders.[43]

The truth of these revelations was impossible to determine, since they came out of duress. Their accuracy went untested in any adversarial proceeding and remained unverified by corroborating evidence. No lawyer was permitted to monitor the questioning, and when Padilla's attorney Andrew Patel was finally allowed to see him, he was instructed by the military not to ask Padilla about the conditions he faced in the brig, a telling restriction on attorney-client communication.

Denying Padilla a lawyer was a deliberate method of instilling a sense of vulnerability, explained the head of the Defense Intelligence Agency, Vice Admiral Lowell E. Jacoby. "Anything that threatens the perceived dependency and trust between the subject and interrogator directly threatens the value of interrogation as an intelligence gathering tool," Jacoby said. "Even seemingly minor interruptions can have profound psychological impacts on the delicate subject-interrogator relationship. Any insertion of counsel into the subject-interrogator relationship, for example—even if only for a limited duration or for a specific purpose—can undo months of work and may permanently shut down the interrogation process."[44] This sounded logical, but the method facilitated the type of abusive setting opposed by the most seasoned interrogators.

It had been during the initial, humane phase of questioning that Zubaydah mentioned Padilla's dirty-bomb plot, according to one of his initial interrogators, Ali Soufan of the FBI. By treating his wounds, inquiring into his worldviews, and lending him a measure of dignity, Soufan said he had gotten Zubaydah to identify Khalid Sheikh Mohammed as the 9/11 organizer and to provide the tip that led to Padilla's arrest. When the CIA began subjecting Zubaydah to waterboarding and other abuse, Soufan objected, and the FBI withdrew its interrogators in protest.[45]

In the end, the torture of Zubaydah and Padilla contaminated everything that had been learned, depriving the government of the most serious charges, which faded away as Padilla was transferred to the civilian justice system. Had Padilla admitted to the gravest plots without coercion, and had the humane interrogation of Zubaydah continued in compliance with the Fifth Amendment, all the statements could have been put into evidence. Instead, the tainted information had to be stripped away to a core of "clean" evidence, which amounted to nothing more than Padilla's presence at a training camp. Although the plan for a dirty bomb had been certified by a Defense Department official's affidavit, and foiling the plot had been advertised by Attorney General John Ashcroft as a victory for counterterrorism, it quietly vanished from the charge sheet.[46] So did the idea of blowing up apartment buildings. Neither appeared in the criminal indictment. The stain of torture could not be scrubbed away.

So Padilla and several others faced trial on the watered-down charge of belonging to a cell that conspired to commit murder overseas. The prosecution presented as its main exhibit his application to an al-Qaeda training camp. The jury convicted him, the government urged life in prison, but the judge gave him only seventeen years and four months, citing his "harsh" imprisonment in the brig and noting that "there is no evidence that [Padilla] personally killed, maimed, or kidnapped." The government appealed to the Eleventh Circut, where a panel, voting 2–1, ordered the judge to lengthen the sentence.[47] Without the torture, he might have gone away for life. Humane interrogations have a long record of success, suggesting that he might have talked anyway. Or, if not, investigators would have been forced to investigate, nail down the facts, and prove his guilt—if he was actually guilty. Once again, torture was a substitute for hard investigation.

THE RIGHT TO SILENCE

Ernesto A. Miranda was not a model citizen, yet a model police practice now bears his name. It has become an adjective, as in "Miranda warning," and a verb, as in "Mirandize," a procedure designed to protect against coercion in the interrogation room. Many officers carry cards with the warning's text for suspects to sign before questioning, and forms printed with its famous words for signature afterward as part of a confession.

Miranda began getting into trouble as early as eighth grade: truancy, burglary, a year of reform school, armed robbery, AWOL from the army, months in the stockade, a dishonorable discharge, driving a stolen car across state lines, a year in federal prison, robbery again, then kidnapping and raping a mentally defective eighteen-year-old woman who could not pick him out from a lineup with absolute certainty.

So the Phoenix police put him in a soundproof room for two hours and questioned him. They told him falsely that he had been identified by the victim. They promised to drop a robbery charge if he confessed, he said later. They did not advise him of his right to silence or to counsel as contained in the Fifth and Sixth Amendments. And although there was no evidence that they beat him, shocked him, put a plastic bag over his head, or otherwise abused him physically, the Supreme Court ruled in 1966 that the "interrogation environment" of isolation without support "is created for no purpose other than to subjugate the individual to the will of his examiner. This atmosphere carries its own badge of intimidation . . . at odds with one of our Nation's most cherished principles—that the individual may not be compelled to incriminate himself."[48]

To ensure that any statement was entirely voluntary, the Court fashioned a four-part warning beginning with the right to silence, designed not only to educate the uninformed suspect, Chief Justice Earl Warren wrote, but as "an absolute prerequisite in overcoming the inherent pressures of the interrogation atmosphere" and to "show the individual that his interrogators are prepared to recognize his privilege should he choose to exercise it."

The thin majority of five justices laid down the rules this way: "He must be warned prior to any questioning that he has the right to remain silent, that anything he says can be used against him in a court of law, that he has the right to the presence of an attorney, and that if he cannot afford an attorney, one will be appointed for him prior to any questioning if he so desires." Rarely has the language of a Supreme Court opinion passed so literally into everyday police work.

Miranda's conviction having been set aside, the state conducted a new trial, this time without his confession but with testimony from his common-law wife that he had told her of the rape.[49] Again he was convicted, and again he was sentenced to twenty to thirty years. Paroled in 1972, he made a meager business selling autographed cards printed with the Miranda warning. Then during a traffic stop, a gun was discovered, a parole violation that returned him to prison for a year. Out again for the last time, he slid into a subculture of low-stakes card games in seedy bars, where he was stabbed to death in 1976 during a fight over a $3 gambling pot.[50] As in many other landmark cases, a noble legacy was left by an ignoble life.

———

Constitutional shields against police power invariably contain holes, some punctured by the courts' lofty second thoughts, others eroded by canny evasions on the ground. The vaunted Miranda warning is such a case. It is a modern device designed to protect the vulnerable from the torture and subtler abuse employed through history. It is also a mundane tool. It fuses a high precept with pragmatism, setting up a struggle not yet entirely resolved. Its application has been trimmed by litigation and shaped to fit inside a criminal justice system bruised by gritty experience with crooks and liars. Yet its central principle, the right to reticence, is rooted in a hallowed tradition.

The accused, facing the options of confession or affirmative defense, may find refuge in a space between the two—in the dignity of silence. It has been recognized as a wise and honorable choice since ancient days. Jesus stood silently at his trial, the Gospels report. "And the chief priests accused him of many things: but he answered nothing," writes Mark. "And Pilate asked him again, saying, Answerest thou nothing? Behold how many things they witness against thee. But Jesus yet answered nothing; so that Pilate marvelled."[51]

Four centuries earlier, in 399 B.C., Socrates had been "silent before his judges," writes I. F. Stone, or had mounted an eloquent defense, as recorded by the contemporary chroniclers Plato and Xenophon. The story of silence, curiously, emerged more than five centuries after his trial and over a century after the crucifixion of Jesus, perhaps to color Socrates retroactively with Christ-like martyrdom, in a silence carried by poise, purity, and innocence.[52]

The right to silence, codified by the Magna Carta in 1215, was invoked fatally in the sixteenth century by John Lambert as he was tried by an ecclesiastical court for heresy. An early Protestant, he insistently maintained that the Communion bread and wine were not turned into the body and blood of Christ literally, but only symbolically, spiritually. He refused to answer the question of whether he had previously been accused of heresy, quoting in Latin the principle "No man is bound to betray himself." In 1538 he was burned at the stake. But by the middle of the next century, the right to silence had been implanted in English common law.[53] It comes to us in the Fifth Amendment.

By the nineteenth century, both English and American courts were taking a dim view of confessions induced by threats and promises, no matter how vague. Scattered throughout accounts of American interrogations were the phrases "You had better own up"; "It might be easier for you"; and

"It will be better for you to confess. The door of mercy is open." These were enough to make many judges doubt that the statements of guilt were wholly voluntary and reliable. The concern was codified in 1897 by the Supreme Court, which reversed a federal murder conviction in *Bram v. United States* because an officer subtly implied leniency by saying, "If you had an accomplice, you should say so, and not have the blame of this horrible crime on your own shoulders." The Court decided that any threat or promise, however indirect, required suppression, but the ruling was persistently ignored by lower courts, and ultimately *Bram* was overturned by the high court itself.[54]

The Supreme Court confronted more explicit coercion well before inventing the *Miranda* protections in 1966. The justices in 1936 heard an appeal of the murder convictions of three black men tortured in Mississippi—all had been whipped repeatedly, and one had been suspended twice with a noose around his neck, then lowered to the ground, still alive. At trial, three of the torturers had described the lashings. ("Not too much for a Negro; not as much as I would have done if it were left to me," one deputy testified.) Yet the confessions had been admitted as the only prosecution evidence, and the men had been sentenced to death. The Court set aside their convictions.[55]

Then the Court in 1940 rejected confessions coerced by other means, less than physical violence, vacating the death sentences of four young black men in Florida who had endured five days and a night of threats and terror that had forced their admissions to murdering a white man.[56] In 1960, the justices threw out as involuntary the confession of a mentally ill black man who had undergone eight or nine hours of nonstop questioning by police investigating an Alabama robbery.[57] Those three opinions were based not on the Fifth Amendment's right against self-incrimination but on the Fourteenth Amendment's guarantee of due process at the state level. Not until 1964 did the Court apply the Fifth Amendment to the states.[58]

Peppering police departments with case-by-case opinions that set no general guidelines did not change behavior very much, and legislatures were not stepping up to their obligation to write unambiguous rules for interrogations. The Court finally did so with clarity in *Miranda*—too much clarity, in the view of many judges, prosecutors, and law enforcement officers. Justice Byron White, in a heated *Miranda* dissent, warned excessively that the rule "is a deliberate calculus to prevent interrogations, to reduce the incidence of confessions and pleas of guilty, and to increase the number of trials." The opposite of his prediction has come true: guilty pleas have risen, trials have precipitously declined, and confessions are still coerced, though less frequently, perhaps, and less brutally.

Some conservative critics argue that *Miranda* extends the rights to silence and counsel beyond the courtroom, where the framers originally placed them, and into the station house, where they can only interfere with police work. As Justice Antonin Scalia observed, a lawyer present at questioning is likely to give only one piece of advice: say nothing. If acted upon intelligently by suspects, he suggested, the Miranda warning would snuff out all confessions, not only coerced, but also voluntary, ignoring the "world of difference . . . between compelling a suspect to incriminate himself and preventing him from foolishly doing so of his own accord."[59]

Scalia liked the way Congress tried to undo *Miranda* two years after the ruling. A provision in the Safe Streets Act of 1968 allowed judges to decide if confessions were voluntary by examining "the totality of circumstances" rather than whether the Miranda warning had been given.[60] This returned federal courts to a looser pre-*Miranda* standard, but the Justice Department didn't take advantage of the relaxation; mostly, it stuck to the requirement that suspects be read their rights.[61] When FBI agents broke the rules and failed to Mirandize an accused bank robber, his incriminating statements made their way to the Supreme Court in 2000 to be ruled upon. Scalia would have admitted the statements under the "totality of circumstances" test, but he was outvoted 7–2 as the justices reaffirmed *Miranda* as a "constitutional decision" and struck down the congressional act. Writing for the majority, Chief Justice William H. Rehnquist observed: "*Miranda* has become embedded in routine police practice to the point where the warnings have become part of our national culture."[62]

The debate since has been softened but not settled. It turns on whether *Miranda*'s requirement is constitutional or prophylactic, a fundamental pillar of rights or merely an expedient rule of evidence that can be revised or withdrawn. For the moment, no confession can be admitted into evidence without having been preceded by the Miranda warning—except . . . unless . . . and with caveats. There are many exceptions, more and more as courts shave away the scope of the rule. These include coerced confessions accompanied by independently obtained evidence sufficient to convict,[63] comments made to cops during traffic stops,[64] statements initiated by defendants before questioning,[65] answers to questions urgently asked to protect public safety,[66] jailhouse confessions to undercover police officers posing as prisoners,[67] and confessions that impeach a defendant's testimony at trial.[68] Also, since *Miranda* applies only when someone is in "custody," courts have shown immense flexibility in defining the term in favor of the police. Even a prison inmate is not "in custody," and therefore not entitled to the Miranda warning, when questioned in jail about another crime.[69]

In 2010, the Supreme Court relaxed the *Miranda* requirements in three rulings that illustrated how subtly constitutional rights can be worn away in small increments, so that they seem whole until they become fragile. In *Florida v. Powell,* the Court allowed police to alter the wording of the warning by omitting the original *Miranda* opinion's requirement that police inform a suspect of "the right to the presence of an attorney" during questioning. Tampa police had told a robbery suspect, Kevin Dewayne Powell, "You have the right to talk to a lawyer before answering any of our questions." Powell then admitted to owning a handgun found in a search, was convicted, and appealed on the ground that the warning had implied his right to a lawyer before, but not during, interrogation. The justices noted that the police had also said, "You have the right to use any of these rights at any time you want during this interview," which the majority believed made clear his right to summon an attorney at any time. Powell seemed to understand as much, since in trial he answered "Yes" when his lawyer asked him, "You waived the right to have an attorney present during your questioning by detectives; is that what you're telling this jury?" But Justice John Paul Stevens, in dissent, argued that the wording could be taken by a suspect to mean "a one-time right to consult with an attorney, not a right to have an attorney present with him in the interrogation room at all times."[70]

The Court went on in *Maryland v. Shatzer* to allow a suspect to be requestioned even after he invoked his Fifth Amendment rights, provided that at least two weeks had elapsed since his release from custody.[71] That ruling was unanimous.

Then, as conservatives moved to cut the *Miranda* protections closer to the bone, more liberal justices peeled away in dissent. The opinion came in *Berghuis v. Thompkins.*[72] It held, curiously, that if a suspect is told of his right to remain silent and he then remains silent, he has not invoked his right to silence. Only if he breaks his silence to affirm his right is he considered to have refused to waive the right; without that waiver, police interrogation is closed off, and statements elicited subsequently are inadmissible. Before this ruling, courts and law enforcement tended to require an explicit waiver, although a previous opinion had recognized that a waiver could be "inferred from the actions and words of the person interrogated."[73] Now the Court, with a bare majority of five justices, reversed the presumption that no waiver had been given, instead interpreting silence as a waiver and holding that a taciturn suspect may continue to be questioned. It is worth recalling that *Miranda* itself was also decided by the slimmest vote of 5–4.

This was a case of trick questioning, in a sense, and the decision seems likely to open the door wider to long interrogations and police manipulation, especially of people with little education, mental dysfunction, or emotional immaturity—including children. Van Chester Thompkins, arrested for a shooting outside a Michigan mall where one man died, was shown a printed form listing his *Miranda* rights, was asked to read one part aloud to test his literacy, and was then asked to sign to signify that he understood his rights. He read aloud but refused to sign. For two hours and forty-five minutes of questioning, he said practically nothing. Then the detective pushed the right button. When he asked, "Do you believe in God?" Thompkins answered, "Yes." Tears welled in his eyes. "Do you pray to God?" the detective asked. "Yes," Thompkins replied. "Do you pray to God to forgive you for shooting that boy down?" Thompkins said, "Yes," and averted his eyes. He refused to write a confession, but his statement was admitted into evidence. The surviving victim also testified, the jury brought a first-degree murder conviction, and the defendant was sentenced to life.

When Thompkins answered the question with a single word, he effectively waived his right to silence, the majority of justices held. *Miranda* had said that "a valid waiver will not be presumed simply from the silence of the accused after warnings are given or simply from the fact that a confession was in fact eventually obtained." But the questions about God broke through his silence. He could have said nothing in response, the Court noted, or "could have unambiguously invoked his *Miranda* rights and ended the interrogation."

In a vigorous dissent, Justice Sonia Sotomayor, a former prosecutor and federal trial judge, condemned the decision for construing "ambiguity in favor of the police," which marked "a substantial retreat from the protection against compelled self-incrimination" provided by *Miranda*. In fact, she said, suspects often invoke their rights with "equivocal or colloquial language." This ruling "invites police to question a suspect at length—notwithstanding his persistent refusal to answer questions—in the hope of eventually obtaining a single inculpatory response which will suffice to prove waiver of rights." She concluded: "Today's decision turns *Miranda* upside down. Criminal suspects must now unambiguously invoke their right to remain silent—which, counterintuitively, requires them to speak."

Furthermore, even the eroding provisions of *Miranda* don't travel well. While the United States claims the right to prosecute crimes committed against Americans anywhere on earth, it does not extend full constitutional rights to suspects interrogated abroad, even when they are later tried in the United States. No Miranda warning need be given unless American agents do the questioning, use foreign police as surrogates, or operate with them jointly.[74] Non-Mirandized statements to foreign authorities are admissible if the government can show that they're voluntary—a big "if," especially during a time of terrorism, as judges and juries face the difficult duty of evaluating confessions that migrate into U.S. courts.

CONFESSION ABROAD, TRIAL AT HOME

In the dense rain forest of Uganda's Bwindi Impenetrable National Park, gunfire broke the dawn, followed by a woman's scream. Some people heard grenades exploding. An American hid silently inside her tent, hoping to be overlooked. A couple quickly crawled out the back of their tent and concealed themselves in the bush. Others were less agile and less fortunate.[75]

So began Monday, March 1, 1999, as a platoon of Hutu militia, seeking English-speaking tourists, swept into a camp. And so, too, began a long and tangled process of investigation, capture, and interrogation. During fifteen months of questioning, three men gave a total of twenty-nine differing statements of guilt. The case became a study in confession as a curse, confession as a blight on justice.

The tourists were there to see the endangered mountain gorillas in one of the animals' final habitats. The militiamen were there to send a message by harming Westerners whose countries supported Rwanda's government. Scattered and exiled after the Hutu-led genocide against minority Tutsis in 1994, the remnants of Hutu forces had regrouped in neighboring lands across the borders, grandly naming themselves the Liberation Army of Rwanda (ALIR). Their ragtag insurgency nurtured hopes of overthrowing the Tutsi leadership that had come to power following the massacres. The militia's Irondelle Company had sent some of its men into the national park.

At the outset, they killed a Ugandan park ranger during a firefight. Then they rounded up tourists, let the French remain untouched, and marched seventeen English speakers out of the camp, where they bludgeoned and hacked eight of them to death: four Britons, two New Zealanders, and two Americans. One American left alive was given a note to convey to the U.S.

ambassador; handwritten declarations were placed on bodies. "This is the punishment of the Anglo-Saxon who sold us," said one. "You protect the minority and oppress the majority."[76]

That two U.S. citizens were among the victims—Susan Miller and her husband, Robert Haubner, Intel employees from Oregon—gave license for the FBI's involvement, which began two days after the attack and gained intensity as Washington swaggered across the battlefield of terrorism. American officials pressed Rwanda for action, offered rewards, and urged that Rwandan forces question Hutu rebels being captured during border-land clashes in 2001. That was done until about ten suspects emerged, eventually whittled down to three.

Rwandan officials worked on the men for a while, then reported them ready to talk. First a State Department security officer at the embassy questioned them. Afterward, FBI agents flew to Rwanda again and again to wander through a labyrinth of more than fifty "interviews." In February 2003, Rwanda released the three to U.S. custody.[77]

Indicted in the United States, they were assigned court-paid defense attorneys and investigators, who also visited Rwanda, gathered witnesses, and then moved to exclude the defendants' statements from evidence. Finally, seven years after the crime, they sat in a federal courtroom in Washington, D.C., where Judge Ellen Segal Huvelle confronted the task of unraveling the circumstances behind the only evidence the FBI had brought back: the men's confessions.

Huvelle conducted a hearing longer than most trials: five weeks of testimony by nineteen people who included Rwandan ex-prisoners and former cabinet ministers, six physicians, and two psychiatrists. She pieced together a narrative she judged credible and set it down in an exacting 150-page opinion, a rare model of judicial scrutiny over the process of interrogation.

The three Hutus were imprisoned at the Kami military camp, whose Tutsi commander, Captain Alex Kibingo, questioned them himself, usually at his house. He carried some baggage. He had been wounded twice by Hutu forces, and when he testified later in Washington, the judge observed "his palpable desire for revenge" and noted that "in his view, the defendants 'are working with ALIR,' and, therefore, 'If they are punished . . . I will be happy.'"

All three began with firm denials. One, Gregoire Nyaminani, insisted that he had been stationed at the edge of the park, nowhere near the killings. The others, François Karake and Leonidas Bimenyimana, claimed no involvement in the murders. These answers did not please Kibingo and his men.

After their statements of innocence, the prisoners testified, the windows of the small rooms where each was kept alone were covered with iron sheets to block out light. Water was splashed inside to force them to sit on wet concrete floors, worsening the harsh conditions: no electricity, no bed or mattress, a can for a toilet, just one daily meal—a small cup of corn and beans contaminated with sand and stones. They lost weight, and hunger gave them dizziness and headaches. One contracted worms, and two, malaria.

That was their reality, from which they were transported from time to time into the artificial propriety of an FBI interview when agents came to town. Back and forth they went from their squalid, darkened cells at Kami camp to a comfortable conference room at national police headquarters in the capital of Kigali, back and forth between brutality and legality, reality and unreality.

With the first suspect, Nyaminani, seated at a long table, the lead FBI agent, Jennifer Snell Dent, instructed a Rwandan interpreter to read aloud the overseas version of the Miranda warning, translating it into Kinyarwanda, the national language. "We are representatives of the United States government. Under our laws, you have certain rights. Before we ask you any questions, we want to be sure you understand those rights. You do not have to speak to us or answer any questions. Even if you have already spoken to Rwandan authorities, you do not have to speak to us now. . . ."

Nyaminani heard it differently, then and every time, as giving him "the right to talk to these people" because he was "not accused." In another session, he understood the translation to mean, "This paper is about my rights, and that I should talk because I'm not accused, and you don't need a lawyer because you're not in court."[78] The various interpreters were themselves interrogators or investigators, hardly neutral.

Printed copies might have helped, but Dent didn't always have any, and when she did, they weren't in Kinyarwanda, only in French and English, which Nyaminani couldn't read. But he signed the form anyway, fearful with Kibingo's soldiers and Rwandan investigators in the room.

He was only on the park's periphery, he told Dent, and he named sixteen men who entered, including the platoon commander, Bimenyimana. The FBI agents said they didn't believe his claim of innocence. They did not ask him how he was being treated.

Back at Kami, Nyaminani's clothes and blanket were taken away.

Four days later, again in the comfort of the police headquarters conference room, he first gave the FBI a two-page written statement reiterating his story, then changed it orally into an admission that he'd entered the park and knew generally about the attack. Only then was he read a mangled variation of his rights. Again he denied involvement in the murders, which he said were committed by a section of the platoon that remained behind and included a man named Karake.

Kibingo then had Karake brought to his house for questioning, but Karake steadfastly insisted on his innocence. A week later, the same denial, and again a day later, this time in a statement that Karake wrote and signed. The third denial brought consequences. Back in his darkened room, soldiers handcuffed his left wrist to his right ankle, and his right wrist to his left ankle, leaving him bent and twisted until the following day.

That evening, soldiers came to Karake's room, unwound him from his painful position, and marched him to Kibingo's house. They sat him in a chair, and Kibingo commanded him to admit that he and Nyaminani had killed. He would not. With the open palms of his hands, Kibingo slapped his ears so hard that Karake "saw something blinking . . . like sparks of fire," a method known elsewhere in the world of torture as *teléfono*, an expert later testified. He fell out of his chair, and Kibingo kicked him.

At last, Karake gave in. He agreed to say whatever Kibingo wanted. To seal the deal, Kibingo beat him with a stick the length of a man's arm, then with a brick inside a sock. A pen and paper were put in front of him, and Kibingo told him what to write: that he had killed one tourist.

Kibingo then passed word up his chain of command that Karake had something to tell the Americans, so the prisoner sat again at the police headquarters conference table with a State Department security officer from the embassy, Bryan Bachmann, who conducted preliminary interviews in the FBI agents' absence. Rwandan investigators were always present, and Kibingo often was as well.

"You do not have to speak to us or answer any questions. . . ."

The overseas version of the Miranda warning explains the right to a lawyer but adds this: *"Because you are not in our custody and we are not in the United States, we cannot ensure that you will be permitted access to a lawyer, or have one appointed for you, before or during any questioning."*[79] Karake did not entirely understand what a lawyer did, but he signed the waiver, because he was afraid not to.

There was bottled water on the table, and bathroom breaks were per mitted. Bachmann asked for more details than appeared in Karake's written statement, which did not specify even the gender of the tourist he supposedly killed. It was a white man with a tattoo of an eagle on his arm, Karake said, the first of many specifics that didn't coincide with facts discovered on the ground: Haubner had a tattoo on his shoulder, but it looked nothing like an eagle.

Eager to avoid the ire of Kibingo, Karake enriched the story. He was ordered to kill, he told Bachmann, so he took an ax and smashed the head of a man lying facedown on the ground, covered with a bedsheet. No sheets were found at the scene, however, and other supposed participants said the victims were not covered. Put together, Karake's various statements had him seeing a tattoo unlike the real one through the T-shirt of a victim covered by a sheet that nobody else noticed and was never found.

Bachmann requested that the Rwandan officials leave the room. Alone with Karake and the embassy's interpreter, a Rwandan who had transported him from Kami and acted as an investigator, Bachmann asked how Karake was being treated. Karake revealed nothing about the abuse, he testified later, because Kibingo "would have beaten me again, and he would have even killed me."

"Kwasa kwasa" was the name of the procedure. Nyaminani's wrists were tied together with two ropes, one leading over his shoulder, the other behind his back. Kibingo once threw him against a wall. He was also handcuffed in the twisted position that Karake endured for long periods, and Kibingo beat him with a foot-long rubber slab two inches thick.

"Even if you have already spoken to Rwandan authorities, you do not have to speak to us now. . . ." At the conference table with the FBI, Nyaminani named numerous men involved but again professed his own innocence. He asserted that Karake talked in his sleep about the killings.

Back in his house on the base, Kibingo beat Karake so fiercely with a wooden stick and a brick that the prisoner's left wrist and forearm were injured, became infected and swollen, and had to be bandaged.

"You do not have to speak to us or answer any questions. . . ." Karake signed the waiver. Agent Dent of the FBI noticed the arm and asked what happened. From blisters, Karake said. She didn't ask the obvious follow-up—where did the blisters come from?—and Karake volunteered nothing, fearing that he "would have been beaten again."

He then gave Dent a piece of what she sought: an admission that he was ordered to kill three white men, killed one, and saw other members of his unit kill two others with an ax.

Again at the Kami camp, Kibingo beat him anyway, threatening that he would "continue hitting" and "would kill" him if he didn't confess to additional murders. So after several more days of beatings, Karake complied, admitting to killing two other men as well. Rwandan officials informed Dent, who did not ask how the Rwandans had managed to acquire information the Americans could not.

"If you decide to speak with us now, without a lawyer present, you retain the right to stop answering questions at any time. . . ." Karake signed the version in English, which he could not read.

So it went for him and the others: antiseptic sessions at police headquarters with the Americans interspersed with torture at the military camp. When an FBI interrogator questioned their denials, the suspects adjusted, because with Rwandans present, every FBI doubt carried an ominous ring, signaling further torture back at Kami.

Gradually, the men succumbed, but their confessions clashed with known reality. One saw red underwear: none was found. The undiscovered bedsheets were mentioned again, along with inaccurate descriptions of the tattoo. Bimenyimana claimed to have seen Karake kill a man and woman together, and Nyaminani said that under orders he'd taken a man and a woman into the forest to be murdered, but in fact men had been killed with men, and women with women. No couple was found dead together. Nyaminani's DNA did not match any material discovered on the bodies.

"If you want a lawyer, but the foreign authorities do not permit access at this time to a lawyer or will not now appoint one for you, then you still have the right not to speak to us at any time without a lawyer present. . . ."

The inconsistencies and contradictions among all the confessions did not seem to trouble Dent or other American agents. They never bothered to visit the Kami camp to see how their suspects were being treated. They never conducted an inquiry into the Rwandans' interrogation methods. The FBI either did not know, pretended not to know, or did not care to know what was happening during the long intervals between their charades of legality. The "evidence" was like food from a filthy kitchen, made to look presentable by clean silverware and starched tablecloths.

Virtually nothing corroborated the confessions, but plenty corroborated the abuse. If the motto of skilled torturers is "leave no marks," Kibingo and his men were sloppy in the extreme. The scars from the handcuffs, the ropes, and the beatings were observed and documented even by the prosecution's medical expert. Karake had "21 distinct lesions or clusters of lesions, some of which contained six or seven individual scars." In an impulse of honesty that impressed the judge, Karake portrayed some as "childhood injuries" and the most pronounced as "deliberate cutting wounds" from rituals. But those he attributed to abuses were deemed consistent with blunt trauma, cuffing, and other techniques he had described to the court.

The U.S. government argued that as time went on, the suspects' statements traveled closer and closer to the truth, while Judge Huvelle suggested that the torture may have propelled them further and further from the truth. Whichever it was, the admissions of guilt shed no light on the truth at all. The FBI had laundered the confessions as the Mafia launders money: by placing the cover of legitimacy over the crime, over the coercion behind the scenes. Instead of revealing reality, confession masked it.

Judge Huvelle found the statements involuntary and suppressed them. Her ruling was so carefully detailed and tightly reasoned that the government didn't bother to appeal. Without other sufficient evidence, the Justice Department dropped the charges, leaving a lesson that law enforcement seems loath to learn: Heavy reliance on the tool of confession is lazy. It aborts justice. As a result, whoever murdered eight people that March day in Bwindi—whether the three defendants or others—was not held to account.

In late 2011, more than a dozen years after the crime, and four years after their confessions were ruled inadmissible, the three Rwandan militiamen remained jailed in the United States, because they did not want to leave the country. Instead, they applied for asylum, arguing that they would be persecuted and tortured if they returned home to Rwanda. Pending an immigration court's decision, or a third country's willingness to accept them, they stayed locked up.

If you've confessed under pressure, you have two chances to nullify your admission. You can persuade the judge to suppress it, as the Rwandans did, or if you fail at that, you can try to convince the jury that it was all a lie exacted under duress. That was the way open to a naturalized American named Muhammad Salah.

When he was arrested during a visit to Israeli-occupied Gaza in 1993, the United States took the unusual step of protesting "the delay in consular access and the condition of treatment."[80] By 2007, though, when the Justice Department wanted to use a confession he'd signed back then, the condition of treatment in 1993 looked just fine—a retroactive absolution of the Israelis.

In fact, Salah contended, the Israelis had abused him into admitting falsely that he had funneled money to Hamas. Under the military law that

Israel applied in Gaza, he had no right to an attorney during interrogation. He was slapped, hooded, kept naked, deprived of sleep, and forced into stress positions, he claimed. After nearly five years in an Israeli prison, he returned home to Chicago, where federal authorities arrested him in 2003 on the same charge.

At a suppression hearing before trial, closed to the public to protect the identities of agents from Shin Beth (the Israeli secret police), the judge heard them rebut the allegations ("I am disgusted by even talking about it," said one interrogator with practiced sensitivity), and she ruled the confession admissible.[81]

But the Israelis' wounded protests failed to charm the jurors, who unanimously rejected the heart of the government's case, finding Salah and another Palestinian-American not guilty of sending funds to the Hamas military wing. Salah was convicted of a lesser charge—obstruction of justice (lying in a civil suit)—and sentenced to twenty-one months.[82]

Another Arab-American tried to escape from his confessions, which were made to Saudi interrogators and imported into his federal trial in the United States. He was Ahmed Omar Abu Ali, a Virginia college student with dual U.S. and Jordanian citizenship who came under suspicion while studying in Saudi Arabia.

He needed either judge or jury to believe his allegations that he had been whipped, beaten, and chained by his wrists to the ceiling to force him to say that as a member of a secret al-Qaeda cell in Medina, he had planned to return to the United States to blow up planes, attack nuclear facilities, and assassinate President Bush with either gunfire or a car bomb. He told the Saudis that he had "moved from his university dormitory to al-Qaeda safehouses" and had "received training in weapons, explosives, forgery, and intelligence gathering," as the Fourth Circuit Court of Appeals summarized his statements.[83]

Bits of independent evidence corroborated his confessions: documents in a safe house containing his aliases and "various weapons, explosives, cell phones, computers, and walkie-talkies found [by the Saudis] in the safehouse, all of which Abu Ali had described," the appeals court noted.

The day before his arrest, U.S. officials had issued a secret, emergency order under the Foreign Intelligence Surveillance Act to a telecommunications company for archived e-mails, which had turned up an exchange, amateurishly encoded, between Abu Ali and a reputed al-Qaeda figure, Sultan Jubran Sultan al-Qahtani. Lamenting recent arrests of Saudi militants, Abu Ali wrote, "I heard the news about the children's sickness. I wish them a speedy recovery," to which al-Qahtani replied ridiculously, "I was saved from the accident by a great miracle. . . . Get yourself ready for the medical checkup because you may have an appointment soon."

Still, "Abu Ali's own repeated confessions provide the strongest evidence of his guilt," said the court, and herein lies the problem. Confessions under the care of foreign police who don't provide Miranda warnings or attorneys, especially in a country with the fragile civil liberties of Saudi Arabia, should never be taken as the strongest evidence of anything. They contaminate the American criminal justice system.

They presented the federal judge Gerald Bruce Lee with the conundrum of figuring out whether they were given voluntarily—not whether they were true or false, just whether they were willing or coerced. For that he needed seven days of testimony via satellite by Saudi officials, including a captain and a brigadier general identified by pseudonyms, and eight more days of live witnesses in his Virginia courtroom, including physicians who inspected Abu Ali's body for signs of torture and psychiatrists who inspected his mind for post-traumatic stress disorder.

To allow the confessions into the trial, the law required only a "preponderance of evidence," meaning at least a 51 percent chance that they were voluntary. This weak but well-established standard allows judges to indulge their hunches, impressions, and instincts. So contradictory was the evidence here that Judge Lee relied on body language, demeanor, and unquantifiable feelings that some witnesses were truthful and others not. There was no way to prove definitively that Abu Ali had or had not been tortured, but the judge was forced to decide.[84]

Although the Saudi officials were visible only on a TV screen, Lee perceived them as credible in their steadfast denials of brutality—even the captain, who swore that he never abused anyone but got confessions or statements from every single suspect he had questioned in his seven years as an interrogator. This might have triggered a touch of skepticism: success records of 100 percent are only slightly more convincing than elections where dictators get 99 percent of the vote.

Judge Lee also credited everything the FBI agents said. They testified that when they observed Abu Ali through a one-way mirror just four or five days after he had supposedly been whipped, he showed no signs of pain but sat comfortably, rocking and swiveling in his chair. Perhaps that was true, perhaps not. The judge believed it.

This was the same FBI that later ignored Abu Ali's complaints of mistreatment. Fearing retaliation by the Saudis, he had said nothing about torture during earlier visits from U.S. consular officers. Only when FBI agents finally interviewed him directly did he take the gamble in what he described as a daring attempt to get help. The abuse, he told them, had impelled him to give false information.[85] The agents' reaction was disappointing. "Oh yeah? I'm going to ask the general," one said, then walked out of the room, didn't return, and reported the allegation only to his supervisor, as Abu Ali told it. No inquiry was made of the Saudis, nor was notice given to the State Department, whose embassies are supposed to monitor treatment of Americans in foreign jails. In short, the FBI showed as much interest as it did in the Rwandans' interrogations.

If the Saudis did torture as Abu Ali claimed, they were better than the Rwandans at leaving no marks. He had been blindfolded and chained to the floor in a kneeling position when he was whipped, he said, but nearly two years later, when doctors for the defense and the prosecution examined him, lines on his back did not have the normal features of scars: they were level with the surface of his skin, neither higher nor indented, as scars usually are. The prosecution's professionals, predictably, did not deem them evidence of whipping. The defense expert, Dr. Allen Keller, a specialist who had interviewed and examined multiple victims of torture, spent eight hours with Abu Ali and found the marks consistent with his account of abuse. Judge Lee resolved this ambiguity in favor of the prosecution, whose dermatologist saw only color photographs of the prisoner's back.

There are also invisible marks on the mind after you have been chained to the ceiling, told that you will undergo the amputation of your hand or your foot or your head, wrapped in a web of sleeplessness from all-night interrogations, and granted little kindnesses to reinforce the sense of vulnerability—all techniques that Abu Ali claimed to have endured. After conducting several interviews and administering a widely used test, a psychiatrist for the defense concluded that he suffered from post-traumatic stress disorder; a consulting psychiatrist for the FBI concluded the opposite and suggested that he was malingering.

The judge chose to go with the FBI's expert and disbelieve the PTSD diagnosis, but for thin reasons. He noted that the defense psychiatrist had grown testy under cross-examination and had failed to interview guards and nurses at the local Virginia jail to check Abu Ali's assertion that his Saudi experience had left him with a fear of all prison personnel. Judge Lee was impressed by the FBI psychiatrist's report from prison staff "that Mr. Abu Ali was smiling when he first arrived . . . was jovial within a few days . . . that Mr. Abu Ali chats with them, gets along with them, and asks favors of many of them." The judge did not mention another interpretation: that out of fear, a prisoner can try to ingratiate himself, precisely the dynamic that interrogators establish.

Lee was also bothered that Abu Ali could not say what instrument the Saudis had used to whip him. Had the judge accepted the diagnosis of PTSD and understood its symptoms, he might have recognized the syndrome in which memory is repressed as a method of self-protection. But while acknowledging that trauma victims sometimes "have difficulty recalling details of the event," Lee then faulted Abu Ali for having exactly that difficulty: "It is noteworthy that Mr. Abu Ali could not recall, even by texture, shape, or dimension, what hit him. Was it a cylinder? Belt? Whip? Stick? Baseball bat? Of course, he was blindfolded and chained to the floor when the beating allegedly occurred so he may not know the exact item used to hit him. However, it seems to the Court that he could, at the very least, provide some basic description of what the item might have been based on how it felt to him."

It was a circular argument: no PTSD, so no excuse for forgetting what didn't happen. Yet the memory loss may have been genuine. Would the young man have been credible had he fabricated a clear story and stuck to it?

Abu Ali had repeatedly asked for a lawyer, but the Saudi system allows no attorney during investigation. He had not been read his right to silence, because no such right exists in Saudi procedure. After what he said were forty-seven nights of questioning and solitary confinement, he was promised a return to the general prison population once he read his statement aloud. He did so, not realizing that he was being videotaped. Punchy from lack of sleep and cheerful that his conditions were about to ease, he clowned around—fatefully, as it turned out.

His thirteen-minute confession impressed both the judge and the jury, but not in the way he wanted. They found him cocky, relaxed, and cavalier, hardly the behavior of a torture victim. He smiled and laughed. He joked about how little good the training in concealing his identity had done and pantomimed himself holding a gun. He was convicted and sentenced to thirty years, a term too lenient for the Bush Justice Department, which got a ruling from the Fourth Circuit that Judge Lee had unjustifiably departed downward from the sentencing guidelines.

In pronouncing the sentence, Lee had observed: "Abu Ali never planted any bombs, shot any weapons, or injured any people, and there is no evidence that he took any steps in the United States with others to further the conspiracy." It was a close paraphrase of another judge's remarks in the Padilla trial. But when the case was sent back down for resentencing, the Justice Department, now under Obama, persuaded Lee to increase the term to life. The judge then shifted ground, noting Abu Ali's "unwillingness to renounce the beliefs that led to his terrorist activities" and declaring, "I cannot put the safety of the American citizenry at risk."[86]

Torture is invisibly insidious, whether practiced by an agency itself or tolerated by an agency indifferent while others do it. During this time of terrorism, the CIA has fit into the first category, the FBI into the second. There were exceptions, among them the FBI agents who complained about the abuses they witnessed at Guantánamo. But as a whole, the institutions allowed themselves to be swept along in acquiescence. A security and intelligence apparatus can be thus destroyed.

In Russia, wrote Vladimir Bukovsky, the human rights campaigner who spent a dozen years in Soviet prisons and psychiatric hospitals, one czar after another "solemnly abolished torture upon being enthroned, and every time his successor had to abolish it all over again. . . . They understood that torture is the professional disease of any investigative machinery. . . . Investigation is a subtle process, requiring patience and fine analytical ability, as well as a skill in cultivating one's sources. When torture is condoned, these rare talented people leave the service, having been outstripped by less gifted colleagues with their quick-fix methods, and the service itself degenerates into a playground for sadists."[87]

Two days after taking office, President Obama abolished torture. A few months later, he reduced the CIA's role in interrogations, making the FBI the lead agency. It remains to be seen whether his successor will have to abolish it all over again.

Wounds will remain in any case. During the liberalization under Mikhail Gorbachev, the Soviet leader who permitted truth telling about the Stalinist past, I sat one day in the offices of a weekly magazine, *Ogonyok*, reading letters to the editor, mostly unpublished. In one, signed with the initials K.A., a former secret police interrogator confessed to inflicting torture decades before, asked his nation's forgiveness, and lamented his haunting dreams: "Now the people in the cases I investigated visit me at night, and instead of fear in their eyes I see that they despise me. How can I tell these people I tortured, how can I explain that my damned life was a tragedy, too?"[88]

The tortured and the torturers share a mutual trauma, Bukovsky said. He remembered a prison doctor near tears as she forced a feeding tube down his bleeding nostrils, his guards pressing for leniency. "Our rich experience in Russia has shown that many [torturers] will become alcoholics or drug addicts, violent criminals or, at the very least, despotic and abusive fathers and mothers."

To America he put this provocative question: "How can you force your officers and your young people in the CIA to commit acts that will scar them forever? For scarred they will be, take my word for it."[89]

CHAPTER TWO

Confessing Falsely

One nasty morning Comrade Stalin discovered that his favorite pipe was missing. Naturally, he called in his henchman, Lavrenti Beria, and instructed him to find the pipe. A few hours later, Stalin found it in his desk and called off the search. "But, Comrade Stalin," stammered Beria, "five suspects have already confessed to stealing it."

—a 1950s joke, whispered in Moscow

BETWEEN TRUTH AND ILLUSION

IF YOU HAVE NEVER been tortured, or even locked up and verbally threatened, you may find it hard to believe that anyone would admit to a crime that he didn't commit. Intuition holds that the innocent do not confess. What on earth could be the motive? To stop the abuse? To curry favor with the interrogator? To follow some fragile thread of imaginary hope that cooperation will bring freedom?

Yes, all of the above. In desperate helplessness, for short-term gain without regard for long-term consequences, the suspect simply concedes, or comes to accept in more complex fashion his own fabrications of guilt. Any policeman or prosecutor who doubts this should read *Darkness at Noon*, Arthur Koestler's masterpiece set in Stalin's Russia, whose protagonist, Rubashov, is maneuvered by his interrogator further and further from reality. "Even he himself was beginning to get lost in the labyrinth of calculated lies and dialectic pretences, in the twilight between truth and illusion. The ultimate truth always receded a step; visible remained only the penultimate lie with which one had to serve it."[1]

It does not take outright torture. In the United States, psychological studies of confessions that have proved false show an overrepresentation of children, the mentally ill or retarded, and suspects high on drugs or drunk on liquor. They are susceptible to suggestion, eager to please authority figures, disconnected from reality, or unable to defer gratification. The prob-

53

lem is not limited to these groups. Mature adults of normal intelligence also confess falsely, and ignorance of constitutional rights and criminal procedure compounds the vulnerability.[2]

Most judges and jurors have not been there, so they can only imagine. And American imaginations are dominated by fantasy worlds of television and movies, where threatening interrogations inevitably produce truth, where tricks and torture magically open minds; Hollywood has little taste for showing tough cops cleverly extracting false leads and phony admissions. So while real-life judges do suppress confessions and jurors do disbelieve them at times, it is not a common outcome. Yet false confessions figured in about 20 percent of the 271 convictions reversed by DNA evidence, according to the Innocence Project's count as of mid-2011.[3] Considering that DNA has been available for only the last two decades, and in just a fraction of criminal cases, many more erroneous convictions certainly occurred, and if one out of every five involves a false confession, the problem is immense.

Furthermore, in every one of the Innocence Project's cases, the confession was given years after the Supreme Court's 1966 *Miranda* decision. Whether recited or written, the warning is supposed to accomplish two ends: to prevent inhumane treatment and to get at the truth. Abusing a suspect into lying obviously subverts the fact-finding goal of the criminal justice system, jailing the wrong person and leaving the criminal free. *Miranda* may have reduced physical harm, but false confessions still abound even where *Miranda* rights are read and signed, as they were by tortured victims in Chicago.

There and elsewhere, suspects have given away their rights under duress, in the same coercive atmosphere that presses them into admissions of guilt. But even where abuse is absent, children, mentally retarded adults, and many others tend not to grasp the concepts in the Miranda warning, which is often given as a perfunctory formality. "The cops are skillful at eliciting a waiver," said Alan Hirsch, an expert on false confessions who teaches legal studies at Williams. "They treat it almost as an afterthought, mere paperwork: 'Just sign, and we'll talk.'" There is no grand announcement, no theatrical recitation that makes the prisoner stop, consider carefully, and take an informed decision. "The awful truth is that *Miranda* has limited utility for protecting the innocent," he said. About 80 percent of those who are not guilty sign and keep talking, usually for the same reason that people consent to searches: the belief that their refusal will sow suspicion and that their innocence will free them.[4]

Detectives Mirandized a sixteen-year-old boy named Felix in Oakland, California, and subjected him to much less than torture, yet he still confessed to complicity in a murder he couldn't have done. He wasn't beaten, electrically shocked, shackled into stress positions, or deprived of sleep. He was isolated, harangued, threatened, and frightened—legally approved techniques designed to break down resistance to telling the truth. The methods surely do that in some cases, but in others they overwhelm resistance to saying whatever the cops want to hear.

During questioning, police themselves are permitted to lie by pretending to have evidence or eyewitnesses, by planting a suggestion that the suspect's memory went blank while he committed the crime. A crafty interrogator can weave fictions into a story that even an innocent may accept.

"It's not like they put him on the rack," said Felix's lawyer, Richard Foxall, a public defender. "It's just the very nature of that door clanging behind you, when they've taken you literally out of the arms of your mother in front of your home. . . . That's the sound of doom. You're fifteen years old, they close that door with that metallic clang, that's as final as final can be."

Felix was fifteen in May 2005 when Antonio Ramirez was murdered. Witnesses who heard gunshots saw two dark-haired Hispanic-looking men in their late teens to mid-twenties run off, leaving Ramirez on the ground with seven bullets in his chest. "That was all the description that was provided," Foxall noted. "There was a direction of flight."[5]

Informants gave the cops the street names of a few hoodlums, which led to other names, and months later Detective Lou Cruz and Sergeant Mark Dunakin brought Felix into an interrogation room at night to ask him about the murder. Oddly, he didn't fit the description, Foxall noted: he looked as young as his age and had such flaming red hair that people called him Red.

Cruz and Dunakin seemed determined to fit the boy to the crime nonetheless. "They were pretty insistent that they knew he did it," said his lawyer. "They used a combination of the late hour, deprivation of the ability to talk to anybody for a couple of hours, a lot of shouting and screaming. He believed they weren't going to allow him to leave. They led him through a story. He nodded. Then they turned on the tape. He didn't tell them anything useful, said he didn't know anything about it, so after ten minutes they turned off the tape." They accused him of lying and assured him that he'd mess up his life if he didn't talk. One got so close that Felix was afraid he was about to be hit and asked the cop to back off.

Foxall hadn't been assigned yet, so the boy had no attorney present, but he asked for his mother, a request that invokes the right to silence. It is supposed to halt the questioning of a minor as decisively as an adult's demand for a lawyer.[6] "They told him he wouldn't get to speak to his mother until he spoke to them," Foxall said.

To defuse the rising tension, Felix "started to make up stuff," which was hard since he didn't know any details of the crime, even the date. So Cruz and Dunakin used the standard ploy of many frustrated interrogators: they primed the pump by asking leading questions embedded with specifics, which Felix then fed back to them.

They wanted a diagram of the crime scene, he told his lawyer later, but whatever he drew bore so little resemblance to reality that the cops never produced it. When he described escaping in one direction after the killing, they told him he wasn't making sense, because they knew from witnesses that the shooter had gone the opposite way. When he didn't mention an alley nearby, they told him about it, and he incorporated it into his statement. "Now we're getting somewhere," said one officer, as Felix recalled to his lawyer.

"The cops started telling him they wanted to hear about the gun," said Foxall, but he denied having a gun. "That's when they really got out of control and started yelling at him. He started to feel personally threatened. He actually did wind up saying something about a gun. He told them he had a gun that night but didn't use the gun."

So where was the gun? In a canny impulse, Felix made up a story: that he had left the gun with his grandfather. "I thought this was brilliant," said Foxall. "If he put something in there that was demonstrably false, there would be something wrong with the confession: he doesn't have a grandfather. Both grandfathers are dead."

Once the badgering had carved the confession roughly into shape, the officers taped it, although it lacked a critical detail, one they had neglected to feed him. Felix learned it three days later in court when he was handed the charge sheet and saw the date of the murder. He stared at the document and realized that he had the perfect alibi: on the day that Antonio Ramirez had been gunned down, Felix had been locked up in a juvenile detention facility.

For that he could thank the tough love of his grandmother. On probation for theft, he had violated the conditions by hanging out in a bad neighborhood that had been declared off-limits. As a punishment milder than jail, authorities offered an ankle bracelet for electronic monitoring, but his grandmother refused to allow her phone to be set up to make the required transmissions. She wanted him in custody—for his own good, it turned out—and so that is where he spent thirty-one days, one of them by lucky coincidence the day of the murder.

The charges were dropped, of course, and Foxall was greatly relieved. "I would have hated to have had to try the case," he said. "It would have been very scary. Juries don't want to believe that somebody will confess to a crime he didn't commit." Judges, either. "When we were standing there with the juvenile hall record, the judge said, 'Well, I don't understand—why would he confess?'"

Most questionable confessions cannot be proven false with absolute certainty, and police and prosecutors who rely on them usually shift and shuffle past new evidence that defeats the lie. Many oppose testing for DNA years after a conviction, and the Supreme Court has refused to find a constitutional right to such evidence.[7] Under the Bush administration, federal prosecutors required defendants pleading guilty to waive any claim to subsequent DNA testing, a policy reversed by Obama's Justice Department.[8] Even where DNA recovered from a rape victim doesn't match a suspect's, new theories of the crime are immediately spun by embarrassed cops and district attorneys: that their man was still guilty as an accomplice, that the genetic material came from another criminal, unidentified. A parcel of doubt often remains.

Not so in Felix's case. The falsehood of his admission was so obvious that it helped open the way to modest reform. At the urging of public defenders in Oakland, the police department instituted, then rescinded, then reinstated a policy of videotaping all statements. It equipped eleven interview rooms to record perpetually, so that the entire run of questioning leading up to the climactic confession—not just the final few minutes—is on record for judges and juries to evaluate. In keeping with professional guidelines on interrogation techniques, the suspect is not told that he is being taped (lest he hesitate to incriminate himself), and if he asks, the police officer "may deny the fact that the interview is being recorded," according to Oakland's manual.[9]

Yet the department took no action against the two interrogators. Detective Cruz remained a prominent homicide investigator for the Oakland Police Department. Sergeant Dunakin switched to a traffic unit where he could do what he loved, ride a Harley-Davidson.[10]

Felix was not unique. A 2004 study found three prisoners who had admitted to crimes that had been committed while they, too, had the perfect alibi of being in jail. Of 125 confessions later proven inaccurate by DNA mismatches or the discovery of the real perpetrators, forty came from minors under eighteen and seven from children under fourteen, whose special vulnerability to tricks of interrogation has been established by extensive social psychology research.

One of the forty, Allen Jacob Chesnet, sixteen, confessed to murdering a neighbor after Maryland police prompted him with specifics, showed him pictures of the crime scene, and pretended that the lab had called with a DNA match. He surmised, as many children do, that he'd be jailed if he kept up his denials and could go home if he confessed, so he gave a statement. It was full of errors and omissions: He said that he'd stabbed the neighbor once, but in fact she'd been stabbed repeatedly, the police knew. He didn't mention—because he didn't know—that she'd also been strangled with her bra strap and hit on the head with a porcelain figurine.

He also told the police that she had stabbed him in the hand and that he had bled. But after the true lab results showed that his DNA did not match blood at the scene, he was still not released. It was campaign season, and the district attorney, in a heated race, didn't seem eager to admit error in such a high-profile case. He kept Chesnet in jail with adults for two months more, until safely reelected. During that time behind bars, the boy was knifed once and raped twice.[11]

Clearly, cops in some departments tend to bear down hard when the crime is serious or sensational. Almost all of the study's 125 false confessions involved murders (81 percent), rapes (9 percent), or arson (3 percent), whose gravity can generate intense pressure for quick arrests. Children who come under suspicion in such cases are easily manipulated.

Researchers find that the lower the age, the higher the willingness to make a phony admission simply to end the unpleasant stress of aggressive questioning. Even while playing the role of suspects during mock interrogations, one-quarter of jailed juvenile delinquents—no strangers to the machinations of criminal justice—said they would falsely confess to halt the process.[12]

Real examples are plentiful. Before finding the actual culprits, police extracted admissions to arson from a nine-year-old in Providence, Rhode Island, and two ten-year-olds in Salem, Virginia, and Galveston, Texas. Anthony Johnson, eleven, confessed falsely to murdering an elderly neighbor in Omaha, Nebraska.[13]

Two Chicago boys, ages seven and eight, caused a national sensation in 1998 when they told police during interrogation that they had killed Ryan Harris, an eleven-year-old girl found beaten on the head, her underpants stuffed in her mouth. The boys, confined for several days in a psychiatric institution, became poster children for the ills of America's inner cities, which seemed shrouded in doom. Then, three weeks later, the lab found semen on the girl's clothing, not within the capability of seven- and eight-year-olds, no matter how malevolent. Charges were dropped, but only against the remarkable reluctance of the Chicago police superintendent and the Cook County state's attorney, who remained gripped by the intoxicating power of the confession. They could not concede error. They could not free themselves from the fiction that the boys were somehow involved, even when the DNA identified the rapist and murderer as Floyd M. Durr, who had previously been accused of three other sexual assaults in the neighborhood where Harris had been found.

All the components of the criminal justice system—police, prosecutors, judges, jurors—lag far behind the understanding of human behavior that has been accumulated during decades of psychological study. That body of knowledge, confirmed by the hard experience of real cases and the recent precision of DNA testing, should make the false confession completely visible in the landscape of social problems, no more obscure or mysterious than crime itself. Yet professionals at every level create conditions that foster lies of guilt. Interrogation trainers teach manipulation, police use deception, prosecutors display a stubborn eagerness to accept admissions containing inaccuracies and contradictions. And the case law assembled by judges over the decades regulates interrogations too loosely.

There is nothing novel about false confessions. Some have been famous, others absurd. Some fifty women in Salem confessed to being witches. About two hundred people offered themselves to authorities as the kidnappers of Charles Lindbergh's baby in 1932, perhaps in some demented lust for notoriety. Psychologists reported that one man admitted to a murder to impress his girlfriend. Another did the same to confuse and retaliate against police who had arrested him at a party for drinking. A woman trying to hide an extramarital affair confessed just to convince her husband that she wasn't where he suspected: Gee, honey, I couldn't have been having sex with Joe, 'cause I was killing that guy on the other side of town![14]

Police sometimes play along with the nonsense. In Florida, they closed about twenty unsolved murders in 1979 by spending four days prompting disjointed, error-ridden confessions from Jerry Frank Townsend, whose IQ between fifty and sixty defined him as mentally retarded. His statements, recorded with frequent pauses, misstated the races and ages of some victims; a thirteen-year-old black girl killed in the daytime was transformed by Townsend into a white girl he said he'd murdered at night. Neverthe-less, despite the lack of physical evidence, he spent twenty-two years in prison, and the real serial killer and rapist, Eddie Lee Mosley, continued his spree.[15]

The psychological literature is clear: while false confessors include people with normal intelligence, those with IQs in the retarded range are especially vulnerable. Many tend to answer yes to every question, even the nonsensical: Does it ever snow here in the summer?[16] "The mentally retarded are slow thinking, easily confused, concrete (as opposed to abstract) think-ers, often lack the ability to appreciate the seriousness of a situation, may not understand the long term consequences of their actions, and tend to have short attention spans, poor memory, and poor impulse control," write the law professor Steven A. Drizin and the psychologist Richard A. Leo. "The mentally retarded tend also to be highly submissive (especially eager to please authority figures), compliant, suggestible, and responsive to stress and pressure. As a result, people with mental retardation are disproportion-ately represented in the reported false confession cases."[17]

THE CENTRAL PARK JOGGER

Interrogation techniques taught by professional trainers influence the questioning that produces false confessions. The methods also produce true confessions; it's just hard to tell the difference.

One police tool is the cunning lie about evidence, carefully concocted to convince the suspect that persistent denial is futile in the face of over-whelming fact. "We are allowed, by law, to use guile and ruse, and we do," Detective Tom McKenna told *New York* magazine. That was thirteen years after he had persuaded a fifteen-year-old that his fingerprints would be found on the clothes of the raped and beaten woman called the Central Park jogger, where no useful prints had been found at all. "People only give things up when you tell 'em you got 'em," the detective said. "But to frame somebody and leave the right son-of-a-bitch out in the street? I'm irate anyone would infer that."[18]

Yet the New York City police did leave the right son-of-a-bitch on the street, and he committed four more rapes in the summer of 1989, murder-ing one victim who was pregnant. Meanwhile, one Latino and four black teenagers were charged on the basis of contradictory confessions, given after fourteen to thirty hours of interrogation, that got most details wrong, including such basics as time and place.

The crime in Central Park set off alarms along the racial frontier. Just after dark that night, dozens of youths from Harlem had rampaged through the park, attacking white joggers and bikers in a random spree they called "wilding." From the sanctuary of white privilege, the spasm of angry pleasure looked like a breach in the firewall that had somehow held back the roiling fury of the ghetto, now released to ignite long-standing stereotypes and fears of black aggression.

One victim became the symbol of the night and of the broader dread. Until she identified herself years later as Trisha Meili, she was known only as the Central Park jogger, and by her most superficial qualities: white, twenty-eight, a graduate of Wellesley and Yale, a promising Wall Street investment banker, just the sort of outline that might sketch the daughter, wife, sister, colleague, classmate, friend of any affluent New Yorker. For hours she lay bleeding into the ground, her moans unheard until a couple of construction workers passed by well after midnight. She had been beaten so badly that her left eye had come out of its socket, and she had lost three-quarters of her blood. After twelve days in a coma, she began a very slow and incomplete recovery, but she left behind every shred of memory about the attack.

Into that vacuum stepped Detective McKenna and his colleagues. From the boys' accounts, the officers appear to have used standard methods of isolation, deception, implied leniency, and reductions of moral responsibility. The teenagers had no contact with parents or lawyers for many hours, and they were deeply fatigued. One was told the fingerprint lie, and others were told they were just witnesses, not suspects. They all said later that they thought that once they confessed, they would be allowed to go home, a typical belief among youth in custody. If the cops had actually made such a pledge, the confessions would not have been admissible, for case law requires interrogators to avoid promises of leniency they cannot or will not keep, especially involving the severity of the charge or punishment. Instead, a skillful questioner weaves a web of implication that induces a suspect to invent his own hopes and expectations, a technique that is hardly different from an explicit promise in the mind of the suspect, yet is acceptable to the courts.

Finally, the teenagers engaged in the common practice, often encouraged by the interrogators, of minimizing their role by picturing others at the heart of the action: I felt pressured by my peers and didn't want to be there; I was standing at the side just watching, not raping, not beating. (In other cases, police sometimes float the notion that the victim provoked the crime. Trainers warn them not to give suspects an argument they can use in their defense at trial.)

The investigators might have been suspicious that four of the boys placed the location of the attack seven or eight blocks from the actual spot and said it had occurred forty-five minutes later than reasonably possible, given other evidence. Moreover, all the accounts differed from one another, and no forensic evidence linked the boys to the place or the victim. DNA testing was primitive then, but hairs found on one youth, originally thought to be Meili's, could not be matched. Nor could a semen stain on her sock. Nonetheless, the police believed the boys' confessions, which were video-taped and admitted into evidence. They were convicted and sentenced to five to fifteen years.

After they had served their time and the statute of limitations had expired, Matias Reyes, a prisoner doing thirty-three years to life for the subsequent rapes and murder, came forward to say that he had attacked the Central Park jogger alone. Unlike the teenagers, he was able to draw a detailed map and describe exactly what happened where.

To his credit, the Manhattan district attorney, Robert Morgenthau, did what few prosecutors are willing to do: he reinvestigated the case and deter-mined that Reyes's DNA matched the semen, that the hairs on one boy's clothes were not the jogger's, and that hair and blood on a nearby rock, supposedly the assault weapon, were not hers either. Eleven months of investigation turned up no connection between Reyes and any of the boys, so the prosecutors were convinced that he had acted alone. But the police department was not, holding to the theory—now an implausible theory—that the boys had been involved along with Reyes or had conducted an initial attack before Reyes happened along. That proposition was based on nothing except the confessions and a stiff-necked refusal to admit a colos-sal mistake.

HUMAN LIE DETECTORS

Absolutes are hard to come by in the criminal justice system, so they are manufactured. A verdict becomes a fact, and a fact is not easily revised, even though it is a synthetic sort of fact, like an umpire's close and disputed call at second base. It creates a new reality, which may not be what really happened. The game moves on as if the runner were obviously out, as if the defendant were clearly guilty.

A confession is the same. Once police and prosecutors obtain it, they

tend to treat it as a fact, and research has shown that it colors their interpretation of the evidence, leading them to credit what confirms the guilt
and discount what does not. "A suspect's confession sets in motion a virtually irrefutable presumption of guilt among criminal justice officials, the
media, the public, and lay jurors," write Drizin and Leo. Police "typically
close the investigation, clear the case as solved, and make no effort to pursue other possible leads—even if the confession is internally inconsistent,
contradicted by external evidence, or the result of coercive interrogation."[19]
Judges set higher bail, prosecutors pursue more serious charges, and juries
are more likely to convict. Confessions carry more weight than eyewitness
testimony or other evidence, and even confessions that later prove false
bring guilty verdicts—in 73 and 81 percent of cases researched in 1998 and
2004.[20]

Furthermore, mock jurors do not disregard confessions that they recognize as coerced, even when instructed by a "judge" to discount them
entirely. In one experiment, volunteers were offered one of three versions
of a murder case: no confession, immediate spontaneous confession, or a
"high-pressure" confession after suffering pain and threats by a gun-waving
detective. Many of the jurors saw the high-pressure confession as involuntary and gave lip service to the law by saying that it would not influence
their verdict. But it had great influence nonetheless, pushing the conviction
rate far above the version that lacked any confession at all.[21]

After conviction, the fact of a confession that has been ruled admissible and accepted by the jury is almost impossible to dislodge. If a hierarchy of appeals courts considers the "totality of circumstances" sufficient
to make it voluntary, then it is deemed reliable. If no other constitutional
rights were violated, the only escape through the courts is by finding new
evidence, presented within a limited window of time, sufficient to justify
a new trial. Otherwise, a pardon or clemency can be sought, but those are
rarely granted. An exception came when Governor George Ryan of Illinois, impressed by DNA's exposure of thirteen erroneous convictions in his
state, emptied death row by commuting the sentences of all 156 prisoners
awaiting execution.[22]

As a rule, then, a collection of confused, disjointed answers in an interrogation room is transformed and hardened into invincible truth. The game
moves on.

The interrogation industry knows the power of the confession, and so
mounts expensive training programs to give questioners tools and techniques to ferret out the "truth" within the limits set by courts. "The first

day, we teach how to assess credibility," said Joseph Buckley, president of John E. Reid & Associates, a leader in the field. Over 200,000 interrogators have attended its programs, where trainers instruct police departments and private corporations in a multistep process that begins with the non-accusatory "Behavior Analysis Interview" of a criminal suspect or an employee under investigation for wrongdoing.

Most striking is the confidence that guilt or innocence can be inferred by asking "two different kinds of questions: investigative and behavior-provoking questions," Buckley explained. "Let's say your neighbor is killed one night. Police say, 'What should we do if we catch the guy?' Guilty people say, 'Gee, I don't know, that's not my decision.'" Asked if the perpetrator should be given a second chance, the guilty often say yes, the innocent typically say no.[23]

This initial interview is non-accusatory and begins with benign background questions designed to identify a person's baseline of normal behavior. Does the subject make eye contact? Does he speak slowly or rapidly? How long does he wait before answering a question, and how long are his answers? Then some fifteen questions are posed about the offense, and the interrogator watches for deviations from the norm, which may indicate involvement.

The innocent tend to suggest solutions to the crime and speculate about possible culprits, displaying what trainers call the Sherlock Holmes effect. By contrast, the guilty are usually less eager to explore the possibilities, since they cannot contribute relevant thoughts without implicating themselves. As a result, their self-portrayals of innocence are less compelling.[24]

The Reid Technique, as the company calls its method, provides an arsenal of probes and tests: Virtually all innocent and most guilty people agree immediately to an interview, says Reid's online Investigator Tips, but "a suspect who puts off the interview without good reason should be viewed suspiciously." Language considered "evasive" includes hedging with such terms as "usually," "generally," and "as a habit." Here, too, it's critical to make comparisons with the person's normal habit of speech, Buckley notes. Direct quotations suggest a fabricated story—who can remember whole sentences verbatim?—while indirect quotations presented as paraphrasing indicate truthfulness. Bad grammar is distributed among both innocent and guilty.

Specific answers also fall into patterns that can be elicited by the behavior-provoking questions. If a store's cash deposit is missing from a safe, it's worth asking employees how they feel about being questioned, according to an article by Buckley and two professors of criminal justice.

An innocent clerk might welcome an interview to prove her innocence and help catch the crook, while a guilty employee might deny having feelings about being questioned, saying she's cooperating just to keep her job.[25]

Interrogators are advised to check suspects' honesty by posing questions with known answers. Ask someone with a criminal record whether he's ever been arrested or questioned by the police. "It is an effective strategy to invite suspects to lie to the investigator," the Reid tips announce. "Innocent suspects usually volunteer the truth, even if the truth reveals possible motives, access, or propensity."

Ask "bait questions," such as "Bill, if we were to review the surveillance video outside the store that day, is there any reason we would see you on the video?" Or, while holding a fingerprint card, "This very recent fingerprint was recovered from a door of the stolen car. Is there any reason this would be your fingerprint?" While the innocent would probably answer categorically, the guilty can be expected to dodge and weave. In the hypothetical case of the missing store deposit, for example, the interviewer might say that many safes have mechanisms to count the number of envelopes dropped into them; if the counter shows one less item than it should, what would be the reason? The innocent might reply that she was sure she inserted her envelope, so the discrepancy couldn't be from her deposit. The guilty might answer, "Gee, I don't know very much about mechanical things, maybe it got stuck or something."[26]

The body can betray the mind, investigators are told. "A truthful subject will exhibit a variety of different postures throughout the course of an interview," but "a deceptive subject," whose lies require so much effort, "may assume an initial posture and never significantly deviate from that posture." Again, deviations from the norm are the key, including smiles and movements of the head, feet, legs, arms, and hands.

The Reid techniques are also replete with caveats and cautionary notes. Don't jump to conclusions on the basis of eye contact, they warn. In some cultures, the averted glance is a sign of courtesy and deference, and even a liar may lock the questioner in a steady gaze during a well-rehearsed answer, a stare that usually breaks when an unexpected question is asked—one reason to put fifteen or twenty questions, not just two or three. Place nonthreatening questions first to establish normative behavior. Don't assume that nervousness or lying is related to the crime; it could be about other wrongdoing, such as unpaid child support or parking tickets.

Still, anyone reading the multiple tips and methods would assume that lies run in only one direction, concealing guilt. The training scarcely aims at revealing false confessions; false denials are the targets. And once the interrogator brands the suspect's denial a lie, the label sticks and leads to the next step—the accusatory interrogation—which assumes that a confession is true and a denial is false. Denial is equated with deception.

Many psychologists scoff at the techniques, ridiculing police who think they hold special powers to divine truth from falsehood, "a folk psychology of human lie-detection that is based on myth, superstition, and pseudoscience," write Drizin and Leo, "more akin to the witchfinding techniques of the 1690s than to the methods of modern science."

In fact, researchers have found that human beings detect lies at little more than chance rates. Reid counters that lab experiments are unlike real settings where the consequences are serious and suspects give off clearer signals.

Some experiments are illuminating nonetheless. In one, police officers were taken in by videos of relatives pleading for the return of missing family members, and failed to spot the deception: the relatives had murdered the missing. In another, college students trained on how to detect lies were less accurate but more certain than untrained students when shown videos of actual interrogations and denials. "The training procedure itself biased observers toward seeing deception, and hence guilt," the researchers concluded. Other studies revealed cops as more likely than laymen to disbelieve people, and inclined more frequently than college students to think a false confession was true. The police officers, too, were highly confident of their judgments, although "professional lie catchers" were correct only 45 to 60 percent of the time.[27]

One detective was quoted as saying, "You can tell if a suspect is lying by whether he is moving his lips."[28]

A devastating application of "folk psychology" set the stage for Martin Tankleff's false and fleeting confession to slaughtering his parents in their upscale Long Island home. The case demonstrated that you don't have to be a poor black kid to have your rights trampled.

Marty was seventeen. On the first morning of his senior year in high school, he woke up early, noticed lights on abnormally throughout the house, and found his mother, Arlene, lying in bed, beaten, her throat slashed. His father, Seymour, sat slumped at his desk, bloody, unconscious, gagging, and barely alive. Marty called 911, followed the operator's instructions to apply pressure with a towel to a gushing neck wound, and was covered with his father's blood when police arrived.

Something peculiar struck the lead homicide detective, K. James

McCready. The boy seemed unemotional. He sat placidly on a retaining wall beside the driveway, rinsed his bloody hands in a puddle, and then waited quietly in a patrol car as instructed, according to McCready's fourteen-page report. Marty gave the police the name of a likely murderer: Jerry Steuerman, who owed his father a substantial debt involving a bagel business. Tension between the two had been growing, and Steuerman had been the last to leave a late-night poker game at the house. But McCready looked in a different direction—the boy's strange calm seemed suspicious.

"I told him that I didn't think that he was very upset about the death of his parents," McCready wrote in his report, "and he said that he was all cried out by the time the Police arrived at his house."[29]

"The police are not psychologists," countered the psychologist Saul Kassin, an expert on confessions. "Psychologists who study reactions to trauma know that some people fly into a state of hysteria, but other people shut down, go numb, and appear emotionless. That doesn't make them killers."[30]

McCready demonstrated no understanding of trauma's multiple effects, so Marty's emotional shutdown looked uncaring, enough to convince the detective within an hour that he had found his murderer. That determination, which satisfied the standard police interview's first goal of assessing credibility, initiated a cascade of questioning aimed at breaking through to the boy's guilt.

At the station house, the two went round and round about when Marty got up, when he put on which clothes, which light switches he turned on in what order, how he got blood on his shoulder or his leg, and "when I saw that I wasn't getting anywhere with the questioning," McCready said, "I came up with an idea. I tricked him, yes I did." The detective walked to an adjacent room within hearing distance and dialed an extension on the next desk. "I picked up the phone in my usual way. I said, 'Homicide, McCready,'" then "I made up a conversation with myself. I said, 'Yeah, John . . . You're kidding! He came out. . . .'"

He went back to Marty and told a legally approved lie about his father. "I made believe that an officer at the hospital called, they'd pumped him full of Adrenalin, he'd come out of his coma, and that he had said, Marty, you did it."[31] In fact, Seymour Tankleff never regained consciousness and died a month later.

The cruel fabrication shook the teenager deeply. Still stained with the blood of his father, he was now shaken by his father's supposed accusation. "My father never lied to me," he said later, explaining what happened to him in those moments of interrogation. Initially, according to the police report, "Marty said if he said that, it was because he was the last person his father saw." He offered to take a lie detector test but wasn't given one. Had he been tested, the police would have been entitled to do what they often do—lie about its results to convince him that he'd failed.

"I was always brought up to trust law enforcement," Marty explained. "I was brought up that cops don't lie. My father was the police commissioner of Belle Terre. We lived in a very good neighborhood, and when the cops turned around and said your father said you did it, I started to doubt myself. I knew that my father would never lie to me. I knew in my heart and my soul I wasn't responsible for this, but when the cops start telling you we know you did it, you start to doubt yourself."[32]

The Supreme Court has tacitly approved police lies during interrogations, and lower courts have developed a body of case law that defines the boundaries of deception, which the Reid Technique is careful to delineate in its training literature. In 1969, the Court let stand a confession given after police falsely told a suspect that his companion had confessed.[33] Since then, trainers have taught police officers how to lie to suspects, but carefully enough to fall within the patchwork of approvals created by state and federal courts.

"Almost every interrogation involves some level of at least implied deceit," says one of the Reid tips. The duplicity begins with the cop declaring that there's no doubt that the suspect did the crime, backed up by references to physical evidence that doesn't exist. The tactic of pretending to have evidence but not actually fabricating it appears in a list of Reid's "suggestions." When false evidence is manufactured to fool suspects, judges have suppressed resulting confessions out of concern that the counterfeit may find its way into a trial. But it's OK to lie about having it. So when Florida police got a murder confession after typing up a lab report with phony DNA results, a state court overturned the conviction.[34] If the cop had just brandished the real forensic test and misrepresented it, however, or had waved any piece of paper, called it a report, and told the suspect that his DNA matched, that would probably have passed judicial muster.

The technique has risks, Buckley cautions. If you say falsely that a witness saw the suspect dash out of a building just before a fire, and the subject actually "stayed in the alley as a lookout while his partner went into the building," Buckley explains, "the investigator loses all of his credibility with the subject. That is why in the baiting technique we never say that we have the evidence."

Yet the online Reid material instructs interrogators on how to draw the line between pretending and fabricating: A suspect can be shown a card bearing a latent fingerprint and be told, "This is your fingerprint. We found it inside that stolen car, so don't insult my intelligence by telling me you weren't inside the car. We know you were." That's legal if the cop puts his own print on the card but not if he fakes it with the suspect's print.

Or the officer may brandish a DVD labeled with the date of the crime, tell the suspect that it's a surveillance video from a store, and say, "I reviewed it this morning, and it shows you going into the store just before the robbery. It's as clear as day; there's no doubt it is you." But he may not fabricate a video showing the suspect.[35] "Again, while this may be legal to do, it is very risky," Buckley remarked. "Consequently, we rarely do it."

The risk worrying Buckley is the loss of rapport between subject and questioner. But there is another risk—that of generating false confessions with these methods. It is occasionally mentioned in the training tips, which caution against lying unless denials are weak. Interrogators are advised against using the tactics on mentally impaired suspects who are eager to please and may believe the investigators more than their own recollections.[36]

This can also happen to mentally healthy adults, a fact ignored by training guidelines, which seem more pragmatic than ethical—probably a reflection of the police culture. Anything legal is moral, it seems. Anything the judge accepts is acceptable. That eases restraints considerably, since courts examine "the totality of circumstances" to determine whether a confession is voluntary. The Reid instructions warn interrogators that "the trickery or deceit employed must not shock the conscience of the court or community," but consciences seem hard to shock these days. The term "shock the conscience" derives from a 1952 Supreme Court case overturning a conviction after police burst into a couple's bedroom looking for drugs, saw the man swallow two pills, pried open his mouth to try to wrench them out, then took him to the hospital, where he was forcibly given medicine that made him vomit.[37] It's a wonder that no judges' consciences were shocked by Detective McCready's callous concoction that a dying father had pointed the finger of accusation at a stunned and grieving son.

"You can imagine Marty at this point kind of like a boxer who's dazed and weak in the knees about to go down," said Kassin, the psychologist. "They lower the boom and McCready goes out and stages a phone call. . . . In doing that, he cites to Marty the person in his life he trusts the most."[38]

"He then asked if he could have blacked out and done it," McCready wrote in his report. Here was an opening to fill the doubt with the mist of a false memory, an expedient way to create detailed confessions out of the thin air of vulnerability. The detective seemed to lead the speculation until Marty guessed that he might have been possessed, and McCready fashioned a narrative that the boy never signed or videotaped. The questioning ended when a sergeant interrupted to say that an attorney—Marty's uncle—had called to request that the session cease.

In experiments, adults who are told convincing fictions have become susceptible to memories of things that never happened—that they had once been lost as children in a mall, had nearly drowned, had been attacked by an animal, or had suffered an accident at a wedding. They may summon up recollections as vivid and imaginary as the details in a dream. A classic study demonstrated the vitality of false beliefs when college students were instructed to avoid hitting a certain key as they typed; an observer stood nearby, watching. When the computer crashed, the students were convinced by fake evidence—a phony printout of their keystrokes and the observer's false testimony—that they had caused the breakdown by hitting the forbidden key. They confessed and believed their confessions to be true, even to the point of providing details of how they pressed the key.[39]

Therefore, psychologists are not surprised that isolating some people in a process that distorts reality, that subjugates them to an authority figure's suggestion, can induce doubts about their own recollections. The phenomenon is called "memory distrust syndrome" and thrives in the setting of an interrogation.[40] Such "illusions of memory," described in a 1908 study of a Salem woman's confession to being a witch, may induce the suspect to imagine that a second personality has split off from her real self and committed the crime.[41] Marty Tankleff alluded to the notion as he pondered the possibility of his guilt.

The result is not just a false confession but an "internalized false confession" in which the suspect comes to think that he actually committed the crime. The admission is often embellished by invented details and motives—sometimes fed by the interrogator—that enhance the story's credibility. As Kassin observes, however, "a police-induced confession is like a Hollywood drama: scripted by the interrogator's theory of the case, shaped through questioning and rehearsal, directed by the questioner, and enacted by the suspect."

As soon as Tankleff was out of interrogation, he recanted his confession, as if coming out of a spell. It didn't help. The trial judge admitted it into evidence, a jury convicted him, and he was given fifty years to life. He got out seventeen years later, only after a New York appeals court vacated the conviction based on new evidence, uncovered mostly by a private investigator, that pointed in the direction of three ex-convicts organized by

Steuerman, who had disappeared several days after the murders, shaved his beard, taken an alias, and moved to California.⁴² Furthermore, Detective McCready and Steuerman may have known each other, according to two witnesses quoted in a book by the private investigator and a *Newsday* reporter.⁴³

New York's attorney general decided against retrying Tankleff, and against charging Steuerman and the others because of insufficient evidence. Tankleff filed a civil rights suit against Suffolk County and the police officers.⁴⁴

THE LAW SLIPS BACKWARD

"Ironically, as more is learned about the perils of false confessions, less is done to safeguard against them," wrote Alan Hirsch after sifting through cases against slaves in the antebellum South. He had discovered something intriguing: judge after judge had thrown out confession after confession induced by oblique, understated suggestions of either leniency or threat. Such rulings would rarely happen today, for the courts have grown permissive.

Before the Civil War, however, some judges in Mississippi, Alabama, and Florida recognized that truth could be sacrificed to the power disparities between slave and interrogator. An Alabama court ruled that even "the slightest inducement" would contaminate a confession's reliability. "A Mississippi court reversed a conviction when a slave confessed after being told that 'it would be better for [him] to tell the whole truth,'" Hirsch reported. "An Alabama court reversed a conviction because the master said, 'Boy, these denials only make the matter worse,' and the slave might 'very naturally have concluded that confessions of his guilt would make the matter better.'"⁴⁵

Concerns over slaves' vulnerabilities were probably magnified by bigotry; some rulings hinted at judges' patronizing stereotypes of blacks as frail in character and intellect, unable to withstand interrogation. In throwing out a confession in 1864, an Alabama court sounded a call to protect "those who are weak, or ignorant, and who might be tempted, or seduced, or overawed, by influences which could not affect the minds of the more intelligent, or more intrepid." Yet courts could not appraise the "constitutional firmness or weakness of each individual," the opinion noted, and so imposed a universal rule to reject induced confessions by anyone, not just slaves.⁴⁶

By the end of the century, the Supreme Court tuned in. Acknowledging the danger of implicit rewards and punishments, the Court in *Bram v. United States* quoted approvingly from a textbook's warning that a confession "must not be extracted by any sort of threats or violence, nor obtained by any direct or implied promises, however slight."

The case was a mystery at sea: During the dark mid-watch on a ship carrying lumber from Boston, an ax or other sharp tool was used to penetrate the skulls of the captain, his wife, and a second mate. An initial suspect with the name Brown, placed in irons, then accused Bram, the first officer, who was also taken into custody. During questioning in port, a detective confronted Bram with Brown's assertion that from his position on the wheel, he saw Bram kill the captain. "He could not have seen me from there," Bram replied, and that was taken as a confession. The detective urged him to name an accomplice to share the burden: an implicit promise of leniency, the Court found as it threw out the statements and ruled that once the accusation was presented, "the result was to produce upon his mind the fear that, if he remained silent, it would be considered an admission of guilt."

"Any doubt as to whether the confession was voluntary must be determined in favor of the accused," the justices declared. "Any doubt" has since grown to require much more: at least a 51 percent chance, a "preponderance of evidence," that the confession was involuntary. Anything less and the confession comes into the trial.[47]

Bram was far ahead of its time, predating the modern research on false confessions; the justices were keen enough to grasp what psychologists have now documented. Yet the opinion never took hold in the judicial system. It was dodged and disregarded as lower courts imagined that the case before them didn't quite fit the model, Hirsch observes, "that the alleged promise was not a promise, or somehow not a sufficient promise," not explicit, specific, or clear enough. Some courts didn't bother to rationalize *Bram* away; they just decided it should not be applied literally, or they simply stopped mentioning it at all, and then they cited one another in a chain reaction of evasion and erosion. In several cases, the Supreme Court was guilty of this itself, before finally laying the opinion quietly to rest in 1991. An excellent principle disintegrated into dust.[48]

The Reid training literature warns that threats and promises combined can generate false confessions, but it then takes advantage of the broadened latitude the courts have given. Interrogators are taught to walk a fine line between making a promise and cultivating hope. They may not say, "We'll get you off without prison," but they may ask, "Was this your idea or did your buddies talk you into it?" The question allows the suspect to consider two possibilities: a moral exemption for being pressured by peers, and a legal chance for a lighter sentence. When the prospect of leniency has been invented inside a suspect's mind, triggered by a police officer's subtle suggestion, courts usually allow the confession. Some judges permit interrogators to get very close to a promise—"I'll let your cooperation be known to the prosecutor," or, "I'll recommend leniency to the judge"—as long as it stops short of a quid pro quo.

"Why is it that antebellum southern judges better understood . . . that the innocent might confess?" Hirsch asked. "The answer may lie in the nature of slavery, an evil so stark as to provide a certain clarity." From that most extreme condition of bondage, the courts extended their misgivings about inducements to all confessions, not just those by slaves—and appropriately so. "To put the point provocatively, all interrogated suspects are slaves," Hirsch wrote. "That is, the conditions of interrogation create a social and psychological reality mirroring that of the slave."[49]

MANIPULATING *MIRANDA*

Hirsch may be right about the social and psychological reality, but the legal reality is quite different, not at all akin to slavery. In the legal realm, the suspect enjoys control he may not sense and options he may not recognize. Therefore, he should be empowered by the Miranda warning. If administered sincerely and explained thoroughly, it is not just a text but a process: the interrogator, in reciting the rights, cedes some measure of authority, conveys the true nature of free choice, and levels the imbalance in the room.

So police officers learn how to Mirandize without jeopardizing their control, without disrupting the flow of questioning, without inviting the suspect to invoke his rights and close down. But of course, innocent people tend to waive their rights, because they believe naively that they have nothing to fear.

"Introduce Miranda casually," the Reid training suggests, and not promptly at the time of arrest, when the suspect "is often defensive and guarded. If he is advised of his constitutional rights in that frame of mind, he is more likely to invoke his rights." Rather, the warnings are better spliced seamlessly into conversation: I want to hear your side, but before I do, I've got to mention your rights, which you probably understand already. You have the right to remain silent. . . . Now, let's talk. OK?[50]

Officers are urged to adopt soft characterizations of the interview as just "routine questions," "to clarify circumstances," "to assist in our investigation." The crime can be called "this thing that happened," and the verb "murder" can be replaced by "cause the death of."

Cops are advised to remove their guns and handcuffs before going into the interview room, so as not to dramatize the force of law enforcement. If the questioning is taped, it should be done surreptitiously, Reid suggests, because visible recording equipment "serves as a huge reminder of punishment, e.g. your words will be used against you later."[51] Therefore, while a skillful interrogation respects the suspect's rights as required by the courts, it does not keep him mentally in the world of legal reality, where his rights give him leverage. It moves him into the psychological realm, where he has less influence.

The strategy is feasible because confession is not just a legal act. It is also a complicated cultural phenomenon. Legally, it carries unhappy consequences, but as a personal, religious, moral step it can expiate guilt and bring redemption. In most settings, it is coupled with forgiveness. It is a religious duty in Christianity, an ethical obligation in family relations, a personal catharsis, a purging, a new beginning designed for salvation to wipe the slate clean of sin. Police officers may play on all these extralegal keys.

Interrogators are encouraged to make appeals to remorse by implying forgiveness morally but not criminally, as in the case of a woman with a long criminal record. To harness her grief and regret, an interrogator collected her mug shots taken over a decade, put them in an album, and slowly turned the pages. In the first photograph, she looked pretty and unspoiled, even naive, but gradually her face grew hardened and scarred by drugs and crime. As she watched herself deteriorating, the officer talked about the pain that her choices had brought in her own life. "By the time the investigator got to the suspect's most recent photograph, she was in tears and confessed not only to the issue under investigation, but implicated a number of other suspects in unsolved crimes."[52]

Like car salesmen who want to close the deal, cops have developed various ways to hurry things up and sell confession as a virtue. Trainers suggest telling the suspect that people naturally believe the original version they hear, so he'd better get his on the table first. Buckley gives this tactic a softer interpretation. "We sell telling the truth," he declares. "Not everyone we interrogate is guilty," and an interrogation should be considered successful if someone is eliminated as a suspect.

That quest for truth is one of the Fifth Amendment's values but, like most noble principles, not universally put into practice. In real life, for example, cops often question before Mirandizing, then slip the warning into the middle of the conversation after someone has made an incriminating statement, and finally build the rest of the interrogation on that pre-Miranda admission. It's a method approved by the Supreme Court.

Federal prosecutors in Washington, D.C., defended it by first arguing in court that a man handcuffed at home during a search was not "in custody" and therefore didn't have to be Mirandized. The police had handcuffed twenty-five-year-old William Davis in his mother's kitchen while they searched the house for drugs. "It is common," said Detective Robert Saunders. "They would go inside and handcuff during a search. You don't want people running around and breaking into weapons." Exemptions are made for women, children, the elderly, and others who don't pose a threat, he said, but Davis had done some time for robbery. His mother, Barbara Destry, was in the kitchen too, unrestrained.

She called him "Bumbles," poor guy, short for Bumble Bee, the nickname he'd been given as a newborn when somebody said he looked like the bee on a can of tuna. Bumbles was mentally impaired, unable to read beyond the level of a second grader, a handicap that worked against him in a fast-paced, tricky situation such as this one.

Officers were searching around the outside of the house when Detective Saunders heard an officer call in and "give a code we use when we recover a weapon." So he turned to Bumbles. "I asked, 'Is there anything we should know about that could get your mother into trouble?' He said, 'There's a gun back there.'"

Destry heard it differently. "He said, 'You have to admit to it, or we're gonna lock your mother up,'" she told me. She was angry at the detective, angry at her son for admitting to a gun, angry that a gun was in a place where children could get it, apparently stashed in a vent on an outside wall. She scolded him. "There are kids out there," she said, and punched her grown son hard enough to knock him off his chair. Only later did she learn that the gun was not her son's, she said, but belonged to a cousin who got it for protection after another cousin had been shot and killed. It was a rough neighborhood.[53]

The cops helped Davis up and took him to the living room, where "I advised him of his rights orally," Saunders testified. The D.C. police usually have suspects sign a form, the PD-47, signifying that they've been Mirandized, but "we don't unhandcuff anybody to let them sign the PD-47," the detective said. Whether or not Davis understood his rights was a question, but in any case the unwarned part of the conversation flowed seamlessly into the post-Miranda phase.

"He appeared to be embarrassed," Saunders recalled as he read from his notes. "He said, 'Please don't take my mother. The gun's mine. It's a black .45. The safety's on.'"

When Davis's defense moved to suppress his statements, the assistant U.S. attorney argued that in the kitchen, before being Mirandized, he was not in custody. The federal judge Rosemary Collyer disagreed. "I find that he was in custody," she said. "I agree that an occupant of a house in handcuffs while his house is being searched is in custody. . . . The question from Detective Saunders was improper and the answer should not be admitted, and I'm going to suppress it."

Davis's statement in the living room, however, after the Miranda warning was recited, "was voluntarily given," she ruled. "I therefore find that it is admissible."

So the police tactic worked: question without the Miranda warning first, threaten to arrest the mother, get an incriminating statement, then recite the rights and build on the first statement to get it again.

The method narrowly received a formal imprimatur in 2004 from the Supreme Court, ruling 5–4 in *Missouri v. Seibert* in favor of an arresting officer who deliberately avoided Mirandizing an arson and murder suspect. After she had confessed, the officer gave her the Miranda warning, confronted her with her earlier admission, and obtained it a second time.[54] If a similar sequence were followed in a physical search—an illegal traffic stop, for example, leading to the discovery of a gun in the car—Fourth Amendment case law would regard the resulting evidence as inadmissible, known in legal parlance as the fruit of a poisonous tree. By contrast, in questioning covered by the Fifth Amendment, judges have decided that the fruit of the poisonous tree can be eaten with no ill effects.[55]

REMEDIES

Courts and legislatures are understandably reluctant to tie police interrogators' hands so tightly that they get no confessions of any kind, true or false. But a false confession is obviously worse than no confession, since it deludes the authorities into thinking they've solved the crime, and it ends with two people in places they shouldn't be: the innocent in jail and the guilty still on the street. That hardly makes society safer. So it seems logical to devise remedies against false confessions, even if that means losing some that are true.

Several steps would eliminate specific tactics that have produced bogus admissions. First, police could be prohibited from lying to suspects by pretending to have evidence that doesn't exist. Second, judges and lawmakers could return to the strict nineteenth-century standards on inducements, outlawing even the subtlest suggestions of leniency. Third, no child should be questioned without a parent or a lawyer present.

Fourth, if the whole interrogation is videotaped, from beginning to end, prosecutors, defense attorneys, judges, and jurors can see the full police repertoire of tricks and maneuvers. This idea is catching on, with several state legislatures and state supreme courts ordering that it be done in capital or other serious crimes. When Barack Obama was an Illinois state senator, he labored and lobbied successfully for legislation in 2003 to require such recording in the wake of the Chicago torture and the DNA reversals of death penalty convictions.[56] The following year, the Massachusetts Supreme Judicial Court ruled that jurors should regard unrecorded confessions with "great caution."[57] A scattering of other states and local authorities now require taping, including Maine, Alaska, and New Mexico.

Police sometimes skate past the rule, using poor equipment so that inaudible words can be resolved in the authorities' favor. Or they record the confession only, which may compound the power of false statements as the judge and the jury see the suspect in the last few minutes of a long session, after he has been broken and is reciting his rehearsed lines. No evidence is more persuasive than a taped confession, especially in the absence of the manipulative interrogation that has preceded it. Some confessions later proven false have been recorded. Very few wrongful convictions are known to have resulted when the entire questioning has been taped from the outset, although that may be partly because recording is still rare.[58]

Full recording in Massachusetts got a murder confession by Shamar Q. White suppressed after the judge could see the interrogator ignore his request for a lawyer. Police told another defendant they wouldn't charge him if he confessed, and then, of course, brought charges based on his admission. With the camera watching, the vulnerabilities of the suspects to interrogators' suggestions become dramatically obvious. Police behavior presumably becomes more professional and responsible.[59]

Yet the confession expert Alan Hirsch has worked on cases where defense attorneys don't want juries to see fully taped interrogations, because even with exculpatory comments early on, or even with obvious police pressure, the final moments of confession remain overpowering. "I've shown laypeople interrogations that convince me of innocence, and it convinces them of guilt. I'll point out X, Y, and Z," he noted, "and they'll say, 'Yes, but why would he admit it if he didn't do it?' Just seeing him admit it reinforces the inference of guilt." So, while Hirsch supports full recording, he has discovered that "it's no panacea."

Recording can actually help police and prosecutors, who avoid unwarranted charges of abuse and end up with unassailable evidence. "I'm a convert," said the chief investigator for the sheriff's department in Kankakee County, Illinois. "When they first started this, I thought they were nuts. I thought there was no way a guy was going to cooperate if he knew he was being taped. Now, I wouldn't do it any other way."[60]

A fifth remedy would require that confessions be backed solidly by independent evidence. While some states bar convictions based solely on uncorroborated confessions, "corroboration" can be a squishy concept in most jurisdictions, including federal courts. Other evidence need only support or bolster the confession, not be proven beyond a reasonable doubt, and judges do not have to instruct juries on corroboration requirements even if asked to do so by defense attorneys, according to several federal appeals courts.

Under the lax standards, confessions replete with inaccuracies have weighed heavily with jurors. The Massachusetts case on recording overturned an arson conviction because interrogators implied leniency by suggesting that the suspect might seek counseling for alcoholism after confessing. They also pretended to have videotaped evidence. And the defendant's confession was wrong on practically every significant fact, including the fire's location, the size of the gas can, the hardware store where it had been purchased, the service station that had sold the gasoline, and the place where the can had been discarded.[61] In reporting on the case, the Reid training material cautions police against accepting statements that don't jibe with established details: "A valid confession should contain information about the crime that could only be known by the guilty person and can also be verified as true." A self-incriminating statement that volunteers specifics and answers questions cogently is not enough. A confession carries great weight, so "it must meet a higher level of proof," police trainees are told.[62] If only the law were as demanding.

Finally, post-conviction challenges to confessions should be assigned to different prosecutors and judges. The district attorney who may have mishandled the case in the first place, and the trial judge whose rulings may have facilitated injustice, are usually normal human beings, seldom enthusiastic about admitting to life-altering mistakes. Even in the face of a DNA mismatch, the original prosecutors can usually be counted on to resist early release or new trials. They are caught in an uncomfortable place between competing roles, as seekers of justice striving for truth, on the one hand, and, on the other, as government advocates pushing for convictions. Few are willing to reverse their own successes. "Part of it is political ambition," says Alan Hirsch, who has urged that cases of DNA exoneration be transferred to new prosecutors. "Either consciously or unconsciously, they think it's not going to look good if they concede they put the wrong person behind bars. And part of it is the belief that innocent people don't confess. You just don't want to believe it."

And yet it is true.

CHAPTER THREE

The Assistance of Counsel

The barrier between government abuse and civil liberties is a
group called criminal defense lawyers.

—Sheldon Perhacs, defense attorney

PROVING INNOCENCE

ANTHONY RAY HINTON has been sitting on death row since 1986, when
his court-appointed lawyer was given too little money to hire a reputable
firearms expert to dispute the questionable findings of a police lab. The
"expert" he found on the cheap, a one-eyed retired engineer who couldn't
operate a comparison microscope, had jurors laughing in ridicule.

Lydia Diane Jones got a life sentence after her lawyer advised her chief
defense witness (who was also his client) not to incriminate himself by
helping her. He would have testified that drugs found in her apartment
were his rather than hers. The judge saw no conflict in the attorney's representing both the defendant and the witness, and Jones spent six years in
jail before wiser judges ruled otherwise.

Ronald Rompilla, convicted of murder, was sentenced to death without his overworked public defenders presenting the jury with mitigating
evidence of his troubled background: fetal alcohol syndrome, abusive
upbringing by violent parents, and mental illness, which might have tilted
jurors toward life imprisonment rather than execution. The Supreme Court
narrowly saved him, seventeen years after his crime.

And so on along a spectrum of violations, from the subtle to the blatant.
The most vivid denials of the constitutional right to counsel this century
have come in the years after 9/11, when lawyers were initially blocked from
seeing a couple of Americans designated enemy combatants and from seeing foreigners imprisoned at Guantánamo Bay. Those cases attracted the
greatest attention and sparked the sharpest outrage, but they were not typical. More perniciously and less obviously, in shoddy courtrooms and decay-
ing jails across the country, legal representation is routinely shortchanged
for thousands of invisible defendants accused of low-grade crimes. Their

hardships predated the terrorist attacks and are likely to continue long after the country recovers its balance.

The law is a labyrinth, best comprehended by the high priesthood of attorneys who fashion and interpret its abstruse language. No unschooled layman, standing nakedly unrepresented before the terrible engine of the criminal justice system, can possibly fathom the hidden dangers of error—or the invisible shields that offer unnoticed protection.

"When I go to court and the judge says something, I hear it," explains Andrew Patel, a New York attorney. "I go to the client, and that client says, 'What did the judge say?' It's not that they didn't understand the words. It's that all they can hear is the beating of their own heart, they are in such an alien situation." That is why "two hundred years ago some pretty smart people set out a road plan," Patel noted, by writing the Sixth Amendment's simple declaration: "In all criminal prosecutions, the accused shall enjoy the right . . . to have the Assistance of Counsel for his defence."

It was an empty platitude for the poor during most of the country's first two centuries. Except in cases carrying the death penalty, lawyers were not provided for indigents until 1938, when the mandate was imposed in federal courts only.[1] In 1942, the Supreme Court explicitly refused to extend the requirement to state and local courts, where about 95 percent of criminal cases were handled.[2]

Then, twenty years later, in among piles of petitions delivered to the columned Supreme Court building, a humble letter, hand printed in pencil, arrived from a Florida prison. In stilted legalese, a drifter named Clarence Earl Gideon appealed his conviction and five-year sentence on a charge of stealing wine and some change after breaking into a pool hall. His story was stark, his argument simple: he had been denied his right to counsel. Destitute, he had requested a court-paid attorney, and his trial judge had apologetically declined, explaining that Florida law authorized no such thing except in capital cases.

Facing his trial alone, Gideon did badly, especially when a taxi driver testified that Gideon had asked him not to tell anyone that he'd driven him from the pool hall. "That was damaging testimony," writes Anthony Lewis. "And Gideon, without a lawyer, let it stand without any cross-examination."

The Supreme Court accepted his appeal, assigned him a prominent lawyer to argue it, and in 1963 ruled unanimously in *Gideon v. Wainwright* that the Fourteenth Amendment extended to the states the Sixth Amendment's implicit obligation to provide attorneys to those who could not afford them.[3] Gideon got a new trial, this time with a lawyer who probed. When the cabbie repeated Gideon's request not to tell anyone about the pickup at the poolroom, the lawyer "asked whether Gideon had ever said that to him before," Lewis reports. "The taxi driver answered, yes, Gideon said that every time he called a cab. 'Why?' 'I understand it was his wife—he had trouble with his wife.'" This jury found Gideon not guilty.[4]

When the lowliest petitions the mightiest in America, dreams are stirred, and so Gideon's Trumpet, as Lewis named the victory, entered the annals of national virtue. A clarion call for justice could be heard. A wayward system could correct itself. A small voice could set in motion a vast reform.

The reform is incomplete.

While insuring the right to counsel, neither the Constitution nor *Gideon* says anything about the quality of counsel—how bad the lawyer has to be to violate the right. Standards have been sketched in subsequent cases that leave much to judges' discretion. To assess a legal defense as "ineffective," the Supreme Court in 1984 established two tests under *Strickland v. Washington*: first, a "showing that counsel made errors so serious that counsel was not functioning as the 'counsel' guaranteed the defendant by the Sixth Amendment," and, second, that the errors undermined the fairness of the trial and the reliability of its result. The defendant must make both showings, Justice Sandra Day O'Connor wrote for the Court, and they must stand against "a strong presumption that counsel's conduct falls within the wide range of reasonable professional assistance."[5]

That burden has been difficult to meet, in part because judges rarely get the full picture. Three trial judges assured me, during a lunch in Birmingham, Alabama, that they could see clearly from the bench whether defense attorneys were functioning well or badly. "We know by reputation lawyers who aren't going to perform properly," one judge said. "I have never encountered in a capital murder case substantial inadequacy that I can recall." Lesser charges may bring less capable defense, he added, leading him once to appoint co-counsel to help an incompetent attorney. "It made me feel better. He should have been in another industry." The judge threw out a conviction years ago because "an old lawyer didn't ask any questions."

The judges were all sure of themselves, as perhaps judges have to be. They were unyielding in their certainty that they could assess the quality of the defense. But a key function of a criminal lawyer's job is to investigate the case outside of court, and that performance is hard to evaluate. How could they tell? They couldn't quite answer. They couldn't describe how they figured out whether the defense had sufficient resources to investigate. Finally, they began to show some doubts. In the end, one conceded,

"I don't know how you'd know if a lawyer has done an adequate pretrial investigation."

Even murkier pictures are presented to appellate courts, said Justice Gorman Houston shortly after he had retired from the Alabama Supreme Court, which agrees to hear only 10 percent of the appeals it receives. At the early stage of determining whether to consider the appeal (by granting a writ of certiorari), the justices have only limited information from the petition, not the intricacies of the whole trial record, which is examined thoroughly only if the court takes the case. "That scares us at times," he said, "because they [the petitioners] may have left out everything important."

Therefore, his court has occasionally used an unorthodox approach. "If we think it's going to be a miscarriage of justice for this conviction to stand, we grant cert." If not, if counsel's borderline performance isn't bad enough to constitute "reversible error," Houston explained, "we have the clerk of the court call and give the lawyer a tutorial. 'This should have been raised, you did not properly handle this or that.'" That might help the lawyer's next client, but it doesn't rescue the current victim of sloppy legal work.

Appeals face other impediments. Defense attorneys loath to admit their flaws rarely support motions to declare their work "ineffective" and even fight to avoid the stigma. That usually leaves the defendant with both the prosecutor and the defense lined up against him, along with a trial judge who's in no hurry to admit his own mistakes. And under the precedent of court rulings, the government is obligated to pay for a lawyer only at trial and on the first level of appeal, not as the case moves to higher courts.[6] The restriction forces impoverished prisoners to rely on pro bono work by nonprofit legal organizations, which have resources to take only the worthiest and gravest cases. As a result, convictions and sentences are rarely overturned for "ineffective assistance of counsel," although ineffective assistance abounds, in large measure because of inadequate funding.

The lack of money torpedoed Anthony Ray Hinton's murder defense, and his lawyer, Sheldon Perhacs, was still bitter about it twenty years later.

Some defense attorneys appointed to defend the poor at low fees may be so greedy that they give their clients short shrift so they can get back to the higher-paying private market. They may be so jaded or burned out that they doze off during trial; there have been such cases. Or they may be so new to the bar, so in need of business, that they're forced financially to take court appointments and inflict their inexperience on the defendants.[7]

But Perhacs was none of these. He was a crafty idealist who had seen the beauty of the system tarnished, and he felt lonely inside the criminal justice culture. "I don't fit into the law game," he told me as he sat at his desk in Birmingham, Alabama. On the wall behind him hung six rifles, part of a collection, from a single-shot Springfield used after the Civil War at the top, down to an M14 at the bottom.

Without robust legal assistance, he noted, you simply can't get a fair trial. He had watched district attorneys and police muscle their way to convictions, taking their burden to prove guilt and turning it upside down into a presumption of guilt. "Prosecutors regularly do something that our Constitution forbids," he declared in a deep voice resonant with indignation. "Once they have selected you and have decided they have enough evidence, you better prove you're innocent, or you're going to jail." (In fact, however, the Constitution says nothing about the presumption of innocence; instead, one might argue that it is woven implicitly into the fabric of defendants' rights.)

Proving innocence is expensive. A dedicated criminal lawyer spends many more hours outside the courtroom than before the jury, retaining costly experts to punch holes in the police lab's work and hiring investigators to counter the police version with a competing set of facts. That's what Hinton needed, but there was no way to get it in the twenty hours of work at $50 an hour authorized for Perhacs, or the $500 provided by the court for a firearms expert. Perhacs needed $10,000 for a qualified tool-marks examiner from New Orleans, because the case against Hinton for two murders rested entirely on a dubious lab report. It purportedly matched Hinton's gun with bullets from the bodies, but the results were more ambiguous than prosecutors let on. Perhacs could not mount a persuasive rebuttal without a true expert, and although he went over his twenty allotted hours, using his own unpaid time worth about $5,000 to $6,000, it was insufficient. Not counting experts, he said, a proper defense in a murder case today would run about $250 an hour, or some $35,000 in Alabama, near the low end of the scale nationwide.

Hinton was arrested after a string of three late-night robberies of fast-food restaurants just after closing time. Each had the same modus operandi: the manager was accosted, forced to the cooler, and shot twice. The first two were killed. The third, Sidney Smotherman, was wounded but survived. As he was leaving, his car was bumped from behind by his assailant, who then forced him at gunpoint to return to the restaurant.

Smotherman was white, Hinton black, and the old racist line "They all look alike" has some bearing on the unreliability of eyewitness identifications across racial boundaries. Smotherman's description, converted into a sketch, led the police to Hinton, despite significant differences in appearance. Smotherman had described the attacker as shorter than Hinton, thinner than Hinton, and without Hinton's scar across the bridge of his nose. The car he was allegedly driving, a dark sedan, did not resemble the red Nissan owned by Hinton, whose green Chevrolet had been repossessed three months earlier. Nevertheless, shown Hinton's picture in a photo lineup, Smotherman picked him out. Executing a search warrant, the police found a .38 in Hinton's mother's house, the same caliber that had fired the bullets in the three crimes.

Oddly, Hinton was not charged in the Smotherman assault, perhaps because he had a solid alibi. At the time of the crime, he had clocked into the locked warehouse where he worked, fifteen miles away, and didn't leave, according to his supervisor and fellow employees. As his appellate lawyers argued, he could hardly have slipped out of the monitored warehouse, switched cars, driven fifteen miles in four minutes, and then returned without anyone noticing his absence.

But the clincher for the jury came in that realm of pseudo-precision known as forensics, as easily corrupted in this case as in the FBI's handling of a fingerprint from the 2004 Madrid train bombings, when a sloppy mismatch sent Brandon Mayfield, an innocent American lawyer, to the brink of prosecution. Here, two examiners at the Alabama Department of Forensic Sciences testified that all six bullets recovered from the three victims showed striations consistent with those test fired by Hinton's weapon. The experts did not disclose (and Perhacs did not know to request) their work sheets, which were pockmarked with gaps. In the columns where examiners are supposed to record the widths and the numbers of lands and grooves—the telltale signatures that a barrel's rifling makes on the twisting lead—no numbers appeared: only dashes and question marks.

This is one reason that you need a real defense expert, Perhacs explained: to tell you what to ask for. "I didn't know the existence of the work sheets until years and years and years later," he said, despite the *Brady* requirement, named after the case in which the Supreme Court ruled that if prosecutors have exculpatory evidence, they must provide it to the defense.[8]

The only witness he could get for $500, Andrew Payne, was a civil engineer by training, had no certification as a tool-mark examiner, and was blind in one eye. Impeded by his vision and his inexperience, he couldn't figure out how to turn on the comparison microscope when he went to the lab, and then he couldn't see the bullets. In withering cross-examination, he was ridiculed by the district attorney, who told the jury: "This man has no idea, he didn't have a clue about what he was doing. . . . This is a one-eyed man, what kind of depth perception does a one-eyed man have? . . . He's no expert, no expert at all."[9]

Under the law, the trial judge could have eased the defense attorney's workload by granting Perhacs's requests to divide the two murder charges into separate trials, by assigning a co-counsel on each as authorized in capital cases, and by approving additional funds for an expert, which Perhacs requested. The judge, James Garrett, seemed unbothered by the obvious handicaps of the defense. He remembered the trial as fair, noting that Payne had been an expert witness in numerous product liability cases. "I thought his testimony was sufficient, and it set forth the issues that the defense wished to raise," he told me. "Obviously, the state's witnesses prevailed, because the jury came back with a guilty verdict." And it took them less than two hours of deliberation.

Hinton's case seemed so extreme that it was taken up on appeal by the Equal Justice Initiative of Alabama, which used charitable contributions to hire three respected tool-marks experts at a cost of about $30,000.[10] Each concluded independently that the six bullets from the three crimes could not be matched to a single weapon, and that none had discernible characteristics that could link them to Hinton's gun. When experts disagree, professional ethics require the state's examiners to meet with the challengers to explain how they came to the original conclusion. But Hinton's lawyers said the Alabama specialists refused to do so; nor did they try to rebut the three defense examiners' assessments.[11] Nevertheless, the Alabama courts kept denying Hinton a new trial until the state supreme court in 2008 sent the case back down for a hearing to determine whether Payne was, in fact, a qualified expert. In the lower court, the judge punted at first, saying she couldn't make an independent finding different from that of the original trial judge. An appeals court then ordered her to decide, so she ruled that Payne was an expert, a finding upheld by the Criminal Court of Appeals. While his options were running out, Hinton sat on death row, waiting.[12]

The ballistics failure in the Hinton case reflects a broader pattern, revealed in an extensive study by the National Academy of Sciences that found incompetent police crime labs throughout the country. No forensic method other than DNA can reliably connect evidence to a specific individual, the study concluded, so the failures of other methods are partly scientific.[13] But also rampant are sloppiness and outright fabrication, malfeasance that cannot be stopped unless defense experts mount expensive challenges with competing experts and testing. In Detroit, for example, the police lab was closed down in 2008 only after an audit found errors in nearly 10 percent of the shooting cases it handled. The audit was prompted by a retired Michigan State Police firearms expert, hired by the defense in a double homicide, who discovered that forty-two shell casings the Detroit lab thought had been fired by a single weapon had actually come from two separate guns.[14] In 2009, the Supreme Court decided that a defendant had a constitutional right to summon forensic analysts to be cross-examined, to fulfill the Sixth Amendment's guarantee of the right "to be confronted with the witnesses against him."[15]

LOCATION, LOCATION, AND LOCATION

If you're accused of a crime and can't afford a lawyer, the quality of your defense (and whether you get counsel at all) depends almost entirely on geography. You're better off in Washington, D.C., for example, than in parts of Texas and Georgia; anywhere in Alabama; and certain counties of New York, Michigan, and Pennsylvania. You're usually more fortunate in federal than in state courts, and in local jurisdictions where indigent defense is funded by states rather than counties.[16] As in the old adage about real estate prices, three factors determine how well you will be represented: location, location, and location.

You don't want to be in a place of financial shortages, overcrowded courts, or jurisdictions where judges invent ways to cut costs at defendants' expense. Some judges withhold assignments from energetic defense attorneys who file lots of motions and petition for high experts' fees. Others define "indigent" so uncharitably that you may not qualify for a court-paid lawyer even if you can't afford one; the tactic is common in parts of South Dakota, Pennsylvania, and New York State. In numerous counties in Texas, you're not considered poor if you can simply post bond. You get either a lawyer or pretrial freedom, not both.[17]

When the American Bar Association (ABA) held hearings on the problems, respected judges and attorneys stepped forward with grim descriptions of that assembly-line processing known in the trade as McJustice. To speed cases along, the prosecutor meets the accused briefly, with no defense lawyer present, pressing him to waive his right to counsel and plead guilty; the shortcut gets the judge's acquiescence or encouragement as a way to ease the overloaded calendar.[18] An ABA consultant witnessed a mass arraignment in Georgia for just that purpose: "The judge informed defendants of their rights and then left the bench. Afterwards, three prosecutors told defendants to line up and follow them one by one into a private room. When the judge reentered the courtroom, each defendant approached with the prosecutor, who informed the judge that the defendant intended to waive counsel and plead guilty to the charges." No defense attorneys were anywhere in view to help the accused grasp what they were doing. Court clerks in another Georgia jurisdiction told defendants who didn't read English that their cases wouldn't be called until they signed complicated waiver forms, which judges routinely accepted without explaining the right the prisoners had forfeited.[19]

Guilty pleas are always the product of carrots and sticks, but guilty pleas without lawyers bear the particular scars of coercion. John Hardiman, chief public defender in Rhode Island, described a judge offering a defendant six months in jail without a lawyer, or three years if he insisted on his right to counsel. A municipal judge in Riverside, California, was quoted by Gary Windom, chief public defender there, as promising to let a group of defendants go home immediately if they pleaded guilty or, if they wanted lawyers, to lock them up for two days, then set a date for trial, and release them only if they could meet bail. Everybody took the plea.[20]

The egregious examples might be dismissed as sensational exceptions to the baseline of competent legal defense provided to the poor in many parts of the country. Yet the problem is even more insidious than the dramatic cases convey. The defects are nourished not just by individual malice but by systemic failure, an uncaring set of priorities that unbalances the adversarial process of criminal justice by pouring resources into one side—police and prosecutors—while leaving the other nearly as impoverished as its clients. It is hard to get taxpayers and their legislators excited about spending money on accused drug addicts, thieves, and assailants. The argument that the funds help maintain the integrity of the constitutional system doesn't get much traction. The truism that jailing innocents leaves the criminals at large has little resonance, although it should be a security concern for the law-abiding. Upstanding citizens have trouble imagining that they, too, could one day find themselves without the rights that they have failed to defend for others.

There are three basic ways lawyers are brought to the defense of poor defendants: by appointment, under contract, or as full time public defenders. Appointed lawyers place themselves on a list, from which they are assigned by judges on a case-by-case basis, usually at much lower rates than the market offers. Contract lawyers or law firms are retained by the court for a flat monthly fee to cover all defendants they're sent, tempting them to hurry through indigent cases and back to private clients. Public defenders work as salaried attorneys of a government institution with its own office, clerks, and investigators. In the well-funded federal system, public defenders do better for their clients than appointed counsel, according to a study by a Harvard researcher: among federal prosecutions that were examined, cases did not drag on as long, sentences averaged eight months shorter, and the costs were lower—$5,800 less per case.[21]

Washington, D.C., may be the model. There, two bodies of full-time public defenders—one for federal, one for local courts—attract graduates of top law schools, including former Supreme Court clerks. They often work as teams, and the offices of the federal defenders, where I spent many weeks, bristle with a synergy far beyond what most paying clients receive from private lawyers.

With forty-five to sixty-five cases simultaneously, though, each lawyer can get stretched thin. One of them, Carlos Vanegas, gave me a snapshot of a few typical days and nights: all day Saturday and most of Sunday in the office, a suppression motion filed Monday, a witness visited and interviewed Monday evening, and a conference with a client until 9:30 p.m. Vanegas left the office about midnight and ran out of time to prepare for an upcoming cross-examination.

His office is staffed by skilled investigators and has enough funds for experts to mount rebuttals as effective as private clients could buy. In one gun possession case, for instance, the public defenders tried to get a confession suppressed by paying a psychologist $225 an hour for testimony that the accused suffered from severe stress during questioning—an ingredient of coercion—as he waived his rights to silence and to counsel. The judge listened attentively to the psychologist, then rejected the argument and deemed the waiver "knowing and informed." The tactic sometimes works, and defense attorneys are obligated to try. A wealthy defendant would certainly have borne the expense; for the impoverished in most parts of the country, it would have been a luxury beyond reach.

All but a handful of federal judicial districts have public defenders who are paid the same as federal prosecutors, so representation in federal courts is generally competent. Exceptions exist, especially in districts along the southern border, where illegal immigrants from Mexico, once processed and deported administratively (and therefore not entitled to government-funded lawyers), have increasingly been charged with federal crimes, swamping prosecutors, judges, and public defenders. Nearly one-quarter of all federal prosecutions in the first half of fiscal year 2011 were for illegal reentry by previously deported aliens. In one of the busiest districts, Texas South, the number of criminal immigration prosecutions jumped by more than six times in two years, from 2,967 in 2002 to 18,092 in 2004, then to an annual rate of 27,000 in 2010. Most troubling, in 2004 and 2005, the median number of days taken to resolve the cases was zero, suggesting that public defenders had no time to defend and that federal magistrates who heard most of the cases moved them through the system on the same day on a conveyor belt of dubious process.[22]

Furthermore, the assistant U.S. attorneys in the districts were so overwhelmed by the immigration offenses they had been ordered to charge that they transferred a lot of serious drug and gun cases to state and local systems where public defender services were minimal.[23] In many states those systems are underfunded, salaries are low, and benefits are tilted in favor of prosecutors, who are entitled to weeks of training at a federally funded institute in South Carolina and can be forgiven their federal Perkins loans for law school.

Public defenders get no such privileges. Idealism lasts as long as the bank balance, and after gaining experience, many lawyers have to move to private practice, leaving the services understaffed and lacking in expertise. Overburdened public defenders have protested by refusing to take new cases in parts of at least eleven states.[24] This has denied defendants investigations while leads are still warm and witnesses' memories are fresh. In Miami-Dade County, average annual caseloads rose to more than triple the recommended maximum (500 as opposed to 150 per attorney).[25]

Courts have come down on both sides. Some judges have held public defenders in contempt for these refusals, but others have ruled that excessive caseloads constitute ineffective assistance of counsel, and have issued threats to release prisoners who are being denied their constitutional rights to lawyers and to speedy trials. Before retiring in 2008, Chief Justice Pascal F. Calogero Jr. of the Louisiana Supreme Court told the state legislature that "unless adequate funds are available in a manner authorized by law, upon motion of the defendants the trial judge may halt the prosecution in these cases. . . . The courts, as guardians of a fair and equitable process, must not let the state take a person's liberty without due process."[26] A superior court judge in Washington State imposed a settlement in a class action suit to limit each public defender's annual caseloads in Grant County to 150 a year per lawyer, and to fund an investigator for every four attorneys.[27]

The hardships worsen during recessions, as in the downturn that began in 2008. "When the economy goes bad, more people qualify for public defenders at a time when counties and localities have less in resources," noted David Carroll, research director for the National Legal Aid and Defender Association. Yet public defenders are less willing to protest. "They're thinking they can't afford to lose their jobs in this economy," he said.

Poverty drains justice from the system, because most of those arrested for street crimes and drug offenses cannot afford lawyers. In Alabama, one of a dozen states without statewide public defender systems, over two-thirds of criminal defendants are poor enough to be provided with court-appointed attorneys.[28] Nearly three-quarters of those locked up in Jefferson County, which includes Birmingham, are awaiting trial, a financial drain at some $60 a day per inmate; the backlog could be eased legitimately by a corps of full-time public defenders. The county attorney's staff recommended as much in a 2001 report; hearings were held, and the Jefferson County Commission stepped to the brink of approval, even picking an office. Most judges objected, however. They were reluctant to forfeit their power to toss favors to defense lawyers, who are often contributors to the judges' election campaigns.[29]

"You don't get that good counsel with an appointed system," said Joe Curtin, an author of the report and a consultant to the county's Criminal Justice Coordinating Committee. "In criminal court, always sitting in the first row are guys looking for appointments. There are guys right out of school, the files are in the back of their car."

You can get good counsel if the appointed or contract system is well funded and monitored by the state, counters David Carroll. He cites Massachusetts, where defense attorneys go through training and submit their case files for review, and Oregon, where a contract system is run at the state level, entirely divorced from the judiciary. Taking judges out of the mix seems desirable; the Nevada Supreme Court did so in a 2008 administrative order.[30]

But the key is to keep caseloads low, which costs money, and impoverished convicts have no political constituency. They've lost their right to vote, and they're despised by most taxpayers. Since the early 1970s, Alabama's repeated attempts to create a public defender system have stalled in the legislature or have been thwarted by judicial districts. "What we keep hearing is, it ain't popular," Curtin said. "Nobody cares about these dudes in jail." He pulled out a summary of the county's inmate population on that day: 223 white, 602 black.

CONFLICTS OF INTEREST

Legal ethics require that multiple defendants in a case have separate lawyers, and that witnesses who need representation during a trial retain their own attorneys individually. The interest of one is not always identical to the interests of all, so in multi-defendant cases a public defender service represents only one of the accused while the others receive assigned, private counsel. Judges are supposed to enforce the practice, and courts have thrown out convictions where lawyers have shown divided loyalties.

But in some parts of the country, the ABA found, law firms that have contracts for indigent defense routinely represent several defendants in a single case, reasoning that the conflict is eliminated when different lawyers within the firm advocate for different clients. It's hard to imagine a law firm doing that in a million-dollar civil suit, but apparently it's good enough for poor people on trial for their freedom.

Defendants just above the poverty line, barely able to pay, don't necessarily get conflict-free lawyers either, as Lydia Diane Jones discovered as she faced a life sentence without parole. It was a drug-trafficking charge, the penalty enhanced by a prior conviction. First with money from her boyfriend, Ronnie Cook, then with $25,000 from the sale of a house that her mother and aunt had inherited, she hired Cook's attorneys, led by J. Stephen Salter, who found themselves wedged uncomfortably between the competing needs of their two clients: Jones and Cook, who was her chief witness. The money did not buy her an exemplary defense.

Like many women at the edge of poverty, Jones had not chosen her men very well. When she was twenty and married to a violent alcoholic, he had dragged her out of bed one morning at two o'clock, forcing her at gunpoint to drive him to a store and wait outside while he entered, stole a purse, then jumped back into the car for the getaway. From the stolen checkbook she forged two checks.

"I was very scared of him. He was very abusive," she told me. "He had a gun on me, so he made me write the checks. I had never been in trouble with anybody. I had never had a traffic ticket or anything. Once I got to court, they made me do eighteen months." Worse, the crime was counted as three felonies: one for the stolen purse and one for each of the two checks. Under Alabama law, the fourth felony defines you as a habitual offender to be locked up for life.

Jones gave birth to three children, divorced her husband, worked in modest jobs, became a computer operator, and then served as a private nurse in a woman's home. She avoided serious problems until she was forty-three, when another man, Cook, brought trouble into her house. In her self-portrait, she again stood as a victim of her sad and innocent helplessness.

When her father became terminally ill with cancer, Jones moved to her parents' to care for him, leaving her apartment on Seventeenth Street in Birmingham in Cook's hands. She professed not to know that Cook was a major dealer in marijuana whom the police and federal agents were tracking, and had no idea, she insisted, that he was storing drugs in her flat.

She was kept busy by chores for her father. "My mother was a schoolteacher, and I stayed with him, taking him back and forth to the doctor, chemo treatment," she said. "I had to do all the running around. I was dropping my mom off at school first, dropping my grandson off at day care and my other two kids at school. That was my routine every morning. Then I'd return to care for my father."

Her parents had no washing machine, so occasionally she took a load of laundry to her own place. She happened to be there one day when the police burst in on a search warrant. "I got the clothes I had in the car, put them in the washer, took a shower," she remembered. "When I got out of the shower, I heard somebody banging. I came out undressed, I saw all these cops, and I said, 'You don't have to break it down! I'm coming!' By that time they had the burglar door off the hinge.

"I was already in the living room. They was hollerin' and yellin' and telling me to get down, putting guns to my head, it was awful. I've never encountered anything like that in my life. It was awful. They didn't even know who I was. They said, 'Who are you?' They handed me a search warrant, and my name wasn't even on the search warrant."

They clearly knew what they were after and where it might be. "They did not go through the house," she recalled. "They went straight in the kitchen and looked under the sink. I heard somebody say, 'Bingo. We got it right here.' They never showed me what they got. They told me it was marijuana." There was enough to charge trafficking, which is often based not on any proof that a person distributed the drugs but on the sheer volume in possession: in Alabama, more than one kilogram of marijuana is considered beyond what someone would keep for personal use.

The police officers asked if Jones knew Ronnie Cook, and she gave them nothing. "They asked me about him, I kept tellin' them I didn't know who he was. One said, 'We're gonna take her downtown and lock her ass up.'" But they didn't, not then. A sheriff's deputy just left his business card with his phone number and asked her to call if she knew anything about Cook, evidently their real target.

She didn't call. Perhaps the authorities arrested her later out of pique that she wouldn't inform, speculated her lawyer, Salter. The assistant district attorney who prosecuted her, Joe Roberts, seemed to say as much. "If she would have given him the information that it was Cook's, my guess is that she would have helped herself," he told me. "I wish she would have taken advantage of the opportunity to work the case off. It was just my opinion that she could have worked it off."

Cook, meanwhile, was doing just that. Arrested later by the FBI on another drug charge, he pleaded guilty and ended up with a relatively modest eight-year sentence by testifying against bigger dealers before several grand juries and in three trials.[31] He was prepared to testify for Jones.

Salter had opened her trial by telling the jury that the drugs belonged to Cook, not Jones, and that as the real culprit Cook would take the stand to swear that they were his. It was a slightly odd assertion, since Salter represented Cook as well. But after the state rested, Roberts, the prosecutor, paid Cook a visit in federal prison to give him a friendly warning: If he admitted under oath to owning the marijuana found in Lydia Jones's house, he would be prosecuted by the state. His plea agreement had been made with the federal government only, and on a different drug crime.

It was a canny threat cleverly combined with affected concern for Cook's Fifth Amendment right against self-incrimination. "I knew what he was going to testify to," Roberts told me. "I don't want to make it sound that I was just a civil libertarian. I didn't want him to testify. I didn't want him to say they were his drugs. That doesn't happen normally if you have counsel to advise you. I just wanted to make sure he understood that he would be prosecuted. If he was going to take responsibility for it, then that was his decision."

By the book, Roberts should have gone not to Cook but to his lawyer. Instead, just the two of them had a jailhouse conversation, as Roberts reported to the trial judge in a later hearing. "I said, 'I would suggest that you talk to your attorney before you testify. Have you done that?' He [Cook] said, 'Well, I am planning on talking to him this morning.'"

What Roberts claimed he did not know was that Cook's lawyer was also Jones's. And when that was revealed in court, just as Cook was about to take the stand, it caused a flurry of concern that Judge Mike McCormick failed to resolve. In a meandering colloquy with the judge, Salter made hand-wringing remarks—"I am sort of in an awkward spot"—and suggested that perhaps a mistrial should be declared and he should be replaced as Jones's attorney. Judge McCormick seemed irresolute, suggesting instead that Cook be assigned another lawyer if he desired and be advised of his rights against self-incrimination, which he could waive and testify if he wished. In a dim recollection of the case, the judge told me that he'd rather

Salter had stepped down as Cook's counsel; McCormick did not realize, apparently, that since Salter's case with Cook was federal, a withdrawal would have required a federal judge's approval.

Salter protested that Cook should not face a state charge while under a federal plea agreement, especially since state and local police had participated in that federal investigation. Neither Judge McCormick nor Assistant District Attorney Roberts bought the argument. "There would be an obvious problem if he confesses to this crime under oath," the judge declared. "It seems to me that the state would not only have the right, but the obligation, to prosecute him under those circumstances."

Salter floated the idea of immunity for Cook, but Roberts wouldn't have it, leaving Salter with two clients holding clashing interests in the same trial. "I did not feel I had a conflict representing Ronnie until the state threatened to prosecute him if he testified," the lawyer told me later in his conference room. The place felt like a small museum of an earlier era. Along the wall, glass cabinets contained elaborate meerschaum pipes and a couple of Prussian-looking helmets. Salter, wearing a black shirt and a short white beard, fidgeted nervously at the end of a heavy table. "It was very unusual, what developed in the courtroom when the prosecution threatened him. It was being held over his head to prevent him from testifying," the lawyer said. "It did put me in an untenable position."

Even Roberts, the prosecutor, told the judge, "I think there is a huge conflict in this case," and the judge agreed, telling Salter, "You have a conflict if you put him on the stand and he makes a judicial admission. You can't represent both clients." So everybody understood the problem, and nobody solved it.

Despite this likelihood of state prosecution, Cook came to court that morning ready to testify that the drugs were his. With the jury out of the room, Judge McCormick questioned him closely to be sure that he understood the probable consequences, and offered to appoint another lawyer to advise him. Cook stood his ground at first, noting that he had already told the police in his federal case that he owned the marijuana. That was different, the judge admonished; swearing to it under oath in open court could get him charged.

Salter then stood up and rambled his way through a most peculiar form of questioning, alternately asking Cook and advising Cook, coaxing him and warning him. He was trying to get Cook's testimony and trying simultaneously to keep Cook from giving it. "It is a little bit of an awkward situation for us to call you as a witness in the case. . . . No lawyer wants to put his client in a jackpot or give them any risk of exposure. I certainly don't want to do that in your case. . . . She would love to have your testimony. I don't want to see you get in trouble. And I am in conflict. . . . Many lawyers, many good lawyers would probably tell you, Don't do it. That's where it becomes a problem for me. She would love to have your testimony. . . . But if that truthful testimony might expose you to some further criminal charge, that's the bind that we are in. . . . And nobody is going to be mad at you if you make a decision not to testify."

After a recess, Salter came back and told the judge that Jones had decided that she didn't want him to call Cook. The judge asked her whether that was true, and she never answered, although the transcript says she nodded. "It wasn't a nod," she told me, remembering far back to that icy moment in the courtroom. "I felt betrayed. I felt like I had just died, you know. I didn't change my mind. I got kind of upset, because it's like Salter switched over. He did a switch on me. I was looking at him like, What are you doing? And they kept asking me, Ms. Jones, are you clear about what's going on here? And I never answered them, because I was dumbfounded. I was like, what did I miss?"

So Cook never testified to the jury, and Jones's lawyers never replaced his testimony with documentary federal evidence of his trafficking, which might have reinforced their opening assertion that the drugs were his. The jury convicted her, and she received the mandatory life sentence without parole. "I didn't cry or anything," she said, "because I knew somewhere down the line that God just wasn't gonna let it stay like that, because I knew I hadn't done anything."

While Roberts, as prosecutor, felt satisfied with the guilty verdict, because he thought she was culpable in letting Cook use her house for drugs, "to be honest, I never felt real comfortable with the sentence she got," he said. "I didn't feel she was adequately represented."

Behind bars, Jones made a smart friend named Paula who read the transcript and knew enough about the law to be more appalled than Judge McCormick had been. Paula "kept writing and writing" until a letter found its way to Bryan Stevenson of the Equal Justice Initiative, who filed an appeal just two days before the deadline. The victory finally came in the Alabama Court of Criminal Appeals, which ordered a new trial. Instead, the prosecution dropped the trafficking charge and let her plead guilty (although she insisted she was not) to simple possession, which got her out on probation. She had been locked up for six years.

Prison changed her. "It's a place that nobody wants to be. The majority of the guards are men. You would have women saying they were sexually assaulted. I did not see it for myself." At least she got visits from her children and her mother. Her father, whom she had left her apartment to nurse, died before her trial.

"I am different. I'm very withdrawn to a certain extent when it comes to outsiders. I feel like I can't trust anyone. I feel down a lot. I really feel that I'm not worthy to be in society because I've done something bad, which I haven't—but I've been in a bad place."

MITIGATING EVIDENCE

After conviction, the penalty phase of a trial can be crucial, especially in a capital case where the jury must choose between prison and execution. To decide, jurors weigh aggravating and mitigating factors: how heinous the crime on the one hand, how abusive the criminal's childhood on the other. This part of the process can divide the effective lawyers from the inept, and those with resources to research the client's past from those without the time and money.

Zacarias Moussaoui, who confessed to a planned involvement in 9/11-type hijackings, escaped a death sentence because nine jurors saw as mitigating factors his "unstable and dysfunctional family" and his alcoholic father's "violent temper" that exploded into "physical and emotional" abuse.[32]

They would have known nothing of this had his public defenders not been granted government funds to assemble a team of lawyers, interpreters, and mitigation specialists who made five trips to Morocco and France, where Moussaoui spent his childhood. They interviewed family members and gathered records showing a pattern of mental illness, hunger, and beatings in his family. They persuaded his two schizophrenic sisters to give videotaped descriptions, which were shown in court, of the hunger and brutality they had endured growing up in a French public housing apartment.[33] Death required unanimity, and the jury gave him life.

The mercy tempered Moussaoui's contempt for the American judicial system. He had been a difficult client, vilifying his lawyers, sending the judge obscene notes, and shouting in court, "God curse America!" He had no expectation of justice to begin with, a view reinforced when he was denied his constitutional right to put on a vigorous defense. He wished to call captured al-Qaeda operatives then in CIA prisons abroad, including the supposed planner of the 9/11 attacks, Khalid Sheikh Mohammed. They would testify that he had not been part of the plot, he argued.

The Justice Department refused to produce them, citing the need for secrecy but clearly worried that the prisoners would talk about being tortured. In response, the judge removed the charges carrying the death penalty. She was reversed by the Fourth Circuit Court of Appeals, which ruled that to satisfy his right, Moussaoui could introduce intelligence summaries of the captives' interrogations. These made his argument but not persuasively, and he turned his back on the process. He pleaded guilty—to a role not in 9/11 but in a future plot to fly a plane into the White House—setting up a penalty phase as elaborate as a full-blown trial would have been.

That such mitigating evidence could be mustered, that a jury would show him something less than vengeance, seemed to crack the shell of his hatred. He filed a motion asking to withdraw his guilty plea, saying, "I now see that it is possible that I can receive a fair trial even with Americans as jurors." There were no legal grounds for granting his request, however, and the judge refused, pointing out that he had waived his right to a trial. He resides at the super-max federal prison in Florence, Colorado.[34]

Ronald Rompilla had lawyers who were considerably less probing. As local public defenders, they were heavy on cases and short on investigative funds, and they accepted at face value the assertions by Rompilla and several relatives that his childhood had been normal and healthy. They failed to look further, even into official documents that told a different story.

During the penalty phase, therefore, the jury that had convicted him of repeatedly stabbing a bar owner in Allentown, Pennsylvania, and setting the body on fire never heard that his parents were both alcoholics who fought violently, that his mother drank heavily during pregnancy, that he probably suffered brain damage from fetal alcohol syndrome, that his father beat the children with belts and sticks and fists and locked him and his brother in a filthy wire-mesh dog pen, that Rompilla and his siblings went to school in rags, that he suffered from mental illness including schizophrenia, and that testing in ninth grade put him at a third-grade level. "There were no expressions of parental love, affection, or approval," wrote an appeals court judge in dissent. "Instead, he was subjected to yelling and verbal abuse. . . . He had an isolated background, was not allowed to visit other children, or to speak to anyone on the phone."[35]

Much of this information was contained in a public file on an earlier conviction for rape and assault, a file kept in the very same courthouse where Rompilla was tried for murder. But his lawyers never read it, even after the prosecutor warned them twice that he would introduce that earlier case as an aggravating factor in sentencing.

"If the defense lawyers had looked in the file on Rompilla's prior conviction, it is uncontested they would have found a range of mitigation leads that no other source had opened up," wrote Justice David Souter for a five-member majority of the Supreme Court, which found ineffective assistance of counsel and overturned the death penalty.[36] Although Pennsylvania had the option to retry the sentencing phase, it chose to enter a plea agreement with Rompilla for life imprisonment.[37]

The case commanded special attention because the appeals court judge who had written the 2–1 opinion rejecting Rompilla's argument was Samuel Alito, then of the Third Circuit, soon to be named to the Supreme Court. He reasoned that the defense attorneys had performed adequately, having heard no suggestion of problems from five of Rompilla's relatives or three mental health workers who had examined him. Alito didn't want to send lawyers chasing needles in haystacks—the same argument later used by Justice Anthony Kennedy in his Supreme Court dissent. Both men gave little attention to the end result: a jury handicapped by ignorance. As Souter said, "Although we suppose it is possible that a jury could have heard it all and still have decided on the death penalty, that is not the test. It goes without saying that the undiscovered 'mitigating evidence, taken as a whole, might well have influenced the jury's appraisal' of [Rompilla's] culpability."

He was quoting from *Strickland,* in which the Court had ruled that a lawyer who made serious errors was not functioning as "counsel," and from *Wiggins v. Smith,* a 2003 case of similar circumstances that had set benchmarks for evaluating lawyers' performances in the penalty phase.[38] Alito did not faithfully observe the precedent, conjuring up differences where few existed. Lawyers for Kevin Wiggins failed to follow obvious leads, he noted, where "Rompilla's trial attorneys had a body of evidence that suggested that a further investigation into Rompilla's family background would not have been productive. . . . They interviewed numerous members of his family."[39] Perhaps if Alito had ever defended a murderer against the death penalty, he would have understood the effort needed to penetrate family denials. But few defense attorneys are elevated to the bench at any level, much less to the Supreme Court.

"In every family there is resistance to talking about family problems and dysfunction and secrets," said Bryan Stevenson, the Alabama lawyer who appealed the Hinton and Jones cases. "The whole challenge in criminal defense is to create a dynamic to get past that and get people to talk about abuse. . . . That's a very different kind of cultural reality for a lot of lawyers. A lot of lawyers feel, 'I'm sitting in this bad neighborhood and I'm doing this for them, and if they don't want to cooperate, I'm gone.' What we learn is that once you actually position yourself as someone who is prepared to listen, someone who is prepared to care, someone who is prepared to help, people are prepared to talk to you. . . . What I love about mitigation work is that it can give voice to a family's plight, a community's plight. It can be therapeutic."

This spirit of inquiry is now woven into case law, but only tentatively. Had Alito risen to the high court sooner, Rompilla would be dead: Alito's appeals court opinion was reversed by only a one-vote margin on the Supreme Court.[40] Such mitigation efforts, often derided as "abuse excuse," are now mandated. In capital cases, at least, going through the motions is not enough. To preserve the Sixth Amendment, defense attorneys have to dig effectively.

WITHOUT REPRESENTATION

A good defense lawyer is essential to justice but not to "justice" as in President George W. Bush's repeated pledge that terrorists would be "brought to justice." His administration tried to avoid the inconvenience of attorneys doing what they do: telling clients not to answer questions, filing motions in court, challenging government witnesses, summoning evidence for the defense, and complaining about abuse behind bars. The culture of contempt for the adversarial system reached from terrorism to white-collar crime.

The hundreds of Muslim men jailed in the Ashcroft Sweeps after September 11 were hidden and moved among scattered prisons in the United States. Their families weren't sure where they were, and lawyers couldn't always find them. Attorneys who visited a jail were sometimes told by officials at the gate that their clients were not there, when they were right inside.

John Walker Lindh, a young American captured as a Taliban fighter during the war in Afghanistan, asked repeatedly for a lawyer to no avail, although the FBI and the Pentagon knew that his family had hired one of the best in the business, James Brosnahan, who had contacted authorities with multiple requests to see him. Lindh didn't even know he had a lawyer, because a letter Brosnahan sent to him via the Red Cross was blocked by the U.S. government; the attorney and the client did not meet until fifty-four days after Lindh's capture, a long while after he was questioned without counsel.

A convert to Islam, Lindh had journeyed to Afghanistan in the summer of 2001, a time when the United States was still cultivating relations with the Taliban. His motive, he insisted, was to fight for a pure Islamic state—

not against his own country, which had not yet invaded, but against the Northern Alliance, which only a few months later became an American client. After Lindh and the remnants of his Taliban unit surrendered toward the end of 2001, they were imprisoned and staged an uprising in which a CIA agent was killed.

In U.S. custody in Afghanistan, Lindh was abused and interrogated again and again. Although a hospital stood five hundred yards away, his shrapnel wounds were not properly treated, a bullet was left in his thigh, and he was described as delirious. Kept naked, blindfolded, taped to a stretcher, and locked in a dark shipping container, he made self-incriminating statements that later formed the basis for a criminal case. Some of these were extracted by an FBI agent under instructions to ignore legal advice to refrain from questioning him without his lawyer, advice that had been provided upon request by the Justice Department's Professional Responsibility Advisory Office.

The breach contaminated the case so badly that Justice Department officials removed relevant e-mails from the file being turned over to the judge, and then hounded and threatened the government attorney who had advised against questioning Lindh.[41]

On the eve of a hearing to suppress his statements, the government offered a plea bargain that would drop terrorism charges and lower the maximum sentence from life to twenty years. He would plead guilty to supplying services to the Taliban and to carrying an explosive during the commission of a felony and would agree to provide information in other cases. He would declare, disingenuously, "The defendant acknowledges that he was not intentionally mistreated by the U.S. military." He would also live the rest of his life under the threat of being designated an enemy combatant, a novel tactic at the time, but one used later to threaten defendants into guilty pleas.[42]

Lindh agreed. Brosnahan didn't think he had much chance before a jury where the government had chosen to try him—in the Pentagon's neighborhood, the Alexandria district of Northern Virginia, which became a favorite venue for major terrorism trials. "I thought we could get some acquittals" on certain counts, he said, but with convictions on two or three of the charges "he'd get life in prison, or forty years." In addition, "our reading was that we were not going to get a lot of pretrial help" from the judge in suppressing coerced statements or allowing Brosnahan to interview potentially supportive witnesses being held at Guantánamo Bay, where the government didn't want lawyers roaming around at all.

Terrorism suspects at Guantánamo were finally allowed to see attorneys under court order, an annoyance to the Pentagon's assistant secretary for detainee affairs, a former navy lawyer named Charles Stimson. He let the Bush administration's culture of contempt for legalities slip briefly into view when, in a radio interview, he named more than a dozen law firms that were sending attorneys pro bono to Guantánamo and slyly suggested a boycott: "I think quite honestly, when corporate CEOs see that those firms are representing the very terrorists who hurt their bottom line back in 2001, those CEOs are going to make those law firms choose between representing terrorists or representing reputable firms." An uproar of outrage followed. Law school deans wrote in protest, and corporate clients including General Electric and Verizon endorsed their law firms' Guantánamo work. Exactly three weeks later, Stimson was out of his Pentagon job and on his way to the conservative Heritage Foundation, where he was treated as an expert on national security and the law.[43]

In more genteel arenas, too, the law-and-order ideologues tried to undermine the vigor of legal defense. For some years, corporations under investigation for white-collar crimes were presented by the government with an unpalatable choice: either the companies could face prosecution as corporate entities, or they could throw their employees overboard by refusing to pay their legal fees, and also waive attorney-client privilege to allow their company lawyers to turn over all internal research on the alleged crime.

The policy was laid out in a 2003 memo from Larry Thompson, deputy attorney general, who urged his subordinate prosecutors, "in determining whether to charge a corporation," to consider "whether the corporation appears to be protecting its culpable employees . . . through the advancing of attorneys fees," and whether the company shows cooperation by issuing "a waiver of the attorney-client and work product protections, both with respect to its internal investigation and with respect to communications between specific officers, directors and employees and counsel."[44]

That broad grant meant that an employee who was required by company rules to cooperate with a firm's attorneys in an internal investigation could find all of his communications with his company's lawyers relayed to prosecutors. The company's lawyers were supposed to warn him that they represented the company, not him, but many a worker got a nasty shock when the feds came rolling around. Furthermore, because of Justice Department threats, he might have to pay for his own lawyer if his contract didn't require his employer to do so. And the complexity of white-collar crime makes the defense costly; legal fees for one executive who was found not guilty ran to about $2 million, his lawyer said; luckily, he was covered by insurance. Without financial backup, many employees simply plead guilty.

Corporations are highly motivated to avoid prosecution, for "in many fields a criminal case is a death penalty case for a company," said Robert Luskin, a prominent attorney in Washington, D.C. The firm can no longer get government contracts, and if it depends on them, he noted, "it can be the end of the company."

In effect, the government tried to get the corporations to do the investigations, but some thought the approach self-defeating. "Anyone who talks to a lawyer knowing that a lawyer may turn the information over to the government is going to be more guarded," said an attorney who has worked on both sides—a decade as a Justice Department prosecutor, and now defending the accused. "Maybe in the short run you learn more about the companies, but in the long run you impede the truth-seeking process. I think it's born largely of an arrogance that the Justice Department is always able to determine and seek out the truth and everybody else—companies and their lawyers—are out to obscure the truth."

After a federal judge ruled the government practice unconstitutional, and following complaints from the corporate legal community, the policy of pressure was abandoned in December 2006. The Thompson Memorandum was superseded by the so-called McNulty Memorandum instructing that "prosecutors generally should not take into account whether a corporation is advancing attorneys' fees to employees," nor should officials "request" waivers of attorney-client privilege for the sake of mere convenience.[45] Later, the judge dismissed criminal charges against thirteen employees whose accounting firm, KPMG, had been forced by the government to deny them funds for legal defense. The dismissal was upheld by the Second Circuit, which found that the Sixth Amendment right to assistance of counsel had been violated.[46]

This was a telling episode of government overreaching—and by conservatives who supposedly valued tight limits on the power of the state. It reflected a view that lawyers could be complicit in crime, both the corporate and the terrorist variety.

Officials were driven by worries that dangerous prisoners might use lawyers to pass messages to confederates outside. So some inmates inside the United States were shackled by the federal Bureau of Prisons' Special Administrative Measures, which subjected even attorney-client mail and conversations to monitoring when "reasonable suspicion exists to believe that a particular inmate may use communications with attorneys or their agents to further or facilitate acts of terrorism."[47] The Justice Department followed up with tough enforcement in the case of Lynne Stewart, who had defended radicals throughout her career. She was prosecuted, convicted, disbarred, and sentenced to twenty-eight months in prison for acting as a conduit of communications to and from her jailed client Omar Abdel Rahman, the so-called blind sheik convicted of plotting to blow up the United Nations building and other New York landmarks. The jury found that she had conveyed his instructions to his organization in Egypt, the Islamic Group, to end a cease-fire.

Some lawyers took this as a more general threat from the government, and some sensed that they were under surveillance: Papers were dislocated on desks, files seemed out of place. A few reported menacing warnings. Karen Pennington, a Dallas lawyer who defended Arabs in immigration and criminal cases, quoted a government attorney with the immigration service (whom she refused to name) as saying "that I am putting my citizenship at risk by representing these people, that I am providing material support to terrorists by providing legal counsel. And my family moved to the Dallas area just after the Civil War!"

Some were reluctant to represent accused terrorists, but others fought fiercely for the right to do so. I met with one of them, Andrew Patel, the day before he flew to Charleston, South Carolina, to visit his client Jose Padilla for the first time.

Padilla, a native-born U.S. citizen, had been arrested on American soil first as a material witness, which is why he had been assigned a lawyer by the court, but was then designated an enemy combatant by Bush and was secretly transferred from a civilian jail in New York to military custody in the naval brig in Charleston. The White House asserted its right to keep him locked up indefinitely without formal charges and without access to courts or lawyers. For twenty months, he had not been allowed any outside contact and had no idea that his appointed attorneys, whom he had never met, had filed brief after brief until they reached the Supreme Court, which they hoped would grant a writ of habeas corpus so that he could get before a judge.

Only on the verge of the Court's decision on hearing the case did the government suddenly resolve a key dispute by inviting Patel and a colleague to see Padilla, but under certain conditions: he could not ask Padilla how he had been treated (recall that Padilla later claimed to have been drugged and tortured), and the military would record the conversation with an officer present.[48]

Such a breach of attorney-client privilege exceeded anything Patel had experienced, even in representing defendants charged with monstrous crimes. Therefore, the lawyer planned to do all the talking. He shipped twenty pounds of legal documents to Padilla in the brig to bring him up to speed, but wouldn't let him say anything during the monitored meeting. "My career has been spent as a criminal defense attorney, which means I deal with aberrant human behavior," Patel remarked. "Usually, it's aberrant behavior by my clients, not by the government."

CHAPTER FOUR

The Tilted Playing Field

I consider trial by jury as the only anchor yet devised by man,
by which a government can be held to the principles of its
constitution.

—Thomas Jefferson

THE POWER OF THE PROSECUTOR

IMAGINE A SOCCER MATCH unseen by referees. They pick the winner
afterward, but there is no tape of the game. They study still photographs
and listen to the accounts of players and fans, then try to assemble the frag-
ments of information into a mosaic depicting the plays, fouls, and goals as
accurately as possible.

Unfortunately for the refs, most of the snapshots are provided by the
home team, and while it's supposed to offer photographs favorable to the
visitors as well, many of those are withheld, at least until it's too late for careful examination. Further, the refs may not realize that some of the "trust-
worthy" witnesses to the game have been given season tickets by the home
club. Finally, a peculiar rule holds that every foul committed against the
home team counts toward the home team's score, even if the refs have only
a strong hunch that the violation occurred and cannot prove it beyond a
reasonable doubt.

In something of the same manner as this imperfect metaphor, the criminal justice system seeks truth and levies punishment. It gives the home-
team advantage to the executive branch—the police and prosecutors who
wield immense discretion to choose what crimes to charge, what pleas to
accept, what evidence to present, and what unproven fouls to cite in advocating enhanced penalties.

Perhaps the judges and jurors who referee the adversarial process get
it right most of the time. Perhaps they don't send innocents to jail in huge
numbers or routinely impose egregious sentences. Yet even if injustice were
uncommon, it would be no more tolerable than the unusual plane crash,
the rare school shooting, or the atypical death from medical malpractice.

An aberration is not benign, especially when it derives from systemic flaws. And these injustices are deeply embedded in rules and laws and standard practices.

They lie on the same spectrum as the dramatic seizure of power by the executive branch in times of war, for just as national security threats enhance executive authority, so do criminal threats. During the Civil War, President Abraham Lincoln suspends habeas corpus, that venerable principle allowing the prisoner to summon his jailer to court. After 9/11, President George W. Bush unilaterally eavesdrops without warrants and imprisons without indictment. And less visibly but more pervasively, the prosecutor also circumvents the courtroom and tilts the playing field. To coerce guilty pleas, she is allowed to withhold exculpatory evidence, hide witnesses' unreliability, and threaten long jail terms to intimidate defendants into waiving their constitutional right to trial. At sentencing, she can get penalties increased by presenting evidence that has been suppressed, not proven, or actually rejected by jurors.

The right to "an impartial jury" as prescribed by the Sixth Amendment occupies a revered place in the Western legacy of justice. From Athens, which assembled a jury of some five hundred for the trial of Socrates, the concept passed to early Rome with jurors drawn from the ranks of nobles, and into the Magna Carta's guarantee that "no freeman is to be taken or imprisoned . . . save by lawful judgement of his peers or by the law of the land." That promise and its breach contributed to the ideals and the resentments that fueled the American Revolution. When the Crown sought to control trade by imposing duties and requiring cargo to be shipped in British vessels, the jury stood as a bastion of defiance, nullifying the hated laws by freeing colonists accused of violations. So Britain created special courts to try the commerce cases without juries, and in the process inflamed rebellion.

The revolutionaries understood that rank-and-file citizens of an orderly democracy can hold decisive authority in only two ways—as voters and as jurors. Only by stepping into the jury box do they gain power in the cloistered hierarchy of the court and, once there, check the autocratic impulses of the police, the zealous temptations of the prosecutor, the compliance or corruption of the judge.

The jury is a human institution, imperfect but indispensable. If all twelve jurors in every case were flawless, the jury room would be as intellectually clean as a sterile operating room, free from the impurities of emotion, illogic, assumption, sloppy thinking, racial bias, and other contamination. No trial is antiseptic, yet the jury remains the obstacle between the vast authority of the state and the vulnerability of the individual at the brink of losing liberty, "the grand bulwark," in the words of Sir William Blackstone, the esteemed scholar who codified English common law.

In the eighteenth century, Blackstone foresaw temptations that now afflict the United States. Expedience may induce "secret machinations, which may sap and undermine" the jury trial, he warned, "as doubtless all arbitrary powers, well executed, are the most *convenient*." He noted that "delays, and little inconveniences in the forms of justice, are the price that all free nations must pay for their liberty in more substantial matters."

For the sake of convenience, the jury trial in America is close to extinction. Only 3 percent of federal and 6 percent of state convictions result from trials, pleasing most prosecutors and judges who push to avoid clutter on the dockets.[1] They collaborate in punishing those who insist on their rights, producing federal sentences five times higher after a jury conviction than after a guilty plea. "When I started practicing in the early seventies, I'd be in trial every four to six weeks," remembers Barry Portman, federal public defender in San Francisco. "You can go years now without a trial."

Pragmatism and efficiency are prized. Yet they go unmentioned in the Sixth Amendment, notes Timothy Lynch of the libertarian Cato Institute, who argues that it's unconstitutional to bribe or threaten citizens into forfeiting their liberties—akin to what happens when the government presses for guilty pleas. "The Framers of the Constitution were aware of less time-consuming trial procedures when they wrote the Bill of Rights," he observes dryly, "but chose not to adopt them."[2]

"We simply don't have the resources to prosecute everything," countered an assistant U.S. attorney on the West Coast, so "there is a lot of discretion on the prosecutor's part, which is good and makes the job attractive. When you speak to kids out of law school, everybody wants to be a public defender, but you can arguably have more effect on doing justice as a prosecutor because there is so much discretion."

The discretion makes justice an elastic concept. It includes the choices not to prosecute or to charge less severely—or even to throw a case, as Daniel L. Bibb conceded that he had done as an assistant district attorney in Manhattan. In 2005, he developed doubts about the guilt of two young men convicted of killing a nightclub bouncer fifteen years before. Although ordered to defend the convictions at a hearing on newly discovered evidence, Bibb dug up exculpatory witnesses and tempered his cross-examinations. As a result, one man was released, the other retried and acquitted. He said, "Prosecutors are supposed to seek justice, not victory."[3]

Many guilty pleas mix justice and victory, but they also snuff out jury trials and rely on a mechanism that is hard to admire. The assistant U.S. attorneys who prosecute federal cases, and the district attorneys who do so at the state and local levels, have had their hands strengthened by laws that entangle judges in webs of sentencing requirements. These have come either in the form of mandatory minimums imposed by legislatures for certain crimes and for "habitual offenders" or through detailed sentencing "guidelines," a euphemism for a rigid system that prevailed for two decades. Until the Supreme Court changed them in 2005 from mandatory to advisory, the "guidelines" were not suggestions, as the word implies, but inescapable restrictions that practically imprisoned sentencing judges in little boxes on a grid.

Composed by about half a dozen judges and former prosecutors and defense attorneys on the United States Sentencing Commission, the federal guidelines are contained in a five-pound volume of some six hundred pages that leave little to the imagination. They tell the courts where on a sentencing table to locate the case: in one of 258 cells formed by the intersection of a vertical column of 43 offense levels relating to the severity of the crime and its circumstances, and a horizontal row of 6 criminal history categories based on the defendant's prior convictions. Many states have similar systems.

While some judges chafe at them, others find them helpful, even comforting. The variations of a criminal's act can be intricate, the law has grown complex, and the particulars of a perpetrator's background may be ambiguous. Meshing these components to arrive at a sentence is easier when they are quantified and put into a matrix. Was it really better before 1984, when a judge could use nothing more precise than gut instinct to pick a prison term within a law's broad range, say, of zero to forty years?

To examine the question, Judge Paul L. Friedman went behind his desk to a small bookshelf and removed a copy of the guidelines, bound in slick white paper. He was a slim man with large glasses and a calm, even demeanor, highly respected in the federal district court in Washington, D.C., where he presided over trials, ruled on constitutional challenges, and imposed sentences. His handsome chambers had an inspiring view of the gleaming dome of the United States Capitol.

He opened the volume to the section on embezzlement, chose the amount of $1 million, figured an offense level of 22, assumed a defendant without a criminal record, then turned to the inside back cover, where the sentencing table was printed. Running his finger down criminal history column I to level 22, he came to a box showing a sentence of forty-one to fifty-one months. "Can I do a better job picking a number?" he asked. "No individual judge is better equipped to pick a better number. Can I say that's not the right number to deter other people or deter him?"

Yet he struggled against certain sentences required by both guidelines and statutes, particularly the hundred-to-one disparity between the crack and powder forms of cocaine. Enacted by Congress in 1986, the law required a five-year minimum for possessing 500 grams of powder but merely 5 grams of crack, and a ten-year minimum came with 5,000 grams of powder and only 50 grams of crack.

Since crack was favored by blacks and powder by whites, prison terms hit blacks disproportionately. Driven by myths that crack induced more dangerous behavior than powder, the disparity played to long-standing stereotypes and racial fears of crack-induced murder and mayhem among African-Americans. It imprisoned low-level street sellers of crack longer than larger traffickers of powder.

One of those, Robert Harris, came before Friedman for sentencing. Arrested at age twenty-one for possessing 68.9 grams of crack, he faced the ten-year minimum, although he had no prior convictions. A young high school dropout, he had worked at low-wage jobs and earned his GED. The crack put him at level 32, or 121 to 151 months, the judge noted, while if the cocaine had been in powder form, the level would have been at 16, for 21 to 27 months.

"In crack-powder cases," Judge Friedman observed later in chambers, "I said to my defendants: 'The sentence I'm about to impose is unfair, but I'm forced by Congress to do it.'" He was not the only judge to apologize for a sentence the law required.

Gerard E. Lynch, a federal judge in Manhattan, called "unjust and harmful" the ten-year prison term he was bound to give Jorge Pabon-Cruz, convicted of advertising and transmitting child pornography on the Internet when he was eighteen, a freshman studying computer engineering at the University of Puerto Rico.

Using the screen name BigThing, the young man was spotted by a New York detective monitoring a chat room. He had no contact with the children shown performing sexual acts, and he did not create the images, but he sent about 11,000 of them, violating a tough law enacted in 1996 and signed by President Bill Clinton. Judge Lynch, a former federal prosecutor himself, took unusual steps to navigate around the long sentence, *The New York Times* reported. "I have some difficulty imagining that ten years in prison is going to do either him or society much good," he declared in a hearing.

First, he tried to get federal prosecutors to bargain down the charges in a plea or reduce them unilaterally, but they refused. Then, during the trial, he proposed including the fact of the ten-year sentence in his instructions to the jury, a ploy quickly appealed by the prosecution and blocked by the Second Circuit as "a clear abuse of discretion." Juries are supposed to convict or acquit on the evidence of the crime alone, not on the penalty, but Lynch reasoned that "we have jurors and not technicians" so they can "act on their conscience," and "jurors' consciences cannot operate if they have no idea what is at stake." They did not hear about the required ten years, and they found him guilty.

Had the young man been convicted of having sex with a twelve-year-old, the judge noted, the sentence would have fallen to about five years. "This leads me to the rather astonishing conclusion that Mr. Pabon-Cruz would have been better off molesting a child."[4]

In Utah, the federal judge Paul G. Cassell was so distressed at having to sentence twenty-four-year-old Weldon Angelos to fifty-five years in prison for his first offense that he took the rare step of urging the president to grant clemency. Angelos had been caught selling eight ounces of marijuana three times to an informant, but the key element in the mandatory sentence was the fact that he had carried a pistol with him twice and that guns had been found in a subsequent search of his home, along with three pounds of pot. He hadn't used his weapons, but possessing them in connection with drug trafficking was enough to mandate five years on the first count and twenty-five years for each additional count.

Angelos was clearly a dealer, and Cassell was advocating more than a slap on the wrist, but not more than the eighteen years recommended by the jury. He urged that the president commute the jail term to that level and that Congress revise the law. The longer term, he said, was "far in excess of the sentence imposed for such serious crimes as aircraft hijacking, second degree murder, espionage, kidnapping, aggravated assault, and rape. It exceeds what recidivist criminals will likely serve under the federal 'three strikes' provision." He continued in a tone of regret: "The court can set aside the statute only if it is irrational punishment without any conceivable justification or is so excessive as to constitute cruel and unusual punishment in violation of the Eighth Amendment. After careful deliberation, the court reluctantly concludes that it has no choice but to impose the fifty-five-year sentence. While the sentence appears to be cruel, unjust, and irrational, in our system of separated powers Congress makes the final decisions as to appropriate criminal penalties."[5]

Yes, but a case can be made that Congress has undermined the separation of powers by shifting immense authority from the judicial to the executive branch. In many areas of government, including criminal justice, the healthy equilibrium has been lost.

A partial correction was made by the Supreme Court in a pair of decisions that reinstated judges' sentencing powers, although the rulings have had more sweeping impact in principle than in practice. In 2004 and 2005 the Court determined that state and federal guidelines, respectively, could not be mandatory, for they calculated prison terms based on facts not proven to a jury, merely asserted persuasively by the prosecution in a sentencing process.[6] Rather than discard the federal guidelines entirely in the 2005 case, *United States v. Booker,* the Court retained them as a starting point for judges who "must consult" the rules and "take them into account."

This twin result came from two unusual coalitions, each mixing strange liberal and conservative bedfellows and sharing only one member in common: Justice Ruth Bader Ginsburg. One group of five found that the guidelines violated the right to trial by jury, the other group of five judged them constitutional if they were not mandatory, a position urged by Justice Stephen G. Breyer, who had been a strong advocate of sentencing guidelines as a counsel to the Senate Judiciary Committee during the 1970s and, later, a member of the Sentencing Commission.

Saving the guidelines with the "advisory" remedy disappointed defense attorneys who thought the Court had given with one hand and taken with the other. They have been proved both right and wrong. *Booker* tilted authority back to judges somewhat, encouraging public defenders in D.C., for example, to avoid plea agreements with the government, advise their clients to plead guilty to the indictment alone (called an open plea), stipulate to no further facts and sign no waivers, and take their chances with the judge. Sentences have drifted downward, according to A. J. Kramer, federal public defender there, and judges who depart from the guidelines have mostly gone lower, not higher.

Some judges now require that facts presented to enhance sentences be proven beyond a reasonable doubt, the standard required for juries to find guilt. In many other sentencing hearings, however, the lesser test—a preponderance of evidence, or a 51 percent probability that an allegation is true—remains enough for judges to raise levels on the grid.

The guidelines benefit from strong institutional momentum, in both the Justice Department and the federal judiciary. All federal appellate courts have told judges to start with the guidelines, which is also what federal prosecutors invariably argue for. Regional differences in sentencing have continued as before, but prison terms for first-time offenders have spread out more widely, both above and below the prescribed guideline ranges.[7] The defense has a better shot at a reduction than before. "There's far more leeway to make arguments that formerly were to no avail," said Kramer.

One of the arguments was on the crack-powder disparity. After *Booker*, Judge Friedman took the unusual step of inviting Kramer to write an amicus curiae ("friend of the court") brief in two crack cases, and the judge used the arguments to sentence lower than the guidelines, as other federal judges around the country were beginning to do. One case involved Robert Harris, whom Friedman reasoned down to below the minimum; he was released from federal prison just under four years following his date of arrest, instead of the ten years he would have received otherwise.[8]

Reflected by *Booker*, the climate on rigid sentencing shifted, and arguments long advanced by the Sentencing Commission for collapsing the crack-powder differences began to take hold. Its recommendation for equivalence in 1995 had been resisted by the Clinton Justice Department and blocked by both houses of Congress. In 2002 and 2004, the commission recommended reducing the disparity to twenty to one, and in 2007 the commission lowered the crack penalties by two levels, or about sixteen months, and then made the reduction retroactive so that some 19,500 inmates sentenced previously could petition the courts for early release.[9] Congress finally moved in 2010, reducing the ratio to eighteen to one.[10]

Meanwhile, the Supreme Court in 2007 had upheld a judge's below-guideline sentence for crack, a partial return of discretion to the trial courts.[11] Still, according to Friedman, judges had no cause to celebrate their liberation from the sentencing guidelines. "We're not free at last, free at last, I can do anything I want to. We're not that free. I don't agree that the guidelines are presumptively the best way to go," but "my pattern has been to go with the guidelines in most cases."

After *Booker*, he said, the Bush Justice Department was "taking names" of judges who departed downward, creating concern that Congress might be provoked into toughening statutory minimums for certain crimes. "Some judges have said that judges feel intimidated," Friedman noted. "It's very hard to say that someone who holds a lifetime appointment is intimidated. But I do think we're cautious, because we don't want Congress to take this discretion away, which they may do anyway."

THE PLEA BARGAIN

Since the *Guidelines Manual* remains the bible for federal prosecutors and the presumptive framework for judges, it is worth looking closely inside to see how it affects the dynamics of power in the criminal justice system.

The text is relentless in its detail yet malleable in the prosecutor's hands. Say you forget to leave your favorite Swiss Army knife or handgun at home when you go to the airport. When it's discovered by security, officials could just confiscate it, or they could turn you over to the local U.S. Attorney's office for possible prosecution. Here, from the guidelines with inserted explanations in brackets, is what you'd be facing:

§ 2K1.5. **Possessing Dangerous Weapons or Materials While Boarding or Aboard an Aircraft**
(a) Base Offense Level: **9** [For someone with no criminal record, this means 4–10 months of probation or prison.]
(b) Specific Offense Characteristics
If more than one applies, use the greatest:
(1) If the offense was committed willfully and without regard for the safety of human life, or with reckless disregard for the safety of human life, increase by **15** levels. [This would take it to level 24: with no criminal record, 51–63 months in prison.]
(2) If the defendant was prohibited by another federal law from possessing the weapon or material, increase by **2** levels. [This would raise it to level 11: with no record, 8–14 months in prison or a mixture of jail and probation; with the heaviest criminal background, 140–175 months in prison, no probation. Those barred from gun possession include convicted felons, the mentally ill, those with dishonorable military discharges, and those convicted of misdemeanors involving domestic violence.]
(3) If the defendant's possession of the weapon or material would have been lawful but for 49 U.S.C. § 46505 [prohibiting guns and explosives in passenger compartments], and he acted with mere negligence, decrease by **3** levels. [This would reduce it to level 6: with no criminal record, 0–6 months, all of which can be on probation.][12]

A couple of the variables are clear-cut: either you are or you are not legally permitted to possess the weapon off an airplane. But item (1) and part of (3) are subject to interpretation: an assistant U.S. attorney, possibly not long out of law school, might have the leeway to read the evidence one way or another to place you in the category of either "mere negligence" or "committed willfully," the difference between zero to six months, on the one hand, and four or five years, on the other.

A judge who thought either sentence inappropriate would have had little choice until *Booker* in 2005. The flexibility introduced by that case has been used to some degree, but since appellate courts have instructed judges to begin with the guidelines, most have ended with them as well.[13] The government can also appeal a sentence it thinks too lenient, and some appeals have been granted, sending cases back down to trial judges with instructions to stiffen penalties.

For the prosecutor, then, Sentencing Guidelines and statutory minimums remain a weapon and a lure. He can threaten the heavier charge if you choose to go to trial, and offer the lighter one if you agree to plead guilty, a tactic approved by the Supreme Court in 1978 after a district attorney in Kentucky had played the life-altering game with Paul Hayes, arrested for forging a check for $88.30.

Hayes had two previous felony convictions, which qualified him for the three-strikes-and-you're-out treatment under state law. Instead, the DA offered Hayes a five-year sentence if he pleaded guilty to "save the court the inconvenience and necessity of a trial." (Blackstone rolled in his grave.) But if he insisted on putting his fate before a jury, the prosecutor warned, a new grand jury indictment would be sought under Kentucky's Habitual Criminal Act, which carried a life sentence. The defendant chose the trial and got life. The Supreme Court narrowly approved, 5–4.[14]

"There's a lot of charge bargaining," with the defendant's criminal record often used as leverage, said Larry Kupers, who has been a public defender in California and Washington, D.C. A prosecutor "can add ten years by filing information that you have a prior drug conviction," Kupers noted, and the threat is often just that explicit. "The prosecutor may say, 'If you go to trial, I'll file, and you'll get ten more years in prison.'" In Northern California, assistant U.S. attorneys "also say if you move for bail, we'll file your prior," reported Steven Kalar, a federal public defender there. "The latest thing is, if a co-defendant files a motion [to exclude evidence, for example], they'll file your prior."

Similarly, a prosecutor can include or ignore elements of the crime. One made a gun magically disappear from a string of robberies to lower the charges and get a guilty plea, Kupers recalled. "I had a client who was very smart, an accountant, who went crazy and did a bunch of armed bank robberies," he said. "The first count with a gun gets 5 years, the second count gets you 20 to 25. He would have faced 150 years, so he had to take a deal for four or five robberies and only one with a gun."

That's a good deal if you're guilty, not so good if you're innocent and want to prove it. Then the risks of a trial are compounded by the guidelines themselves. For an admission of guilt, called "acceptance of responsibility," your sentence is lowered by two levels, and by a third level if you give "timely" notification of your willingness to plead, "thereby permitting the government to avoid preparing for trial," the guidelines state.[15]

The result can significantly reduce time behind bars. "Let's say it's at offense level 26," explained Kalar. "If you plead guilty before the pretrial conference, you can get three 'acceptance' points. So you go from 26 to 23, from 120–150 months to 92–115 months. So you'd save up to two years if you plead guilty."

But it's not up to the defendant and his lawyer alone. "This has to be on the motion of the prosecutor," Kalar observed. "You cannot even have a trial date set." And if you suspect a weakness in the prosecution's case, because of either an illegal search or a corrupt police officer, you need to think twice before moving to suppress evidence, he cautioned. "If you file a suppression motion saying the cop is dirty, they say you don't get the reduction, so you lose the three 'acceptance' points."

Furthermore, in the most Kafkaesque provision of all, if you are truly innocent, go to trial, deny the crime under oath, and are wrongly convicted nonetheless, the guidelines elevate your sentence by two levels for "obstructing or impeding the administration of justice." The same increase is imposed if a witness testifies on your behalf and is disbelieved.[16]

Court decisions have also deprived defendants of information that could be crucial in helping them decide whether to plead guilty. To guarantee a fair trial, the Supreme Court has ruled that the prosecution must give the defendant evidence that is favorable to his case or unfavorable to prosecution witnesses. Under *Brady v. Maryland* in 1963, a conviction can be overturned if the prosecution fails to disclose exculpatory evidence,[17] and under *Giglio v. United States* in 1972, if the prosecution withholds facts that may impeach a witness's credibility. These can include leniency in exchange for testimony if the witness is facing prosecution or deportation.[18]

But that's in a trial. The Court has denied the accused a right to such helpful information when contemplating a guilty plea, which is essentially a voluntary waiver of a host of constitutional rights: against self-incrimination, to a jury trial, to confront witnesses, and to due process as bolstered by access to exculpatory and impeachment evidence.[19] Police don't want to identify informants and undercover agents unless absolutely necessary, and some prosecutors require defendants to sign waivers of their rights under *Brady* and *Giglio* as part of the plea agreement, primarily to avoid later appeals. It was one such waiver that was found constitutional by a unanimous Court in 2002.[20]

That doesn't mean that all prosecutors conceal their hands. Even during plea bargaining, some willingly reveal facts that tend toward exoneration. "I disclose all evidence that I have," said an assistant U.S. attorney in California. "I have a colleague who came from the Southern District of New York, and she said that's not the way it's done there. She said they disclose only the minimum." Such variations occur not only from region to region, defense attorneys observe, but within the same office.

When information is not forthcoming, defense lawyers often fly blind as they give their clients advice under pressure to make a "timely" decision on a plea. They may not know that the police turned up evidence calling the defendant's guilt into question, or that a key witness has a background of unreliability, or that an informant charged with a crime is being paid off with a lower sentence in another case. Sometimes, if the prosecution witness is not a U.S. citizen, he is rewarded for his testimony by having his crime reduced below the level at which deportation is mandatory—a fact that the accused may not learn unless prosecutors choose to tell him.

As a result, says the public defender Kalar, "cops that are dirty are not tested. Informants that are dirty are not tested. The only check on the law enforcement procedure is the adversary process." Yet Kalar would not plead an innocent defendant guilty. That would be unethical. "Usually, we don't ask," he said. "My first question is not, 'Did you do it?' I'm not interested in that question until we're close to a plea." And many lawyers never know for sure.

THE SENTENCE

It's an irony that the more intricate the legislative branch makes sentencing provisions in the law, the more power is transferred to the executive branch, by way of the police and prosecutors. This was not the intention when Congress enacted the federal sentencing guidelines in 1984. They were designed to eliminate judges' disparate sentences, which had put black convicts in prison for much longer terms than whites, one scourge of a racially biased justice system.

The plan did not succeed. At first, in 1984, blacks and whites received equivalent sentences averaging just over two years, but by 2004 the gap had widened again, to six years for blacks and four for whites.[21]

Moreover, the guidelines created new problems. At the sentencing hearings that followed guilty pleas or convictions, prosecutors could argue for increased prison terms by making assertions about the defendant and the circumstances of the crime. Before the guidelines, judges were generally free to accept or reject the arguments, and in so doing, many indulged their biases, racial and otherwise. With the guidelines in place, however, judges were less able to disregard "enhancement factors," which had to be proven only by a preponderance of the evidence, not by the higher standard—beyond reasonable doubt—required for juries to find guilt.

In tens of thousands of cases since the guidelines were enacted, therefore, sentences have been based on weaker evidence than a jury needs to convict. That continued even after *Booker* shifted the guidelines from mandatory to advisory, since they remain the preferred benchmark for most judges and prosecutors. "In this circuit you can use quadruple hearsay: a snitch to an informant to a cop to a prosecutor," complained Kalar, the public defender in San Francisco. "I have to tell my client, 'We're probably not going to prevail on this.' It's harmful to the truth-finding process. It encourages them to use informants in sentencing hearings, shaky informants that could not withstand the trial."

Furthermore, even what you win at trial you can lose at sentencing. If the jury acquits you on four of five counts of crack possession, the judge can still include those four not-guilty counts in calculating your offense level, as long as he doesn't exceed the statutory maximum enacted by Congress for the one count of conviction by the jury. That is the only upper limit, but it's hardly limiting: those maximums in the law are usually high, so they barely impede sentence increases based on what is called "acquitted conduct," legal shorthand for a device so widespread that it rates a label.

Robert Mercado Jr. and Daniel Bravo, two alleged members of the Mexican Mafia, got caught by this practice. A jury convicted them of racketeering and conspiracy to distribute narcotics but found them innocent of more serious charges that they had participated in three murders and two armed assaults and had conspired to commit a fourth homicide. The judge lengthened the sentence by citing the murders nonetheless, replacing the jury's finding with his own that the crimes had been sufficiently proven.

The box where they fit in the guidelines grid put their sentences at around three years for the convicted charge of drug trafficking. Had they been convicted of murder, it could have been life. The judge couldn't give them life, but the high statutory maximum for drug trafficking allowed him considerable room to move upward, and so he sentenced them to twenty years. Their appeal failed 2–1 in the Ninth Circuit, prompting the dissenting judge, Betty Fletcher, to declare plainly: "By considering acquitted conduct, a judge thwarts the express will of the jury," thereby marginalizing the jury and undermining the Sixth Amendment. "Such a sentence has little relation to the actual conviction," she wrote in stating the obvious, "and is based on an accusation that failed to receive confirmation from the defendant's equals and neighbors."[22] Mercado and Bravo were denied review by the Supreme Court.

At least ten federal circuits following *Booker* upheld trial judges' discretion to use acquitted conduct in sentencing, including the Second Circuit in a much-quoted opinion by Sonia Sotomayor.[23] The Supreme Court allowed the practice to continue. Perhaps the unusual, fragile coalitions of liberal and conservative justices were too close and fluid to refine the *Booker* decision that they had assembled—the decision that guidelines violated the right to a jury trial when they were compulsory but abridged no right when merely advisory. So, in the parallel universe of jurisprudence, sentences based on allegations unproven to a jury were unconstitutional if mandatory and constitutional if discretionary.

Even an implausible confession, given under duress and disbelieved by the jury, could be spun into a long sentence, at least in the federal judge William H. Alsup's San Francisco courtroom. There, at the prosecutor's urging, a conviction for insurance fraud was magnified by Alsup into terrorism by arson, a charge the jurors had unanimously rejected. They had found Luis Gonzalez guilty of essentially faking the theft of a car to collect insurance, a crime that normally carried a sentence of probation or several months in jail, his attorney figured. Judge Alsup gave Gonzalez eight years instead.

A hard-nosed Clinton appointee, the judge built the sentence on an uncertain foundation of constitutional rulings that weakened Gonzalez's efforts to protect his Fifth Amendment right against self-incrimination and his Sixth Amendment right to trial by jury. As a result, the case began to work its way up the ladder of appeals, where the precedents did not favor defendants.

The crime came out of financial desperation, as so many do. In May 2006, four months after Gonzalez's wife, Katherine Paiz, had taken a loan to buy a $32,000 Honda, the car developed severe engine trouble not covered by the warranty because of "driver abuse" by "over-shifting," the dealer claimed.[24] Evidently unschooled in the art of challenging automobile manufacturers and unable to afford the repair of $5,000 to $7,000, Paiz upgraded her insurance to cover damage from "fire, theft, tree, hail, flood, act of God." Then, before her evening shift at Lowe's department store, she parked beyond the range of surveillance cameras, in an area avoided by employees because of vehicle break-ins. When she left work at 10:00 p.m. and saw that her car was missing, she called 911 and reported it stolen.

The police told her that the Honda had been discovered ablaze about an hour and a half earlier in a cattle pasture of dry grass near a small airstrip. A gasoline can, found in the backseat, led suspicious insurance investigators to notify the FBI, which got a quick confession from Paiz to the fraud but not to the fire. An unnamed acquaintance, she said, "gave me the idea to get rid of my car. They took it from Lowe's parking lot with the valet key they received from me. I didn't know what they were going to do with my car. I just knew they were going to take it. They said just report it stolen, and insurance would take care of it."

Two FBI agents then questioned Gonzalez, but in a manner raising Fifth Amendment concerns, according to his lawyer, Daniel Blank. Since he was a suspected gang member on probation for an earlier crime, he was subject to the instructions of his probation officer, Julie Nie, and was vulnerable to being returned to prison for a violation. So the FBI had Nie summon him to her office for a visit that was hardly voluntary. She ordered him to provide a urine sample for a drug test, talked to him for a while, and told him to wait at her desk while she left the room to let the agents know they could question him.

When they walked into the office, the agents formally established that he was not in custody—a prerequisite for avoiding the Miranda warning. He was not under arrest, they said, nor did he have to speak with them. But he agreed to answer questions, and they led him to another room "with one of the agents situated between Gonzalez and the door," according to his appeals brief.

For ninety minutes, Gonzalez insisted that he had known nothing of the theft until his wife had called him from Lowe's; he had borrowed his father's car to pick her up. He "stated that he did not set the car on fire and that he did not know who did." The agents persisted, asking if he would take a lie detector test. He agreed, but it was never given.

When he finally asked about a lawyer, the agents replied that he did not need one and was free to leave. Yet when he stood, "one of the agents also stood and approached him," his brief reports, and "reminded him that he was on felony probation," which gave them the authority to search his house without a warrant or probable cause. "Feeling threatened by the words and actions of the agents, Gonzalez did not leave," his lawyer told the court. He sat back down.

The agents then played a scary card, according to Blank. Since the burning car was found near an airport, they declared, it may have been a "terrorist-related event." The tactic appeared to be part of a widespread practice after September 11, when the FBI and the Justice Department inflated their counterterrorism numbers by relabeling many common crimes as terrorism. "They said, 'Your wife is on the hook for a terrorism offense,'" Blank reported. "'Why don't you help her out?'"

The ploy drew Gonzalez into a rebuttal. It was not terrorism, he declared. The agents cleverly parried his denial. They needed more than his word, they told him, to convince headquarters that his wife was not into something extremely dangerous. They prodded until Gonzalez finally burst out, "I burned that shit up." The caper "was purely an insurance fraud" that had "nothing to do with terrorism," his brief quoted him as saying. He was trying to protect his wife by taking the blame entirely on himself.

But his confession contained nonsensical elements. He told the agents that he hadn't seen any dry grass, when the field was actually covered by it. He said that after setting the fire, he had walked fifteen miles home in time to get Paiz's call from the parking lot just ninety minutes later, making a record-breaking walking speed of ten miles an hour. Unfazed by the obvious falsehoods, the FBI and the Justice Department relied wholly on his confession to charge him with conspiracy to commit wire fraud (calling the insurance company to report theft) and using "fire or an explosive to commit" the crime, a charge carrying a statutory minimum of ten years.[25] There was no other evidence, Blank said.

Gonzalez and Paiz were tried separately, Gonzalez first. Blank argued that his confession should be suppressed because he had effectively been in custody, had not been Mirandized, had requested and had been denied a lawyer, and had not been truly free to leave despite the FBI agents' statements otherwise. In short, his Fifth Amendment right against self-incrimination had been violated, and the confession was patently false. Judge Alsup disagreed. He rejected the contention that the agents had intimidated Gonzalez into staying and talking; found the situation noncustodial, which meant that no Miranda warning was required; and denied the suppression motion.

So the jury learned of the confession, but their doubts about it were helped along by testimony from a close friend that he'd been with Gonzalez at home when the car was burned. Gonzalez was pronounced not guilty of the fire but guilty of wire fraud. Separately and also before Judge Alsup, Paiz's jury then found her guilty of both fire and fraud. He sentenced her to ten years and one month. Then he turned to Gonzalez.

Defendants and their attorneys do not often have much power at sentencing. They can present mitigating factors, testimony to the convicted person's otherwise good character, pleas for mercy. But it is not always a full evidentiary hearing, not a retrial of the facts, and so swirls of rumor and innuendo can turn the courtroom into a surreal echo chamber where half-truths are repeated over and over and magnified until they haunt the facts.

Gonzalez was thus afflicted. By sliding in beneath the jury's high standard of proof, Judge Alsup accepted his confession—nothing else linked him to the crime—and found the arson established by "clear and convincing evidence," which is lower than the "beyond reasonable doubt" required of the jury but one notch above the "preponderance" considered acceptable for sentencing. Having created an alternative reality, Alsup then logically found that the alibi witness could not have testified truthfully, and that the defendant must have suborned his perjury, earning Gonzalez an increase of two offense levels for obstructing justice. The judge gave him ninety-six months. Lewis Carroll could not have written it more acutely.

A repair would be quite straightforward: either Congress or the Sentencing Commission could simply bar courts from considering acquitted conduct in sentencing. This fix was suggested by none other than Judge Brett M. Kavanaugh, an extreme conservative named by President George W. Bush to the D.C. Circuit. Given precedent, Kavanaugh and his two colleagues did not feel free to overturn the enhanced prison term of Tarik Settles, who was sentenced for carrying a gun during a drug deal, although he'd been convicted of only gun possession, not selling drugs. Kavanaugh quoted from the sentencing hearing, when Settles made the point directly: "I just feel as though, you know, that that's not right. That I should get punished for something that the jury and my peers, they found me not guilty."[26]

To arrive at a fair sentence, a judge needs to know a good deal about the convicted man or woman standing before him, a picture sketched largely by the probation department that presents a presentencing report and recommendation. The portrait's ingredients, called "relevant conduct" in legal parlance, may be accurate—or may be salted with unproven allegations immune to effective rebuttal at a sentencing hearing. The strict rules of evidence used in trials would hamper the wider inquiry allowed at sentencing, filtering out elements of background and character that might guide the judge. But the very flexibility to probe into the defendant's behavior also raises troubling questions of due process that have been repeatedly litigated up to the Supreme Court.

On balance and within limits, the Supreme Court has entrusted the judge with the burden of determining sentence. In a 1949 homicide case, the justices ruled that a judge could override a jury's recommendation of life imprisonment and impose the death penalty based on unproven reports that the murderer had committed some thirty burglaries (none of which had brought convictions) and on a probation officer's assertion that his "morbid sexuality" made him "a menace to society." The Court held that while the determination of guilt or innocence at trial should not be influenced "by evidence that the defendant had habitually engaged in other misconduct," it is precisely such misconduct that needs to be known to the sentencing judge. "Highly relevant—if not essential—to his selection of an appropriate sentence is the possession of the fullest information possible concerning the defendant's life and characteristics," wrote Justice Hugo Black for the majority, so "that the punishment should fit the offender and not merely the crime."[27]

The question, however, is how to test the allegations for accuracy. The Court has answered this with the preponderance standard, interpreted as meaning more chance than not that a given incident took place, as little as 51 percent. It is a subjective test susceptible to various judges' disparate interpretations. It is embedded in precedent, however. In 1986, a Pennsylvania law was upheld imposing a minimum five-year prison term for carrying a firearm during certain crimes, where the gun possession had been determined by the sentencing judge, not the jury, and on the basis of preponderance, not beyond reasonable doubt. The sentence was permitted because the penalty with the gun did not exceed the statutory maximum without the gun: the five-year minimum fell within the range of sentences that the law provided for an unarmed criminal.[28]

But when the judge finds facts by a preponderance that takes the sentence above the statutory maximum for the crime of conviction, he violates the right to have a jury consider the charge, the Court has ruled.[29] In *Apprendi v. New Jersey*, now considered a defining opinion, the justices set down the requirement that juries, not judges, rule on additional facts that make the convicted crime eligible for a sentence above what would otherwise be the statutory maximum. Charles Apprendi, who shot several times into an African-American family's home, pleaded guilty to gun possession for an unlawful purpose, which carried a prison term of five to ten years.

The prosecutor then moved to lengthen the sentence because of the shooting's racial motivation, putting it into the category of a hate crime. After a full evidentiary hearing in which the defense called a psychologist and seven character witnesses, plus Apprendi himself, the judge agreed that bias had been demonstrated by a preponderance of evidence and imposed a twelve-year sentence, two years above the maximum allowed by law for the gun possession charge alone. The Court overturned it, 5–4, ruling that the hate-crime component had to be proven to a jury beyond a reasonable doubt.[30]

As long as prosecutors and judges stay within the broad ranges in the law, however, "enhancements," as they're pleasantly called, can factor into sentences all kinds of untrustworthy or questionable elements, even evidence suppressed because of an unconstitutional search.

So it was for Clemente Zavaleta, a.k.a. Oliver Espanol, who was sitting at curbside in his Cadillac when the "gang violence suppression patrol" of Oakland, California, drove along in two cars looking for suspicious vehicles, people, and behavior. Zavaleta fit a few profiles, apparently. He spun out from the curb and nearly collided with a van, the police said, then sped through two stop signs.

When the cops pulled him over, they thought he seemed nervous and unsure about where he lived—Oakland or Seattle—and couldn't produce a valid license, although one from Washington was later found in his wallet during a pat-down. He was placed under arrest for driving recklessly and without a license, and was asked for permission to search the vehicle. He consented, the officers claimed (Zavaleta denied it), and their search of the trunk turned up a kilo of cocaine inside a gray metal tackle box, "wrapped in black electrical tape and laundry detergent," according to the police report. "That's not my cocaine," the report quoted Zavaleta as saying. "I'm just bringing it to a bar."[31]

Without a warrant, the squad then went to his house nearby and asked his wife, Irene Felix, for permission to search. Granting consent would have waived her Fourth Amendment right "to be secure" against a search unless a judge had signed a warrant. A Spanish-speaking officer, E. Ayala, testified under oath that he had made the request politely, telling her that he worried that items dangerous to children might be inside.

Her account, also given under oath, was quite different: She asked if he had a search warrant, and when he said no, she insisted that she would not let him in without one. He grew angry, raised his voice, told her that she was probably in the United States illegally, could be jailed, might lose her house, and could see her children taken away. Preying on a mother's elemental attachment to her children is an effective tactic by agents of some oppressive regimes. Yet Felix was in America. She stood steadfast for ten or fifteen minutes, keeping the screen door closed and not allowing Ayala inside. The argument continued until her fears overcame her rights, and she signed a consent form. The police found six more kilos of cocaine in the attic and a nine-millimeter pistol in the bedroom closet. Then Ayala threatened her again with arrest and the loss of her children to get her signature on a statement that she had not been threatened.

The federal judge accepted her version, not the cop's. "Her testimony was generally consistent, forthright, and believable," Judge Saundra Brown Armstrong wrote. "Officer Ayala improperly threatened Ms. Felix in order to gain entry into the residence," rendering the consent involuntary and the evidence from the house inadmissible. The exclusionary rule applies to evidence seized in violation of the Fourth Amendment during searches, as it does to information obtained in violation of the Fifth Amendment during interrogations; it is the main deterrent to unconstitutional behavior by law enforcement. So, once Judge Armstrong excluded the cocaine and the gun from the house, the prosecution was left with only the kilo of cocaine from the car, which carried a sentence of up to five years. Zavaleta pleaded guilty to the lesser charge.

Then things got strange. The prosecutor, Assistant U.S. Attorney Lewis A. Davis, urged the judge to include the suppressed drugs and gun from the house as "relevant conduct" in calculating the sentence. "If the court were to rely solely on the one kilogram," Davis said at the sentencing hearing, "it has a picture of the defendant as one type of narcotics trafficker. When it considers seven kilograms of cocaine, the court must have a different view of this cocaine trafficker. . . . It changes the whole complexion of his offense and the nature of his conduct. And it seems to me that conduct is important for the court to consider in toto in fashioning the appropriate sentence."

Zavaleta's lawyer, Jerome Matthews, cited precedent for ignoring evidence at sentencing when it was obtained in "egregious" circumstances. Judge Armstrong, who had been the first African-American policewoman in Oakland, seemed torn at first. But in the end, speaking of Officer Ayala, she declared, "I have to say I did not find his behavior to be egregious." So a federal court determined that threatening to take a mother's children away if she didn't consent to a search of her home was not egregious.

"Your argument has visceral appeal," Armstrong told Matthews, "but I, unfortunately, don't sentence based upon my visceral reaction."

Matthews urged her to see that considering wrongly seized evidence would undermine the exclusionary rule's deterrent effect; if police could enhance a sentence by bullying their way over the Fourth Amendment, he argued, they'd have nothing to lose by trying coercion. Armstrong disagreed. Suppressing the evidence in trial was sufficient deterrent, she said; it could be removed from sentencing if the illegal search had been designed deliberately to increase the drug amounts as a scheme to lengthen jail time, but she saw no such motive.

It was a close call, she conceded, but she doubled Zavaleta's sentence to ten years, the most that the law would have allowed if the house had been searched under the purity of a warrant.

An appeals court had to set things right by sending him back to Judge Armstrong for resentencing. "It was plain error to expose Zavaleta to a higher statutory maximum sentence than would otherwise apply on the basis of this uncharged and unproven drug quantity," a panel of the Ninth Circuit declared. The judges added, however, that they would not explicitly rule out considering the suppressed evidence—the six kilos and the gun—in fashioning a sentence up to the statutory maximum for the one kilo found in his car. This left intact the principle that the fruits of an illegal search could enhance a sentence, to a point. Armstrong had to reduce the penalty and chose the most she could give for the single kilo of cocaine. Zavaleta was released after five years.

REVOKING PROBATION AND FORFEITING ASSETS

The protections of liberty are most clearly visible when they are gone. Into their absence flow the police and prosecutors with unproven suspicions, flimsy evidence, and life-altering decisions. Without enough to gain criminal convictions, they can still imprison certain people and seize certain property by operating legally behind a facade of due process, making a kind of Potemkin justice.

The bad results come from penalties enacted for good reason: the forfeiture of assets used in or derived from crime, and the forfeiture of freedom by a released convict who violates the rules of probation. The trouble is, neither allegation has to be proved beyond reasonable doubt, only by a preponderance of the evidence, the hunch that something is more likely to have happened than not. This has given truth a casual quality.

The good reasons are compelling. The narcotics trade flourishes on money, and terrorism plots need financing, so the power to confiscate property can be a quick, supple weapon, effective if employed with judicious

precision. The targets can include a car or a boat believed to have transported drugs, a house thought to be a place of storage or sale, and funds
that seem to have come from the trafficking. Yet they can be seized before
any judgment on whether they meet the criteria of the law. In everyday
practice, cash is taken from black and Latino drivers pulled over on rural
Southern highways, whole bank accounts are emptied, real estate is frozen
long before trials are held. In asset forfeiture, the punishment precedes the
verdict.

Similarly, monitoring inmates who are out on probation following their
prison terms is wise and often helpful; in the federal system, probation is
aptly called "supervisory release."[32] But accusations too weak to stand up
at trial are routinely referred by prosecutors to probation officials who use
lower standards of evidence to send people back to jail.

Neale Jenkins went through exactly this experience when prosecutors
didn't think they had a case strong enough to convict him for rape, so they
used the probation system to lock him up for a year before he was finally
exonerated.

He had been doing well during the four months since his release after
serving a five-year sentence for narcotics and guns, according to one of his
lawyers, Tony Miles. He lived with his mother, kept his probation appointments, tested clean for drugs every time, and held a decent job at a restaurant in Bowie, Maryland. He also partied with old friends in Washington,
D.C., with unhappy results one night.

In the wee hours of a January morning, his former girlfriend, Sabrina
Knott, then engaged to another man, returned to the apartment where she
lived with her fiancé. When he heard her story, he called 911.[33]

With her fiancé present, she told a detective that as she had left a
friend's house about 3:30 a.m. (after drinking alcohol, smoking pot, and
taking Ecstasy, she later admitted), she was accosted by Jenkins, who held
a gun to her head as a masked accomplice grabbed her keys and drove her
car away. Jenkins forced her into a red car and, from behind the wheel, beat
her with a belt, she charged. He took her into the corridor of an apartment
on Sheriff Road, brandished a knife, pulled down her pants, and raped her
anally and vaginally, she claimed, then took her to a 7-Eleven, where the
masked man gave her back her keys and her car. She drove home and was
taken to a hospital, where a nurse found tears in her anus but no sign of
trauma or bruising elsewhere.

The police arrested Jenkins the same day, and Knott began amending
her account as the detective drove her to a "showup," which is like a lineup
with only one person (the suspect) available for identification. On the way,

she told the cop that the rape had actually occurred in a Travelodge on New York Avenue, not an apartment. She'd made up the apartment detail, she explained, so her fiancé wouldn't be angry that she'd gone to a motel with her old boyfriend, even under duress. But everything else was true, she insisted.

Poised to bring a criminal indictment against Jenkins, the assistant U.S. attorney on the case put Knott before a grand jury, where she repeated what a federal judge later called "version one," altered by the switch from the apartment to the motel. Worried by her lack of credibility, the detective challenged her with his doubts, and she changed her story again: no accomplice, no gun, no red car, no beating, she now said, but threats nonetheless; in this version she had to drive her car as he directed her to the motel, where she was forced inside at knifepoint, grabbed by the hair, thrown down, and raped. The 7-Eleven disappeared from her story, and she drove herself home from the Travelodge.

As the government shifted its narrative of the crime to match Knott's revisions, the detective and the prosecutor, Elana Tyrangiel, realized that their one and only witness might not get them a guilty verdict, so they decided to go the easier probation route instead. Asked why by the federal magistrate judge John M. Facciola, Tyrangiel said frankly, "Your Honor, there's a difference, clearly, in the burden about what we must prove, and beyond a reasonable doubt is a very difficult standard. The preponderance of the evidence standard is much slimmer. It's not nothing, but it's a significant difference."[34]

Shopping around for the least exacting forum and the lightest burden of proof should be closed as an option, Tony Miles believed, and he saw a clear solution to such practices: prohibit reincarceration for alleged probation violations that cannot be proven beyond a reasonable doubt. Courts have ruled otherwise, however, leaving the lesser standard in place, and leaving Jenkins in an unusually uncomfortable spot.

He was jeopardized doubly, you could say, because he fell under the jurisdiction of both the federal supervisory release program and the District of Columbia parole system. In a complicated plea bargain five years earlier, he had admitted guilt to both a federal and a local crime, which meant that he now had to convince two entirely separate authorities that he should not be returned to prison.[35] In effect, he had to prove his innocence both to Magistrate Facciola, who would make a recommendation to a federal district judge, and to an officer of the U.S. Parole Commission handling D.C. cases.

On the federal side, Facciola conducted a long hearing, at which Knott again changed her account: in this version, Jenkins asked her for a ride as she left her friend's house, Knott agreed and took him into her car, he told her where to turn at each intersection, then compelled her to enter the Travelodge and, once in a room, poked at her with a knife, then raped her anally and vaginally and called her a "bitch" for breaking up with him when he went to prison.

She had insisted all along that she had not seen much of him since his release, but Miles found pieces of evidence that undermined her credibility further: Jenkins's cell phone, which showed incoming calls from the house where Knott was staying; two neighbors who saw them together earlier that evening; and a jerky video from a Travelodge surveillance camera showing her walking into the motel not like a captive but ten feet behind Jenkins, carrying his sweater as a willing companion. Contrary to her contention, "the videotape displays no such fear," Facciola found. She accompanied Jenkins when he checked in, showed his true ID, and got the key to a room.

"I appreciate that, as every 'date-rape' case shows, the sexual relationship can go from being romantic to violent in an instant," Facciola wrote in his recommendation. "But, if I cannot credit Knott's testimony that she was forced to go to the Travelodge, I have to harbor significant doubts about the truthfulness of what she said occurred in the room." He observed that "Knott is an admitted perjurer and liar" and that on the witness stand "she indicated no remorse or shame whatsoever" for her perjury. "I left the hearing with the distinct impression that she thought it was perfectly proper to lie under oath to achieve Jenkins's imprisonment."

The case had not even met the lower preponderance standard, he found, and he bridled at the government's concept that Knott was more credible when that standard of proof was less demanding. "Knott is either telling the truth or she is not," Facciola declared. Then he made a statement that might well be hung on every prosecutor's wall: "Truth cannot be quantified and does not admit of modifiers." Judge Paul L. Friedman accepted the recommendation that no violation be found.

Jenkins had been in jail eight months. He would have been free to go, except that the U.S. Parole Commission had not yet ruled on the local, D.C. case, and the government wasn't giving up. Without knowing Facciola's findings, which happened to be issued the same day as the commission hearing, Commissioner Robert Haworth came to the opposite conclusion, ruling that Jenkins had violated his parole by raping Knott.

Jenkins's legal team wasn't giving up either.[36] His lawyer in the D.C. case, Thomas L. Dybdahl, dispatched an investigator for the Public Defender Service to the neighborhood and found another witness, Patrice Kelly, who had hosted the party in her apartment. Her account devastated Knott's claim. "Sabrina and Neale were all over each other," Kelly said in a signed statement. "They were making conversation about where they were going to have sex at. . . . Sabrina said to me, we are going to go to a hotel. I saw Sabrina and Neale leave together to go to the hotel."

Kelly even provided a motive for Knott's rape report. Two weeks earlier, she said, "I had told Sabrina about the Victim's Rights Program. I had gotten busted in my lip by my friend, and I was supposed to get $1,500 for relocation money. The man lived in my building. When I told Sabrina this, she said, damn, they gonna give you $1,500? I told her if you ever get victimized (battered or raped) on these streets, they will give you money so you can move."

With that account plus the Facciola decision, Dybdahl appealed the Parole Commission's ruling to its National Appeals Board, but that's as much as he could do. "It's frustrating," he said. "Essentially, there's no redress. The court says the lower standard for parole violations is constitutional. You're at the mercy of these commissioners," and while procedural and constitutional matters can be appealed to a court, findings of fact cannot.

More than two months later, Dybdahl said, "I actually got a call from Commissioner Haworth, who told me upon reviewing the information he had changed his mind and the commission agreed with him, and they were voiding their earlier action and making a finding of no violation." On January 5, 2006, just three days short of the one-year anniversary of his arrest, Neale Jenkins was released.

You could say that the system worked, but barely, and not without inflicting pain. Sometimes you can hear the pain in a voice, as I did over the phone with Benjamin Molina, who'd had $18,000 in cash seized by local police as he was driving through southern Virginia. After four months, he'd just gotten it back (minus $100 deemed counterfeit and $1,000 for his lawyer). It was more of a victory than most victims of highway forfeiture can claim, but his wounds had not healed, as betrayed by his lingering tone of astonished anger.

He was forty, with no criminal record and no earnings at the moment, a carpenter here legally from El Salvador, recovering from a kidney transplant and surviving on disability payments from Social Security. He had sold a house and had drawn $18,000 from his bank so he could buy a used car if he saw one he liked as he drove between his New Jersey residence and North Carolina, where he kept a mobile home. Only paper currency could be used for a roadside sale, he explained in halting English. "They want $10,000, 'I give you cash right now.' They're not gonna take check from nobody they don't know."

This was not a story acceptable to officers in the struggling little town of Emporia, Virginia, population 5,700, median household income $38,000. Police departments get to keep a good portion of the property they confiscate, providing a high motivation for seizures, especially from vehicles with out-of-state plates and black or Latino-looking drivers. In Barbour County, Alabama, one of the nation's poorest, the sheriff's department has used forfeited "drug money" to buy guns, bulletproof vests, and nine out of its fourteen cars.[37] The Kingsville Police Department in Texas bought Dodge Chargers, digital ticket writers for $40,000, and assault rifles for its town of 25,000 souls.[38] James Woodford, a forensic chemist who testifies as an expert witness, notes that some departments keep the money in a box and just spend it at will.

As part of a federal narcotics program, local police departments seized $1.58 billion worth of assets in 2007, triple the amount four years earlier, according to Justice Department figures. The most lucrative fishing expeditions are conducted by police in border states, who would rather get money going south than drugs coming north, so are "more interested in working southbound than northbound lanes," according to John Burnett, who spent nine months investigating forfeiture for National Public Radio.

"If a cop stops a car going north with a trunk full of cocaine, that makes great press coverage, makes a great photo. Then they destroy the cocaine," Jack Fishman, a former IRS agent, said on National Public Radio. "If they catch 'em going south with a suitcase full of cash, the police department just paid for its budget for the year."[39]

Such a grant of executive power invites abuse, and the Supreme Court has acted as enabler. In 1996, Tina B. Bennis was told by the Court that the automobile she owned jointly with her husband could be forfeited, even though she was entirely innocent of the crime committed in the vehicle: his "gross indecency" with a prostitute. He screws around, she loses her car. As Justice Clarence Thomas observed wryly in concurring, "This case is ultimately a reminder that the Federal Constitution does not prohibit everything that is intensely undesirable."[40]

The Court thereby set the stage for this one, described by Richard Foxall, a public defender in Alameda County, California: A prostitute's husband was arrested for drugs while driving her car, which was seized. When she objected to the forfeiture, a cop demanded free sex, released her car, and kept stopping by for his periodic rape until she retrieved a condom he'd thrown out the window. She had the DNA tested, sued the police department, and got him fired.

Forfeiture is an old practice, employed by the British against American colonists who evaded the Navigation Acts' requirements that all trade be carried in British ships, subject to customs and excise duties. After independence and well into the nineteenth century, the federal government depended on tariffs as a main source of income, so with prisons scarce, forfeiture remained the swiftest deterrent to smuggling and other violations. "A ship loaded with merchandise was the most valuable thing in America at the time," notes David B. Smith, an attorney and expert on forfeiture. "They even forfeited ships with slaves."

After the income tax was enacted in 1913, forfeiture tapered off, becoming a "backwater of law until 1970," Smith says, when Congress passed antiracketeering and antinarcotics statutes. "Both had a criminal forfeiture provision, which was a new thing in American law," he observes. "There had been criminal forfeiture in medieval times. . . . If you were convicted of a felony, your estate was forfeited to the king, to take away the economic power of the landowner. That had died out. And Congress got the idea, why don't we just attach forfeiture penalties to the criminal proceeding—things that were used in the crime and proceeds from the crime? But law enforcement agencies didn't use these statutes for about ten years."

At the urging of Senator Joseph Biden, then chairman of the Judiciary Committee, federal prosecutors began employing the provisions, says Smith, who was deputy chief of the Justice Department's Asset Forfeiture Office at the time; he was assigned to write the manual on how to apply the laws, which grew in scope. In 1978, Congress added to the drug statute a civil forfeiture provision to confiscate proceeds, which replaced the favored tactic of having the Internal Revenue Service prosecute a drug dealer for failing to pay taxes on his ill-gotten gains.

As a result, income from a crime, or property that facilitates the felony, can now be forfeited in one of two ways: by criminal or civil means. The criminal route comes with higher due process protections, although its consequences can be far more severe, of course. The guilt of both the person and the property must be proved beyond a reasonable doubt, and acquittal for the crime means the property goes free as well.

Civil forfeiture has easier standards. Only the property is charged, not the person, hence the strange-sounding titles of cases: *United States v.*

$242,484 in U.S. Currency, or *One Lot Emerald Cut Stones and One Ring v. United States*. Except for real estate and vast sums of money, which require a judge's order,[41] the assets can be seized by the police in an administrative, nonjudicial process that may never advance to court if the owners don't object.

And many don't. "When we pop somebody and we know he's got $50,000 in the trunk of a rental car," said one federal prosecutor, "he may choose not to come forward and say, 'I want the money back,' because it's like confessing." On the other hand, "if he writes and says I want my stuff back, then the administrative process halts and the prosecutor decides whether or not to proceed to try to forfeit this stuff through the judicial process. If so, we have to file a forfeiture action in court."

In a civil forfeiture, though, the standard of proof is merely a preponderance of the evidence in a federal case, less in some states. In effect, you have to prove that your cash or your car is innocent. If the beyond-reasonable-doubt test applied, it seems safe to say, police would be deterred from easy assumptions and cavalier behavior.

The Emporia police pulled Benjamin Molina over for tinted windows, a convenient catchall when cops want to make a traffic stop. (Some officers, such as those in Washington, D.C., carry tint meters to measure the amount of light getting through side windows, to justify a stop as a pretext for investigating more serious crime.) Molina had his money in his pockets, $10,000 in one, $8,000 in another. "They said, 'Step out of the car. Do you have money in the car? Do you have drugs? What do you have?'" Molina recounted. "I said, 'What do you think I have?' I never had problems with that. Nobody ever asked me that question. 'You have something in your car?' I said no. They said, 'Money in car?' 'No.' 'You have money on you?' 'Yes.' 'How much?' 'Eighteen thousand.' 'What?'"

So an officer opened the door of Molina's Toyota Corolla, told him to put the cash in the car, divided the bills into three bunches in three envelopes, and brought a drug-sniffing dog that happened to be on hand to check cars with tinted windows. The cop put each envelope in a different spot—on the floor, the seat—and no matter what the location, the dog signaled the presence of drugs by sitting.

"He said, 'The money's ours now.' 'What do you mean?' 'It comes from drugs.' I said, 'That's from my bank—what do you mean?' 'So the bank gave you money from drugs?'" If he'd had his bank receipt with him, his money might have been rescued on the spot, as it finally was when his lawyer sent in the bank's paperwork.[42]

After all these months, a flabbergasted Molina could not stop protesting the absurdity. "How's a guy like me—I'm sick. If I do something like that, I lose Social Security. I lose my medication. I can even get deported for something like that." Indeed he could; a drug conviction usually means deportation of a noncitizen, even a legal resident.

But there was no drug conviction. There was not even a drug charge. Only the money was accused of being generated by the drug trade. Molina didn't even get fined for the tinted windows. "He don't give me no ticket. He don't give me nothing. He just want the money. He even took the little knife that I had to open cardboard. I paid $20 for that thing, and they keep it."

Such is the pattern across the country. Especially in the rural South and near the southern border, highway patrolmen, called "police pirates" by one group fighting asset forfeiture, collect cash they think is drug money bound for Mexico. And much of it may be. The Drug Enforcement Administration estimates that about $12 billion for drug cartels travels annually from the United States to Mexico, with millions in cash seized on the way, discovered secreted inside tires and hidden compartments.[43]

When dog alerts are the only indication that the money comes from narcotics, however, the evidence has come under question. Studies since the 1980s have suggested that most paper currency circulating in the United States bears traces of cocaine, which clings to bills, gets transferred among them, and is widely spread by banks' counting machines. "The odor that the dogs alert to is methyl benzoate," said James Woodford, a chemist who discovered that the substance is released as cocaine molecules degrade in moist air. The synthetic version he developed and patented, he said, has "become the standard training for dogs," which are taught with Pavlovian rewards to recognize the sweet smell. One problem is that it's also found in some foods, perfumes, and pesticides.

Dogs learn to detect other drugs by other smells. "Ecstasy gives itself away through the cherry-pie scent of piperonal," writes Avery Gilbert, an odor scientist, "and methamphetamine has a characteristic cherry-almond scent from benzaldehyde."[44] Marijuana, whose odors derive from a multitude of chemicals, can smell like lime peelings or pine trees, Woodford notes.

He first recognized the ubiquitous presence of cocaine when he was hired as a defense expert in a criminal case in Atlanta. "It came to my mind that people roll dollar bills and use them to sniff cocaine—maybe it's on some percentage of the money," he recalled. "So the court said: Get money from the bank and see." He went to the Federal Reserve. "I was just shocked. They gave me shredded money. I got bails of it. Ninety percent had cocaine."

In most subsequent tests by other researchers, cocaine traces were also found on significant amounts of currency: 96 percent of the bills taken from Los Angeles and other cities;[45] 97 percent of those from banks around the country tested by the Dade County medical examiner's office in Miami; one-third of a sample from Chicago banks and the Federal Reserve that were examined by the DEA's own lab there;[46] and 79 percent of currency tested in another study, whose researchers concluded: "The exchange of illicit cocaine for money by drug dealers is an everyday occurrence in cities in the United States. There is ample opportunity during the exchange, storage, and use of cocaine for paper currency to become contaminated. . . . Cocaine contamination of currency is widespread throughout the United States."[47] A dog even once signaled there was drug residue on bills in Attorney General Janet Reno's purse.[48]

"Unless it has come straight, hot off the Bureau of Engraving and Printing press," said Smith, the forfeiture specialist, "it's going to have drugs adhered to it." And not only drugs. About 94 percent of $1 bills sampled in Ohio tested positive for "pathogenic or potentially pathogenic organisms."[49] The bugs can make you sick, but you probably have a better chance of recovering your health than recovering your cash.

Prosecutors have countered the contamination claims with two main arguments, neither of which has stood up well to rebuttals. First, their experts contend that methyl benzoate evaporates within hours, so its presence must indicate recent contact with cocaine. The chemist Woodford, when testifying as a defense expert, responds that the evaporation test has been performed on bills that have just been washed in methanol, which removes the reason that drugs cling: oils from hands, called sebum, the same oils that leave fingerprints on smooth surfaces. In a competing test, Woodford took a circulated bill, spiked it with methyl benzoate, placed it outdoors in a light wind, and thirty-six hours later could still smell it well enough to pick it out from ten others while he was blindfolded. And he was a mere human, lacking a drug-sniffing canine's discerning nose.[50]

Second, government officials "came up with the superdog theory," said Smith. "Now they claim they have better trained dogs that will only alert to a large amount of cocaine residue, not just the ordinary amount which covers every bill in the country. I frankly doubt that that is the case, that these dogs are so carefully trained. But even assuming that that is the case, I don't believe it proves anything. Even if some bills have more, that doesn't mean [the owner] was the cause of the drugs getting on the money." In other words, a drug on money doesn't mean that it's drug money.

Nor are the dogs infallible, as numerous experiments have demonstrated. Dissenting from a Supreme Court ruling that a dog alert provided probable cause for a search at a routine traffic stop, Justice David Souter listed cases with error rates from 8 to 38 percent. "In practical terms," he wrote, "the evidence is clear that the dog that alerts hundreds of times will be wrong dozens of times."[51]

Woodford seconds the doubts, noting that a properly trained dog costs $10,000, more than many small police departments are willing to spend. "They go to the pound and get a dog," he said. "They do what's called play-reward conditioning. They play with him, take some drugs from the police department evidence room, put it under the dog's nose, and reward him for learning." Without complex, double-blind training, in which neither the handler nor the dog knows whether the sample substance is a drug, you get "living, walking detection instruments" that do not measure up to court-established standards for crime lab procedures and expert witnesses.[52]

Some judges and juries are appropriately skeptical, but many are not. "Everybody loves a dog," Woodford remarked. "You can imagine being an expert going in after they bring in this lovely-looking dog. That's a hard act to follow."

As unreliable as the dogs may be in legitimizing a search, depending on them when forfeiting cash is more decisively unjust. The victim cannot mount a court challenge without a lawyer skilled in this specialty, which can cost more than the amount confiscated. Those targeted on the highway are often financially insecure, without credit cards, checking accounts, or the wherewithal to find an attorney who understands the complex laws of forfeiture. Most people standing on the hot pavement watching their cash disappear have no clue that legal fees can be recovered if a lawsuit is successful, and many lawyers don't know either.

In civil cases, as opposed to criminal, the indigent don't usually get government-paid lawyers, and that's the way it was in civil forfeiture prior to 2000. Then the rules were changed by a federal reform called CAFRA, requiring judges to provide appointed counsel if a primary residence is seized and allowing them to do so for other confiscated property.[53] "But in most courtrooms today nobody knows to tell the judge of these provisions," says FEAR, the Forfeiture Endangers American Rights Foundation.

The Legal Services Corporation, whose lawyers were made available, reported only one request from the courts nationwide between 2000 and

2003, "several additional requests" the following year, and merely one a month as of February 2008.[54]

It's often worth contesting the forfeiture. Since the 1990s, reservations about dogs' dependability have penetrated federal appeals courts. The Ninth Circuit ruled in 1994 that a dog alert was insufficient.[55] The Eleventh Circuit, in 2003, decided that "the dog alert, at best, tells us that this currency (like most circulated currency) may have been exposed, at some point, to narcotics." The dog would be significant only "when combined with more compelling evidence of a connection to a narcotics transaction."[56]

The trend is hardly unanimous, however. What some judges think is "more compelling evidence" is so vaporous that the truth-finding process seems to float untethered to facts. As recently as 2006, after more than a decade of doubts had piled up about the questionable dog alerts, a federal appeals court ruled that other factors, equally dubious, should be given weight in defining drug money. If someone simply had lots of cash, kept the money prudently out of sight, and displayed a natural nervousness when pulled over and questioned by police, the elements were ample enough to connect cash to drugs, the Eighth Circuit decided.

By the narrow margin of 2–1, the panel overruled a district court judge who had found insufficient proof that $124,700 taken from Emiliano Gomez Gonzolez by a Nebraska state trooper was drug related. The cash had been collected for a business investment, Gonzolez explained—$65,000 from one friend, $20,000 from another, and $40,000 of his own money—to buy a refrigerator truck from a Chicago acquaintance. He'd carried the bills onto a plane from California, discovered in Chicago that the truck had already been sold, so arranged to return. Told that it was "bad" to carry more than $10,000 by air, he got a friend to rent him a car.

Scared of being robbed, he wrapped up the cash and hid it in a cooler, a reasonable precaution. When he was stopped for speeding, he was rattled, and his nervousness propelled him to obfuscate. The two appellate judges had only one explanation for this: drugs. What they failed to grasp about their own country was something widely known in the vulnerable subcultures of immigrants. Even many who are here legally live in a twilight of anxiety, constantly alert to being violated by officialdom, especially since 9/11.

Furthermore, Gonzolez's mixture of Spanish and English was poorly understood by the troopers, and every slip on the side of the highway was magnified later in the judges' minds. When asked if he had ever been arrested, he said no, although he had been, for drunken driving, as a trooper quickly discovered by computer. Then, questioned explicitly whether he had been stopped for drunken driving, Gonzolez said yes, explaining later that the trooper had first asked if he "had any crimes" or "had been a prisoner."

When questioned about whether he had large amounts of cash in his vehicle, Gonzolez said no. The name he gave of the car renter didn't match the paperwork. "He said that he lied about the money and about the names of other parties involved, because he believed that carrying large amounts of cash might be illegal, and he did not want to get his friends in trouble," the court reported. Nevertheless, he consented to a search of his car, as many frightened drivers do. A dog signaled the presence of drugs.

Although appeals courts are not supposed to second-guess trial judges' findings of fact, this panel did so by pretending that it wasn't doing so. The trial judge had heard Gonzolez and his friends, who had journeyed to Nebraska to confirm his story, and found all their testimony "plausible and consistent." But the two appellate judges, playing with semantics, called this characterization "different from a finding that the court actually *believed* the testimony." Without defining the difference, they imagined it as giving them enough room to *disbelieve,* and so performed a rhetorical contortion.

The opinion is worth studying, because it carries the overtones of arbitrary rule. It was written by Steven M. Colloton, nominated by Bush the Younger in 2003, and joined by Morris S. Arnold, named in 1992 by Bush the Elder.[57] Their search for truth was easily satisfied, and with such facile clarity as to suggest more caprice than jurisprudence.

First, "possession of a large sum of cash is 'strong evidence' of a connection to drug activity," they reasoned, an unusual twist on the meaning of "evidence." Second, hiding money was essentially a confession, even if it wasn't hidden very well. "We have adopted the common-sense view that bundling and concealment of large amounts of currency, combined with other suspicious circumstances, supports a connection between money and drug trafficking." In this novel definition, "common sense" apparently applies to someone who is content to leave wads of cash in view of every passerby.

Third, "Gonzolez had flown on a one-way ticket, which we have previously acknowledged is evidence in favor of forfeiture." So, if you don't want to fly back or don't know your return date, you're probably a drug trafficker. Fourth, "he gave a vague explanation, attributed to advice from an unidentified third person, about why he elected to return by car." Yet his explanation and the advice turned out to be precisely right, given that bundles of money, at high risk of being discovered by airport security, would be seized based on this very court's loose assumptions.

Fifth, the truck-buying mission struck the judges as incredible. "This testimony does not inspire confidence in the innocence of the conduct." So now the man has to prove his innocence—or, more accurately, the innocence of his money, since no cop or drug agent bothered to follow up and investigate this alleged drug trafficker and the source of his funds. Gonzolez and his friends are free, after all, while considerably poorer.

Finally, "the false statements to law enforcement officers" about his drunk-driving "criminal history," his money, his friends, and the like added up "to the inference that Gonzolez was involved in illegal drug activity." So "inference" is now equivalent to a preponderance of the evidence.[58]

This is justice on autopilot. It is also lazy law enforcement—grab the money but not the supposed drug ring. In jumping to its conclusions, this court revealed its remoteness from the reality of America, where legions of marginalized workers can't get credit cards, don't trust banks, and deal in a shadow economy of cash and barter.

There are many reasons why people conduct their affairs in cash. Not all of them are legal. Narcotics, gambling, tax evasion, extortion, bribery, and other crimes are facilitated by evading the banking system, where transactions are easily traceable in a computerized age. But some legitimate small business is also done in paper currency, and sometimes the upstanding laborers and entrepreneurs are olive-skinned speakers of Spanish and blacks with braided hair.

Michael Annan, a Ghanaian immigrant with dreadlocks who didn't trust banks, forfeited $43,720 from years working at various jobs, most recently on a dredging barge, when he was stopped in Georgia. He eventually got it back, less the $12,000 he had to pay in legal fees.[59]

Christopher Hunt's $5,601 came from his auto-detailing business in Atlanta, he insisted, and he was taking it to his mother's house for safe-keeping over the weekend, when he was pulled over for speeding in Lamar County, Georgia. He was black, his braids hung down behind each ear, and he wore a sleeveless white undershirt, fitting the profile often used to stop drivers. He had a handgun on the console, properly licensed. The police claimed to have smelled burned marijuana, but they found no drugs in the car. He was not given a ticket, but his cash was taken from his pockets to the station, where a dog smelled drug residue.

When the money was deposited, a bank teller identified two $10 bills as counterfeit; the balance was turned over to the DEA, and to what his lawyer, David Smith, called an "incredibly stubborn" federal prosecutor, who insisted on the forfeiture despite the relatively small amount. Smith accused the feds of "pursuing this on behalf of a corrupt local sheriff's office, which seized the money and has a pattern of doing this and basically robbing black motorists on the highway when they find them with a lot of currency." Smith learned later that Hunt had an arrest record (not for drugs, though, and with no conviction), making him a more likely suspect; he got only half his money back in a settlement.[60] NPR found fourteen other such currency seizures in the same county during the previous four years.[61]

These official assaults on currency sometimes backfire on the government. Javier Gonzalez lost $10,032 in profits from his used-car lot in Austin, Texas, when sheriff's deputies ninety miles north of the Mexican border pulled him over. He was on his way to buy a vehicle, according to an NPR report, and he filed a federal civil rights suit, eventually winning not only his money back and his legal fees but also $110,000 in damages.[62]

In the case of Benjamin Molina, the man with the pain in his voice, the DEA "even did a sophisticated ion scan test" on the money, said Smith, his lawyer. "The prosecutor sent them to me. This purported to show that Molina's money had twice as much cocaine on it as ordinary money in circulation." Yet he got the bills from a bank, as his receipt proved. "The test may be perfectly accurate, I wouldn't know. So what? He didn't put the cocaine on the money. He got it from a bank."

Molina remains nervous, because he still makes that drive through Emporia on his way to and from North Carolina. So I took the liberty of explaining that under the law, he didn't have to consent to a search. He uttered a sound of surprise. I explained again. He replied: "Then they will arrest me. They do whatever they want with the law."

CHAPTER FIVE

Below the Law

May Allah bless America.

—Imam Mirja Abu Beig

THE TRAPDOOR

IF YOU ARE ARRESTED for a minor crime—shoplifting, say, or stealing a lottery ticket from the 7-Eleven where you work—your lawyer might suggest that you plead guilty even when you're innocent, as Evelyn Greene's advised. In exchange, she was sentenced to ten weekends of community service rather than jail time.

But then, if you are not an American citizen, as she was not, you could end up behind bars anyway on your way to deportation. No matter that her husband and three children held citizenship, or that she had years of legal residence in the country after fleeing civil warfare in Liberia, or that she dutifully applied to renew her work permit. That's when she was caught, appearing obediently at immigration offices to provide more information, as requested. The request was a ruse to get her there, so she could easily be jailed under a merciless federal law that gives practically no grace.[1]

Deportation is the immigration system's most decisive sanction, and it targets two main categories of foreigners: those who overstay their visas or smuggle themselves into the country, and also legal immigrants who have been convicted of crimes, such as Evelyn Greene. Both groups contain relatively benign offenders: The "illegal aliens" include long-term residents who have established families and businesses, paid taxes, and provided essential services. The criminals include the pregnant shoplifter and the casual pot smoker. Yet the penalty of "removal," as it is officially called, cannot be calibrated with a sense of proportion. It is absolute, blind to the varied situations of the real people it punishes.

We citizens have decided that we do not want in our midst noncitizens convicted of what federal law terms "aggravated felonies" or "crimes involving moral turpitude," so our Congress has made "removal" mandatory for vast categories of misbehavior much less serious than those labels indicate.

"Aggravated felonies" include offenses that are neither aggravated nor felonies, but mere misdemeanors under some state statutes. The law sweeps away not only the gangster, the drug dealer, the forger, and the murderer but also practically anyone who commits (or admits to committing) a crime deemed so minimal that the court imposes the lightest of sentences: probation or community service. The heaviest sentence of all, the one you cannot contest before an independent judge or jury, may be the loss of your adopted country.

Evelyn Greene was pregnant. Since everyone born in the United States is automatically an American citizen, her fourth child would be delivered simultaneously into the privileges of citizenship and the restraints of Virginia's Hampton Roads Regional Jail. This prospect made her weep, and it made Debi Sanders, a visiting pro bono lawyer, weep with her.[2] It can take months to arrange deportation, meaning months of imprisonment.

Hampton Roads was the most humane of the jails visited regularly by Sanders's team of lawyers, and therefore the only one that would allow me inside to have a look. Its two superintendents, one white, one black, came with interesting résumés: David Simons had gone to law school after years as a cop, including as police chief in a small Virginia town. Moses Pollard was a licensed Baptist minister. They tried to keep the jail decent by keeping it accessible. Teams of volunteer attorneys, GED tutors, writers like me, and other visitors were welcomed. "We are always open to scrutiny," Simons declared, a contrast with most prisons.

He and Pollard sat down routinely with lawyers who had just made rounds and had talked with inmates. It was a remarkable scene: around a conference table, the attorneys conveyed complaints from prisoners to the two superintendents and several guards, who took notes and, lawyers said, actually acted on the problems. In many other local facilities contracted by the federal government to hold immigration detainees, the prevailing routine included epithets, physical abuse, and medical neglect.[3]

Nonetheless, Hampton Roads is what it is supposed to be: a prison, an oppressively high-tech, soulless, antiseptic array of large boxes of white concrete built in 1998, each box a "pod" connected at a central control room. "No Weapons or Ammunition Beyond This Point," says a red sign at a metal detector. The guards, in pressed uniforms of dark green, smile and wave, as if they too were inmates happy to have their boredom relieved by visitors.

The windowless hallway, its gray concrete floor painted with yellow lines as boundaries for inmates as they move, has an austere smell of artificial hygiene, as if cleanliness were as sacred as security. Entering a pod is like moving through an air lock: A door heavy with thick glass slides open electrically, we step into a compartment facing another door, the first door slides closed behind us with a swoosh and a thump, then the second opens, and we walk through. It closes, sealing us into the central guard area, where we stand before a looming control room that is raised above the floor like an airport tower. Through its windows, the guards who are secured inside can see us, and they can speak to us through an intercom. They check our names against a list, then direct us toward another air lock into one of the pods.

The lawyers, organized by the Capital Area Immigrants' Rights (CAIR) Coalition, are trained to sort quickly through inmates to find who might be helped. There is no point devoting precious volunteer hours to prisoners who have already hired attorneys, or to those facing inevitable deportation, as most are. Only where the lawyers discover people who may have a case but no lawyer do the volunteers, many from high-rolling Washington law firms, zero in.

Unlike poor criminal defendants, whose Sixth Amendment right to counsel has been interpreted by the Supreme Court to require the government to pay for indigents' attorneys, immigration detainees come under civil law that gives them "the privilege of being represented" but "at no expense to the Government."[4] So detainees have the right only to attorneys they can afford or can get to work for free; the executive branch has never provided immigration lawyers for the poor. Their "privilege" derives from the Fifth Amendment's vaguer guarantee of due process, not the more specific right to counsel, and can therefore be manipulated more easily by administrative rulings.[5]

Still, there is little that lawyers can do for most immigrants convicted of crimes, even if they have been in the country legally for many decades. The law, as amended by the Republican-led Congress in 1996, opposed by President Bill Clinton's immigration officials, but signed by Clinton nonetheless, added numerous crimes retroactively to the deportable list, making noncitizens subject to removal for offenses committed before the law was passed. The Supreme Court in 2001 limited the retroactivity by ruling that immigration judges could waive deportation for guilty pleas prior to 1996, but not for convictions in trial.[6]

The law mandated detention pending deportation by denying bail to those with past convictions for a host of crimes, including "aggravated felonies," drug and gun crimes, and two or more offenses involving "moral turpitude." As a result, many thousands have been imprisoned for many months, even years, often in brutal local jails. Here, too, the Supreme Court stepped in, ruling in 2001 that people could not be held indefinitely while the authorities tried to arrange for other countries to take them. It set six months as a reasonable maximum, requiring release if no foreseeable opportunity for deportation existed.[7] The ruling, often ignored, did not prevent a Somali named Keyse G. Jama, for instance, from spending six years locked up after drawing a one-year sentence for getting into a knife fight. At a cost to taxpayers of $200,000 or more, he was flown by a private security company on a chartered jet to a remote part of his homeland, where he was rejected by Somali authorities and returned to jail in Minnesota.[8]

The 1996 measure narrowed the grounds for waivers, leaving little flexibility to immigration judges, who are not independent in any case; they are administrative employees of the Justice Department, beholden to their bosses and subject to dismissal. That means the entire mechanism resides in the executive branch, without the separation of powers to check and balance the use of the authority to deprive individuals of their freedom as they face immigration charges.

The judges can be quite erratic in those areas of immigration law with murky, subjective standards, varying considerably in granting or rejecting claims of political asylum, for example.[9] Where minimal discretion is allowed, as in deportation after a criminal conviction, an ill-trained judge can easily overlook errors in the government's case against an immigrant. The law may be unforgiving, but it is not simple—it took eighteen pages of concise shorthand for one immigration attorney, Mary Holper, to describe it in a memo for defense lawyers. Yet some of the immigration judges hired by the Justice Department have no experience in immigration law, according to a study by the Transactional Records Access Clearinghouse of Syracuse University. They get less training by the department than they would receive in a single law school course on the subject, and their knowledge is tested inadequately: new judges take an untimed exam online immediately after a day's instruction on a topic, rather like an eighth-grade quiz on yesterday's lesson. They are then empowered to alter people's lives.[10]

Justice Department officials under George W. Bush admitted using political and ideological criteria to hire immigration judges and make appointments to the fifteen-member Board of Immigration Appeals, ensuring that they were Republicans, most of them recommended by the White House Office of Political Affairs. The law prohibits such political discrimination. One of the beneficiaries, Garry Malphrus, had burnished his credentials by working on the "Bush-Cheney Florida Recount Team" during the disputed

2000 election and had recommended candidates for immigration judge-ships based on "loyalty to the Bush administration." After just three years as an immigration judge, he was named to the appeals board.[11]

Only a careful and informed judge will see the narrow possibilities for a legal immigrant convicted of a crime to escape deportation, and only a good immigration lawyer will find the openings. The task is mostly hope-less, "something akin to being an oncologist," said the late Michael Maggio, who was a private immigration attorney in Washington, D.C. "Sometimes you can save a person or postpone the inevitable, but you're mostly help-ing people to adjust to a huge loss. Our clients, just like cancer stages, go through stages: Denial, this can't be, I'm gonna go see my congressman. Rage. Sometimes, acceptance."

The best way to avoid deportation is not to commit a crime, obviously—or at least not to accept certain plea agreements. Since lawyers who prac-tice criminal law may know little about immigration law, they mistakenly advise clients to take pleas that may keep them out of jail but get them kicked out of the country. A lawyer bargains and gets what seems like a good deal: instead of a six-month prison sentence for theft, let's say, a one-year suspended sentence with no actual jail time. The trouble is, that counts as one year under immigration law, which classifies a long list of crimes as "aggravated felonies" if the defendant receives at least a twelve-month term, suspended or not. This is so even if the offense is labeled a misdemeanor, not a felony, by the state where it occurs.[12] So if you want to stay in the United States, it is better to go to jail for less than a year than to get a year suspended, which strikes most prosecutors and defense attor-neys as counterintuitive.

Evelyn Greene and her attorney did not know this until it was too late. Although she insisted that she had not stolen a lottery ticket from the 7-Eleven where she worked, her lawyer warned that it would cost too much to contest the charge. Erroneously, he assured her that since the crime was a misdemeanor, it would not mean her deportation, and the prosecu-tor agreed to a suspended sentence and community service. No similar discretion was shown by government lawyers in the immigration system, however; they launched deportation proceedings against a pregnant mother who posed little or no threat to society.

As the deportation law has been enforced more vigorously since 9/11, immigration attorneys have tried to educate prosecutors, defense lawyers, and trial judges, who are not used to imagining consequences beyond the criminal case at hand. "For example, possession of stolen property is a removable offense, but resisting arrest is not," explained Bryan Lonegan of the Legal Aid Society in New York City. "Let's say a person is charged with both. Our recommendation would be to plead to resisting arrest as opposed to possession of stolen property. It's a criminal conviction, they can get whatever sentence, but it's not going to have the immigration consequences."

Some criminal courts began to require that defendants be clearly advised of the immigration implications of pleading guilty—or at least not be misinformed by counsel. Twenty-eight states and D.C. enacted laws requiring judges to warn of the consequences when taking guilty pleas. But the demand was far from universal. Under a pair of New York Court of Appeals decisions, Lonegan noted, a criminal defense lawyer was "ineffective" only if he gave inaccurate immigration information but not if he refrained from telling his client anything at all. This position, supported years later by the Obama administration, would have had bizarre consequences if sustained. Since few attorneys enjoy being deemed ineffective, even to get a client's conviction overturned, the rulings encouraged silence instead of informed advice.[13]

But the Supreme Court changed the game in 2010, ruling that a defense lawyer's failure to warn a noncitizen that a guilty plea could result in automatic deportation constituted ineffective assistance of counsel, a violation of the Sixth Amendment. A Kentucky man—a legal permanent resident for over forty years, charged with transporting a large amount of marijuana in his tractor trailer—was assured erroneously by his attorney that he "did not have to worry about immigration status since he had been in the country so long." The lawyer seemed to believe that the immigration law was humane and sensible. So the defendant pleaded guilty instead of going to trial.[14]

From inside the fortified Hampton Roads jail, a train whistle could be heard, beckoning. In the small gym, with one basketball hoop, inmates and lawyers paired up to discuss cases. A man from Trinidad, his face desperately mournful, had come to the United States at the age of twelve, and some time ago had done a year in jail for youthful cocaine possession during "a five-year period when I messed up in my life." He now had three kids, ages eleven, two, and three months. His wife was American. "I have no family left in Trinidad. It's atrocious."

The prison gym was deep in sorrow. Some prisoners arrived with papers in file folders, some with documents folded in quarters and stuffed into shirt pockets. A Vietnamese immigrant, formerly in the South Vietnamese navy, had escaped by fishing boat as Saigon fell in 1975, had been picked up by the U.S. Navy, and had been in the country since. In 1990, he had been convicted of sexually abusing his daughter, given a ten-year suspended sentence, and sent to treatment. They had reconciled, at least from his viewpoint. "I said I'm sorry. Still daughter and father, you know."

But the sin could not be expiated in the eyes of the immigration apparatus. He was targeted by Operation Predator, a sweep of noncitizens with records of sexual crimes. Agents of ICE, the appropriate acronym for Immigration and Customs Enforcement, had appeared at his home at 6:00 a.m., asked him deceptively to come to the immigration office for paperwork involving his citizenship application, and on the way to the car put him in handcuffs.

A tall black man with a goatee, who had arrived from the Netherlands Antilles in 1970, had been ordered deported for two convictions of drug possession and wanted to appeal. He thought he might be a U.S. citizen, since his father had been naturalized before the age of eighteen. The law on such "derived citizenship" is complex, and his mother had hired a lawyer who "took the money and told me he can't do nothin'," the man said bitterly.

The CAIR attorney sitting with him in the gym, Paromita Shah, was not taking any money and was instead giving him compassionate candor, explaining the law, the limited grounds for appeal, and the prospective lockup time. He'd stay in jail waiting for a hearing, and after the final order the government would have ninety days to deport him, adding up to months more behind bars. He would be escorted by two federal marshals, part of the cost to American taxpayers to rid the country of nefarious characters. "You're basically choosing to stay in jail to fight your case," she told him. "It stinks. The burden's on you to prove that you derived citizenship."

Proving anything from a cell is a hardship, and for immigrants with limited English or relatives who are estranged or unsophisticated it is nearly impossible. While the Vienna Convention gives detainees the right to contact their respective consulates, asylum seekers fleeing their own governments certainly don't want to do that, and some others get no help when they do. Prison systems charge several dollars a minute for collect calls, which are routinely rejected by certain consulates, especially when officials hear that the immigrant has a criminal conviction. "There's no uniform behavior you can rely on," said Shah. Saudi Arabia often pays for lawyers, "but India and many African countries are obnoxious." When they hear it's a collect call, they hang up.

Incarceration is doubly useful to the authorities, therefore, both to make sure that people don't become "absconders," as those who dodge deportation orders are officially labeled, and to make them so fed up with jail that they'll just agree to leave. Challenging an order is mostly fruitless anyway. The pro bono lawyers of CAIR do not have time to drive around to local courthouses to pull records to see if some error was made in a criminal case, some mitigating circumstance overlooked. They depend on relatives to do the legwork, and that doesn't always happen. "We know almost every form of release depends on the family," said Mary Holper. "We can't put our resources into it if we can't even get family involved."

Bela Modi, for instance, was afraid to get her father's file from the courthouse in Virginia Beach, Virginia. "My driving record is ridiculous, and Virginia Beach is where I have a bench warrant out for me because I missed a traffic court hearing," she said. "I'm twenty-three now. I think it was driving on a suspended license, suspended on points for speeding."

So her father, Sevantilal, languished at Hampton Roads jail because of a dubious conviction that an appeals court might have overturned, since he had no lawyer. The case began as a family dispute, as he described it, when he and his wife, later divorced, owned a motel. As his teenage daughter was waiting for him to drive her somewhere, Modi hastened to put a new TV set into the room of a long-term tenant, he said, a woman who "fabricated the accusation that I asked her for a sexual favor" to reduce her rent. A few weeks later she told his wife, who urged her to call the police. They arrested him for "sexual battery."[15]

He first turned down appointed counsel because he thought his wife would help him hire his own, but when she refused and he realized that he could not arrange or afford an attorney himself, he requested a state-provided lawyer. Too late, the court told him, and he had to represent himself at trial. He didn't get a jury, because the charge was merely a misdemeanor, which sounded dubious to Holper, who understood Virginia law to provide a right to a jury if the sentence could exceed six months. The judge found him guilty and gave him the magic number of twelve months, suspending three of them, which instantly converted the misdemeanor into an aggravated felony for immigration purposes. He served 138 days. The following year, when he applied for citizenship, he was denied because of "moral turpitude."

Then, nearly a decade later, long after he thought that he'd paid a wrongful debt and closed the books, ICE agents came to his door at five o'clock one morning.

"Double jeopardy," he said again and again in anguished disbelief as he sat on a stainless steel stool at a stainless steel table in the jail. Technically, it wasn't double jeopardy, which applies to criminal charges; immigration actions are administrative. But the effect was similar: jail time, plus the end of a life he had made in America. Modi was stunned. He had lived in the United States for thirty-six years, all as a legal immigrant, had worked as an engineer in nuclear power plants, and now suffered from diabetes, macular degeneration, and other ailments that he was sure would kill him if he was forced to move to India, where he had only distant relatives. He looked older than his sixty-three years, with a round, exhausted face, wispy white hair, a short white beard. He was losing weight in prison. Finally winning temporary release for medical reasons, he had to report every ninety days. Before ICE could send him back to India, he died in Virginia Beach of colon cancer.[16]

Modi's judge and others who sentence lightly probably don't imagine the hidden sentence they are also imposing. Had the judge given him one day less than a year, the conviction would not have triggered the removal process.[17] Had Modi's right to counsel and jury been observed, he might have been acquitted. But the flaws of the criminal justice process are magnified by the unyielding deportation machine.

Such was the experience of Hemnauth Mohabir of Guyana, whose story was told by his lawyer, Bryan Lonegan. Mohabir arrived in the United States in the early 1990s, married an American, had a child, and acquired technical skills at an air-conditioning school in New York. He loved music, played with a band, and reveled in the freedom to record whatever he wished, something he could not do in Guyana. Everything was going well.

"And then, in 1996," said Lonegan, "he's heading to his studio and gets approached by a derelict who says, 'I desperately need some crack. Where can I get it?'" Mohabir says he doesn't sell, the derelict begs him, please, please, please, so Mohabir says, OK, give me the money, "takes the guy's $10, goes around the corner, gets it from one of the street sellers, comes back and gives the guy the crack, is immediately arrested." The "derelict" was an undercover cop.

Charged with a misdemeanor carrying a minimum of two to six years, Mohabir was offered the standard plea since he had no prior record: an attempted sale and five years probation. "Everybody takes it," said Lonegan, "'cause just the risk of going to trial, your word against the cop's, you just don't want to deal with it. He refused. He said, 'No, I'm not pleading guilty, because I'm not a drug dealer.'" He presented a difficult defense alleging entrapment, and he won. "The jury found the guy not guilty of criminal sale of a controlled substance. But they did find him guilty of possession of the bag of crack, which was a misdemeanor. And the judge sentenced him to a $250 fine."

That ended the criminal case. But in 2002, Mohabir's mother was taken ill, he flew to visit her in Guyana, and when he returned, his conviction popped up in the customs computer at the airport. Drug possession does not have to be an "aggravated felony" to trigger deportation or "inadmissibility" to the country. First-time possession of cocaine is not a felony under federal law, but it's a deportable offense, and removal can be canceled only if the immigrant has resided in the United States continuously for at least seven years. The only drug crime that doesn't activate deportation proceedings is the possession of thirty grams or less of marijuana for personal use.[18]

If Mohabir had not left the country, and if seven years had run before his crime, he would have been eligible for a waiver (now called "cancellation"). As an "arriving alien," however, he was ruled "inadmissible" and was subject to mandatory detention without bond. "The judge had no choice but to order his deportation," Lonegan explained, "and the judge apologized. He said, 'I'm sorry. I think this is an example of what's wrong with our system, but I have no choice.'"

Mohabir mounted an immigration appeal but abandoned it when he ran out of money for legal fees. His imprisonment continued. He went on a hunger strike and agreed to resume eating only after Lonegan promised to see if the district attorney's office in Queens would reopen his criminal case, which would permit a late appeal, which in turn would mean that the conviction was not yet final, and the immigration judge could vacate the removal order.

"The district attorney's office would not do so," said Lonegan. "They basically said: 'We don't agree with the jury's verdict; we think he's a drug dealer.' So much for the jury system." He was deported in April 2004 after spending two years in jail. "So now his wife and child need to seek public assistance. They're here. His twelve-year-old son is now without a father. And we've done a really bang-up job, for a conviction for a possession of drugs that a judge didn't think was worth more than a $250 fine, that he wouldn't have had, had not an undercover cop asked him to go buy it. The situation to me is just absolutely appalling, and it's not an infrequent scenario."

Trying to defend clients in the immigration system is a bit like trying to catch a ball in zero gravity: the familiar laws of physics do not apply. The judges' lack of independence is one problem, but it might matter less if normal constitutional protections existed. The fact that a noncitizen has no right to be in the United States is the starting point from which other rights erode, even as the person awaiting deportation is locked in the same jail as a criminal convict. If he is charged with auto theft, the Constitution protects him; if he is charged with overstaying his visa and jailed pending deportation, the Constitution is barely relevant. (It kicks in only if his illegal entry is prosecuted as a federal crime, which has been done increasingly in certain jurisdictions along the Mexican border.)

The Supreme Court has ruled that deportation, a civil not a criminal process, does not violate the Eighth Amendment's ban on cruel and unusual punishment. The Fourth Amendment's search warrant requirements are waived by federal law to give immigration agents authority, "within a reasonable distance from any external boundary of the United States, to board and search for aliens any vessel . . . railway car, aircraft, conveyance, or vehicle." Within twenty-five miles of the border, private land, but not dwellings, may be searched and patrolled without warrants.[19]

The Fifth Amendment scarcely applies, and you have to be brave and savvy to invoke it. Immigration agents have the "powers without warrant . . . to interrogate any alien or person believed to be an alien as to his right to be or to remain in the United States," says the statute.[20] This can happen anywhere in the country. The supposed alien could refuse to answer, and the government would then have to prove that she is not a U.S. citizen before proceeding. But it takes a rare grasp of the law to keep silent in the face of insistent questioning about whether you're a citizen. And if you lie, you can be charged with falsely claiming citizenship and be barred from the country indefinitely.

Just as police may question people not in custody without advising them of their rights (and people may refuse to answer), so immigration agents may ask about immigration status without providing any warnings. Even in custody, immigration detainees have no constitutional right to a Miranda warning if they don't face criminal charges. A federal regulation does mandate that ICE agents give similar warnings to people they put into deportation proceedings: the reason for the arrest, the right to an attorney at no government expense, and the possibility that anything they say may be used against them. But these explanations are often provided on forms printed in English, a language some detainees can't read. Only if criminal prosecution is brought—for illegal reentry into the country, for example—is the Miranda warning required.[21]

Once in immigration court, a detainee facing removal could invoke the Fifth, since criminal charges may be possible. In practical terms, however, a potential deportee may have to testify to make his case effectively, "in light of the alien's burden of proof," the Seventh Circuit noted.

"A guy actually has more rights in criminal cases than he does in immigration cases," said Lonegan. "It's not so much that they're violating due process as it is that there's a lack of due process."

The federal rules of evidence, customary in criminal courts, do not apply. "I'm not always entitled to even get a copy of the client's immigration documents," said Paromita Shah. Instead, she would file a request under the Freedom of Information Act, a process that could take at least two or three months. "It leads to a noncooperation ethic" among ICE agents and government attorneys, and "you have to negotiate," she said. At the hearing, the government may present documents that she has never seen; the judge may either give her adequate time to study them or require that she glance through them then and there, and proceed. Furthermore, documents are frequently "redacted," that euphemism for "censored," with names of arresting officers blacked out. ICE moves prisoners from jail to jail, so their lawyers can't readily find them. There is no firm right to summon government witnesses for cross-examination. Their written statements are presumed to be reliable, and most immigration judges won't require the live testimony of an arresting officer, for example, without substantial evidence that calls his statement into question.

Finally, the rules seem to change all the time. Immigration lawyers have blogs to share anecdotes, observations, and news of the latest clues to current policy gleaned from remarks and actions by officials of the Justice Department, where immigration judges work, and the Department of Homeland Security, which now houses ICE and other immigration agencies. After 9/11, some regulations that had rarely been enforced were abruptly transformed into ironclad dicta, while others slid along unobserved. A visa overstay was ignored one moment and punished with brutal incarceration the next.

People slipped out of legal status not always because of their own mistakes but also because of official errors by immigration authorities. James Ziglar, the head of the Immigration and Naturalization Service on 9/11, discovered later that boxes of completed forms and uncanceled checks had been sent unprocessed to storage in a Midwestern warehouse. The system was overwhelmed by massive amounts of paper, leading to either honest error by clerks or a desire to clear their desks. In the process, they left immigrants "out of status," subject to deportation.

It seemed as if the speed limit were constantly changing, but Dina Haynes, a law professor and former immigration attorney for the government, took the analogy another step. "This is like the speed limit is a secret," she said. "One day we're going to enforce it at thirty-five and the next day at seventy, and you don't know. And the enforcement will be different based on the color of your skin and whether you have a turban on your head."

NARROW ESCAPES

Nevertheless, outcroppings of mercy can be found in the midst of this cascading misery. The law provides tiny islands of refuge, and if a detainee happens to fit onto one of them, he may end his nightmare by waking up back in the same place he began, albeit with an added sense of vulnerability and estrangement from his adopted country.

Robert Conteh came from Sierra Leone at age eleven, was arrested for having a small amount of marijuana at age sixteen, was sentenced to rehabilitation classes, graduated from high school, served in the U.S. Marines, was arrested again at age thirty-one for possessing under half an ounce of marijuana, and again was sentenced to rehab and probation. Six years later, ICE handcuffed him and prepared to send him back to a land he scarcely knew.

He wore his hair in dreadlocks. He was dressed in a blue prison uniform. Surrounded by sliding doors and concrete walls, he seemed in shock. "When somebody is arrested, shouldn't they give you time to get a lawyer and prepare?" he asked, making a gesture of helplessness at the walls. All he had been able to do was to call the Marriott, where he worked as a chef, and say "an emergency came up and I needed a leave of absence."

If only he had taken up the suggestion, made by the marines, to become a U.S. citizen. "When I came to the U.S., I wanted so much to be an American," he recalled. "As a child, coming to a new environment, you want to be accepted and fit in. I got myself involved with the wrong types of friends. My family was hard on me: go to school, never really had the opportunity to go out and play. During those years, me trying to be more American" meant going along with friends who smoked pot.

Who was he, though? He looked for himself in the marines, was discharged for a medical problem, went to college for a couple of years, then reached for his roots. On a trip back to see family in Sierra Leone, "I had a whole different perspective about where I came from and wanted to know more." That took him to a different attitude about U.S. citizenship. "I said no, I didn't want to. I would stay an African."

So the immigration bureaucracy, polishing its efficiency with computer-ized databases, picked up his adult marijuana conviction, which Virginia law called a mere misdemeanor but which bore the more dramatic label of possession "with the intent to sell, give, or distribute."

Federal immigration law considers any drug-trafficking conviction an "aggravated felony" for deportation purposes. That's what this sounded like. But Conteh was lucky enough to have skilled volunteer lawyers who dug up decisions by federal courts and the Board of Immigration Appeals that defined trafficking as "unlawful trading or dealing" of a "business or mer-chant nature."[22] Trafficking under Virginia law was broader. It didn't have to be a business venture but could include just the "intent to give or dis-tribute marijuana only as an accommodation to another individual and not with intent to profit thereby."[23] A trafficking conviction in Virginia, there-fore, did not necessarily rise to the federal definition of trafficking.

The immigration judge accepted the argument and ruled that Con-teh had not been convicted of an aggravated felony, so deportation was not automatic. He wasn't quite out of the Byzantine labyrinth of the law, however, for the Virginia statute called his crime "accommodation," which implied more than the simple possession that would have made his offense non-deportable. Instead, it suggested that he was giving the pot away, not necessarily for profit, but not for his own use either, and that put him under the federal statute permitting, but not mandating, removal.[24]

Then came the balancing test between factors that argued for and against his deportation. He fit through one of the few openings for a waiver: being a legal permanent resident for at least five years, and living at least seven crime-free years in the country before the conviction. Conteh quali-fied on both counts.

Moreover, returning to Sierra Leone, his lawyers argued, would create medical hardship, since he was HIV positive and required two injections daily of a medication that he couldn't get back home. His industrious attor-neys got the manufacturer to confirm that the drug would be unavailable there.

Combining compassion with admonition, the judge canceled his depor-tation order but lectured him bluntly that he would not get another waiver if he continued his marijuana use (for medicinal purposes, Conteh claimed) and would instead go home to die alone in Sierra Leone. The government chose not to appeal the judge's ruling, and after three months in jail Robert Conteh was free—as free as he could be.[25]

———

Unlike columned courthouses the land over, no chiseled words labeled the immigration court in Arlington, Virginia. Its judges sat in an anonymous office building, up an elevator, through a reception area devoid of grandeur. Beyond a security desk, Courtroom No. 3 was furnished with a red carpet and blond wooden benches as hard as church pews. On the left-hand wall hung a map of the world, showing all the countries to which those passing through this small room could be deported, and behind the bench, on the Great Seal of the United States, an eagle in flight held an olive branch in one set of talons and a cluster of arrows in the other.

At the front right-hand corner of the courtroom stood a television set. This was how most detainees made their appearances, as faces broadcast from scattered prisons to spare the government the bother and cost of transportation to a building considered insecure. From the top of the set, a camera was aimed at the defense counsel's table, at which Trevor Abel's fiancée and three of his daughters gathered, looking into the lens as if posing for a family photograph. When Abel suddenly materialized on-screen and saw them at his end, he beamed with delight, waved, and said, "Hi, everybody."

He wore a dark green prison uniform against the white cinder-block wall of the county jail in Farmville, Virginia, where he had been awaiting "removal" to Jamaica, the place he had left for the United States twenty-two years earlier. As the immigration judge read through the papers, the smile disappeared from Abel's face.

This was his chance to fit through the eye of the needle, and Judge Wayne R. Iskra would decide. The judge looked the part—black robe, glasses, a shock of white hair—and was respected by immigrants' attorneys as fair-minded, so there was hope. With no stenographer present, he inserted a cassette into a tape deck to make an official record.

There is no privacy in a hearing to consider a waiver or "cancellation of removal," which probes into character and draws up a raw balance sheet of faults and virtues. A waiver here was possible only because Abel met narrow criteria: his crime—possession of eight grams of marijuana—came in below the thirty-gram ceiling and was committed after he had been in the United States for seven years without a conviction, and after five years of permanent residence without an aggravated felony.[26] His attorney, Paromita Shah, was arguing his case for free, because the CAIR Coalition happened to encounter him on a routine visit to the jail. The factors lined up about as beneficially as they ever do.

The detailed turbulence of his life was paraded before the court, largely through Abel's own testimony—he had no incentive to exercise a right to silence in this proceeding. He had nineteen children and stepchildren by several women, including three by his former wife, Sonia. His work record seemed solid: steadily employed as a janitor at the National Institutes of Health, as a welder, a locksmith, then as an electrician.

His scrapes with the law were ambiguous: a girlfriend made a stalking complaint, later withdrawn, and she would testify by phone on his behalf; a charge of battery against Sonia was dropped; an arrest for narcotics when he was swept up with a bunch of Jamaicans at a store never went to prosecution because "I had no drugs on me," he said.

"Do you pay your taxes?" his lawyer asked him.

"Sometimes I do." He had filed only intermittently. Shah asked why he skipped some years, even when he was working. "I didn't have the proper papers. I lost my green card and Social Security card. I didn't have no form of ID." The lame excuse had brought no legal action by the Internal Revenue Service, however. His only conviction, the sole provocation for his deportation order, had come as a result of an altercation with Sonia on Christmas Day 1991, when he had gone to deliver presents for her and the children. She called the police. They arrested him, charged him with battery (later dismissed), and found the pot in his jacket pocket.

He denied it was his and wanted a trial, but his court-appointed lawyer advised him to plead guilty and take six months of probation—the typical pattern. He agreed, not realizing that he had made himself inadmissible if he left and tried to come back. "I never bothered Sonia again," he told the immigration judge. "It was terrible, terrible. It was a mistake, and I apologized to everybody, and I'm sorry."

When his mother died in Jamaica thirteen years later, the funeral was delayed until he could fly down, on a ticket bought for him by his employer. He checked with immigration authorities to be sure he wouldn't have difficulty returning and was told that everything was in order. But when he landed at Dulles International Airport outside Washington, D.C., officials ordered him to appear the next day with all his papers. He dutifully complied, presenting every police report. He was arrested immediately.

"To me it doesn't make any sense," said his sixteen-year-old daughter Tania before the hearing. "It's something that happened so many years ago, and he already did his probation. For them to pick it up and bring it back up doesn't make any sense." On the witness stand, she testified to his generosity. "I would see him every Friday, on payday. He would call me and we would go out and eat. I've had problems with math, and he was real good with math. When I would have problems, I would call him and he'd help. Christmas he got me clothes. I got him shirts. My mom bought them because she knows what he likes. He would give me $50 on payday, 'cause my mother's sick. I would give it to her to buy medicine." The judge looked bored, and Abel looked pained.

"He's a very nice man," Tania added. "I know he has his ups and downs, but he's very nice."

Shah presented four other witnesses: The ex-girlfriend said she remained his good friend and had no fear of him, despite the stalking complaint, which she'd made after he'd gotten another woman pregnant. A twenty-five-year-old daughter testified to his caring warmth, saying she "would be devastated" if he were deported. His stepdaughter valued him as a father, since she had never known her own. And his fiancée, a registered nurse who had flown up from Miami, confirmed that he had "a good heart, a warm heart. He's always there when you need him."

"Have you ever seen him do drugs?" Shah asked her.

"No. If he did, I wouldn't be here. It's not my style."

Shah had also brought a supporting affidavit from Sonia, who was too ill to attend, and had collected letters from Abel's employers. Her closing argument emphasized his "continuous working history," arguing that "he is not a danger to society." In rebuttal, the government's lawyer recited his brushes with the law and contended (inaccurately) that he showed no remorse and no inclination to take responsibility. The government's case for deportation seemed weak, and Judge Iskra seemed to think so as well.

On the one hand, Iskra said slowly, dictating his ruling onto the tape, Abel had some arrests but no other convictions, the assault on his wife occurred a long time ago, and while the court did "not condone the incident," it did "place weight on the affidavit of the wife." The ex-girlfriend's lack of fear and continuing friendship took on "great weight," the judge declared. "I balance the negative factors against the lengthy residence of respondent in the United States, and with respect to his family, at least three of his children and grandchildren are present in the United States. Respondent is an ideal father and has good relations with his children. He is working and supporting his family members. . . . It is the opinion of the court that the favorable factors outweigh the negative factors. I grant relief under Section 212(c)."

Abel's face on the screen didn't show that he understood. Finally, when Shah explained that he had won and would be released, he broke into a broad grin. "Thank you, thank you," he said. "Thank you, everybody." Judge Iskra allowed himself a kindly smile.

It seems reasonable to imagine many such waivers being granted if the law allowed them for slightly more serious crimes, if the government provided attorneys for the immigrants, and if the country accepted the concept that once someone has "paid his debt to society" for a criminal act, he should not be punished again, with banishment. Understandably, we do not like sex offenders or drug users or thieves, but we also believe in redemption.

ORPHANED

Because her father was thrown from his motorcycle and killed when she was four, Dr. Waheeda Mani Tehseen considered herself an orphan. Her mother, struggling with six children in the North-West Frontier area of Pakistan, taught school for $5 a month and wrenched a hard living from the ground. "We had animals, we had buffaloes," said Dr. Tehseen. "We used to sell them, and we sold chicken eggs. We grew vegetables in our backyard and sold vegetables." She did not say this with the melodic pride of having risen out of destitution to the heights of education and accomplishment. She said it in a minor key of sadness—perhaps because she had now fallen so far.

In an unlucky coincidence, she spent her childhood in the town of Nowshera, near Afghanistan, a tribal region where the Taliban and al-Qaeda established themselves decades later. Mani (as her friends call her) learned multiple languages of the region and the world: Urdu, Pashto, Punjabi, English, and Arabic. Her mother prodded her to college in Peshawar, and from 1983 to 1985 she taught high school at Landi Kotal in Khyber, where her first job every morning "was to collect all the guns from the children, put them in a closet, and lock it," she said. "I had tags for all the guns."

In 1988 she received a scholarship for graduate study at the University of Illinois. She came on a student visa, her husband and three children followed, and in 1993 she earned her Ph.D. in toxicology after winning a grant from the National Science Foundation for a "difficult and ambitious project to characterize pollutants along a large stretch of a river in Pakistan," according to one of her professors.[27]

Her husband belonged to a minority sect of Islam, the Ahmadis, who in Pakistan are considered non-Muslim heretics, often persecuted and physically attacked. So he applied for and was granted asylum, along with his family. Ahmadis have been killed in recent spasms of Taliban violence (ninety-five were slaughtered in two mosques in 2010), but outright government oppression has been episodic, allowing him to return periodically to Pakistan without consequence.[28]

Mani made a solid professional life for herself in America, even while hardship hit her family. Their fourth child, Manahil Chohan, who was born in the United States, has been impaired by benign brain tumors. The next older, Warda Chohan, is mentally retarded.[29] Their schooling required attentive monitoring, and because Mani's husband worked only sporadically, the burden of providing support fell mainly to her.

She was employed as a toxicologist for five years at the Illinois state Environmental Protection Agency, but lost her position after she overstayed a fifteen-day leave to care for her ill mother in Pakistan. Getting fired was frightening. "I was the only breadwinner in my home," she said. "I was desperate to get a job." So she applied to the U.S. Environmental Protection Agency, was interviewed on the phone, and was so delighted to be hired that she made her first mistake.

She either did not read or did not understand or did not want to grasp a key condition of her new job. After moving her family to a Virginia suburb outside Washington, D.C., in 1998, she went to work reviewing tests of pesticides on animals to determine appropriate conditions of the chemicals' use—the maximum quantities, the minimum waiting times between application and harvest, and other restrictions to avoid harm to humans or livestock. A week into her employment, the human resources department gave her the usual forms, which mentioned that anyone filling her position had to be an American citizen. She was not. She held a green card signifying her permanent residency, which had put her on a path to naturalization as a citizen. "I may be a Ph.D. in toxicology, but I am not a Ph.D. in immigration," she explained. "I wasn't clear that it was a green-card requirement or a citizenship requirement. I was hired, and the pay was double." So when the papers asked about her citizenship, "I lied," she admitted, "but I didn't think it was a heinous crime."

Six days after the attacks of September 11, 2001, she applied for naturalization. The form is demanding enough that immigration specialists often recommend that an applicant consult an attorney in filling it out. Mani did not. Her husband completed it as he applied for himself and their daughter Warda, she contended, and she signed it without reading it—the second mistake, a fateful one. Where the form asked for her work experience and her current employer, the EPA was omitted. Where the application asked, "Have you **ever** claimed to be a U.S. citizen (*in writing or any other way*)?," an X was placed in the box marked "No." The signature panel contained a warning that the questions were answered "under penalty of perjury," and later she swore to her answers in a personal interview. Officials had no reason to doubt her, and she became a citizen the following year.[30]

As Mani tells her story, the American invasion of Afghanistan in 2001 swept her back to the traumas of her early life. "The news really hurt me," she recalled, especially pictures of women and children fleeing across the border into Pakistan. "I stopped watching the news because it triggered my childhood. People just can't imagine what would happen to a woman if she becomes widowed. She would have to go to the street for a piece of bread, into the garbage for food." So Mani felt driven to help.

In November she took $4,000 or $5,000 of her own money to Chaman, across the frontier from Kandahar. Her brother-in-law, a senior Pakistani army officer, obtained 1,000 blankets and 500 sweaters at discounts from a factory and delivered them in army trucks. "Refugees were coming," she said. "They were wounded, they were sick." There was chaos. "It really hurt in my heart to see all the children crying, the women. You can do this only if your heart is triggered."

Back home, she campaigned for contributions at the EPA and elsewhere. She left a container in her open garage so people could fill it with used clothing, and took the donations three or four times to the border regions. She established a charity called Help Orphans and Widows; obtained nonprofit status from the IRS; and created a vocational institute in a refugee camp where widows and orphaned girls were taught sewing, carpet weaving, and other crafts. "I bought 2,000 clay pitchers. I bought sweaters and basic food items: flour, oil, tea, sugar, rice, lentils—dry food items—and some medicines, rehydration, painkillers." The EPA gave her its Unsung Hero Award "for providing care, funds, and needed articles through your own resources and contacts to isolated refugee camps often not reached by international aid groups."[31]

Eager to expand the assistance, "I was looking for a bigger Muslim organization to put up money," she said, so she rented a booth at an Islamic convention in the United States. Trolling for help, she happened upon a display by the Islamic American Relief Agency (IARA), whose representative "got very sympathetic," then visited her booth and promised to talk to his director. This struck her as a hopeful prospect, but it set in motion a chain of misery. IARA was a Khartoum-based organization with a U.S. office in Columbia, Missouri, run by a Sudanese-American, Mubarak Hamed. He called Mani later, not with an offer of financing, but with a proposal that she facilitate the creation of an orphanage for boys. IARA would send the money directly to its sister organization in Peshawar.

Unbeknownst to Mani, IARA was already under investigation by the FBI for possibly funding organizations involved in terrorism. It was not yet listed as a terrorist group by the Treasury Department, but it was under surveillance, whether through ordinary criminal wiretap warrants or the more flexible orders that could be obtained secretly through the Foreign Intelligence Surveillance Act or, possibly, the warrantless eavesdropping by the National Security Agency authorized by President Bush. Later, Mani also came to suspect that the FBI had been called by a new manager at the EPA, upset that she was taking so much accumulated leave to travel to Pakistan. However it happened, she appeared on the radar as she organized the orphanage. IARA had given her names of Pakistanis who could help, and she called them. "I had no clue who these people were," she said. "Even IARA didn't know these people. They knew the people in Peshawar, didn't know the field people."

The building chosen for the orphanage had been abandoned by its owner, a common occurrence in that turbulent region. Mani understood well how others simply moved in and took over such abandoned property, but she worried that "I open up the orphanage and people come [back] and it's a rough culture. If we spend money, they could come kick us out." So she asked questions on the phone: "To whom does this building belong?" The FBI was listening.[32]

What they allegedly heard was the name Gulbuddin Hekmatyar. It was not a name that Mani knew, and it may seem naive now, looking back, that she thought only about the durability of the lease, not about terrorism. Hekmatyar, a former Afghan prime minister, led a mujahideen faction that had helped to defeat Soviet forces with U.S. assistance. But the fickle alliances had shifted, and by 2003 his affiliation with the Taliban and his alleged support of al-Qaeda got him listed as a terrorist by the State Department. In the late 1970s, with a land grant from Pakistan, he had founded Shamshatu refugee camp, which contained the building in question.[33] There is no evidence that he was in the area when the orphanage was established or that he received any money from IARA. But the possibility evidently excited FBI investigators.

They opened a quiet investigation of Mani. "Initially, I think they thought I was affiliated with terrorists, which is completely false, 100 percent false," she declared. "They talked to my professors," she learned later. "Everybody gave very good, positive, extremely good information, and they could not find any flaw in my life, not in money, credit cards." The one thing they found was her lie on the EPA documents and, consequently, on the citizenship application. In the law, the transgression is classified as naturalization fraud.

It's not difficult to imagine FBI agents' glee in discovering this hook, this opening to extract information and cooperation. Immigrants are especially vulnerable, even after they have been naturalized as U.S. citizens, for their citizenship can be taken away by a judge if they have lied to acquire it.

Once agents had this leverage, they wanted more, it seemed. Their instrument came as a stranger calling herself Amanda Davis. She phoned Mani with an enticing story that her grandmother had left money to be donated to worthy causes, and asked to visit Mani to talk about her work in Pakistan. Several times Davis came to her home, looked around, once took her to lunch, and discussed the newly established orphanage housing two hundred boys. "She kept asking me, 'When are you going to go back again?,' and I told her probably after a couple of months." Davis offered to give Mani $10,000.

Whatever the scheme in preparation, it went awry when Mani decided to fly on short notice to Pakistan to see her husband, who had traveled there amid marital difficulties. Only at the last minute did she remember her promise to let the putative donor know when she was going. "I called Amanda Davis and told her I was leaving today," Mani recalled. "She said what time. And I said in one hour. And she panicked. I think the plan was to catch me red-handed. She vanished. During the questions, they asked who is Amanda Davis, and I said I don't know her well. And they smiled a little bit, so I think she was their person."

A sting might not have worked anyway. On the one hand, Mani did not know the U.S. law: if you're carrying $10,000 or more, you must declare it to customs as you leave or enter the country, then you may take it after a record is made. On the other hand, she knew the law of survival in Pakistan: even if Davis had managed to get the cash to her in time, Mani wouldn't have flown out with it. "I would be the last person, knowing my country, to take $10,000 to Pakistan on my body," she said. "People shoot you dead for $1,000."

The authorities were ready for Mani nonetheless, and when she arrived at the airport and put her passport on the check-in counter, two agents arrested her for naturalization fraud. "I was shocked," she said, and was certain "that there was some misunderstanding." They searched her thoroughly and seemed surprised not to find the money. For three or four days she was locked in a cell the size of a small bathroom, a terrifying time that became the pivot point of all that she later sought to avoid.

They also got a search warrant for her house, carried away many boxes of documents, and peppered her with additional threats: about some unspecified errors in her mortgage application, about what they claimed were counterfeit labels on clothing her brother had brought her from Pakistan. The possible charges were piling up.

It soon became clear that the FBI wanted her "cooperation," an elastic word in law enforcement that can mean anything from tightly focused testimony to a long-term role as an informant. "I was under the impression that they wanted to make me a spy," she said. She knew the tribal areas, after all, could blend in, spoke all those languages. She imagined that the authorities had something like that in mind, although they never got far enough with her to say so explicitly.

If federal officials considered making expansive use of her skills, they were less than adroit. "Total dumb people come into these jobs," Mani declared, "not knowing anything and having preconceptions in their head, and will do anything to get ahead." The real help they needed from her, she thought, was an education on Pakistan. "They didn't understand me at that time, and I didn't understand them. Whenever they asked me any questions, truthfully whatever I knew I told them. But in their perspective I was not telling them everything and I was hiding something from them. In their mind I was related to some big terrorism and I could go to those areas, and being a woman, I could do a lot for them."

The government did not seem to know how to woo her. Instead, it ratcheted up the pressure. She was threatened with prison time for her naturalization fraud, which carried a maximum of ten years.[34] The FBI stationed a vehicle ostentatiously in front of her house, not for stealthy surveillance (it was in plain view), but to compound her stress. The phone at home would ring day and night, and when she picked it up, she heard only silence. "Since I was scared, I was an easy target for them," she said, and recounted the threats: "OK, if you don't cooperate, we will make another case regarding your mortgage, a case against your son—so they kept making all kinds of stories of what they would do." Her son was nineteen. "They take him out from his college and took him out for two or three hours for investigation," she said. "He was a child, and he was very scared. They were telling him to push me, if you cooperate with us and tell your mother to cooperate with us—otherwise we will make a case against you about some money."

She lost her job at the EPA, although she was warmly praised by the supervisor who had hired her. Her health deteriorated, both physically and mentally, as documented by a thick file of medical records provided later to the court. "I was under eight medications," she said. "I had high blood pressure, anxiety problem." She was losing her memory, her ability to concentrate. "I was on high doses of so many medications, sleeping pills, panic attacks, attention deficit disorders." Diagnosed with depression, she was so "fragile," said one professional who dealt with her case, that she could not have survived prison. And it was avoiding prison that became her obsession. "I think *I* was the most terrorized person—by them," she declared.

Yet the bullying did not work, not immediately. Her lead prosecutor, Assistant U.S. Attorney John T. Morton, suggested in writing that her "assistance" might include providing information on relatives, which she understood to mean her husband, whose occasional return to Pakistan had raised officials' suspicions about his asylum claim. Morton wanted her "to answer questions that I or agents assisting me wish to pose her concerning her activities and those of her family and associates over the past few years."[35]

When asked to testify against IARA, she worried that she would be damaging innocents, so she hesitated and then refused. What she would have gained from cooperating was unclear. She would not have been able to save her American citizenship—Morton would get her "denaturalized" anyway because of the false statements in her citizenship application. Nor did she remember being promised that she would be allowed to stay in the United States—she would be deported, sooner or later. This is confirmed in a letter from Morton to her lawyer, which offers only that her removal could be "non-custodial" (read: no jail or handcuffs) and could be postponed as long as the government needed her cooperation. No possibility of permanent residency was raised.[36]

The government seemed to be toying with her, requiring her commitment and giving none of its own, which is typical in such matters. "Assistance" was nebulous, and the consequences of providing or withholding it were equally vague. Perhaps she would have prevailed at a trial, given the minor nature of the falsehood on her application, but Morton gave no ground to sympathy or proportion, and going to trial seemed too risky for a woman too vulnerable to go to jail. Her lawyer negotiated a guilty plea with no prison time, but with an acute punishment nonetheless. She was stripped of her citizenship and deported, which drove a wedge of nearly half a world between her and her young adult children, who remained in the United States as American citizens.[37]

She dared not take Warda, her retarded teenage daughter, with her to Pakistan. "In Pakistan people believe in superstitions and in most cases the mentally retarded people are considered being possessed by the evil ghost," wrote Dr. Riffat A. Chaudhary, head of the psychiatry department at the National Institute for Handicapped in Lahore. "Often such patients are taken to the ghost doctors and the treatment . . . is so torturous, inhuman and horrible. . . . The mentally retarded patient is tied with the tree, beaten with the whip, lighting of fire around him and engulfing him in smoke. . . . Mentally retarded females are often abducted, raped, and murdered. If Warda Chohan return to Pakistan, she is likely to face the same fate. . . . It will adversely affect her personality and it may shorten her life too."[38] So Warda stayed in the United States with her older brother and sister.

Even in Pakistan, the FBI was not finished with Mani. Two months after her deportation in 2004, IARA was listed by the Treasury Department as a "specially designated global terrorist,"[39] and as the case developed, Mani started receiving requests from Pakistan's security agency to sit down with FBI agents at the U.S. embassy. "I thought, OK, if I don't go, this is a country, they can pick me up," she told me by phone from Islamabad. "In this country anything could happen. I'm tired of being scared."

The American agents asked her politely if she would return to testify before a grand jury. They played on her pain of separation, promising that she could see her children. Mani struggled for weeks. "I just can't forget my children. I am a mother. I have lost everything," she said to me. Yet "the way I am hurt," she added, "I can't hurt anyone. I don't want to be a part of that."

Besides, her professional life had been restored. Pakistan's National Engineering and Scientific Commission had hired her to create a poison control center, she said, and to establish radiation limits to protect workers in the nuclear field. She would be managing hundreds of employees. It would be a sensitive position, however, and her travel would be restricted. "If you are in that job, your passport is in the hands of government," she explained. "Even going out of the country is with their permission."

As she longed for her children, the FBI kept calling, kept promising or at least implying that she could return to the United States and receive an S visa, known in the trade as a "snitch visa," which might lead to a green card once again. Pakistani officials told her that she had to make a choice: Pakistan or America. She could not keep her job if she went to testify in the United States.

Finally, she agreed to go in 2007 and was flown at U.S. government expense to Kansas City, where she was put up in a hotel while she testified for only a few minutes before a grand jury. "They asked questions about the orphanage, very specific questions," she said. "They asked me all the financial details."

But her Justice Department handlers would not let her fly to Washington, D.C., to see her children, and her children did not have the money to fly to see her. She returned to Pakistan with two empty hands—without having embraced her son and daughters and without a job.

Mani is a slight woman with a white shawl across her right shoulder, a small gold stud in her nose, and an endless weariness in a face that seems not to have been graced by a smile for a very long time. She was born in 1957 and worries that she looks much older, but I think she looks much younger than her voice sounds. It is thin, exhausted.

She has put out a bowl of nuts and a plate of cookies and has brought mugs of green tea. In the town house she can barely afford to rent, indistinguishable from all the others in a colorless Virginia suburb near Dulles International Airport, she has hung a picture of her mother, looking strong and kind, who died several years earlier.

A gangly teenage boy comes in. He is one of four orphans of Pakistan's 2008 earthquake whom Mani adopted, as if her need to give and care were insatiable, a way to fill the emptiness. "I believe I was doing very, very similar to Mother Teresa, what she was doing," Mani says, not as if it were a boast or a delusion, just a plain explanation.

She has been here since April 2009, when the U.S. government flew her and her adopted children from Pakistan so that she could be a witness in a trial of IARA's director, Mubarak Hamed. Officials did a few things for her. Because adoption in Pakistan was like guardianship, the FBI got her an attorney pro bono to complete the adoptions here to comport with U.S. law. The Justice Department gave her a stipend for living expenses at first, she says, and obtained a work permit for her. But her naturalization fraud has so far prevented her from getting hired as a toxicologist. With her Ph.D., she has been cleaning houses, visiting food banks, and begging for money from friends and churches. She has worked recently summarizing news stories for the Pakistani embassy.

After her grand jury testimony but surely not because of it, Hamed and others at IARA were indicted. Among the charges was their transfer of $130,000 to renovate buildings owned by Hekmatyar—namely, the orphanage—an accusation still left unproven. Indeed, prosecutors dropped the count as they accepted a guilty plea to something entirely different. Hamed admitted funneling money to unspecified people or organizations in Iraq without a license, violating the sanctions imposed on Iraq after the 1991 Gulf War. His lawyer insists that the funding went to charitable ends, including an orphanage and a program to slaughter cattle for distribution to the poor,[40] the kind of humanitarian aid that might have been granted a license by the Treasury Department, had Hamed applied. It may be, then, that Hamed's guilt was the equivalent of driving safely without a license, not driving so as to endanger others. There is a difference.

Mani knows nothing about the Iraq connection, and the guilty plea obviates the need for a trial. So the entire reason for her tribulation has evaporated. Her "assistance" is not required. It probably never was, not even to get the indictment, which relied on records of bank transfers and wiretaps. She has received her promised S visa, and hopes that the authorities will deign to permit her to remain with her children in the United States. She cannot look to any due process in such a case, for there is no transparency and no set of rights, just the whim of the powerful.

She is orphaned again, this time by both her adopted country and even her native land. "In Pakistan now I am defamed," she says, because she was deported and then returned to the United States and because of her slight cooperation with the FBI. She is afraid of going back to a country where people vanish without explanation.

Around her, people have disappeared in another way. Her arrest in 2004 frightened away almost all her friends and colleagues, especially fellow Muslims who may have imagined themselves suffering guilt by association. In the region below the law, people do not welcome the magnifying glass of governmental authority, no matter how innocent they may be. "Nobody calls me. I don't get a ring," she says. The words "isolation" and "seclusion" appear in her conversation. "You are not in jail, but you are in *a* jail."

Losing what she had gained has been a constant theme of her grief. "Imagine an orphan child coming to this level of life," she told me in 2006, from Pakistan. "And having seventeen years of accomplishment snatched away for what? Some small error? Every single night I cry profusely. I can't sleep. . . . I was so self-confident and independent."

And in 2011, sitting in her Virginia living room: "I don't know what to do. I don't know where to go. Everything is gone. I am living, but I'm a dead person. You have no idea how difficult it is for an orphan child to reach this position and get a Ph.D. I stand nowhere."

Was it worth crushing Dr. Waheeda Mani Tehseen for the lie on her form, for the charity work that led her to IARA, for her slimmest testimony, which produced only an unproven charge? The man largely responsible, Assistant U.S. Attorney Morton, was a low-level official of thirty-eight at the time, but he then rose meteorically through the ranks of law enforcement until President Obama made him director of ICE, the agency that seizes and deports immigrants. Looking back, did Morton think his retribution on Mani was proportional to her crime? How did he reckon the gains and losses on the balance of justice? He wouldn't say. Requests for his assessment went unanswered.

Who is guilty and who is innocent in this affair? Mani? Morton? Hamed? Agents of the FBI? Or was tragedy produced by various strains of guilt and innocence intertwined in each of them?

THE ASHCROFT SWEEPS

On September 15, 2001, a car carrying three Middle Eastern men was stopped in Manhattan for a routine traffic violation. Their appearance, their accents, and their names invited a closer look by jittery police officers, who searched the vehicle and found plans to a public school. All three were arrested. Their employer, who was contacted the next day, confirmed that the men were merely construction workers who needed the plans for a job. Nevertheless, they were classified by the FBI as being "of interest to the September 11 investigation" and were held by the Immigration and Naturalization Service as part of a broad, two-month sweep that caught about 1,200 people in its net.

They were thrown into a legal limbo devoid of due process. Held for immigration violations, they were presumed guilty of terrorism, abused in prison, and released or deported only after being cleared by the FBI and the CIA, which took months in many cases. Not a single "terrorist" was found among them—no surprise, given the randomness of the arrests.

Driven by President Bush's admonition "Don't let this happen again," Attorney General John Ashcroft sent immigration and FBI agents scurrying to check every tip, no matter how absurd or venal, about foreigners (particularly Muslims) possibly living in the country illegally, possibly plotting, possibly harboring attitudes toward America that were less than adoring. FBI offices were flooded with calls and e-mails from landlords, neighbors, spurned lovers, ex-spouses, disgruntled co-workers, and others to the point where some FBI agents felt queasy taking them seriously.

An Arab shop clerk told a customer that he'd like to learn to fly, and he was locked up. A grocery store that seemed to be operated by "numerous Middle East men . . . too many people to run a small store," as a caller suggested, was raided, and a worker there was jailed. When one person was targeted, all those with him who lacked valid visas were detained as people "of interest."

Because the government wanted to recruit informants and deny terrorists a mosaic of its "investigation," the prisoners' names were not released, and their eventual deportation hearings were held in secret, where the men were condemned by classified "evidence." This prompted Judge Damon Keith of the Sixth Circuit to write a line that instantly became a catchphrase: "Democracies die behind closed doors." He led a unanimous panel in ordering the hearings opened. In reality, there was no investigation, only a scattered array of capricious arrests that added up to nothing. But the Supreme Court later accepted the fiction, bought the government's rationalization, and let stand two other appeals court rulings endorsing the secrecy of the detentions and hearings.[41]

Many were held without access to counsel. A phone call to a lawyer was counted as complete when an answering machine was reached. When a guard would ask, "Are you OK?" and an inmate replied, "Yes," that was taken to mean that the prisoner did not want to contact an attorney. Lawyers arriving at jails were told wrongly that their clients were not there. In the hard prison culture, all presumption of innocence disappeared, and "correction officers" exacted their own punishments. They "slammed and bounced detainees into the walls . . . twisted and bent detainees' arms, hands, wrists, and fingers," according to a report by the Justice Department's inspector general. Prison guards called them "bin Laden Junior," "fucking Muslims," and other epithets accompanied by threats: "You're never going to leave here"; "You're going to die here just like the people in the World Trade Center died"; "Don't ask any questions, otherwise you will be dead."

During a medical examination, a physician employed by the Justice Department's Bureau of Prisons told an inmate, "If I was in charge, I would execute every one of you . . . because of the crimes you all did," which, of course, they had not done. The doctor's "cruel and unprofessional" treatment of other prisoners, the inspector general reported, earned "a verbal reprimand."[42]

What happened in county jails and federal prisons, for which eleven federal guards were later indicted, was something of a preview of the abuses later committed in Guantánamo. Islam was mocked, and copies of the Koran were thrown on the floor, according to Mohammed Maddy and Ashraf Ibrahim, Egyptians who wrote separate, detailed accounts after they were deported. During most of their six to seven months in jail, they had been in the federal Metropolitan Detention Center in Brooklyn.

Both men described being smashed repeatedly face-first against walls while shackled, told they would never see their families again, and subjected to a range of insults and deprivations. Guards stepped on their ankle chains while they walked, making them trip, then dragged them by clothes or handcuffs. Maddy's glasses were taken away when he was arrested, yet he was made to sign blurry legal documents, and when he was finally able to contact his wife, a new pair she sent was returned to her twice by prison authorities. Ibrahim said he was also forced to "sign a document that I did not read."

Little indignities loomed large. In Maddy's cell, he reported, no cups were allowed except during meals, and the water was often cut off, so he could drink only from the shower—often a cold shower, with no hot water. Minimal toilet paper was provided—just two feet a day—and the air-conditioning was turned on full blast in the winter. "We was freezen," he wrote. The bad food came in child-sized portions, and he lost forty pounds. During four months he got no haircut, he said, and had no way to clip his nails except to bite them.

Ibrahim made similar complaints: no soap, no toilet paper, no toothbrush or toothpaste, inadequate food, lights left on twenty-four hours a day, and guards "shouting and banging the cells doors all the time and for no reason just to prevent us from sleeping. . . . There were no radios, television, newspapers, or even information about anything. The officers refused even to tell us the time!!!" he wrote.

Unlike the tortures inflicted by the CIA, these measures seemed motivated by sadism more than intelligence gathering. Periodic interrogation by FBI and immigration agents struck the prisoners as pointless. "They asked me very silly questions," Ibrahim reported, "such as, 'Do you go to any mosque in the U.S.?' 'Do you pray regularly?' 'Why aren't you married?'" At one point, "they threatened me that if I did not give them some information about 9/11, I would be detained in jail for a long time!!" But he did not have any information to give, which the FBI eventually came to realize. After having been arrested in September 2001, he was sent to Egypt in March 2002, with a final humiliation: "I was strip searched and given a very bad and large shirt and an xxx large jeans without a belt and a pair of boots size 13 without shoe laces! . . . In Cairo, the Egyptian state security investigation officials kept me in custody in one of the worst jails for 4 days. Now I am seeing a psychiatric regularly."

His New York landlord told him that the FBI had taken everything from his apartment, including cash, clothes, watches, cameras, books, documents, and credit cards. The agency—or the agents—kept the loot. He was unable to get anything back.

In an eight-page handwritten statement from Cairo, Maddy characterized the Metropolitan Detention Center: "It is another country inside U.S.A., no roules, no laws." During his ten years in America, he had come to love the United States as "my second nation," and he concluded with this lament: "No go back to U.S.A., they killed my life, no job."

The criminal justice system provided retribution, but the civil side of the system did not. The indicted guards at the Metropolitan Detention Center were convicted or pleaded guilty. Among them were Captain Salvatore Lopresti, who got fifty-one months for conspiring to violate the civil rights of an inmate, obstructing justice, and making three false statements regarding the beating of a prisoner, and Lieutenant Elizabeth Torres, sentenced to fifteen months for obstructing justice by covering up a beating.[43] That was the result of a criminal prosecution.

Civil action failed, however, and in so doing left a damaging legal legacy far broader and more durable than the abuse of detainees. When deported prisoners sued Ashcroft, FBI director Robert Mueller, and various prison personnel for violating their rights, they were thwarted by a 5–4 Supreme Court finding that they could not even proceed without providing more detail in advance showing that the high officials had intentionally engaged in ethnic or racial discrimination. This is a hard point to prove without getting inside people's minds—or without seeing memos and other concealed evidence that could be pried loose in the process of discovery after a lawsuit is filed. Until this case, *Ashcroft v. Iqbal*, traditional rules allowed civil suits to go to discovery unless laced with obviously absurd and fanciful claims. But under the ruling now, judges are licensed to dismiss suits at the outset, before any fact-finding, if they don't find the claim "plausible." How they would know without giving the plaintiffs opportunity to force evidence into the sunlight the justices did not explain. Instead, they set up a new Catch-22 under which the courts won't allow you to gather the facts unless you already have them in hand. Depending on various judges' predilections, this could be a boon for government and corporate secrecy, whose protectors on the bench moved quickly in hundreds of cases to slam the courthouse door in the face of aggrieved detainees, employees, and others confronting powerful institutions.[44]

In the Ashcroft Sweeps, the government used administrative measures outside the courts to conduct a campaign of preventive detention, although the authorities didn't really know whom they were detaining or what they were preventing. They would have done even more under a proposal floated when senior officials gathered in a secure room at FBI headquarters on September 11. "What was originally contemplated was far more draconian than what happened," recalled James Ziglar, head of the Immigration and Naturalization Service. They discussed doing "some big sweeps" in "any community where there was a large concentration of Arabs, to basically do a door-to-door," he said. "We ended up doing something sort of semi-that, but it wasn't quite that."

Ziglar thought of himself as "quite a Bill-of-Rights kind of guy," a Goldwater Republican with a libertarian streak. "I was the only guy in the room who raised his hand and said, 'Wait a minute. We've got something called the Fourth Amendment here. We don't do sweeps in this country. We had a revolution over warrantless searches.'" The comment may have broken the momentum, but the reaction from some was hostile. "You've got to understand, this was September 11, and the level of hysteria was huge," he said. "Once you raise an idea, anybody who says that's a stupid idea is somehow unpatriotic or soft on terrorism." Yet "some people after the fact came to me and said, 'I'm really glad you did that, 'cause it calmed down the situation.'"[45]

The FBI began trying to find people it had been watching, taking along INS agents so that anyone out of status could be picked up on immigration charges. Immigration law became the handiest tool since it required no proof of wrongdoing except a person's presence without documentation. That in turn sometimes resulted from clerical oversights, as in the case of Enayet Ullah and his family.

He was caught as officials screened airport workers, a potentially sensible precaution dubbed Operation Tarmac. When Ullah's name came up on a list of baggage handlers at John F. Kennedy International Airport, the immigration records showed an outstanding deportation order, one that he had never received, although he hadn't changed addresses; he'd lived for years in the same ground-floor apartment in Brooklyn. Perhaps the ruling had been sent to his lawyer, who had failed to notify him—not an infrequent slip, and one that can get a removal order reversed for ineffective assistance of counsel.

Ullah had applied for political asylum in 1994 after fleeing persecution as secretary of a pro-democracy party in Bangladesh, where he had been jailed and beaten for five days. A criminal case was begun against him there, so upon release he had gone into hiding; government thugs had visited his house, threatening to kidnap and kill his little daughter if his wife spoke against the ruling party. It seemed like a strong claim of persecution, and the U.S. embassy issued visas to the whole family, who departed in full view of the disorganized Bangladeshi bureaucracy, thanks to a relative employed at the airport in Dhaka.

Yet no decision on his asylum petition had ever been reached by an American immigration judge, as far as he knew. Twice his immigration lawyer failed to show up for hearings, drawing a warning from the judge; finally, the attorney appeared and applied for an extension. "And after that, no answer," Ullah said. "I told the lawyer, what can we do? We do not get any answer from the immigration office, what can we do? He said if you go over there, you'll get deported. So you should do nothing, because they don't say anything."

That may have been good advice in the 1990s, when the most dysfunctional agency in the federal government couldn't keep track of its own decisions and the law went largely unenforced. By 2002, however, targeted pockets of efficiency had been created. One concentrated on immigrants working at airports.

Before their carefully constructed lives started to be disassembled, the Ullahs could have been a poster family for a beneficent America. Instead of trying to be rid of them, a clever government could have touted them in the Muslim world as an exhibit of America's virtue as a refuge, albeit a difficult one, for achieving, principled people courageous enough to uproot themselves from their own cultures and languages and professions, and begin again on alien soil.

Gathered in their neat and comfortable apartment, they seemed so gentle, despite the time of high tension and uncertainty. Enayet Ullah, who sported a mustache and wore reading glasses, buried whatever anger he felt under a quiet sweetness. His wife, Razia Sultana, wore a cream-colored head scarf, marking her as an observant Muslim and drawing nervous glances after 9/11. "They're afraid," she said sadly. "People look at me like I did something. Sometimes they don't even want to give me a seat." To come here, she had taken a step down professionally, from lecturing in psychology at a Bangladeshi university to working for an accountant in New York—a typical compromise for educated immigrants. Occasionally, she descended into tears, softly, not harshly.

Two of their three children were not in danger of deportation: their oldest daughter, Rahnuma, a student at Hunter College, because she was married to an American; and their youngest, a boy named Tasfiq, because he had been born in the United States and thus into American citizenship. Razia and the middle child, Tarnima, were as vulnerable to removal as their father, who was out on $15,000 bail.

And what had this done to their opinions about America? A long silence settled on the room, and finally Rahnuma spoke: "I mean, at first, I mean, my dad came here for opportunity, for freedom."

"For safety," he added.

"But now, see, here we don't have any safety," said Rahnuma, "no freedom, actually." Her clear English came in a thin, light lilt that made her sound as if she were smiling. She was not. "We are actually being judged because of our religion, like he did something wrong."

It had been a Tuesday in November 2002, her father's day off from his job with a private contractor for United Airlines. The phone rang early in the morning, the manager calling to ask that he come to work immediately. Only later did his boss apologetically describe the scene: FBI and immigration agents bullying him into making the call, staying at his side while he did so, telling him that he could not leave the office until he reached their quarry—in other words, an illegal detention of the supervisor. "They watch him," Ullah said. "They think if he go out, he can call me and tell me don't come."

As Ullah rode up the escalator in Terminal 7, he saw at the top three men in plainclothes who had his picture. As he stepped off, one cuffed his wrists behind him. He was questioned for eight or nine hours and was not allowed to call anyone, neither his wife nor a lawyer.

Razia was nagged by worry. She tried and tried his cell phone but could not reach him. Finally, around 3:00 p.m. a call came from his brother, who also worked at JFK, saying that he'd heard that Ullah had been taken by the FBI and immigration. "She fainted," Rahnuma said of her mother. "I was there." And then, "we actually left home" and hid in a friend's house, she said, an old survival reflex from Bangladesh to avoid agents who might come looking for the rest of the family.

For three months, much longer than he had been jailed in Bangladesh, he was held at a detention center in Elizabeth, New Jersey. He was not brutalized, perhaps because the earlier abuse elsewhere had begun to gain publicity. His new attorney, Sin Yen Ling, then of the Asian American Legal Defense and Education Fund, got him out on bail, which was raised by five friends and relatives.

Ullah went back to work while Ling revived his asylum application. Each morning, he headed out the door at 4:00 for the airport (where he was no longer allowed to cross through security), leaving Razia suspended in anxiety that when his shift was over at 1:00 p.m., he might not return. But he did return, and thanks to an old copy of his arrest warrant from Bangladesh, plus credible evidence of what he might face if he were sent back, Enayet Ullah and his family were ultimately granted political asylum in the United States of America. After failing, the system sometimes works.

The frenzied efforts to ferret out potential terrorists rode on the latest episode of anti-immigration sentiment, a periodic feature of American history.

The current aversion had gathered force in the early 1990s, propelling California voters to pass Proposition 187, which denied access to government benefits, even public schooling, to illegal immigrants and their children, including those who were citizens by virtue of being born in the United States. The ballot measure, later found unconstitutional, electrified politicians all the way up to President Clinton, who understood that he could not win a second term without California's electoral votes.

Clinton was a master at defusing the right by adopting some of its positions—on welfare reform, for example—so he did the same with immigration. He endorsed tougher deportation measures. He avoided even symbolic gestures of regard for the venerable process of acquiring American citizenship. "I tried the whole time I was at INS to get Clinton to a naturalization ceremony," said Doris Meissner, who headed the immigration agency from 1993 through the end of his administration. The White House staff never agreed, she complained. "Isn't that something?"[46]

Then came the attacks of September 11 and a convenient confluence of fears—of terrorism and of immigrants. After years of scant enforcement, the immigration laws were suddenly mobilized like a weapon carelessly deployed, wounding the harmless along with the nefarious, causing untold collateral damage with unforeseen social costs.

Like the Palmer Raids against foreign-born "anarchists" early in the twentieth century, the Ashcroft Sweeps, early in the twenty-first, focused on entire groups, not just individuals. Attorney General A. Mitchell Palmer had ordered the roundup of some 6,000 people, mostly immigrants, after a series of bombings in 1919 included an explosion on the porch of his house. Had the 2001 attacks occurred in that earlier age, before the society's rising sensitivity to racial and ethnic profiling, wholesale internment of Muslims might have been accepted, as the confinement of ethnic Japanese had been during World War II. The preferred method now, a haphazard substitute of sweeps and raids, was more restrained but based on similar assumptions: cast the net for Muslim men, hold those in violation of immigration law, and a few guilty catches would inevitably be found. All nineteen hijackers were Muslims, after all, performing their atrocity in the name of a twisted notion of religious duty. All but three, however, were in the United States legally.

The authorities singled out Muslims in various ways. Ashcroft issued a demand that males sixteen and older who were not permanent residents, from any of twenty-five heavily Muslim countries, present themselves to immigration offices to be fingerprinted, photographed, and questioned. The "special registration" requirement was short-lived, running from November

2002 to April 2003, producing no terrorists willing to show up and declare themselves. But in five months it worked considerable hardship on hapless illegals among the 83,000 who complied. Some 13,000 who were out of status, sometimes because of technical or clerical errors by the INS itself, were greeted at immigration offices with deportation orders, often handcuffs. Many disappeared into jails for months. Their families knew nothing except that they had never returned from their visits to officialdom, so officialdom became anathema.[47]

Several thousand panicky, undocumented Pakistanis, the largest group of immigrants among the twenty-five, gave up on their American dreams and uprooted themselves from their homes, schools, jobs, and small businesses. They fled, either back to Pakistan or north to the border with Canada in search of asylum *from* the United States. When Canadian authorities couldn't process them fast enough, they congregated in northern Vermont, cramming into churches and homes, sheltered by the Salvation Army, taking refuge in their own vehicles during the deep of winter. Some, given Canadian appointments a month later, were arrested when they returned without American visas to the U.S. side of the border.[48]

They left behind decimated neighborhoods. Little Pakistan, along Brooklyn's Coney Island Avenue, saw its vibrant street life wither, its crowded mosques and flourishing restaurants decline, some classroom desks stand empty, its Urdu-language newspaper lose most of its advertising.[49]

The spasm of fear at the highest levels of government was mirrored by fear in the lowliest neighborhoods of immigrants. Women "come to us, their husbands are beating them, and we ask them if we can proceed with the law. They say, 'No, no, I will be deported. I'm illegal, and I have children,'" reported Muhammad Tariqur Rahman, director of the Islamic Circle of North America in New York City. "Even legal immigrants robbed in the subway, they won't go to the police because they think they'll see them as a suspect."

These are not unfounded fantasies. When Rita Cote called police in Tavares, Florida, to help her Spanish-speaking sister in a domestic violence incident in 2009, the officers arrested Cote instead. She spoke with an accent and looked Latino, so they demanded her passport and found an old, undelivered administrative removal order from her childhood. She was locked up for several weeks, away from her husband and three young children, while the American Civil Liberties Union petitioned for her release, successfully in the end.[50]

Some Muslims worried that the most innocent gatherings might be viewed as suspicious, so two New York taxi drivers from Pakistan stopped getting together with friends in Brooklyn to watch cricket matches on satellite television, lest a building superintendent report them.[51] "The advice people give to each other is, if at odd times you hear a knock on the door, don't open the door," said Rashida Abdul-Hakim, a caseworker for the Islamic Circle. None of this was irrational, since ludicrous tips were aggressively investigated and arrests were routinely performed between midnight and five in the morning, when agents figured their quarry would be home. The crackdown sharpened the edge of vulnerability, and many immigrants grew less willing to complain about exploitative landlords who charged high rents and employers who paid low wages.

As always in America, though, opposites coexisted: alienation and assimilation, anxiety and pride. One March day as crisp and clear as September 11, I happened on a funeral at a mosque in Queens where the pulse of fear became a weak counterpoint to a show of patriotism.

The street was closed by police cars with lights flashing, led by a ranking officer with gold braid and a plainclothesman with an earphone. A large crowd of men spilled across the street outside the mosque. American and U.S. Army flags were fluttering above the green of army uniforms, a hearse parked at the curb.

Six soldier pallbearers marched in quickstep to the back of the hearse, and a Muslim flag was placed on the coffin, which they carried into the mosque. Inside was the body of Azhar Ali, a national guardsman killed in Iraq, a young Muslim dying for America's cause. The face of his mother, who was robed in black, was the color of ash. "Please pray so we do not have to say another prayer, and another," intoned the imam after prayers for the dead. "Thank you all for showing your patriotism and coming." He concluded, "May Allah bless America."

UNINTENDED CONSEQUENCES

It's a safe bet that the legislators who fashioned the rules of deportation, and the officials who enforced them zealously after 9/11, did not mean to deter abused wives from calling the police for protection against their violent husbands, or to break up families by deporting a parent who leaves a spouse and children behind. Surely they didn't intend to create a humiliating spectacle in northern Vermont, which probably undermined American moral authority in the Muslim world more effectively than any al-Qaeda propaganda. Against this tide of anxiety, FBI officials struggled constantly to keep open communications lines with immigrant communities, meeting frequently in public forums to hear concerns and explain policies, even while their undercover agents were infiltrating worship services and deploying informants with hidden recording devices.

Among the most devastating results of the deportation assault has been the scattering of family members. It's been too much of a hardship for one deported member to pull the rest out of their American lives, and spouses and children have often stayed in the country after the "alien" is "removed." Berly Feliz, here illegally, went innocently to an immigration office to renew her work permit and was handcuffed and flown back to Honduras with no chance to say good-bye to her husband and eight-year-old daughter, both American citizens, left behind in the Bronx.[52]

Hassan Raiss of Morocco was forcibly separated from his American wife after he neglected to notify immigration authorities when he moved. Early in the 1990s, such a minor infraction had not usually been punished, said his lawyer, Lawrence Gatei. This was partly because "processing change-of-address forms is one of the lower-priority tasks," which didn't always get done, according to Doris Meissner, who headed the INS under Clinton. In the wake of the 9/11 attacks, however, the benefit of the doubt was rarely given.

Raiss's oversight created a snowballing series of violations: First, when his wife was too ill to attend his green-card interview, as required, the interview was rescheduled, but the notice of the next appointment was sent to his old address and returned, prompting the authorities to launch deportation proceedings. A subsequent order to appear before an immigration judge never reached him, and his removal was ordered in absentia. He achieved a serious-sounding new status: "fugitive alien."

Then came bizarre deception, which often characterizes immigration arrests. Authorities worry that if potential deportees know what's about to happen, they'll run and melt into immigrant communities. ICE recruited Detective Andrea Purcell of the Massachusetts Bay Transportation Authority Police, who visited Raiss's house and left her number. He called her when he got home, according to Gatei's account. She said that someone had used his car for unlawful activity. "He said, 'Wait a second, I sold that car in May.' She said, 'Do you have a receipt for selling the car?' 'I have it here. Would you like to see it?' 'Yes, I'd like to see it.'"

He wanted to contact his lawyer first, but she assured him that he didn't need one and urged him to come with the documents. "The next day she went to his house, but she didn't find him," Gatei said. "She left a message saying she was there, for him to contact her. She went to the hotel where he worked, but he had left for the day."

Although Gatei was skeptical about Detective Purcell's story, she promised the lawyer by phone that nothing more was involved. So he accompanied Raiss to the police station, car receipt in hand. The detective met them, excused herself immediately, then quickly reappeared with two ICE agents, who made the arrest.

The exasperated lawyer felt used. He also thought this was a gross misuse of transit police. "Every day we're hearing of women riders being assaulted," he said, "and they have detectives running all over enforcing federal mandates? And they're not even trained to do that." He complained to the chief of the transit police, who admitted that lying to an attorney was "improper" and declared that enforcing immigration law "is generally best left to the federal agencies established for that purpose."[53]

That principle has been breached in both the Bush and the Obama administrations by the Department of Homeland Security, which now houses ICE, Customs and Border Protection, and U.S. Citizenship and Immigration Services. As of late 2010, it had entered into agreements to train and authorize seventy-one local law enforcement agencies in about half the states to detain and report undocumented immigrants, mainly by using the improving databases to check the immigration status of anyone who seems foreign when stopped for traffic violations or arrested for more serious crimes. By August 2011, 1,502 jurisdictions in 43 states had signed up to send fingerprints of everyone booked to Homeland Security under a program named Secure Communities, which officials hoped to extend to all police departments in the country by 2013.[54]

It's a prescription for racial and ethnic profiling eagerly embraced by some local departments, while others firmly reject playing immigration agent. They don't want to jeopardize immigrants' cooperation with local law enforcement. "I'm concerned that people who are victims of a crime, whether citizens or not, are not calling us because they're afraid we're going to check status only," said Dave Rohrer, police chief in Virginia's Fairfax County.[55]

Enlisting locals to enforce immigration law has created problems both practical and constitutional. During a two-year sample period, 42 percent of people whom the database failed to list as legal were, in fact, properly documented; many of them were wrongly detained.[56] Fourth and Fifth Amendment rights have been invaded as well, often against American citizens who look "foreign."

The fear of wide-scale profiling and rights violations drove national protests after Arizona passed a law in 2010 directing police officers and government agencies, during "any lawful contact," to check anyone's immigration status "where reasonable suspicion exists that the person is an alien who is unlawfully present in the United States." The term "any lawful contact" was taken to mean that cops could approach and question people solely for immigration purposes, without requiring a traffic violation or other suspected offense as a prerequisite for a stop. "Lawful contact" might apply to the most benign encounters: an officer who is asked for directions, sees a law-abiding driver, or merely notices a pedestrian on the street. Furthermore, "reasonable suspicion," the least demanding form of justification for a police inquiry, could be aroused by little more than skin color, accent, and other attributes of ethnicity that would surely catch non-Anglo U.S. citizens in demands that they show their "documents."[57] An array of civil liberties and human rights organizations, joined by Obama's Justice Department, challenged the law in federal court and won a temporary injunction in a case ultimately destined for the Supreme Court. A flurry of similar laws, passed later by other states, faced similar challenges.

ICE officers may legally ask for immigration papers. But to be constitutional under existing case law, immigration inquiries by local police must follow legitimate *Terry* stops for ordinary, non-immigration offenses, governed by a 1968 Supreme Court case requiring either reasonable suspicion that a person is armed or probable cause to believe he is involved in a crime.[58] Without that prerequisite, a stop is unconstitutional, and if information about the person's immigration status is obtained as a result, it has been obtained illegally.

The practice on the street is considerably less pure, judging by cases that lawyers see. Police sometimes manufacture minor crimes to justify arrests, or they simply ask people for their documents. Citing security concerns in the months after 9/11, for example, local officers approached simple landscapers working near the Pentagon, who were suspected of nothing at all, and demanded documentation of their legal status. In Woodbridge, Virginia, police adopted a habit of arresting day laborers for loitering in front of a 7-Eleven where contractors picked them up for jobs, then asking about immigration status. Elsewhere in the state, local officers were simply "going up to immigrants and asking for their immigration papers," according to the attorney Mary Holper.

If they concede to being undocumented, the foreigners are turned over to ICE, which places them in removal proceedings. Even if the stops are illegal, the admissions given to police or ICE cannot readily be suppressed in immigration court unless egregious coercion can be shown. This is because the detainees face only civil consequences (deportation preceded by jail), which are not governed by the same constitutional protections as criminal cases—even though permanent removal may bring heavier catastrophe than prison terms. By violating the Constitution, then passing the detainees into the immigration system, police who are enlisted in the hunt for illegal aliens evade two crucial rights: to be free from unreasonable search and from a form of self-incrimination.

It doesn't take a great leap of imagination to picture the kind of country in which traffic cops or foot patrolmen are free to approach any citizen or foreigner who has a swarthy complexion, a Spanish accent, or a Muslim head scarf and demand proof of legal presence, ask intimidating questions, and effectively threaten to take apart a person's world. That is what is happening here and there, in the patchwork of local immigration enforcement, under local authorities who do not observe the strictest constitutional rules.

The alarm was sounded six months into the Obama administration by two dozen civil rights organizations, which expressed their stunned condemnation of Homeland Security for expanding the program, known as 287(g) after the section of immigration law that authorizes it. "In Davidson County, Tennessee, the Sheriff's Office has used its 287(g) power to apprehend undocumented immigrants driving to work, standing at day labor sites, or while fishing off piers," said the groups' statement. "One pregnant woman—charged with driving without a license—was forced to give birth while shackled to her bed during labor. Preliminary data indicate that in some jurisdictions the majority of individuals arrested under 287(g) are accused of public nuisance or traffic offenses: driving without a seatbelt, driving without a license, broken taillights, and similar offenses."[59] Virginia police reported some immigrants so terrified of encountering local cops that they were hiding in their homes and hoarding food.[60]

And then, in a corrosive phenomenon too shameful for Muslim leaders to talk much about, those wrongly arrested have sometimes been shunned in immigrant communities riven by fear. The government's presumption of guilt by association has invaded the apprehensions of Muslims who try to appear squeaky-clean. They do so by avoiding those who come under suspicion, even unjustly. With excruciating diligence, they have ended friendships and even cut family ties.

So it was for a political refugee from Iraq whose refuge felt suddenly unsafe. His life plunged into loneliness.

THE PURSUIT OF HAPPINESS

He stood out, a stocky man with graying hair and an olive complexion, spotted by border patrol agents in the train station of Havre, Montana, about thirty miles from Canada. Under immigration regulations implementing the federal law giving them warrantless search powers, the agents were "within a reasonable distance" of the border as long as they were within one hundred miles, and they routinely met the two Amtrak trains that stopped daily, heading east and west. They walked through the railroad cars and the station looking for anyone "believed to be an alien," as the law allows. The question, about to be tested, was whether that belief could legitimately be based on apparent ethnicity.

Abdulameer Habeeb had not been out of Iraq long enough—perhaps he never would be—to shed the reflex of averting his eyes when a uniformed officer looked directly at him. So that's what he did. He was traveling by train from Seattle to Washington, D.C., where he was to begin a new job, because he wanted to get a look at his adopted country, he explained. "I want to see everything—the land, the forests, the farms, everything." So when the train made its thirty-minute stop, he got off to see a bit of Havre. He had time to admire a statue of the founder of the town and, as an artist and sculptor himself, thought it "very nice." He had time to try to buy a Pepsi from a machine, but it didn't accept cash, and his debit card was depleted. He walked back toward the train and encountered the agent's steady gaze.

Habeeb came from a prominent Shiite family in southern Iraq, where his father, a respected sheikh, commanded the allegiance of a large clan with potential ties to Iran. The Shiite south was rebellious and problematic in the brutal politics of Saddam Hussein, who tried to threaten and bribe leaders into offering endorsement and support. Habeeb's father was a target, and his son became the unwilling conduit of the dictator's demand.

As Habeeb told it, his artistic skills as a calligrapher drew the attention of ranking army officers after basic training. Instead of deployment to a unit, he was asked—actually, taken—by an official in the presidential palace to teach art to children of Saddam's relatives and aides. He was also assigned to create ornate calligraphy not just of the customary verses from the Koran but of sayings by Saddam.

Soon Habeeb realized that his position "was like a cover for something else. They really wanted to force my dad" to honor Saddam, and Saddam's son Qusay delivered the request to Habeeb himself. "They asked me many times to persuade my dad to say yes." His father's answer was unequivocal. "He said, 'Now I'm an old man. All I need is to leave me alone.' When I told the government that, they did not accept that."

Habeeb was arrested several months later, ostensibly for failing to finish some artwork on time, and placed in a special prison for high-level government officials who had run afoul of the regime. "They hit me, they shocked me by electric, they broke my fingers, they broke my feet, they did things I can't say." He was released, rearrested, released, rearrested. "They took me many, many times to the jail" for months at a time.

In between, Habeeb tried to practice his art, opening a shop, doing pieces for houses and gardens. But his repertoire was politically limited. "Many pieces they don't like," he said. "One of the pieces I did, it was about life in Iraq, so they said no. This one you can't show this in any gallery or you can't give it because this one talk about something that is not happening. We are a happy life and golden times. It was a sculpture—one woman with her little baby, and she is poor, her baby is dead between her hands. So they said no."

Meanwhile, his father's farms, livestock, and houses were confiscated, and their return was promised if only he would stand up for Saddam. He would not. One day in 1998, his father parked his car, opened the door, stepped into the street, and was run down and killed by a vehicle that had been following him—no accident, the family concluded.

An older brother had been murdered earlier, a younger brother had fled to Seattle, and his mother, trying to save him, told Habeeb to leave while he could. Well-placed bribes got him a passport and clearance at the border into Syria, where his story was verified by the United Nations High Commissioner for Refugees and by American officials who granted him refugee status. He flew from Damascus to Amsterdam to Los Angeles and now wanted to see his new country.

So, on April 1, 2003, not long after the United States invaded Iraq to overthrow the regime Habeeb had fled, he aroused suspicion by glancing away from the uniformed man on the platform in Havre, Montana.

Sir? What is your name? Where are you from? Are you legal here? Do you have any documents to prove you're legal? This was Habeeb's muddy recollection of the questions, coming to him in a language he barely understood at the time. He showed a Washington state ID (issued in lieu of a driver's license), a Social Security card, and an I-94 immigration document testifying to his refugee status.

Habeeb could have kept walking, refused to answer questions, and boarded the train. But he didn't know that, and certainly didn't feel free to do so, especially after the agent was joined by two others, one in uniform, the other in plainclothes. "They scared me," he said. And if he had ignored them? "They shoot me."

If you don't feel free to leave, you can make a case that you have been "stopped" in legal parlance, and a stop requires some level of suspicion beyond your ethnicity or the direction of your glance.

Immigration agents can legally chat with people without "stopping" them, courts have held, but a stop, the Supreme Court has ruled, cannot rely solely on race or ethnicity to be "reasonable" under the Fourth Amendment; those are factors that can be considered only if other elements lead to the belief that someone is in the country without authorization. The Court unanimously threw out a stop by the border patrol near Mexico when the only ground for suspicion was the agents' impression that the vehicle's occupants looked Mexican.[61] Therefore, the encounter at the Montana station was not only unpleasant but probably illegal.

"He asked if I had gone to registration," Habeeb recalled. "I did not understand. 'Can you explain that to me?' He said you have to go to registration every three months to be fingerprinted and be photographed. I said I didn't know about that. He said we publicized it on TV, in newspapers. I said even on TV I didn't understand." He remembered the plainclothes agent then saying, "Take him."

He was handcuffed, agents retrieved his luggage from the train, and he was put into an office with microphones, cameras, and an intimidating picture of a bearded, blindfolded man tied to a chair. "Next to me, a cage too small to sit up or stand or lie. Nobody in there." Habeeb took it as a threat. "They asked me if I have guns or bombing. I said no. I'm an artist. I have colors and brushes and art books. They asked me to open my bags. I opened."

Then they asked whether he knew anyone who spoke against the U.S. government, whether he had Saudi or Pakistani friends. "This is McCarthyism," said his lawyer, Jesse Wing. "They asked him who he was associated with. If you are associated with somebody who gets arrested for an immigration violation, you are in somebody's little black book."

Habeeb found the lockup in the local Montana jail "very scary," full of white men with long hair and tattoos who called him "Saddam Habeeb." In a complicated form he couldn't read, he was given written notice of his right to a lawyer but was not offered the proverbial phone call to contact one; this was not a criminal matter, although he was jailed like a criminal, with criminals.

After several days, Habeeb was flown back to Seattle and placed in an immigration detention center whose inmates turned out to know the law better than either the border agents, the government's attorney on his case, or even an immigration judge. From his cell mates he learned that refugees were not covered by "special registration," so the entire premise for his arrest was wrong: he wasn't required to register.

He told this to his pro bono lawyer when he got to court, and to the judge, who asked the government attorney whether it was true. The judge wasn't sure, and neither was the government attorney. They adjourned to do a little research, which didn't prove difficult. The government's lawyer finally "dismissed the case after one of my partners called and said that refugees were not required to register," said Wing. "The attorney said, 'Send me what you have.' My partner said, 'Why don't you look at your Web site?' My partner faxed him a printout of the Web site." Under "Exceptions," it plainly listed among those excluded from the registration requirements "refugees, individuals who have been granted asylum, and individuals who have applied for asylum" before publication of the new rules.

After eight days in jail, Habeeb was released, but his exoneration did not restore his relations with fellow Muslims. "I used to have many Iraqi friends here in Seattle," he said, "and when they heard about my case and the border patrol stopped me and the FBI interrogated me and arrest me, nobody say '*salam aleikum*' again."

The job he'd been promised in an Islamic cultural center in D.C., doing art for a newspaper and Web sites, evaporated. A man who had offered him a place to live there reneged, begging him not to mention his name to anyone. When Habeeb decided to appeal for his job in person in D.C., he took the same train again, staying aboard this time as the same agents came through the car and didn't mess with him. That small victory was more than he got when he approached his erstwhile employers in the nation's capital. "They said to me, 'We think you have a problem with the government.'"

Worse, the imprisonment, as relatively brief as it was, reignited the trauma from his years in Iraq. He now kept a phone by his bed, for "every night when I sleep I feel someone come and kill me." When he told me this in his lawyer's office, Jesse Wing prompted him to talk about the Statue of Liberty.

Habeeb lapsed into silence, breathing hard, looking down at the table to hide the tears welling up in his eyes. He stayed that way for a very long time, until I came to his rescue by saying that I'd call him to follow up. No, he replied, he wanted to speak now. So he gathered his words.

"When you see the Statue of Liberty and when you believe this is a free country and you come to this country and do whatever you like and especially if you're an artist or a writer, and when you come here and find this is a big joke, you be in deep frustration." That was the best he could do in his limited English, but "frustration" hardly seemed adequate.

He returned to work loading furniture on trucks in a Seattle warehouse. He did not practice his art. He lived alone. With the help of Wing and the American Civil Liberties Union, he also sued the border patrol agents for violating his Fourth Amendment right to be free from unreasonable seizure, and his Fifth Amendment right to due process.[62] His lawsuit was summarily dismissed by federal judge Sam E. Haddon, who used to be an immigration patrol inspector and found that no "seizure" had occurred of Habeeb during the platform questioning, in that he was free to leave. But Habeeb's case was regarded as so strong that the Justice Department saw only risk in defending it in the courts.

A three-part settlement was offered, and Habeeb accepted: damages of $250,000, a decision by Judge Haddon vacating his ruling as erroneous, and a letter of apology from the Justice Department. The last sentence of the letter from Justice to Habeeb might be a fitting epitaph for this era once it ends, once the book can be closed on the latest time in its history that the country has seriously strayed from the path of liberty: "The United States of America regrets the mistake."[63]

CHAPTER SIX

Silence and Its Opposite

Every idea is an incitement.

—Oliver Wendell Holmes

MIGHTIER THAN THE SWORD

FIVE DAYS AFTER September 11, amid the country's tense anxiety, seven young men in Northern Virginia gathered for dinner to talk about their fears of vigilantism against Muslims and to hear from Ali al-Timimi, a cancer researcher who had earned a reputation as an erudite lecturer on Islam. His words that evening were later judged to have crossed an invisible line that had been drawn and redrawn over many decades—the ambiguous boundary between the exercise of liberty and the commission of a crime.

The First Amendment does not say that Congress (now taken to mean all levels of government) is allowed to make *some* laws abridging speech, the press, religion, and the right to assemble. It says, "Congress shall make *no* law," unqualified language that may tempt absolutists to ask judges and legislators, "What is it about 'no' that you don't understand?"

Yet the framers were not categorical, and courts and legislatures have never treated any part of the Bill of Rights as absolute. Instead, every provision has been woven into a matrix of exceptions, compromises, escape clauses, waivers, and fuzzy limits that enlarge or reduce the umbrella of protection. The shelter of the First Amendment has been broadened considerably since ratification, especially in the last half of the twentieth century, but it does not shield every statement, symbol, or expressive act. Outside its preserve lies speech whose consequences are deemed so severe that government is granted the authority to punish. Seldom rising above the fleeting moments of history, judges draw those boundaries at what they perceive as the balancing points of liberty against order, individual interests against community welfare, overarching constitutional principle against the particulars of a given circumstance.

Timimi may have thought he was free to say anything. Born in the United States a year after his parents emigrated from Iraq, he attended an elite private school in Washington, D.C., before moving at age fifteen with his family to Saudi Arabia, where he spent five years in Islamic study. Then he returned to college in the United States. "Many of my best qualities are simply because I am an American," he told *The Washington Post*. One of those qualities may have been a belief that he was entitled to state his opinions, even those "counter to the mainstream of American society," as he described them.[1]

When he spoke to the young Muslims that evening, Timimi made three points in his hour-long talk, according to Milton Viorst, a writer whose son had been Timimi's school chum years before. First, he held "that the 9/11 attacks augured the imminence of the end of days. Muslims, he said, had a duty to repent their sins." Second, he suggested that "they and their families might best leave America, following the precedent of the Prophet Muhammad," who in A.D. 622 fled to Medina from persecution in Mecca. "As his third point, Ali reviewed—rashly, as it turned out—the Islamic doctrine of jihad as holy war, and pointed out that his listeners could serve the faith as mujahideen in Kashmir, Chechnya, or Afghanistan."[2]

The government would make much of the fact that Timimi had asked that the phones in the house be unplugged, the blinds pulled down, and the discussion kept secret.

Speech is our essential liberty, yet Americans' freedom to speak expands and contracts with the nation's sense of security. In times of threat, the First Amendment's shield narrows. In periods of tranquillity and comfort, it broadens as government and citizens tolerate widening dissent. That has been the general pattern of history.

The American experience since the attacks of September 11, 2001, has seen a mixture of crosscurrents. Unpopular opinion has been stifled sporadically by law enforcement agencies and protected inconsistently by the courts. Nevertheless, vitriolic propaganda has exploded on shout shows and the Internet, and voters have felt free to lambaste politicians at town meetings. Competing impulses of liberty and conformity have coursed through the landscape.

In wars past, the parameters of acceptable debate have been restricted by both law and culture. The outside enemy has been seen taking up residence within, provoking an edgy vigilance aimed at "others" within the country, meaning foreigners and minorities. They have been the ones most tightly bound by restraints on speech, which have gradually ensnared the larger citizenry.

The "war on terrorism" has continued in this unworthy tradition, to a degree. Some Muslims in the United States, placed in the government's crosshairs because of their statements, have ended up in prison. Several U.S. citizens overseas have been killed in drone strikes, most notably Anwar al-Awlaki, an al-Qaeda propagandist whose online appeals in colloquial English were so influential that President Obama ordered his assassination in Yemen without any judicial proceeding. Yet perhaps because this has not been quite the "war" that President Bush called it after 9/11, the violations of free speech have been less egregious than before, as if the country were on a learning curve. During the last century, as courts have blocked one or another form of suppression, authorities have adapted with different methods, usually less overt and less coordinated. As a result, World War II was not quite as tough on the First Amendment as World War I, the Vietnam War was not as severe as World War II, and the impediments placed on dissent following September 11 have not silenced the raucous debate.

After his evening discussion, Timimi was carried along by the flow of a tortuous legal history. The Supreme Court had begun sketching the modern contours of the First Amendment with ad hoc inadvertence, a case-by-case assessment of how society could be kept both free and orderly. Only sporadically did one or another justice lift his gaze above the parochial political fears of the day to the long, lofty views of sweeping liberty. Grand statements of momentous constitutional principles, first buried in dissents, gradually migrated into majority opinions, but not before citizens had been fined and imprisoned for unorthodox ideas and associations.

That judicial record tells more about the society than about the Constitution. Especially in the realm of speech, the law is a product of the political mood. Strip away the facade of legal reasoning in the line of early First Amendment cases, peel apart the neat attempts at precision of thought and language, and what often remains is a rationalization of a statute designed to silence the unpopular and the outrageous.

It is a tribute to America's capacity for self-correction that oppressive acts look ugly in the cold light of history. From the distance of time, the anxieties behind censorship seem as trivial as a storm at sea appears from a high jetliner. Few justices gain such perspective, however; most stand on the pitching deck, braced against the wind and spray. We confirm them for life to insulate them from the gale, and instead they often hunker down, crouching into the status quo, clinging to a safe narrowness that pinches freedom. The exception is called a "landmark," not only because it marks a turning point, but because it is so rarely seen.

"It was abolitionists, in the 1830s, who first argued that Southern states shouldn't be able to ban antislavery tracts because of the remote possibility they might provoke an insurrection; the Supreme Court took another

130 years to enshrine the underlying principle into law," writes Jeffrey Rosen. Similarly, he notes, the Court protected the speech of communists and Ku Klux Klan members "only when they were no longer perceived as a serious threat by national majorities."[3]

So the right of free speech is somewhat time-bound, reliant on the moment. Defendants such as Timimi, prosecuted for what they say, might benefit if their trials weren't so speedy. Decades later, after passions cool, it can seem ludicrous that their words were once deemed "a clear and present danger."

That famous dictum was coined by Oliver Wendell Holmes in his 1919 opinion for a unanimous Court upholding the conviction of Charles Schenck, general secretary of the Socialist Party, which had mailed leaflets calling the draft a despotic method by the rich to force the poor to fight World War I on behalf of Wall Street. The flyers advocated resistance by citizens and soldiers, urged a peaceful petition to repeal conscription, and pleaded with Americans to "assert your rights" and "not submit to intimidation." Schenck was sentenced to prison under the 1917 Espionage Act, which made it a crime to obstruct military recruitment during war.[4]

U.S. participation in the war was hotly controversial, and in Schenck's leaflets Holmes and his colleagues found "a clear and present danger" to the country's ability to raise an army. He drew the limits of the First Amendment this way:

> The most stringent protection of free speech would not protect a man in falsely shouting fire in a theatre and causing a panic. It does not even protect a man from an injunction against uttering words that may have all the effect of force. The question in every case is whether the words used are used in such circumstances and are of such a nature as to create a clear and present danger that they will bring about the substantive evils that Congress has a right to prevent. It is a question of proximity and degree. When a nation is at war many things that might be said in time of peace are such a hindrance to its effort that their utterance will not be endured so long as men fight and that no Court could regard them as protected by any constitutional right.[5]

The definitions were left vague. You could not *falsely* shout "Fire!" so presumably you could if it was true. But if your words created danger, how clear and how present did it have to be to constitute a crime? Holmes and his colleagues tinkered with the question in other opinions, even during the same session of the Court. In several subsequent cases upholding Espionage Act convictions, Holmes loosened the standard. Instead of requiring that speech present "a clear and present danger" before being suppressed, he ruled that it could be silenced if it merely "had a natural tendency to produce the forbidden consequences."[6]

Very soon, also in 1919, Holmes began to turn the danger test around, using it to oppose convictions. Usually, he found himself in the minority as he wrote in dissent that the words being prosecuted posed no clear and present danger. In *Abrams v. United States,* he argued that the danger had to be "immediate," and he voted to overturn the conviction of five people who had circulated leaflets urging a general strike to protest American involvement against the Bolsheviks in the Russian civil war.[7] The danger must be "imminent," Justice Louis Brandeis wrote several years later.[8]

By 1925, Holmes's fear of flagrant speech had abated, and he derided the notion that the United States stood precariously on the brink of revolution. When a majority of his colleagues fumed that "a single revolutionary spark may kindle a fire that . . . may burst into a sweeping and destructive conflagration," Holmes refused to sign on. The Court was upholding the conviction of Benjamin Gitlow, a young New York legislator and socialist who drew a five- to ten-year sentence for a pamphlet asserting the inevitability of proletarian revolution.

Holmes agreed with the majority in one respect: *Gitlow v. New York* expanded rights significantly by extending the First Amendment to the states, thereby opening the door to Supreme Court review of state laws restricting freedom of speech and the press.[9] But he saw no "clear and present danger" in Gitlow's pamphlet. "It is said that this manifesto was more than a theory, that it was an incitement. Every idea is an incitement," he thundered. "Eloquence may set fire to reason. . . . If in the long run the beliefs expressed in proletarian dictatorship are destined to be accepted by the dominant forces of the community, the only meaning of free speech is that they should be given their chance and have their way." For the sake of liberty, Holmes was willing to take risks his colleagues were not.

Nevertheless, like a weapon whose inventor could not control its use, the clear-and-present-danger test was expanded well beyond the national security purpose Holmes envisioned. One celebrated victim, a Jehovah's Witness named Walter Chaplinsky, was caught in the constitutional question as he distributed leaflets in 1942 denouncing organized religion. A crowd that gathered in Rochester, New Hampshire, grew agitated and alarmed the police, who led him away. Chaplinsky asked the city marshal to arrest those responsible for the disturbance, but the marshal replied that Chaplinsky should just come along. Angered, the leafleteer allegedly told the officer, "You are a God damned racketeer" and "a damned Fascist, and the whole government of Rochester are Fascists or agents of Fascists." (Chaplinsky admitted to saying all the words except "God.")

The Supreme Court unanimously upheld the broad state law under which Chaplinsky was convicted; it prohibited "any offensive, derisive or annoying word to any other person who is lawfully in any street or other public place." The justices found that "the appellations 'damned racketeer' and 'damned Fascist' are epithets likely to provoke the average person to retaliation, and thereby cause a breach of the peace." No public interest permitted "the lewd and obscene, the profane, the libelous, and the insulting or 'fighting' words—those which by their very utterance inflict injury or tend to incite an immediate breach of the peace."[10]

Since then, however, the Court has not affirmed a conviction for using "fighting words" against a public official and in a 1992 case effectively erased the fighting-words doctrine.[11] You may now insult police officers, if you're so inclined, as long as you don't harass them or interfere with their work.

More relevant for Timimi was the 1951 case of a dozen Communists, including the party's general secretary, Eugene Dennis, who had been prosecuted despite serious reservations among government lawyers. Although the Communist Party was tiny and marginalized, it loomed excessively large amid the peculiar sense of fragility that afflicted the United States following World War II. Justice Robert H. Jackson imagined its members "secreted in strategic posts in transportation, communications, industry, government, and especially in labor unions," and he warned, "Through these placements in positions of power it seeks a leverage over society that will make up in power of coercion what it lacks in power of persuasion." The Communists' "strategy of stealth" may preclude the need for force or violence, he said, "because infiltration and deception may be enough."[12]

As evidence of the Communists' threatening plans, the government used Lenin's exhortations to Russian workers more than three decades before; Dennis and his colleagues countered that the "classics" were not applicable in America, that their party's constitution eschewed violence, that the party relied on education—not force—to persuade Americans of socialism's virtues. The jury didn't buy it and convicted them. They were sentenced to five years.

They appealed and lost in the Supreme Court, which upheld the Smith Act of 1940, under which they had been convicted.[13] Citing the test of "a clear and present danger," Chief Justice Frederick Vinson declared, "Obviously, the words cannot mean that before the Government may act, it must wait until the putsch is about to be executed, the plans have been laid, and the signal is awaited." Echoes of this reasoning were heard after 9/11 in the government's accusations that groups of young Muslims lay dormant in "sleeper cells" waiting for instructions.

The *Dennis* indictments suggested how distant the Communists' abstract words stood from an actual threat. "The defendants were charged, not with attempting to overthrow the government," observes the constitutional scholar Geoffrey R. Stone, "not with conspiring to overthrow the government, not with advocating the overthrow of government, but with *conspiring to advocate* the overthrow of government. How does one make sense of 'clear and present danger' when the 'danger' is so far removed from the defendants' acts?"[14] Forty-five years later, Timimi was indicted, similarly, for the indirect crime of "inducing others to conspire" to support terrorism.

SIMPLY OUT OF FEAR

A key difference between Timimi and the Communists lay in the fact that something actually happened after Timimi's talk at dinner. Later that September evening, a few of the men bought a phone card and placed a call to Pakistan and over the next few days applied for visas—although at least one of them already had a plane ticket before hearing Timimi speak. They had been playing paintball in the suburbs of the nation's capital not merely to let off steam in a combat sport, federal authorities decided, but to hone their skills for the real thing. By September 22, four were on their way to training camps of Pakistan's Lashkar-e-Taiba (LET; Army of the Pious), the Islamic movement organized two decades before to fight on the pro-American side against the Soviets in Afghanistan. LET was not yet on the terrorist list, but like the American-backed mujahideen who transformed themselves into Afghanistan's Taliban, it had spun far beyond American influence, spearheading attacks on the Indian presence in disputed Kashmir. (Its operatives were to attack hotels, a train station, and a Jewish center in Mumbai in 2008.)

The four men first went to lounge on the beach for a long while before going to the camps, where they received weapons training, and returned to the United States after a few weeks. A year and a half later, following what defense attorneys speculated was illegal, warrantless surveillance by the secret National Security Agency, they and seven others were charged with an assortment of conspiracies to fight against India in Kashmir and Russia in Chechnya, possessing firearms in connection with a crime, and providing material support to LET following its designation as a terrorist organization in December 2001. Six pleaded guilty and five contested the charges, with some opting for bench trials rather than depending on jurors from the heavily military neighborhoods near the Pentagon. Judge Leonie M. Brinkema acquitted two, convicted three, and handed out substantial sentences ranging from three years to life.

Timimi had not gone to the camps or anywhere else; he had merely spoken, but he was charged the following year, and three who testified against him were rewarded with release, at the request of the prosecutor, after just three years of their ten- and eleven-year sentences.[15] One had been Timimi's host at the dinner, Yong Ki Kwon, a Korean convert to Islam. Another, Muhammed Aatique, told the jury in Timimi's 2005 trial, "He encouraged us to participate in the coming jihad. . . . He said the battle in Afghanistan was imminent and that the Americans were going to attack." Aatique quoted Timimi as calling the victims of 9/11 "combatants, not civilians," since their taxes funded the war against Islam. Following Timimi's talk, he said, "me and everyone else at that meeting was excited and charged up."[16] A year after his testimony, Aatique was freed from federal prison, seven years early.

The premature releases drew a sardonic comment from Timimi's lawyer, Edward B. MacMahon Jr. "I thought we were about protecting the American people," he said, "and here the U.S. Attorney is releasing the actual terrorists. Have they been rehabilitated?"

The jury took seven days to convict Timimi. Judge Brinkema sentenced him to life plus seventy years for inducing the young men to conspire to levy war against the United States and for inducing them to conspire to use firearms and explosives in criminal acts.

The jurors evidently accepted the government's strategy: project him onto a large screen, magnify him into the "spiritual leader" of young jihadis, portray him (in the prosecutor's words) as a "rock star" held "in awe" by young men who would do "their best to do what he told them to do," although in fact he hardly knew them.[17] The narrative confirmed the story line that many Americans were braced to hear after 9/11: a kind of Voldemort, preaching invisibly from the mysterious depths of a hostile Islam, intoxicating youth with poisonous ideas—and right in our own backyard, embedded in suburban Virginia. This is how terrorists sow terror.

The man uttered offensive words, no question. Against him, the government used even those unrelated to the case, devoting nearly two of the indictment's sixteen pages to his long statement celebrating the crash of the space shuttle *Columbia* in 2003. It was hardly a public call to his "followers," as pictured in the indictment; his lawyer, MacMahon, countered that it had been made in an intercepted phone call to a friend in Saudi Arabia, and "none of them had ever heard it until an FBI agent played it for them."

When he learned of the *Columbia*'s demise, Timimi told his friend, "My heart felt certain good omens," the indictment alleged. The name of the shuttle, derived from Columbus, was "a strong signal that Western supremacy (especially that of America) that began five hundred years ago is coming to a quick end, God Willing." Then, with the presence of an Israeli astronaut in the crew, Israel's "hope and ambitions were burnt with the crash and burning of the shuttle." And with the news that the crash had occurred near Palestine, Texas, "I said to myself, 'God is Great.' This way, God Willing, America will fall and disappear."[18]

It is not hard to find such rants among religious lunatics of various stripes, but they don't usually get life in prison. "Some of it, frankly, rises to the level of hate speech," MacMahon acknowledged to the jurors, then relied on them in vain to uphold Timimi's "First Amendment right to have these opinions. You don't have to agree with him to realize he has a right to free speech."[19]

Furthermore, MacMahon tried repeatedly to have Timimi's statements to the paintball crew ruled as protected speech, given that the remarks did not meet the test of inciting imminent crime. Judge Brinkema decided against him before the trial by allowing Timimi's words into evidence. She did instruct the jurors that they could acquit if they found no imminence. After conviction, MacMahon raised the First Amendment issue again, requesting the judge to conduct a constitutional analysis of the statements in question, which she declined to do.

That left free speech impaired. A trial is not a precedent, but it can be a point of reference, and here the line between protected and unprotected speech had been moved to a place remote from a violent act that had not even occurred. "The case really sticks in my craw," said MacMahon, "because it's not just what he said at the dinner party. It's the use of his religious speeches," which were excerpted selectively and introduced by the government into evidence. As such, MacMahon believed, Timimi was condemned for his religion—for a distorted version of his religion. The prosecutor told the jury that Islam approved of lying.

"The way our law is developing in the United States right now, there's two sets of rules," said MacMahon. "There are terror defendants and regular defendants. If it was a business case and I said Bernie Madoff [of the

Ponzi scheme] is a Jew so he stole all the money, you'd laugh at me. But if you said Ali al-Timimi is a Muslim so he's at war with the United States, that's taken seriously."

With no court willing to do a searching review of the First Amendment issues in the case, there could be no broader correction to the government's power to prosecute for speech. That may still come if more such indictments are brought and are scrutinized with the same standards used to end the criminalization of Communists' utterances during the Cold War.

High-level misgivings were evident years before prosecutions of Communists were closed down. Even as the Supreme Court upheld Eugene Dennis's conviction in 1951, Justice Felix Frankfurter, while concurring with the majority, worried that ideas would be suppressed when they were coupled with calls for illegality; it would be hard to disentangle them—precisely the problem in Timimi's case more than a half century later. Justice William O. Douglas took the argument further in a passionate dissent in *Dennis*. The open market of belief and expression had rendered communism in America "crippled as a political force," he observed. "Free speech has destroyed it." The movement's adherents "are miserable merchants of unwanted ideas; their wares remain unsold."[20] It can only be hoped that Islam's violent aberration will suffer the same.

But terrorists are real, and many are inspired by charismatic preachers. Actual Communist agents were in government, too, as files in Moscow revealed following the collapse of the Soviet Union. Most of the real spies and subversives were missed by sweeps following *Dennis,* however, because authorities concentrated on open speech rather than criminal behavior. In the six years after the Court delivered its opinion, while espionage flourished secretly, the FBI arrested the party's overt leaders throughout the country, prosecuting 145 Communists for violating the Smith Act by teaching or attending classes on the writings of Lenin and Stalin, who had advocated violent proletarian revolution. There was no evidence that the defendants had any such plans.[21]

The net of arrests caught Oleta Yates, a Communist Party leader whose case illustrated how the vicissitudes of fear determine the scope of free speech. She was sentenced to five years along with fellow party members in California for espousing Marxism-Leninism. But by the time her appeal found its way to the Supreme Court, the climate in the country had changed, and so had the Court's composition. Four new justices had been seated, including Chief Justice Earl Warren. Stalin was dead and had been denounced by his successor, Nikita Khrushchev, leading Russia to a slight internal thaw. The Communist-hunter Senator Joseph McCarthy had been censured by the Senate. The tense anxiety over Communist infiltration had eased.

Writing in 1957 for a majority of six, Justice John Marshall Harlan deftly narrowed the interpretation of the Smith Act without reaching an opinion on its constitutionality. The law did not bar the "advocacy and teaching of forcible overthrow as an abstract principle, divorced from any effort to instigate action to that end," even if such advocacy "is engaged in with evil intent," he wrote. "The statute was aimed at the advocacy and teaching of concrete action for the forcible overthrow of the Government, and not of principles divorced from action." The Court overturned five of the convictions and sent the other nine back for retrial.[22] The government dropped the charges against those nine and other party leaders across the country.

"*Yates* sounded the death knell for the Smith Act as a weapon in the campaign against American Communists," Stone notes. "Thereafter, the Court eviscerated virtually all of the anti-Communist loyalty programs that had been instituted in the 1940s and 1950s. In a series of decisions, it held unconstitutional a law denying Communists passports, invalidated denaturalization orders based on membership in the Communist Party, held unconstitutional a statute denying Communists property tax exemptions, and set aside a federal law making it difficult for individuals to receive foreign 'Communist propaganda.'"[23]

In 1969, the Supreme Court appeared to close the door firmly on government's power "to invade that sanctuary of belief and conscience," in Justice Douglas's words, by extending the shelter of the First Amendment to a leader of the Ku Klux Klan, Charles Brandenburg. He had gathered Klansmen for an organizing rally on a farm near Cincinnati, and the Court overturned the Ohio law leading to his conviction and ten-year sentence. In a concurring opinion, Douglas sketched the damage done to the rights of speech and association by the Court's varied applications of Holmes's ambiguous standard over the previous fifty years.

"Out of the 'clear and present danger' test came other offspring," Douglas wrote. One was the tool of forcing a citizen under oath to confirm or deny his membership in the Communist Party, to expose him either to prosecution for belonging or to blacklisting for invoking his Fifth Amendment right not to incriminate himself by answering. "And so the investigator roams at will through all of the beliefs of the witness, ransacking his conscience and his innermost thoughts." A criminal act can be prosecuted, Douglas continued, but "all matters of belief are beyond the reach of subpoenas or the probings of investigators."[24]

Not all, not today. Today, Timimi is regarded as such a grave national security threat that he is held under the Bureau of Prisons' Special Administrative Measures, denied the right to speak publicly or to contact other inmates. He is allowed out of his cell for one hour a day.

So, in his final exercise of his right to speak freely before disappearing into prison, Timimi projected himself onto a large screen, too, telling the court that he claimed innocence not "because my Muslim belief recognizes sharia law rather than secular law, as somebody might argue. It is merely because I am innocent." To believe that "an individual who has never owned or used a gun, never traveled to a military camp, never set foot in a country in which a war was taking place, never raised money for any violent organization, would be—*could* be—the author of so much harm" meant that a conviction came "simply out of fear," he declared.

"In the end, Your Honor, I too, like Socrates, am accused and found guilty of nothing more than corrupting the youth and practicing a different religion than that of the majority. Socrates was mercifully given a cup of hemlock. I was handed a life sentence."[25]

SYMBOLIC SPEECH

Very few Americans can identify with Timimi—he is an outlier on the spectrum of opinion, a Muslim of Arab background whose religious politics make him a minority within a minority. Hardly anyone can imagine thinking or saying what he did, and therefore we can't imagine ourselves being arrested for our speech.

The assumption seems reasonable until more thought is given. Since constitutional rights apply to everyone, so do their violations. Too many mainstream Americans who couldn't imagine their speech being suppressed have learned that once a tool of censorship is sharpened, it can be turned in any direction, including back on them. First Amendment guarantees, said Justice Hugo Black, "must be accorded to ideas we hate or sooner or later they will be denied to the ideas we cherish."

The concept had not taken root in the Colorado town of Alamosa when John Fleming relied on that bible of American values, the *Boy Scout Handbook,* instructing that the American flag may be hung upside down as a sign of distress. He did just that in the front window of his book and music store, the Roost, to signify the distress he saw his country causing by invading Iraq.[26]

Fleming stood on firm constitutional ground, but as he quickly discovered, it's ground that has to be constantly reinforced against the floods of popular outrage. The right to use a flag as a symbol of speech protected by the First Amendment has been developed in a line of cases reaching back to *Stromberg v. California* in 1931, when the Supreme Court courageously invalidated one clause of a California law banning the red banner as an "emblem of opposition to organized government." In that instance, it was the red flag of the international workers' movement, raised every morning over a Communist youth camp while the children stood and pledged allegiance to "one aim throughout our lives, freedom for the working class." A camp supervisor, a nineteen-year-old woman, was arrested, tried, and convicted. The Court found the law so vague that it could prohibit any criticism of government, including by peaceful means.[27]

Tested by war, religion, and other contentious issues, a divided Court then expanded the First Amendment's shield in using the American flag for dissenting views. In 1969, a slim majority ruled that contemptuous words about the flag were not punishable (in this case, "We don't need no damn flag"). "It is firmly settled that under our Constitution the public expression of ideas may not be prohibited merely because the ideas are themselves offensive to some of their hearers," the Court declared.[28] In two 1974 cases growing out of Vietnam War protests, the justices ruled it permissible to tape a peace sign to a flag,[29] and to deride the flag by wearing it on the seat of your pants.[30]

Those opinions laid the groundwork for the landmark ruling on flag burning, *Texas v. Johnson*. The case emerged during the 1984 Republican convention in Dallas, when Gregory Johnson was handed an American flag taken from a flagpole by a fellow protester in a march against government and corporate policies under the Reagan administration. In front of city hall, he poured kerosene on the flag and set it ablaze. While it burned, demonstrators chanted, "America, the red, white, and blue, we spit on you." Johnson was arrested for violating a Texas law prohibiting the "desecration of a venerated object," which explicitly included state and national flags. He declared at his trial: "The American flag was burned as Ronald Reagan was being renominated as President. And a more powerful statement of symbolic speech, whether you agree with it or not, couldn't have been made at that time." He was convicted and sentenced to a year in prison and a $2,000 fine.

When his appeal reached the Supreme Court, Chief Justice Rehnquist was able to gather three other justices to his minority view that the law was constitutional. A burning flag was equivalent to fighting words that could provoke violent reactions, he wrote, and the curb on free speech was insignificant: "The Texas statute deprived Johnson of only one rather inarticulate symbolic form of protest—a form of protest that was profoundly offensive to many—and left him with a full panoply of other symbols and every conceivable form of verbal expression to express his deep disapproval of national policy." Rehnquist supported his legal argument with a mawkish rehearsal of the flag's history in battle, quoting at length from "Barbara Frietchie," John Greenleaf Whittier's melodramatic poem:

> "Halt!"—the dust-brown ranks stood fast.
> "Fire!"—out blazed the rifle-blast.
>
> It shivered the window, pane and sash;
> It rent the banner with seam and gash.
>
> Quick, as it fell, from the broken staff
> Dame Barbara snatched the silken scarf.
>
> She leaned far out on the window-sill,
> And shook it forth with a royal will.
>
> "Shoot if you must, this old gray head,
> But spare your country's flag," she said.

Five justices, however, recognized flag burning in this circumstance as "expressive conduct" intended to communicate ideas, similar to picketing, protest marches, and sit-ins at segregated lunch counters. "The government generally has a freer hand in restricting expressive conduct than it has in restricting the written or spoken word," the majority acknowledged, but the governmental interest in doing so must be compelling and not aimed at suppressing speech. So protesters who block traffic can be arrested for blocking traffic, not protesting. A flag burner could be arrested for violating a fire code but not for expressing antipathy toward the United States.[31]

Texas had given two reasons for prohibiting the act: to prevent disorders and to preserve the flag as a symbol of nationhood and national unity. On the first point, Justice William J. Brennan Jr. observed in writing for the majority, "no disturbance of the peace actually occurred or threatened to occur because of Johnson's burning of the flag." The act wasn't directed at anyone as a personal insult, so couldn't be construed as "fighting words."

The second goal, nationhood and unity, "is related to the suppression of expression," the Court found. Had Johnson disposed of a torn or dirty flag by burning it ceremonially, the method approved by federal law, he would not have been arrested, Brennan noted. If flag burning in protest were out-lawed, then the symbolic act would be legal when it meant one thing and not another, producing an unconstitutional regulation of content: silencing a particular message.

"If there is a bedrock principle underlying the First Amendment, it is that the government may not prohibit the expression of an idea simply because society finds the idea itself offensive or disagreeable," Brennan declared. "We have not recognized an exception to this principle even where our flag has been involved."

And what of the public's reaction to such an act? "We can imagine no more appropriate response to burning a flag than waving one's own, no better way to counter a flag burner's message than by saluting the flag that burns, no surer means of preserving the dignity even of the flag that burned than by—as one witness here did—according its remains a respect-ful burial. We do not consecrate the flag by punishing its desecration, for in doing so we dilute the freedom that this cherished emblem represents."

Justice Anthony Kennedy wrote in concurrence: "It is poignant but fun-damental that the flag protects those who hold it in contempt."[32]

It is hard to imagine a purer form of symbolic expression than inverting the American flag as John Fleming did, covering it with messages, tram-pling it underfoot, or even setting it ablaze. No libel is committed, nobody is incited to violence, no threat is issued, no falsely induced panic is pro-voked. No one else's property is damaged or destroyed if the flag belongs to you.

The worst accusation that can be leveled is hypocrisy: that you are using the freedom the flag represents to damage or destroy the very symbol of that freedom—a cherished symbol, to be sure, but merely an arrangement of shapes and colors. The rare protesters who actually burn flags, as opposed to just hanging them upside down, may be guilty of nothing more than committing paradox. A more fitting gesture for opponents of the Viet-nam War was suggested in 1969 by Norman Thomas, the perennial Social-ist candidate for president: "If they want an appropriate symbol they should be washing the flag, not burning it."[33]

The "bedrock principle" so visible to the Court's slender majority keeps getting covered by the debris of cheap patriotism. Within half an hour after John Fleming hung his inverted flag in his bookstore, half a dozen outraged citizens called the police chief, who paid Fleming a visit and told him he was breaking an old state law making it a crime to "mutilate, deface, defile, trample upon, burn, cut or tear any flag in public," none of which he had done. Part of the statute had been ruled unconstitutional thirty years before, but Fleming didn't want to be arrested, so he removed his flag and then called the American Civil Liberties Union, which threatened a suit and got the town to retreat. Fleming, who was nicknamed "Coyote," became the target of a threat himself as someone dumped the bloody carcass of a coyote on his doorstep, after cutting off the ears to get the bounty.[34]

Under the Supreme Court's current interpretation of the First Amendment, you may burn a flag but usually not a cross, and never a draft card. "Speech," in the Court's view, also means speech plus conduct, as in marches and sit-ins. But the Court has drawn lines between expression that is protected by the First Amendment and expression that is not. Unprotected speech may be suppressed if the government's interest is "compelling, substantive, subordinating, paramount, cogent, or strong," as Chief Justice Earl Warren wrote in a draft-card case, *United States v. O'Brien*.[35]

On March 31, 1966, less than a year after American ground troops were sent to Vietnam, four protesters, including David Paul O'Brien, went to the steps of the South Boston Courthouse and demonstrated their anti-war positions by burning the Selective Service registration certificates that all males eighteen and over were required to carry. After several onlookers began attacking the protesters, O'Brien was taken to safety inside the courthouse by FBI agents, who then arrested him. He was convicted, and he challenged the law as a violation of his right to free speech.

Federal law had imposed up to five years in prison for anyone "who forges, alters, or changes" a draft card, a reasonable prohibition that had nothing to do with political expression. Then, to quell the card's use in protests, Congress in 1965 added two offenses: "knowingly destroys" and "knowingly mutilates."[36] Now the statute was a different animal, aimed at countering "the defiant destruction and mutilation of draft cards by dissident persons who disapprove of national policy," according to the Senate report, which predicted excessively: "If allowed to continue unchecked this contumacious conduct represents a potential threat to the exercise of the power to raise and support armies."[37] (It was the same argument used to justify arrests of draft opponents during World War I, under the 1917 Espionage Act.)

Revising the draft-card law, Congress had openly stated its goal of silencing "dissident persons," yet in rejecting O'Brien's appeal, the Supreme Court looked the other way and focused on the act of destruction. "When 'speech' and 'nonspeech' elements are combined in the same course of conduct," the Court ruled, "a sufficiently important governmental interest in regulating the nonspeech element can justify incidental limitations on First Amendment freedoms." Such limitations must be minimal, the justices cautioned, and the government's interest—in this case, raising an army through conscription—must be "unrelated to the suppression of free speech."

Draft-card burning has passed out of fashion in the absence of an active draft, but cross burning still occurs occasionally as the most poisonous symbol of white supremacy and the fiercest gesture of hatred against blacks and Jews. Whether government may criminalize the fiery cross depends on its purpose. "Cross burnings have been used to communicate both threats of violence and messages of shared ideology," the Court noted in a 2003 case, *Virginia v. Black.* Therefore, criminal prosecution is constitutional only if the cross is burned with the intent to intimidate, and such intent must be proved separately at trial, the Court ruled 6–3. The majority held that the symbol could not be considered automatically intimidating, and so struck down part of a Virginia law that read, "Any such burning of a cross shall be prima facie evidence of an intent to intimidate a person or group of persons."

The two cases, which the Court sent back for retrial, seemed to fall on each side of the line that the justices had drawn. In one, Ku Klux Klan members set a cross on fire in an empty field; in the other, a blazing cross was placed on a black family's front lawn. As "a sign of celebration and ceremony" at a Klan rally, burning a cross might be "core political speech" protected under the First Amendment if no purpose of intimidation can be proved, the Court noted. By contrast, doing so in front of someone's house might fall into the category of "unprotected speech," defined in a long line of cases to include intimidation, obscenity, fraud, libel, and incitement to imminent crime.[38]

From 2000 through 2007, sixty cross burners were convicted in federal courts, and some drew heavy sentences: fifteen months for Kyle Shroyer of Muncie, Indiana, who set a cross ablaze in front of a biracial family's home; three years for Ronald Joshua Youngblood, who ignited a cross in Michigan and then set off an explosion so a black family would run outside, see the display, and hopefully move away; and ten years for Matthew Curtis Marshall, one of five who lit a cross outside a black family's home in Texas.[39] State prosecutions have gone forward in Massachusetts, Mississippi, Idaho, New York, and elsewhere. As an example of the spreading suppression of offensive symbols, New York State in 2006 made the display of a swastika, along with the burning cross, a felony punishable by four years in prison.

But flags have struck chords of special resonance. The world around,

pieces of colored cloth are elemental symbols invested with deep signifi-
cance. They summon and rally various peoples to their historical narratives,
ethnic roots, ancestral languages, and divine faiths. Groups identify themselves as distinctive, worthy, and superior under banners that can unfurl
the passions of conquest and yearning, defiance and dignity, suffering and
pride. All this from dyed fabric sewn into one pattern or another.

Both Confederate and Union flags were banned by Johnson County,
Kentucky, whose population was split between sympathies for the North
and the South.[40] During the Vietnam War, bolts of blue material, used in
Vietcong flags, were confiscated by the South Vietnamese government in a
vain attempt to stop the symbols of communist allegiance and control from
erupting all over the countryside. For years after Israel occupied the West
Bank and Gaza Strip in the 1967 war, its troops tore down Palestinian flags
and arrested Arabs for displaying them—until 1993, when Israel accepted
the concept of Palestinian statehood and its emblem. The American right
claimed exclusive patriotic virtue by expropriating the Stars and Stripes
during Vietnam, crudely equating love of the country with support for the
war. And today, a century and a half after the American Civil War, the stars
and bars of the Confederate flag are still woven with intertwining messages
of regional honor and traditional racism, stirring pride and exultation in
some, anger and insult in others.

After September 11, 2001, the American flag blossomed. It hung from
highway overpasses and flew from fire trucks, decorated storefronts and
restaurants, and was used as a kind of talisman that Muslims nervously
hoped might ward off evil assumptions about their loyalties as they drove
taxis and operated small businesses.

The flag reflected the nation's moods, stirring raw emotions at both
ends of the political spectrum. Three Miami firefighters who thought their
country had not held firmly to principles were suspended for refusing to fly
a flag on their fire engine. A school bus driver was ordered to remove the
small flag he'd taped atop his side mirror, supposedly a safety violation.[41]
Most troubling, the local policemen who threatened John Fleming and
other antiwar protesters for hanging the flag upside down did not know the
Constitution or the case law, did not understand that freedom extends to
expression in many forms, verbal and symbolic: a word, a song, a painting,
a demonstration, a flag. The Supreme Court's rulings had not penetrated
to the grass roots.

After 9/11, flags used by protesters as counterpoints to the drums of war
provoked constitutional violations by authorities across the country. Two
Grinnell students in Iowa flying an inverted flag from their dorm window

on September 26, 2002, were threatened with arrest by a couple of police officers who had been poorly advised by county prosecutors, all of whom the students then sued successfully.[42] A Montana couple who hung an inverted flag to protest the Obama administration ("chock full o' Marxists") said they'd "received much criticism, angry visitation, and undue police surveillance."[43]

A rougher confrontation occurred in Asheville, North Carolina, in July 2007, when Mark and Deborah Kuhn pinned protest signs to a flag—including a picture of Bush labeled "Out Now"—and hung it upside down on their porch. Unwanted attention came their way. A police officer visited after a complaint, then a man in fatigues appeared at the door, and a passerby took pictures ostentatiously. A week later, a sheriff's deputy showed up with a copy of North Carolina's flag desecration ordinance and asked for their identification so he could write them a citation. They refused and allegedly slammed the door on his hand; he supposedly pushed his way into the house, and the couple was taken to jail. Bailed out for $1,500 in a few hours, they had all charges dropped after ACLU intervention. But the sheriff kept their flag.[44]

Terri Jones hung a flag upside down in Iowa to protest inadequate mental health services after her son committed suicide following his return from combat in Iraq. She was not arrested, but officials in another county filed a misdemeanor charge against a friend of hers, a farmer named Dale Klyn, after he signaled his sympathy by flying an inverted flag from a tall pole on his property. The Iowa flag desecration statute was also brought to bear on Scott Wayne Roe, who hung a flag upside down in a less exalted protest—against overly zealous cops who interrupted his rock band's loud rehearsal after complaints from neighbors.[45]

Together Klyn and Roe won a summary judgment in federal court that the state ordinance violated the Fourteenth Amendment's guarantee of "due process of law" because its ban on showing "disrespect" to the flag was vague and subjective. That made it susceptible to unpredictable enforcement on the whim of an official's personal taste, and therefore a denial of due process. Vagueness inhibits freedoms in two ways, courts have ruled: imprecision gives excessive discretion to the police, and it forces citizens into a guessing game about what behavior is illegal, thereby chilling the exercise of rights.[46]

One might think that these antiquated desecration laws would fall into ruin against their obvious unconstitutionality, that officials would be ashamed to enforce them, much less enact them anew. But just a week after the court's decision, the Iowa House unanimously passed a slight revision, cynically attached to a bill establishing a veterans' mental health program to meet Terri Jones's demand. It defined "disrespect" more exactly, an effort to meet the judge's objections, and thereby remained on the books awaiting a fresh challenge.[47] Further, in creative defiance of the Supreme Court, an Indiana judge ordered David H. Stout not to touch any American flag while he was out on bail pending a trial for exercising his constitutional right to burn one in September 2001.[48]

In other words, employing the flag in protest may be a fundamental liberty, but it has to be repeatedly defended, litigated, and subjected to legislative debate. Forty-seven states still have laws modeled on the 1917 federal statute barring the flag's desecration or its mere appearance in advertising or publicity. The prohibition was cited by Iowa authorities that year in ruling that newspapers couldn't print the flag at the top of their editorial pages.[49] If enforced today, the laws would bring woe to most political candidates when they saturate stages and TV commercials with the Stars and Stripes.

Instead of making sure that the law conforms with the Constitution, some politicians repeatedly try to make the Constitution conform with their notions of proper behavior. Again and again, Congress has introduced amendments to prohibit flag "desecration." Using a religious term to describe a political act suggests how fervently the self-righteous seek immense state power to enforce a shallow reverence.

A flag amendment, a unique exception to the First Amendment, would insert a caveat unlike anything else in the Constitution. This is no idle threat. In 2006, the last time it was attempted, the amendment came within a single vote of mustering two-thirds of the Senate. Democrats Harry Reid of Nevada, Dianne Feinstein of California, Evan Bayh of Indiana, and Mary Landrieu of Louisiana joined the Republicans. There were just enough senators to defeat the measure, barely enough willing to be accused of coddling wretched flag burners. One more vote and the proposed amendment would have been on its way to the state legislatures, where three-fourths of them might have ratified it.[50]

With a flag amendment in place, it is not hard to imagine a future line of cases decided by an increasingly pro-government judiciary that would find little difference between burning a flag and burning the president in effigy, or showing the president satirized and ridiculed on a poster. The president is duly elected, after all. Would vitriolic attacks on his image, especially if he is popular in a time of war, not sully the entire nation, insult the whole people, and "desecrate" a symbol of America as surely as burning the flag itself? This view would not be entirely unprecedented. Recall that John Adams sought a certain immunity from derision by imprisoning editors under the Sedition Act, and Woodrow Wilson employed the force of law against his wartime critics.

The Court warned of that slippery slope. "To conclude that the government may permit designated symbols to be used to communicate only a limited set of messages would be to enter territory having no discernible or defensible boundaries," the majority said in *Texas v. Johnson.* "Could the government, on this theory, prohibit the burning of state flags? Of copies of the Presidential seal? Of the Constitution? In evaluating these choices under the First Amendment, how would we decide which symbols were sufficiently special to warrant this unique status? To do so, we would be forced to consult our own political preferences, and impose them on the citizenry, in the very way that the First Amendment forbids us to do."

This may sound alarmist in an era of boisterous protest and debate. But the best constitutional minds always caution against trespassing on rights in ways that seem innocuous at first. Once breached, the wall is more difficult to sustain, mainly because judges often commit the sin of incrementalism. They may move inch by inch away from the original holding, using each slight erosion as a new benchmark from which to travel another short distance, until the original is virtually obscured. We avoid these ends, as Justice Robert H. Jackson wrote decades earlier, "by avoiding these beginnings."

He used the phrase in upholding a right that seemed only peripheral to the core liberty of free political speech: the right of schoolchildren to refuse to salute the flag and recite the Pledge of Allegiance. Requiring that ritual, Jackson argued, could lead to broader demands for expressions of specific ideas and loyalties.

The Court had flipped back and forth on the salute and the pledge. In 1940, the year before entry into the war raging in Europe, the justices upheld, "in the promotion of national cohesion," a 1914 law in the small Pennsylvania town of Minersville forcing schoolchildren to salute the flag; oddly, the school used the straight-armed, palm-up gesture that had already been adopted by the Nazis. The appeal was brought by Jehovah's Witnesses, the parents of Lillian and William Gobitis, ages twelve and ten, who were expelled for not performing an act they considered a violation of the biblical injunction against worshipping a graven image. Making them do so was justified, Justice Frankfurter wrote for the majority, because "national unity is the basis of national security."[51]

The denial of the right to refuse did not last long. The Court reversed itself three years later when another Jehovah's Witness, Walter Barnette, successfully challenged a flag-salute mandate that West Virginia had enacted following *Gobitis*. Now, writing for a majority of 6–3, Justice Jackson declared plainly: "The flag salute is a form of utterance. Symbolism is a primitive but effective way of communicating ideas . . . a short cut from mind to mind." Citing *Stromberg*'s red-flag opinion, he proclaimed, "If there is any fixed star in our constitutional constellation, it is that no official, high or petty, can prescribe what shall be orthodox in politics, nationalism, religion, or other matters of opinion or force citizens to confess by word or act their faith therein." So here and in other cases, fundamentally religious citizens defended free speech for all citizens.

Jackson then rebutted Frankfurter on "national unity." To achieve it when moderate methods fail, Jackson noted, leaders both good and evil "must resort to an ever-increasing severity." The "ultimate futility of such attempts to compel coherence is the lesson of every such effort from the Roman drive to stamp out Christianity as a disturber of its pagan unity, the Inquisition as a means to religious and dynastic unity, the Siberian exiles as a means to Russian unity, down to the fast failing efforts of our present totalitarian enemies. Those who begin coercive elimination of dissent soon find themselves exterminating dissenters. . . . It seems trite but necessary to say that the First Amendment to our Constitution was designed to avoid these ends by avoiding these beginnings."[52]

This might be called the worst-case-scenario theory of constitutional law. It's the reason the ACLU and other defenders of civil liberties know no politics as they pick their cases, defending cross burners as well as flag burners, Nazi marchers on the right as well as antiwar demonstrators on the left. In contesting even minor violations, the ACLU's purpose is often preventive, not unlike the FBI's preventive approach to terrorism. Both predict the most dreadful possibility and try to head it off. The civil libertarian belief holds that a denial of one person's rights on a single day can be repeated until it becomes acceptable in culture or in law, so it's better to put out brush fires before the flames consume the Constitution.

That is why Americans' right of free speech is guarded so jealously and worried over so anxiously, even while the country stands safely unrestrained amid the raucous rhetoric that has come to dominate political debate. There appears little danger to the free-flowing expression of opinion in the United States, no matter how noxious. Yet to defend this vast homeland of liberty, little fights on behalf of free speech occur almost invisibly at the distant boundaries of the ground protected by the First Amendment. They may seem marginal, even trivial, but in a judicial system resting on precedent, minor skirmishes can shape constitutional principles that are then applied across the broad landscape.

These small tests often bring narrow victories. During the Vietnam War, for example, a California law prohibiting "offensive conduct" that would "maliciously and willfully disturb the peace or quiet of any neighborhood or person" was used to prosecute Paul Robert Cohen, who wore a jacket emblazoned with the words "Fuck the Draft" in the hallway of a Los Angeles courthouse. He made no noise, threatened no violence, provoked no disorder, and was convicted solely for the content of his speech.

By the bare majority of 5–4, the justices found no obscenity (the language not being erotic) and no "fighting words" (the slogan not being aimed insultingly at any individual). They dismissed the argument that the unwilling viewers, who included children, should not have been subjected to such an offensive message, holding that privacy interests wane outside the home. "To shut off discourse solely to protect others from hearing it . . . would effectively empower a majority to silence dissidents simply as a matter of personal predilections."[53] In other words, permitting an insignificant statement tenuously preserved a greater right.

SMALL VIOLATIONS OF LARGE PRINCIPLES

"We Will Not Be Silent," declared the young man's T-shirt, in Arabic and English. The letters were vividly white against black, and the sinuous Arabic script must have looked gracefully sinister. The man had suspiciously olive skin and a closely trimmed beard and mustache, like the desperate faces being televised from war-torn Iraq. His accent when he spoke was slyly softened by the purr of the Middle East. He sat alone waiting quietly, eating a small breakfast in the gate area of New York's John F. Kennedy International Airport, two days after an airliner bombing plot, unraveled in London, had sent a pulse of anxiety across the Atlantic.

His name was Raed Jarrar, and what happened to him was such a small story. It was an indignity and an inconvenience, not typical and not monumental enough to make a landmark court decision, perhaps not even a footnote in the sweep of American legal history. But it violated a founding principle. And so, like other minor trespasses onto the vast territory of free speech, it tripped an alarm.

On August 12, 2006, Jarrar passed through the metal detector without a beep, en route to a JetBlue flight home to Oakland, California. To avoid hassles at security over new restrictions on liquids and gels, he had checked all his luggage and had only his cell phone, wallet, boarding pass, and the clothes he was wearing. He was pulled aside for a second screening. He was frisked, and his shoes were tested for explosives residue.

Cleared again, he got some cash from an ATM, bought breakfast, and settled down to eat and wait for his flight at Gate 16. Then he saw a uniformed agent of the Transportation Security Administration (TSA) approaching.

"He said, 'Do you have a minute?' and he showed me his badge. He asked me to walk with him," Jarrar recalled. "I was terrified."

Born in Iraq and raised under Saddam Hussein, Jarrar was schooled in the arbitrary power of the state. Now safely married to an American, he held a green card signifying his legal status as a permanent resident of the United States, but he actively opposed the war and was mindful of his vulnerability as a noncitizen, as an Arab. So as the episode at Kennedy Airport unfolded, he tried to balance his fears against his rights, delicately.

The TSA official, later identified as Supervisory Aviation Security Inspector Garfield Harris, led Jarrar to the JetBlue counter and told him that passengers at the screening checkpoint had, in Harris's words, "expressed displeasure" at his T-shirt, which he would have to remove.[54] Evidently, it took only a couple of narrow minds to mobilize the federal government.

Shock tightened Jarrar's fear. "I would never have expected that in the U.S.," he said later. "It reminded me of how I would feel when approached by security forces of any authoritarian regime: you're in trouble and you might get in huge, huge trouble if you didn't act like a good citizen. I was being very polite and very communicative in dealing with them, without giving away my rights."

Surrounded by a small group that included JetBlue crew members, he submitted to Harris's unjustified questioning: Where did he live, where did he work, where had he traveled, when had he come to New York City, and for what purpose? "I didn't say, 'It's none of your business,' or get into a confrontation, especially considering that many other Arabs or Muslims were shipped out of the U.S. to be tortured for doing less."[55] When Jarrar opened his wallet to pull out a business card, Harris spotted his green card, asked to see it, and wrote down the personal information it contained, which included his country of birth.

Jarrar resisted only one demand: that he remove his shirt. "I said I would take it off if you present me a lawful order. Otherwise I prefer to keep it on because I consider it's my constitutional right."

"People in the U.S., they don't know anything about constitutional rights," one of the uniformed men told him—whether an agent of the government or the airline he wasn't sure. "He wasn't actually being hostile," Jarrar remembered. "He was being friendly. He was just informing me: Who is this naive newcomer?"

The naive Jarrar tried to convince Harris of his shirt's innocence. Its creators, a small organization called the Critical Voice, had given him one when he'd spoken at an antiwar rally in Washington three months earlier, and thousands had been made with the same message in many languages. The slogan had originated in 1942 with the White Rose, a student resistance group in Nazi Germany, which had distributed an antiwar leaflet pledging, "We will not be silent. . . . We are your bad conscience. . . . The White Rose will not leave you in peace!" Its members were executed.[56]

Jarrar might have mentioned this noble history had he known, but the TSA agent may not have been moved. He seemed fixated on the Arabic writing, arguing "that it was impermissible to wear a shirt with Arabic script at an airport, since that was analogous to a person wearing a T-shirt at a bank stating, 'I am a robber,'" Jarrar stated in a later lawsuit.[57] The message was no such threat, Jarrar insisted. Harris wasn't persuaded. Without a translator, he countered, agents couldn't be sure it didn't say something quite different from the English. He allegedly ordered Jarrar to turn the shirt inside out if he wanted to board the aircraft.[58]

As the standoff continued, Jarrar grew gradually more nervous about missing his flight or being arrested. Although the airline later denied threatening to bar him from the plane,[59] the group confronting him was joined by a JetBlue man who "appeared openly hostile and threatening," according to Jarrar's complaint. Compromise began to seem sensible, so when a female JetBlue agent offered to buy him another shirt, Jarrar considered and reluctantly relented.

She proposed "I Love New York," but Agent Harris suggested a plain T-shirt, "to avoid the impression that Plaintiff was being asked to endorse a particular message," he told the court. Jarrar heard it another way: that Harris, having stereotyped him as hateful, thought it would be unreasonable to force him to announce his love for America's largest city.

Whatever Harris meant, he and the JetBlue crew guarded Jarrar while the airline employee went to an airport shop and bought a gray T-shirt blandly labeled "All Original New York Authentic Blend." As they kept close watch, Jarrar put it on over the offending Arabic and English message, all the while promising a lawsuit, which he later filed against both Harris and JetBlue with the help of the ACLU.

Humiliated and still worried that he could be arrested or deported, Jarrar avoided the stares of other passengers by waiting a distance from the gate. JetBlue evidently wanted him out of sight, too: a ticket agent allegedly tore up his boarding pass, changed his seat from 3A in the front to 24A in the back, and escorted him onto the plane before anyone else. A Department of Transportation investigation found unjustifiable behavior by the airline based on perceptions of Jarrar's ethnicity.[60]

His lawsuit claimed that both Harris and JetBlue had violated the Civil Rights Act by "intentional discrimination" and that Harris, as a government agent, had abridged both the First Amendment's guarantee of free speech and the due process provision of the Fifth Amendment, which encompasses equal protection under the law.[61] Jarrar's lawyers were asking the courts to play their dual role, to apply the law to a specific infraction and also to judge the constitutionality of government behavior.

Jarrar had not been arrested, he had not been deported, he had not even missed his flight. Yet his wife, Niki, an Iranian-born, naturalized American, was left with a residue of apprehension. When they drove across country together, "she hid all her books in Arabic or Farsi in a bag," he said. "She buried them as deeply as she could."[62]

Angered by what he'd seen firsthand of the war before fleeing Iraq, Jarrar was neither starry-eyed nor cynical about the United States. He gave a touching nod to America's ideals by working as a consultant for the American Friends Service Committee, speaking across the country on the devastation of Iraq, testifying before Congress, putting U.S. legislators in touch with their Iraqi counterparts. He respected America's fears, too.

"I would support the right to get any suspicious person off an airplane or a bus," he said. "But to cover someone's T-shirt and put him in the back of the plane because of the language, that's another thing. I didn't object to the TSA taking me to a secondary check. I don't have a problem with safety and security, but I have a problem with Islamophobia or this general tendency of calling brown people terrorists or suppressing my right to express myself."

Once Jarrar's story hit the news, a sassy blogger wrote on his Web site: "What the hell, this guy got a free T-shirt and he's complaining?" But others made sure the shirts appeared at many airports. White Anglo passengers wore them onto JetBlue planes without interference, reinforcing Jarrar's belief that he had been singled out as an Arab.

He decided to keep his own in a drawer while his lawsuit proceeded, "because I wanted to get a legal ruling from the court whether wearing this T-shirt was my constitutional right." This test of American principle he was not willing to dodge by agreeing to a settlement for mere money; he wanted a jury trial. "I'm not interested in settling unless the settlement will create a legal precedent," he declared firmly. He envisioned the court issuing an order prohibiting airlines and the TSA from treating passengers as he had been treated.

In a civil suit such as his, though, the most he could win was money, and he could lose something along the way: JetBlue and TSA attorneys dug into his family and subpoenaed his friends for long depositions in an effort to sully his reputation and "intimidate me so I would drop my case," he said. "I was against taking money," he lamented. "There are people who sue McDonald's because coffee falls on them. I don't want to fall into this group of people."

But one day the judge asked why the parties hadn't settled, prompting JetBlue and two TSA agents to dangle $240,000 even as they denied wrongdoing. Jarrar very halfheartedly agreed. He'd won but didn't feel vindicated. Skeptical, he could only hope that his attorney, Aden Fine, was right in saying, "The size of that settlement really sends a message that this should never have happened, and what they did should never happen again." From his proceeds, he donated $50,000 to cover the ACLU's out-of-pocket expenses, a fraction of the hundreds of thousands of dollars' worth of time the organization had spent.

Jarrar had envisioned a purer victory. He'd imagined a jury of Americans being indignant: "I thought in ten minutes they'd say, 'What the hell did you do to this guy?' But I was advised by my lawyer that a jury might not look at you the same way because of where you come from. That's a bad feeling." The money did not erase the bad feeling.

Having to pay the money didn't even deter the TSA from an alarmist reaction to Arabic writing three years later, this time more abusively, when Nicholas George, returning from summer break to Pomona College in California, dutifully emptied his pockets at security in Philadelphia's airport. He pulled out a set of English-Arabic flash cards, the standard tools of a language student, a weapon in the war on insularity and parochialism. The TSA held him and interrogated him, then called the Philadelphia police to handcuff him and lock him in a cell awaiting the FBI, which finally let him go after five hours. The quality of investigation was revealed by a TSA supervisor's questions: "You know who did 9/11?" Osama bin Laden, George answered. "Do you know what language he spoke? Do you see why these cards are suspicious?" George sued, too, and the Obama administration actually defended its officers.[63]

PUNISHING WITHOUT PROSECUTING

There are many ways to muffle dissent short of bringing criminal charges. There are zealous federal agents, for example, who smell some violation of something when the president is the target of protest. Secret Service agents, charged with checking out possible threats, knocked on an apartment door in Durham, North Carolina, about six weeks after September 11, where a nineteen-year-old college freshman named A. J. Brown had hung a poster on her wall. It showed President Bush as a hangman, holding a rope supposedly leading to a noose, with drawings of hanging bodies in the background, and the words "WE HANG on Your Every Word. George W. Bush Wanted: 152 Dead," the number executed while he was governor of Texas. It was a protest against the death penalty, but to some anonymous neighbor or classmate who called the authorities, it was "anti-American," the agents told her. They asked incongruously if she had any information about Afghanistan or the Taliban. She said no and complied with their request to fill out a form with her name, race, and other personal information.[64]

The FBI and the Secret Service visited Barry Reingold, a sixty-year-old retired telephone worker, after he mouthed off in a gym in San Francisco, where he went routinely to lift weights and pontificate. "Discussion turned to bin Laden and what a horrible murderer he was," Reingold told *The Christian Science Monitor*. "I said, 'Yeah, he's horrible and did a horrible thing, but Bush has nothing to be proud of. He is a servant of the big oil companies, and his only interest in the Middle East is oil.'"

As the rhetoric heated up, one of the other men threw a question: "Aren't you an American?" Agents rang his bell a few days later, and Reingold went into the hall to meet them. "We've heard that you've been discussing President Bush, oil, Osama bin Laden," one of them said; sardonically, Reingold replied that as far as he knew, such speech was still allowed. "They said, 'You know, you are entitled to freedom of speech.' And I said, 'Thank you. That ends our conversation.'" He closed his door, hearing one of the agents remark, "But we still need to do a report."[65]

Doing reports and checking out every tip after 9/11, no matter how preposterous, agents even showed up at a tiny Houston art gallery half an hour before opening for an exhibit titled *Secret Wars,* on American covert operations, which had been reported to them as "un-American." After two hours sneering at various art pieces, they deemed the show "not dangerous."[66] National security was preserved.

Some federal agents dislike this sort of hyperscrutiny, as demonstrated by a strange 2006 incident in Colorado that turned members of Vice President Dick Cheney's Secret Service detail against one another. It began when Steve Howards made a slight detour while walking his seven-year-old son through a mall to a piano lesson. Noticing Cheney shaking hands with people, Howards went up to him and said something like, "I think your policies in Iraq are reprehensible." He may have lightly touched Cheney's shoulder. Nothing happened to him then, but when he returned to the area about ten minutes later with his other son, an agent asked him, "Did you assault the Vice President?" Howards, "in shocked amazement," as he put it to the court, said he had not, but he was handcuffed in view of his son and hauled off to the police station. The charge was reduced from assault to harassment and was then dismissed by the district attorney. Howards sued, provoking a public rift among Secret Service agents who tried to blame one another for the embarrassing arrest.[67]

The high emotions that brought federal agents to Reingold's and Brown's doors took an ugly twist when Marcia Perez got into a spat with her son's roller hockey coach, Pete McGurty, who had lost friends in the World Trade Center. Right after a game on September 28, 2001, "I gave him my condolences," Perez recalled, "and I told him that I hope the U.S. begins to reconsider its foreign policy." In other words, she pushed the button that seemed to say: we were at fault.

"He got really antagonistic and said, 'What does foreign policy have to do with what happened in New York?' I said, 'I simply don't think bombing women and children in Afghanistan is the answer.' He stated to me in a loud voice, 'I don't care if they bomb those fuckers and their families too.' I told him I agree that what happened in New York was very saddening, the death of anyone was saddening. He said the answer was to go after the terrorists and kill them all. I told him innocent lives should not be sacrificed, that my husband was an orphan because of U.S.-trained death squads in Guatemala, that we understand the costs of war. He was ranting and raving. He didn't have a political view except just rage in his heart. He called them sister fuckers, right in front of the kids. My son was hearing this."

Then it got "racial," she said. "If they bomb East L.A., how would La Raza feel?" she quoted him as asking, and as he did, he made a gesture of slicking his hair back. "How would Mexicans feel?"

She replied, "I don't know. I've never been Mexican in East L.A." Perez is half Mexican, half Japanese; her Guatemalan husband was standing there, too, listening, along with other parents.

When I called McGurty to check this account with him, three years later, he got mad at me for just asking. The question revived all the pain of loss, he said, and he refused to offer his version, except to flail at Perez.

"She was so cruel," he practically shouted through the phone, his voice breaking in anger and near tears. "She was cruel, she was mean and inhumane. She was a cold, heartless woman. I'm from New York, and my personal friends passed away that day in New York. She was cruel. She picked on somebody who was emotionally devastated. She was inhumane. . . . I was in mourning then, and I'm probably going to be in mourning the rest of my life."

Their argument might have ended as a sad rift at a terrible, raw moment of the American experience. But several days later, Perez got a call from Mike Stallings, director of parks and recreation for Daly City, south of San Francisco, which ran the hockey league. "He called me into his office," she said. "He offered me my money back for hockey. I said no, my son's playing hockey. He loves hockey. He said he can't play anymore. We've made a decision that your son be removed from the league." He'd heard that she supported the attack on the Trade Center, he told her. She set the record straight. "I said, 'So you're saying that my eight-year-old son can't play hockey because the coach disagrees with the political views of the parent." She threatened to sue, and she's a lawyer.

Here was local government punishing a small child for the political views of his outspoken mother. The error must have been recognized by someone in city hall, for Stallings soon sent her a letter of compromise moving the boy, Marcelo, to another team after a week's suspension ("We will issue a refund . . . for the value of one week of the program"). It was still a hardship for a lad of eight. "The Ranger's [sic] coach has requested that your son, Marcelo, be placed on another Pee Wee hockey team," Stallings wrote on official letterhead. "Marcelo will <u>not</u> be able to play hockey this week on the Rangers and will begin with the Wild on Oct. 8." He added a censorship order to Perez: "Please remember that this is a youth recreation hockey program and that conversations with the coaches should be about hockey."[68]

Marcelo took it badly. "He cried. He really cried," his mother remembered. "He said, 'Why do I have to leave the team, Mama?' Actually, it's his first lesson in racism and, I guess, overzealous patriotism. And I explained to him when people don't agree with you and they have power over your life, they do these things. I explained that this is an issue of control and power, and your coach is a white male and I'm a female and I'm brown, and my opinion doesn't really matter to them, nor do your feelings. This is his first real-world lesson in racism and fighting for his rights of free speech."

After his new team, the Wild, played his old, the Rangers, the kids and coaches lined up to shake hands. When he got to Coach Pete McGurty, Marcelo pulled his hand away.

Acting like thought police, some guardians of decorum have silenced discordant Americans to keep the comfort zone placid, anodyne: don't disturb the harmony, don't let bothersome ideas from the margins rankle the general mood of unanimity. Proprietors do not want ripples of resentment and offense. Owners of shopping malls seem to fear unpleasant thoughts interrupting customers' bland contentment as they glide from store to store. Employers worry about conflicts distracting workers who are getting paid to work. Colleges want to protect their minority and female students from racist, sexist sneers and epithets.

The First Amendment restricts only government, so with some exceptions, private actors can muzzle unwelcome speech without legal sanction. If Marcelo's hockey league had been run by a Rotary Club or a YMCA, his mother would have had no leverage on the free speech issue alone, only on her charge of ethnic discrimination. If Raed Jarrar had been hassled by JetBlue without the federal TSA's involvement, he would not have had a First Amendment case, which in his lawsuit he reserved for the TSA alone, accusing JetBlue of discrimination only.

This creates a complex First Amendment culture, with private actors often imposing their own sanctions on dissent in ways that government cannot.

When the singer Natalie Maines of the Dixie Chicks told a London audience how ashamed she was that President Bush came from her home state of Texas, the group got death threats, had to install metal detectors at their concerts, and became the target of a privately organized boycott in which some American radio stations stopped playing their music.

When the German composer Karlheinz Stockhausen called the attack on the World Trade Center "the greatest work of art imaginable for the whole cosmos," a performance of his work scheduled at the Cooper Union in New York was canceled by the Eastman School of Music's Ossia Ensemble. A concert was also canceled in Hamburg. He later explained apologetically that he was referring to the art of Lucifer, the prince of destruction who takes a role in his opera *Licht*.[69]

When the artist Christopher Savido created a portrait of Bush composed of tiny images of chimpanzees, the entire exhibition in which the work appeared was ordered closed by a director of the Chelsea Market in Manhattan, who threatened to seize all sixty pieces of art and have the organizer, Bucky Turco, arrested and evicted from his rented office.[70]

When a few librarians at Florida Gulf Coast University in Fort Myers wore "I'm Proud to Be an American" stickers after 9/11, their superiors asked them to remove them, lest they offend foreign students. "If some people are offended by another person's speech," countered Howard Simon of the ACLU, "that's the price of freedom in this country."[71]

At another library, in Topeka, Kansas, supervisors banned an employee, Bonnie Cuevas, from speaking at work about the Supreme Court ruling that overturned a Texas law used to prosecute homosexuals for sodomy. After a few colleagues expressed delight with the decision, and reporters called her for comment, she was told by two managers that another employee had complained about her pro-gay conversations creating "a hostile work environment." A private firm might have had the right to impose censorship, but this was a government-run library, and federal case law bars the government from silencing speech on a public issue just because someone is offended.[72]

Privately owned facilities open to the public are another matter. They fall into an ambiguous category overseen by a variety of disparate state constitutions and court interpretations that have allowed the owners of shopping malls to test the limits of their censorship powers. At the Westlake Center mall in Seattle, a week before the Iraq war began, a security officer ordered a shopper either to remove a small, one-and-a-half-inch "No War" pin or to leave the building.[73]

Around the same time in upstate New York, Stephen Downs went into the Crossgates Mall in Guilderland with his adult son, Roger, to perform a test of their own. They asked a store in the shopping center to make them two T-shirts, for which they paid $22 each. Stephen's said "Give Peace a Chance" on one side and "Peace on Earth" on the other; his son wore one reading, "No War in Iraq" and "Let Inspections Work."

They put the T-shirts on over their other shirts and went to a food court to eat. All was peaceful in the mall until the inflammatory messages promoting peace were spotted by two security guards assigned to keep the peace, who told them to remove the T-shirts or leave. "I said I wasn't going to take off the T-shirt," reported Stephen, an attorney who was then chief counsel in the Albany office of the Commission on Judicial Conduct.

The guards disappeared, returned a few minutes later with a policeman, and informed the father and son that they were causing a disturbance, which seemed odd, since the group was surrounded by nonchalant shoppers who were calmly consuming, as Americans were advised to do by their president after 9/11. The only disturbance came from the peace officers objecting to peace messages and threatening to lock up the father and son.

The two had decided in advance that Roger would avoid arrest, so he took off his shirt, and Stephen, who had a Subway sandwich in one hand and a drink in the other, held them out in front of him, saying, "Do what you have to do."

Then he felt something new. "After they handcuffed me, I had an out-of-body experience," he said. "I'm a lawyer but was surprised. You're really helpless."

He was arrested not for unpleasant speech—which would have been patently unconstitutional—but for trespassing, the most common tool used by government to enforce private censorship. At a police station inside the mall, Stephen and the cop sparred for a while. "The basic premise was that if I went to somebody's house and I was doing something that offended the people and they asked me to leave, I should get up and leave. This was like a person's house, private property. I said this is more like a marketplace, people coming and going."

And that is precisely the divide that the Supreme Court has left to state courts and legislatures to sort out. Some have interpreted state constitutions as protecting speech in privately owned malls because they are public forums (California, Massachusetts, Oregon, and New Jersey, for example), and others allow malls to curb messages they deem offensive (Connecticut, New York, Arizona, Georgia, Pennsylvania, South Carolina, and Minnesota among them), creating a patchwork across the nation.[74]

Crossgates dropped the trespassing charges against Downs, but he sued the company, which retained a vaguely worded code of conduct on its Web site. A section titled "Please Dress Appropriately" declared: "The wearing of apparel which is likely to provoke a disturbance or embroil other groups or the general public in open conflict is prohibited."[75]

A saving grace of open societies is this: in most cases of suppression, the offending statement receives more publicity than it otherwise would. The Dixie Chicks may have suffered some at home, but the remark about Bush gained circulation far beyond the audience in London, and the group continued to perform globally and sell a lot of CDs, setting a record for a country-music act of $62 million gross that year.[76] The Bush portrait made up of chimps was widely viewed when published in *The New York Times*. And Downs's shirt was added to the T-shirt collection of the New York State Museum in Albany.

The conclusion from all these episodes, whether they are momentous or merely minor scuffles at the margins of free speech, is that Americans do not like to be told what to say or what to think. At least that is what we want to believe about ourselves. Although national trauma does not foster reasonable discourse, as we have seen since 9/11, the idea of America remains the din of ideas. Our founding truth makes room for a multitude of truths, spoken by each of us in our own voice, clashing and competing and drowning out orthodoxy.

This right to speak serves as the wellspring nourishing other rights. Art cannot flourish, literature cannot inspire, the powerless cannot dissent, the press cannot probe, the voter cannot choose wisely, the space for dialogue cannot remain open, and our system cannot be self-correcting without the First Amendment's guarantee.

That makes free speech bigger than an individual possession, for the right to be heard is also the right to hear: your freedom to speak determines my freedom to know. As citizens of dictatorships discover, imposing silence on one imposes deafness on all. They lose the privilege of listening, and into silence marches tyranny.

CHAPTER SEVEN

A Redress of Grievances

Democracy is not a quiet business.

—Anthony D. Romero, executive director, ACLU

DECORUM AND DISSENT

THERE IS NO STRONGER magnet for protest than the nation's capital, and no more intimate opportunity for face-to-face (or in-your-face) encounters with power than the white-domed Capitol and the flanking House and Senate office buildings. Nowhere else can a dissenting citizen so easily cross paths with the legislators who write laws, shape budgets, and determine the course of the country. If you stroll the corridors, you can buttonhole senators and representatives as they hurry to floor votes or committee hearings, which are almost always open to the public.

Until May 10, 2007, Gael Murphy freely roamed those hallways and hearing rooms as a leader of two groups trying to end the war in Iraq: the congressional co-chair of United for Peace and Justice, and co-founder of the women's movement that named itself Code Pink in a spoof on the Department of Homeland Security's colored levels of alert, which usually stayed at Code Orange or Red.

That day, as a Senate committee hearing ended, she tried to unfurl a banner reading "Stop Funding War." She was immediately arrested, jailed overnight, and then banned by court order from the entire Capitol grounds, including all office buildings and surrounding streets. The "stay-away order" lasted ten months, and although she managed to get a slight relaxation from the judge, she could not lobby as before. She could attend specific hearings only when armed with an invitation from a sympathetic congressional aide, so she could not hang out in the offices to chat with staff members, drop in on last-minute hearings, or talk on the run with legislators. Her effectiveness was practically extinguished.[1]

It would be hard to argue that Code Pink hastened the withdrawal from Iraq. It certainly didn't prevent President Obama from adding troops in Afghanistan. As an exercise in First Amendment rights, demonstrations are usually born of frustration, and their impact is debatable. They typically open space for dissent where authorities have stopped listening, but they don't usually force policy change without becoming intensely dramatic, either by incurring violence from the police, as during the civil rights movement, or by their overwhelming size and persistence, as during the war in Vietnam—two rare successes in the annals of American street protests.

The marchers against segregation in the South prevailed mainly because their opponents, represented by beefy white civilians and cops, played the thugs by attacking peaceful protesters with dogs, fire hoses, and truncheons, as if fulfilling roles in a pageant of injustice. Civil rights leaders understood very well how powerfully the televised scenes of crude brutality against passive resistance would mobilize the conscience of the country against the segregationists.

The Vietnam protests grew so huge, and their spin-offs so intrusive on college campuses, that they amplified the larger public's gathering doubts about the failing war and eventually propelled the American withdrawal. Other grievances were pulled into the vortex of the demonstrations, including the draft—which was ended before the war ended. Students who occupied university buildings against imperious administrators won major revisions in parietals and other campus policies, so that today's undergraduates can thank the protesters for ending the rules that women be in their dorms by 10:00 or 11:00 or midnight and have no male guests after hours.

Typically, though, most demonstrations are futile, so it's remarkable how eagerly government tries to impede them. That happens especially during wartime, when the right to free speech is most needed and most vulnerable, when the country requires candor but cries for common purpose. Among the many strengths that war demands, and one of the hardest to muster, is the power to listen.

But listening to Gael Murphy or seeing her banners did not appeal to the congressional leadership or the Capitol Police, who applied the stay-away order as a convenient countermeasure. It is a tool normally used to prevent real crime, usually issued as a condition of release pending trial for drug dealing or domestic abuse—a method of keeping the defendant away from a neighborhood, a witness, or a victim.[2]

Stores, libraries, and other institutions have issued banning orders without court authorization to exclude suspected shoplifters and vagrants. Washington prosecutors routinely request them to suppress demonstrative messages on Capitol Hill, and the practice has caught on elsewhere. Police slapped one on Andrew Silver as they expelled him from the 2007 North Carolina State Fair. His offense: wearing a sandwich board and collecting signatures on a petition urging that Vice President Dick Cheney and President George W. Bush be impeached.

"They took me to the police precinct at the fairground," said Silver. He smiled while they snapped his mug shot and posted it on their wall along with pictures of shoplifters and drug dealers who were banned. The cops "said I'd be arrested if I ever came back. There was no end date on it."

So blatantly did this violate the First Amendment that the American Civil Liberties Union quickly got it reversed with a phone call or two, and Silver was given his own booth a couple of days later near restrooms—an ignominious but well-trafficked spot.[3] As he was setting up, Silver recalled, a policeman who had not been involved in the arrest strolled by, looked around to make sure nobody was listening, and then "stopped and said, 'You beat the Nazis.'"

In Washington, Gael Murphy's "crime" was no worse, nothing more than a lack of decorum, if that. She had committed no violence, had made no threat, and had not even disrupted the committee's hearing. Code Pink activists had shouted down witnesses in the past, but they hadn't done so this time, and Murphy deliberately sought to avoid arrest by sitting quietly during testimony by Secretary of State Condoleezza Rice. Satirical stunts are Code Pink's trademark, and that day Murphy and others wore pink police-style hats and pink shirts labeled "Pink Police," and they appeared here and there to "arrest" war criminals. She waited until the hearing was adjourned and Rice and the senators were walking out before she reached for the banner. She didn't even get it unfurled before police officers took her and a colleague away.

When Republicans were in charge, unfurling a banner got a person ejected but rarely arrested, and sometimes not even ID'd by the police, Murphy said. But as antiwar pressure increased after the Democrats won majorities in the House and Senate, pressure also built on the Capitol Police to keep order. They did so dramatically when a second-grade teacher and Code Pink member, Desiree Fairooz, dyed her hands blood red and waved them inches from Rice's face just before another hearing. The rattled cops lost their cool, video shows. They grabbed others dressed in pink—who were not protesting, just sitting quietly wearing pink crowns reading "Shame"—and twisted their arms while hauling them roughly out of the room. As Fairooz was led away, she yelled at Rice, "War criminal! War criminal!" and then as she disappeared out the door, "Take her to The Hague!"

As the police ratcheted up their response and got judges to issue stay-away orders, a sense of unpredictability overcame the protesters. "All of a sudden we were being arrested for things we'd done for six months," Murphy said. "We've been given permission to unfurl banners in hearings. We've struck deals with chairmen and staffers." The protests had settled into such a routine that in a skit on *Saturday Night Live,* a chairman formally announced the next item on the agenda: a six-second disruption by Code Pink, and a few women in pink then chanted for precisely six seconds, before the hearing resumed. In real life, Murphy said, chairmen lost their tolerance or their influence over the police, and activists grew uncertain about the threshold that would trigger arrest.

The consequences of civil disobedience could be serious. If you went limp or questioned a cop, you got charged with "assault on a police officer," which sounds as if you threw a punch but covers anyone who "opposes, impedes, intimidates, or interferes with a law enforcement officer."[4] The charge was invariably dropped or reduced, she noted, but it was scary. Even a misdemeanor such as "unlawful conduct," the accusation against Murphy and two fellow protesters, ended up in a database that prevented her two colleagues from entering Canada.[5]

"It is unpleasant that every time you're arrested now, you'll spend a night in central cell block, in pretty ugly conditions," she said. "Once you enter the [federal] marshal system you are absolutely guilty. That's how you're treated. They have a row of stainless steel cages, and that's where they keep you." And when you're released, you have to walk to a Capitol Hill police office to pick up your wallet and money. "You have nothing," she said. "Some people are let out late at night."

The methods became a deterrent. "I'm obviously much more careful," Murphy said. "I'm very wary of being arrested, that's for sure. If I felt I was moved to do something in a hearing, like unfurl a banner, or stand up and challenge a lie, I would most likely be arrested and held overnight. But it would make me think whether being arrested is worth it. I look more carefully at actions and what the consequences would be. I'm more discerning."

There is a narrow line between free expression and disruptive conduct, especially in a congressional hearing, so Murphy's stay-away order may or may not have survived a constitutional challenge, had there been one.[6] In this and other areas, demonstrators and police jostle each other through a legal landscape with too few signposts, and those that exist are often ignored by the authorities.

On the grounds outside the Capitol and other federal buildings, police periodically evade the courts' rulings. There, as in flag burning, the same First Amendment principle has to be defended repeatedly: demonstrations around monuments are clearly protected speech, provided they don't obstruct entrances, disrupt passersby, interfere with government business, or deface buildings. This has been codified in a line of cases since 1972, when the Supreme Court affirmed a D.C. Court of Appeals opinion striking down a statute prohibiting demonstrations on the Capitol grounds, and in 1983, when the justices declared that sidewalks around their own Supreme Court building, like those elsewhere, were "areas of public property that traditionally have been held open to the public for expressive activities." The Court could hardly have done otherwise in that case, which involved the arrest of a nun, Sister Mary Grace, for carrying a sign bearing the words of the First Amendment.[7]

But even in a system devoted to the rule of law, it seems, the police skate past decisions of the courts; even in a judiciary that values precedent, the battles have to be fought again and again. Even after the rulings from 1972 to 1983, police banned leafleting and demonstrations on the sidewalk at a Capitol entrance. When an artist, Robert Lederman, refused to move 250 feet away, he was arrested. He held a sign reading "Stop Arresting Artists" as he handed out leaflets about a pending lawsuit to secure artists' rights to sell their works on New York City's sidewalks.

In 2002, a unanimous three-judge panel of the federal Court of Appeals for the District of Columbia found the prohibition unconstitutional. Although the Capitol sidewalks had been declared a "no demonstration zone" by the Capitol Police, Judge David Tatel, writing for the court, ruled them a "public forum," citing the thirty-year line of cases. He derided the government's argument that the broad ban was legitimately aimed at facilitating access. Only those who expressed viewpoints were cleared from walkways, he noted wryly: "If people entering and leaving the Capitol can avoid running headlong into tourists, joggers, dogs, and strollers—which the Government apparently concedes, as it has not closed the sidewalk to such activities—then we assume they are also capable of circumnavigating the occasional protester. . . . We likewise reject the proposition that demonstrators of any stripe pose a greater security risk to the Capitol building and its occupants than do pedestrians, who may come and go anonymously, travel in groups of any size, carry any number of bags and boxes, and linger as long as they please."[8]

The "public forum" designation is critical to determining where free speech rights exist. Since demonstrations involve speech plus conduct, government's right to regulate the conduct is repeatedly tested. Beginning in 1939, the concept of a "public forum" was introduced by the Supreme Court,[9] and then it was expanded from streets and meeting halls to a state capitol's steps,[10] the streets around a capitol building and a courthouse,[11] the sidewalks and streets near a school,[12] and the vicinity of embassies.[13] The Court refused to grant "public forum" status to buses,[14] areas near jails,[15] military bases,[16] sidewalks on U.S. Postal Service property,[17] and airport terminals.[18] The label is significant, because government restrictions on "expressive activity" in public forums "survive only if they are narrowly drawn to achieve a compelling state interest," as Chief Justice William H. Rehnquist wrote in the 1992 airport case, while in nonpublic forums the limits need only "satisfy a standard of reasonableness."

It was deemed "reasonable," then, for officials to block Jesse Ethredge several times during more than three decades as a civilian employee at Robins Air Force Base in Georgia—not a public forum. He liked to adorn his truck with stickers denouncing various Republican commanders in chief. He was admonished by base authorities in 1984 for one reading "To Hell with Reagan." In 1990 he was given a ticket for "provoking speech on a truck" after driving onto the base with a sticker saying "Read My Lips Hell with Geo. Bush." When he got a letter from the deputy base commander in 1991 warning him not to enter the base with "bumper stickers or other similar paraphernalia which would embarrass or disparage the Commander in Chief," he sued and lost in the Eleventh Circuit. Then, just before September 11, 2001, the Secret Service paid him a call about his stickers reading "Thief, Liar, Two Faced Murderer Geo. W. Bush," and "Hell with Bush and All Damn Republicans." The agents decided he was not threatening the president.[19]

Since 1941, the Court has upheld "reasonable" limits on the "time, place, or manner" of demonstrations that stop short of censorship, affirming the convictions of Jehovah's Witnesses who defied a town's permit requirement and carried signs while they marched along a street, albeit single file.[20] Reasonable does not always mean sensible, though. In 1967, the Court affirmed the decision of an Alabama judge to enjoin a civil rights march in Birmingham, which had taken place in 1963, and to hold Martin Luther King Jr. in contempt of court for violating the order. In a South that used the courts and the police to enforce segregation, the Supreme Court split hairs over the failure of the demonstrators to apply for a permit, to file motions in higher courts, and to play in a rigged game of legalities that they would surely have lost.[21]

POLICE SURVEILLANCE

One of the easiest intelligence operations for police departments and federal agencies is spying on peaceful opponents of government policies, as if the most serious threats were posed by dissenting citizens rather than dangerous terrorists. Hardly any protest groups are secretive, and they're eager for volunteers, so intelligence officers who want to follow the path of least resistance can readily watch and infiltrate the antiwar community. As a result, the dossiers contain a lot of peace activists who raise their voices, not their fists.

The specter of surveillance intimidates would-be demonstrators, it is argued, inhibiting free expression. When a volunteer turns out to be an undercover cop, trust and cohesion disintegrate, some people get scared, and effective organization deteriorates. So goes the reasoning.

Captain Jeffrey Herold thought otherwise and portrayed the watchfulness as essential and benign. His uniform was perfectly pressed, his hair was meticulously trimmed, and he presented himself as a precise thinker with balanced priorities. He had a demanding job: head of intelligence for the Washington, D.C., police department's Office of Homeland Security and Counterterrorism. But he spent most of his time in front of a computer screen, he said, checking what he could learn from protest groups' open sources. Since they advertise to garner public support, they usually plan overtly. He noted that they had been targeted by more undercover officers back in the 1970s and 1980s, before the window provided by the Internet.

To assemble the right equipment and manpower at a demonstration, he explained, the police need to know whether illegal acts are likely and what tactics might be used. Making that assessment also requires direct surveillance, he conceded, and gave as an example preparations for the protests in 2000 against the International Monetary Fund. "We asked Home Depot, 'If you get people who don't look like plumbers buying a bunch of PVC pipe, give us a call.' They called. We started surveilling Home Depot." Police stakeouts saw people buying huge amounts of PVC, which protesters use for "sleeping dragons" to lock themselves together, so the cops knew to take the necessary tools to the march: Jaws of Life, bolt cutters. Separating demonstrators to arrest them can be tricky. They sometimes fasten bike locks around their necks, Herold said, so you have to exercise great care when cutting them off. "Some put ropes around necks so if you pull, you strangle them."

In addition to monitoring Web sites and doing stakeouts, "there is undercover work," he added. "But there's got to be a criminal predicate there," meaning a preceding indication of a crime. "I wouldn't see wasting police resources going into Code Pink, for example."

Gael Murphy and her Code Pink colleagues felt under close scrutiny, though, maybe not by the city's police, but certainly by the Capitol Police before and after her ban. "Everywhere on Capitol Hill we're followed. When we go to lunch, a table of policemen are next to us. I'm assuming my phone is tapped. I wouldn't be surprised if our group is infiltrated. They're on our e-mail list." As she and her colleagues walk through hallways, they can hear the crackle of police radios: "Pinks in the house."

The surveillance fires indignation in some activists, resignation in others. Murphy seemed nonchalant. "We come from a premise that we don't have anything to hide," she explained. "We're not doing anything illegal; we're not doing anything violent."

Her group does take precautions if it wants to pull a surprise. "When we're planning some civil disobedience, we are careful about not using cell phones or discussing it over e-mail—even landlines if we can help it," she said, then added: "Usually, we come to find out that the police are fully aware of our plans. That's how we know that there's likely infiltration," as it seemed one day when activists quietly organized a little guerrilla theater to stage a mock die-in on the west terrace of the Capitol. There's a rule against lying down on non-grassy areas, to prevent that kind of demonstration, and by the time protesters approached, the area was sealed off with "bicycle rails and layers and layers of police," she recalled, "so it was impossible to even get near the terrace."

If activists suspect one or another of being an undercover cop, doesn't that taint relationships within the movement? "Not really," Murphy said. "It makes you wonder sometimes about people, I mean, where do they come from? Sometimes some odd people show up, and you don't really expect them. So it makes you wonder."

You wonder also who doesn't join a protest, who keeps silent, who is intimidated by the very belief that surveillance is active. You wonder whether that is precisely the objective when the government gets heavy-handed, as it did with Drake University in Iowa. The school was served with a federal subpoena demanding the names of leaders, annual reports, and details of a forum held in 2003 by the campus chapter of the left-wing National Lawyers Guild, including names of attendees and issues discussed. The subpoena contained a gag order on college administrators, caused a public uproar nonetheless, and was withdrawn as the American Association of University Professors issued a defiant declaration: "To demand the naming of all persons who attended a lawfully registered campus conference will undoubtedly chill protected expression, and deter participation at similar events in the future."[22]

That seems logical. "An individual planning to attend a political meeting or a rally protesting the war in Iraq, for example, will be much more hesitant to attend if he knows FBI agents may be taking names," writes the constitutional scholar Geoffrey R. Stone. "Such surveillance, whether open or surreptitious, can have a significant chilling effect on First Amendment freedoms."[23]

Yet when nothing comes of the information gathering, citizens may not feel the chill. If police don't disrupt or arrest in advance, does the mere suspicion of surveillance inhibit free speech and organizing? "The only thing I think it inhibits is illegal activity," said Herold, the police intelligence officer. "That argument sounds good, that it's going to scare people. But I've seen officers standing next to protesters who are right in your face, screaming and yelling at you, using words you wouldn't bring home with you." Had it happened to him? "Yes, and I've been standing there in uniform."

Still, there are the non-zealots, the citizens in the gray areas between conformity and activism, the folks who might feel a quiet apprehension tugging against their impulse to step out. They are unseen, they may prefer to remain that way, and as long as they do so, they cannot be counted.

Furthermore, intelligence gathering itself contributes to a mind-set among officers about protesters as adversaries and lawbreakers, as documented by internal police files that have been made public. If you stand back and list the threats facing the society, and how we'd be smartest deploying the limited resources of law enforcement—to combat terrorism, drugs, guns, sophisticated white-collar crime, and so on—conducting surveillance on nonviolent peace movements would hardly rank as a priority. Yet if dissent is tarred with the brush of danger, which it often is, then license is given to monitor, infiltrate, and gather intelligence as if the protest group were preparing an attack. The Maryland State Police logged nearly three hundred hours of undercover surveillance aimed at opponents of the death penalty and the Iraq war and found no criminal activity, yet entered some of the names in a database of suspected terrorists and drug traffickers.[24]

From 2001 through at least 2006, the FBI devoted untold man-hours to monitoring and investigating the Religious Society of Friends (Quakers), Greenpeace, *The Catholic Worker,* and People for the Ethical Treatment of Animals (PETA). According to a book-length report by the inspector general of the Justice Department, an FBI agent was dispatched to an antiwar rally in Pittsburgh to look for suspected international terrorists, but without any indication that any would be there. Before leaving his office, he glanced through a book of faces but, once at the demonstration, found that he couldn't remember them well enough to do matches.[25]

The Pennsylvania Office of Homeland Security hired a contractor to do bulletins on possible terrorist threats, which included upcoming meetings of an environmental group opposing the use of hydraulic fracturing to drill for natural gas. The contractor's uncorroborated reports sent state police chasing false leads.[26]

The Denver Police Department and other Colorado agencies spent considerable resources closely watching peace activists even before 2001, as revealed by multiple documents obtained from internal police files, each labeled "Intelligence Bureau Information Summary."[27] One report lists the license plate numbers of cars near a demonstration on March 27, 1999, at Peterson Air Force Base in Colorado Springs, with owners' names (blacked out) and addresses. "This was a peaceful demonstration, lasting approximately one hour," the officer typed at the bottom, with a sentence revealing that a tail had been put on a representative of the Colorado Coalition for the Prevention of Nuclear War and the director of the American Friends Service Committee (AFSC), a Quaker organization of devout pacifists: "Four vehicles left 901 W. 14th Ave., and car pooled to the demonstration."

Another file lists license numbers of cars in the parking lot at a conference called "Space, Nukes, and International Law" conducted February 6, 1999, by the AFSC and Citizens for Peace in Space. The name of each registered owner was deleted before the report was made public, but the home address, tag number, or make and year of each vehicle remained.

A police intelligence report dated April 12, 1999, names the officers of the Pikes Peak Justice & Peace Commission, the editorial board of its newsletter, and about a dozen "additional persons who have been identified that are associated with PPJPC or Citizens for Peace in Space." Their addresses are included.

Most comically, Officer Larry Valencia, "wearing a transmitter," was sent undercover to a 2000 meeting at the AFSC office, where a small group discussed forming an umbrella organization to plan demonstrations and mobilize protesters to go to Washington. "It was announced that there would be a meeting for developing a mission statement on the following Wednesday May 11th at Alfalfa's," the officer reported. "A thin female wearing glasses and having a fair complexion stated that the police and F.B.I. were also invited and she stated that they were probably in attendance now. I decided to quit writing notes so as not to look obvious."[28]

The head of intelligence for the Denver police rebuffed my efforts to get an explanation of why, in an age of dangerous, violent crime, he would assign officers to cruise parking lots writing down peaceniks' license numbers.

Not only local police but the FBI and military intelligence have monitored protest groups since 9/11, as they did during the Vietnam War. Back then, the CIA illegally provided the FBI with over 1,000 domestic intelligence reports a month, and the army gathered intelligence on more than 100,000 opponents of the war, including Martin Luther King Jr., who was under military surveillance when he was assassinated in Memphis in 1968.[29]

The FBI's infiltration and disruption of antiwar and civil rights groups, under the rubric COINTELPRO, supposedly ended after the embarrassing disclosures by congressional investigations in the 1970s. For a quarter century, Justice Department guidelines barred the FBI from monitoring any organization because of its First Amendment activity. The CIA was prevented administratively from sharing intelligence with the FBI, and the FBI was precluded from surveillance of political or religious organizations. Agents could not even attend public meetings without specific justification for a criminal investigation.

After September 11, those restrictions were erased by Attorney General John Ashcroft. Local FBI field offices no longer needed high-level approval to send agents undercover to lectures, forums, religious services, and organizational meetings, where they posed as activists. And Congress passed the Patriot Act, which permitted intelligence to be shared with criminal investigators.

However, evidence that the FBI never quite stopped monitoring is contained in one document, unearthed from before the 9/11 attacks, describing protest groups in extreme terms. A memo dated May 23, 2001, by the Los Angeles field office reports from "a reliable source" on a demonstration at Vandenberg Air Force Base by the "Catholic Workers Group," which promotes civil disobedience to impede missile launches. It "also advocates a communist distribution of resources," says the FBI file. Members of a second organization the memo calls "Rukus" (presumably the Ruckus Society, which trains in demonstration techniques) "advocate property damage, advocate anarchy [and] an end to capitalism in America."[30]

The reports suggest that intelligence officers, whether civilian or military, drift easily from watching out for violence to watching out for protest in general. This confusion about the mission was illustrated by TALON, a Defense Department database designed for intelligence reports on terrorist threats to military installations in the United States. Launched in 2003, it quickly became a repository of information on nonthreatening groups that merely picketed bases and recruitment offices.[31]

Not all demonstrations were peaceful, to be sure. Some involved vandalism, but they could hardly be called terrorism. A truly violent attack occurred when a recruiting office in Times Square was bombed at 3:45 a.m. on March 6, 2008, evidently timed to destroy property, not lives (nobody was hurt). Significantly, it had nothing to do with the sort of public demonstrations being monitored by military intelligence.

A window into the military's surveillance came from Pentagon documents, first reported by NBC and then pried out of the Defense Department by an ACLU lawsuit under the Freedom of Information Act. With a whiff of hysteria, the intelligence files portray antiwar activities as highly dangerous.[32]

One memo, labeled "Suspicious Activities/Incidents," is designed "to alert commanders and staff to potential terrorist activity." The "potential terrorist activity" includes a rally in Akron, Ohio, under the slogan "Stop the War NOW!" It is announced in an e-mail received by a federal agent from the AFSC, the pacifist Quaker organization. The army intelligence report reveals that the group "will have a March and Reading of Names of War Dead" and that the march "goes past a local military recruiting station and the FBI office."

Another report begins: "This update is submitted to clarify why the Students for Peace and Justice represent a potential threat to DOD personnel." Notice the word "threat." Army intelligence knows what threats are. Threats are bullets. Threats are rockets, grenades, roadside bombs, all the bad stuff that happens in Iraq and Afghanistan. Here they're talking about that other front in the war on terrorism, the University of California at Santa Cruz.

"Students and community allies shut down the annual career fair, where recruiters from the Army, Navy, and Marines had set up tables. The activists demanded that recruiters leave immediately and turn their tabling spots over to student counter-recruitment activists. Also"—and here we learn the nature of the terrorist threat—"two of the recruiter's vehicles were vandalized while parked on the campus. . . . Students for Peace and Justice conducted an impromptu march to the Army recruitment offices in Dobie Mall. . . . The protesters blocked the entrance to the recruitment office with two coffins, one draped with an American flag and the other covered with an Iraqi flag, taped posters on the window of the office and chanted, 'No more war and occupation. You don't have to die for an education.'

Recruitment officers who were on duty during the protest had no comment and told protesters who tried to enter the recruiting office to leave unless they want to enlist." At least one recruiter had a sense of humor.

The military report lumps together all political protest, sinister and otherwise, by including it under the ominous heading "This information is being provided only to alert commanders and staff to potential terrorist activity or apprise them of other force protection issues." And these reports on upcoming peace protests get wider distribution than might be expected; copies are listed as going to the Joint Terrorism Task Force, made up of local police and federal authorities.

The official files offer insight into the intelligence world's capacity to conflate violent and nonviolent lawbreaking, and to misunderstand the worthy tradition of civil disobedience. "There is an intense debate among the protest groups concerning whether to be nonviolent or to conduct civil disobedience," as if the two were contradictory, says one military report on planned protests at recruiting stations in New York City. "While a group may publicly call for nonviolent protests, individually many of the individual members actually favor civil disobedience and vandalism." So "nonviolent" seems to mean obeying all laws, and civil disobedience is "violent," with no recognition that most acts of civil disobedience, like the sit-ins and marches of the civil rights movement, are deliberately nonviolent—refusing to be herded into a "free speech zone," for example, blocking an entrance, or crossing a police line.

The intelligence officer here misses a key principle of political protest: that there are many ways to break laws without using violence, a point made by an e-mail from the organizers, quoted in the very same memo. They advocate "Gandhian nonviolence" and firmly instruct demonstrators: "We will not use physical violence or verbal abuse toward any person," and, "We will not carry weapons." This seems clear enough, but it gets reported under the title "Potential Terrorist Activity," suggesting how reliable U.S. military intelligence might have been in selecting "terrorists" for imprisonment overseas. Intelligence performs best by understanding the country being watched—this country in this case, with its traditions of Thoreau's civil disobedience, King's pacifist methods, and the passive resistance of the peace groups under surveillance. They are all respectable components of American history and culture that go unnoticed in these Pentagon documents.

Monitoring the antiwar movement has missed the real dangers. The Maryland State Police watched pacifists more closely than they did an eighty-eight-year-old Annapolis resident whom they knew well for his

234 / RIGHTS AT RISK

menacing, anti-Semitic, racist rants. He took a .22 rifle into the Holocaust Museum's entrance in 2009 and shot a black security guard dead. Nor did the military's fascination with peace groups translate into security when a Muslim convert, recently returned from Yemen, opened fire in an Arkansas recruiting center, killing one soldier and wounding another. He had not been involved in any organized activity. Neither had Major Nidal Malik Hasan before he fired on soldiers at Fort Hood, Texas, killing thirteen and wounding dozens of others. A psychiatrist, he had questioned whether Muslims should be killing Muslims in Iraq and Afghanistan, and he had queried a radical Yemeni cleric about Islam in e-mails that were intercepted by intelligence and referred to the FBI and a Defense Department investigator, yet dismissed as nonthreatening.[33]

"Peaceful civil disobedience is still illegal activity," observed Captain Jeffrey Herold. True enough, and he gave an example from 1995, when Justice for Janitors, a union campaign protesting low wages and cuts in the D.C. education budget, blocked Roosevelt Bridge across the Potomac with a yellow school bus during morning rush hour, a demonstration that right-wingers dubbed "traffic terrorism."[34] "Are we supposed to just let that go and not be able to handle that just because it's nonviolent?" Herold asked. "I'd say no. There's nothing in the Constitution—you come outside the Constitution when you're involved in illegal activity."

Of course, but most police departments aren't good at calibrating their responses to the difference between breaking the law by passive resistance and by assault—the difference between refusing to disperse, for example, and hurling stones. Departments will be criticized more for failing to preserve order than for failing to protect free speech, so they tend to expect violence and prepare for it. Like an armed force jockeying for military advantage, the police operate in a thick fog of misunderstanding and false assumptions about groups they see as adversaries. This may be the most damaging aspect of extensive surveillance: the state of mind that it creates in law enforcement.

Studies of police behavior indicate that unverified intelligence and training sessions that anticipate violence can feed anxiety, leading to preemptive curbs on free expression. Facing protests against the World Bank and International Monetary Fund in 2000 and 2002, the D.C. police "inflated crowd estimates and exaggerated dangers," reported Mary Cheh, a law professor later elected to the city council. "The police made plans for infiltrating, disrupting, and preempting the protestors," she wrote after conducting an investigation. "For example, on Saturday, April 15, 2000, the day before the largest scheduled demonstration, the MPD [Metropolitan Police Department] and City fire officials entered the anti-globalization groups' headquarters, or 'convergence center,' on the pretext of a fire inspection. Fire officials issued multiple fire code violation notices and closed down the center, thus seriously disrupting the plans of the demonstrators and displacing many out-of-town protesters who were staying at the building. Officials confiscated property of the demonstrators and sealed the building, only letting individuals return two days later—after the demonstrations had ended."[35]

Officers were shown films of massively violent European demonstrations beforehand, she reported. "There were not even examples in North America of that degree of violence," she said, and the films obliterated the officers' capacity "to have any nuance or proportionate response, or to separate what might be dangerous from what was not dangerous," she observed. "It got them into a mindset of looking at all these demonstrators as the opposing army, and giving them a hair-trigger mentality."

As a result, the police herded peaceful, orderly demonstrators and bystanders into Pershing Park on Pennsylvania Avenue, closed them in, and arrested nearly four hundred, without having issued any order to disperse. Protesters were held for at least twenty-four hours, some with one wrist handcuffed to the opposite ankle so they couldn't straighten up (resembling a torture used in Rwanda), and the police chief gloated that they would be missing the demonstrations. The arrests were so baseless that no one was prosecuted.

Advanced technology has given both organizers and authorities new tools. In August 2011, transit officials foiled a demonstration in San Francisco's subway system by pulling the plug on cell-phone service, denying organizers the means of texting and Twitter to orchestrate a protest over a fatal police shooting. The Bay Area Rapid Transit officials took a leaf out of Egypt's book, where the dying authoritarian regime had shut down the Internet in a futile effort to impede the pro-democracy movement. The San Francisco action was denounced by the ACLU as a violation of the First Amendment.

In Miami, an investigating commission found that constitutional rights were underplayed in training before a meeting of the Free Trade Area of the Americas in November 2003. As police prepared to confront violence, emotions were whipped up by scare tactics. "Three days were devoted to the sophisticated devices employed by protesters in recent demonstrations held elsewhere," the panel reported, "One hour was devoted to legal issues restating the basic principle that protesters and demonstrators have the protection of the First Amendment to freely express their opinions and the right to peaceful assembly."[36]

Press coverage contributed to the hype. In the days before the Miami demonstrations, local television put police officers on edge by repeatedly broadcasting videos of violence during the 1999 Seattle protests against the World Trade Organization. Clashes were then rewarded with extensive play on the evening news, part of a universal pattern: since placid demonstrations rarely get the media coverage they deserve, some protesters look for confrontation, and cops often give it to them. Officers in riot gear practically sealed off downtown Miami, fired beanbags and rubber bullets into nonviolent crowds, hit some people in the back as they were retreating, and rounded up large numbers in mass arrests. More than two hundred were kept in oversized cages without toilet facilities.

SPIES IN NEW YORK

The demonstrators' "sophisticated devices" mentioned in the Miami investigation are featured prominently in New York City intelligence estimates done before the 2004 Republican National Convention, as if police and protesters were in something of an arms race, with each group ratcheting up its tools and techniques to counter the other's tactics. The most dangerous methods are used by a small minority of demonstrators, yet they occupy a prominent place in New York Police Department (NYPD) documents. Any officer reading the intelligence reports, which lack proportion and perspective, would naturally brace himself for a battle when he goes to a protest march.

That is what happened before the convention, a story told by 603 pages of intelligence files, called "end user reports," gathered by the NYPD and released under a judge's order in a lawsuit. Taken together, they help explain why the NYPD cracked down on demonstrators so vigorously and preemptively. (A lawsuit by some of those arrested failed to win release of a further 1,800 pages of "field reports" by undercover police agents who infiltrated various protest groups.)[37]

Some of the most aggressive surveillance of dissident groups is done by the NYPD, and the spying has a long history. In one of the less admirable episodes, a police division infiltrated the Black Panthers and accused twenty-one members of plotting to blow up department stores; it turned out that the plan had been the idea of the police agents themselves. After years of litigation in a suit brought against the unit, a federal judge in 1985 approved a consent decree that barred monitoring and infiltration without "specific information" of a group's link with criminal activity.

Arguing after September 11, 2001, that the decree tied its hands, the NYPD got a judge to relax the restrictions to coincide with FBI rules, which are weaker, and to eliminate a requirement that surveillance be documented with a paper trail that could expose any abuse.[38] Freed by the loosened guidelines, the New York police geared up for a rash of demonstrations when the Republicans came to town in the summer of 2004.

Some of the intelligence documents make exciting reading, especially descriptions of demonstrators' devices and tactics.[39] Undercover cops who are discovered pretending to be protesters are sometimes marked with ultraviolet paint, their locations transmitted via cell phone or Webcam, the reports say. Jammers are used against police radios. Gas balloons filled with metal shavings are sent toward power lines. When police barricades impede marches, demonstrators have torn them down with crowbars, grappling hooks, and sledgehammers, tools often hidden in huge puppets ("Trojan Horses") to avoid detection until the last minute.

Helmeted officers who use wedge formations to split demonstrators' ranks, then trap them without escape routes and arrest them one by one, now find some protesters locked to signposts or linked together in "sleeping dragons" made by putting arms inside three-foot pipes rigged with inaccessible catches—the sort the Washington police saw being bought at Home Depot. Policemen singling out specific demonstrators for arrest have been evaded with "Black Bloc" tactics: protesters dress in three layers of clothing—an outer layer of dark garments to make activists indistinguishable from one another, a second layer exposed during illegal activity, and a third layer of ordinary street clothes to blend in during escape.

When police use tear gas, some protesters don gas masks—violating an archaic 1845 New York statute prohibiting three or more masked people from loitering. When police videotape demonstrators breaking the law, the protesters mask themselves with bandannas and T-shirts they've brought along for the purpose.

Given the history of police officers breaking up protests violently, a small number of activists have countered with homemade weapons. As listed in NYPD intelligence reports, they include frozen water balloons dropped from buildings onto police cars; flammable or noxious chemicals in toy water guns or inside eggshells; marbles or ball bearings scattered before police horses; lacrosse sticks and slingshots to hurl rocks, bottles, and other missiles; and a "Tiki Torch" of burning liquid in a can at the end of a long stick that can be raised high and swung forward to spatter the police thirty to fifty feet away.

How often and where such assaults have actually occurred is not made clear to officers reading the intelligence, however. So there is no way to acquire perspective from the NYPD reports. They are written in hyperbolic language, the dastardly possibilities are woven into the benign, the violent is mixed in with the nonviolent, and the unlawful with the lawful until a dizzying spectacle of "anarchists" and "extremists" anticipates mayhem on the streets.

"Instructions Given to Anarchists," says one heading. "Anarchist Checklist for Action," says another. Some protesters are self-declared anarchists, but the police spread the term more broadly than warranted, casting demonstrators as nihilists who have no political position or consequential viewpoint. They come across as dangerous, dark, and mysterious, like black holes of chaos.

One group branded that way, Critical Resistance, states idealistically on its Web site that it "seeks to build an international movement to end the Prison Industrial Complex by challenging the belief that caging and controlling people makes us safe. We believe that basic necessities such as food, shelter, and freedom are what really make our communities secure." The group advocates "community-based alternatives for safety and conflict resolution." Police intelligence labels this "anarchist." End of discussion. Cops aren't enthusiastic about eliminating prisons.[40]

The reports contain shared intelligence from police authorities across the country. Much is blacked out in the copies made public, but with enough left uncensored to indicate extensive infiltration: One hint of internal spying is seen in documents with numerous references to activists "considering" this or that tactic. West Coast organizers were reported to be planning a reconnaissance trip to New York. An undercover officer or an informant joined a walking tour by the group Surveillance Camera Players, which maps closed-circuit cameras around the city.

As the NYPD files filled up with confusing threat assessments from across the country, more obscurity than clarity developed. From Philadelphia, for instance, a report during the 2000 Republican convention noted that protesters had deployed lawyers wearing badges labeled "legal observers" to watch police conduct. The intelligence document called it "an effort to intimidate uniformed personnel." Yes, if uniformed personnel would be intimidated by lawyers watching for brutality and other illegal behavior.

Looking through the lens of combat makes every innocent defense look like part of the offense. So when a group advertised tips on treating for tear gas, pepper spray, and physical injuries before the 2004 convention in New York, police intelligence reacted with suspicion, warning: "The above indicates that participants of direct action protest(s) may be willing to physically resist and confront disorder control personnel." Yes, or it may indicate that the participants anticipate being gassed, sprayed, and injured by "disorder control personnel."

The intelligence professional's passion to collect everything possible is nicely illustrated in an NYPD report under the rubric "Secret," and beneath a blacked-out box that may have contained notes from an infiltrator. The censored document declares ominously in large type: "LOCAL ACTIVIST GROUP TO USE ART MURALS IN ORDER TO SPREAD PEACE MESSAGE; GROUP MAY USE DIRECT ACTION METHODS IN CONJUNCTION WITH STREET THEATRE." It describes the organization as "a collective of artists dedicated to using artwork to spread the word of peace." It uses "murals, banners, posters, and street theatre during its actions."

It's logical that police want to know about demonstrators' plans, but it's hard to see how this overdose of mislabeled information can possibly be useful to patrolmen or commanders making quick decisions on handling crowds. In the jumble of impressions from the intelligence reports, the occasional acknowledgment that a certain group plans "passive acts of civil disobedience" is overwhelmed by the dangers attributed to other organizations. But who can tell the various protest groups apart when they're entangled in the streets? How can cops differentiate between those devoted to lawful protest and those planning to violate the law? And how does the surveillance prepare officers to react to lawbreakers with a sense of proportion?

Dire intelligence leads police to expect the worst and act accordingly, often losing perspective on the severity of the infraction. "The way the police are deployed during demonstrations, the model is not policing, the model is military," said Mary Cheh of the D.C. City Council. "If you keep that in mind, then you understand. They don't want to resolve the problem or handle it, they want to remove the adversary. They want to remove them. Any minor act is a precursor to chaos, so arrest everybody." There is a difference between blocking a sidewalk and throwing a stone, but officers tend to pull out the handcuffs for both.

The NYPD ordered 26,000 pairs of flexible cuffs (at ninety-five cents apiece) before the Republican convention, rented a pier for containing prisoners, and issued a memo stating that no mere summonses would be written; every infraction would result in arrest. The ACLU surmised that the purpose was to build a fingerprint database of demonstrators.[41]

Armed with an intricate legal memorandum prepared beforehand, New York police officers had a handy guide listing which law could be used to charge which offense, from criminal acts down to the most insignificant violations of the administrative code. Of 1,827 people swept up and locked away for a day or so, 1,342 were charged with minor administrative infractions (such as riding a bike on a sidewalk) or "disorderly conduct," a catch-all usually applied to someone who ignores an officer's instruction to move.

"Distinguishing between protected First Amendment activity and criminal conduct is often difficult," the police memorandum declares, adding that while many demonstrators are "cooperative with the police and cause few problems," others "are less agreeable and engaged in conduct that pushes to the limit the delicate balance between the right to demonstrate and public safety."

As a cautionary note to cops who might want to slap on the cuffs when a protester hurls nothing more than an epithet, the guidelines warn, "It is virtually impossible to sustain in court a charge of harassment based on verbal insults directed at a police officer." But if "the words were part of a scheme to harass or annoy," or if they were accompanied by "physical contact, however slight," then harassment under the state's Penal Law, section 240.24, could be charged.

The guidelines tell officers to allow signs but not poles that could be used as weapons, and advise charging "criminal possession of a weapon" (article 265 of the Penal Law) for hiding sleeping dragons and other implements inside large puppets. "If an officer is physically injured" while trying to dismantle a sleeping dragon, the guide states, "consider charging their possessor(s) with Assault in the Second Degree, Penal Law § 120.05 (D) Felony."

Taking down police barricades can be charged as inciting to riot (Penal Law section 240.05), but the memo warns that incitement requires that ten or more persons be urged toward "tumultuous and violent conduct" that is *likely* to bring public harm. Those engaging in passive resistance can be arrested for obstructing governmental administration (Penal Law section 195.05), according to a PowerPoint presentation shown to officers before the convention.

The guidelines state that if demonstrators on sidewalks or in streets don't obey orders to move, police can arrest them for blocking vehicular or pedestrian traffic, provided the protesters are doing so "with intent to cause public inconvenience or alarm," and not inadvertently. The charge is disorderly conduct under Penal Law section 240.20(4), under which 548 demonstrators were seized during the convention. And so on, wrapping protesters in a blanket of ordinances.

If enforced literally, New York City's laws and regulations can be stifling. I learned as a reporter in the 1970s, investigating corruption in the construction industry, that it was practically impossible to build a building legally in the city. If the cops wished, they could stand and write a ticket every time a truck spilled a little dirt while it crossed a sidewalk at a construction site—hence the weekly payoffs to the precinct.

So it is with demonstrations, as a lanky twenty-five-year-old technical whiz named Joshua Kinberg learned to his distress. He had prepared for the convention by rigging his bike with a dot matrix printer to spray water-based chalk on the pavement, like skywriting. As messages were sent to his Apple PowerBook computer or to his cell phone, he would transmit those he chose via Bluetooth from his computer to the writing device—a novel and quite innocent form of expression.

Kinberg thought that chalk, easily washed off, wouldn't count as graffiti, but he was wrong. As an MSNBC interview with him was ending (conducted by Ron Reagan, of all people), police arrested the biker and confiscated his bike, which he'd equipped as his master's project at Parsons School of Design. The NYPD's legal guide pointed out that defacement of property under the city's Administrative Code, section 10-117, is "a class B misdemeanor and does NOT require any actual damage (i.e. chalk markings)."

The law also prohibits riding on the sidewalk (called "Reckless Operation on Sidewalks") unless you're under fourteen and your bike has a wheel diameter under twenty-six inches. Traffic rules for bikes are so detailed in requiring certain lights and reflectors that most cyclists are probably vulnerable to citation, which allowed cops to arrest biking demonstrators preemptively to forestall massive congestion—or the worse possibilities the police imagined. "Intelligence detectives questioned me about 'violent protesters,'" Kinberg told *The Village Voice*, "but seemed disappointed to learn that I am an artist and only know other artists, and had no knowledge of any violence being planned."[42]

Anyone who reads the preambles to the NYPD's Legal Guidelines and the *Police Student's Guide: Maintaining Public Order* is transported happily into a universe of constitutional perfection where "force can never be used by police officers to punish," but "only when necessary to prevent crime, to arrest, or for their protection or for the protection of others"; where "the role of the Police Department includes protecting the right of protesters to peaceably express their view and protecting the right of non-protesters to go about their daily life unaffected by public disorder"; and where "the rights of assembly and the freedom to peaceably protest [must] be zealously protected."[43]

Both manuals quote the First Amendment, and both stress the police officer's obligation of impartiality. "Regardless of your personal feelings towards the demonstrators or the object [of] their protest," says the student guide, "you must remain neutral." It adds: "All attempts to regulate activities that are classified as *pure speech* have failed constitutional muster. . . . When the activity is more than pure speech and there is a real likelihood that it will affect the public in general, the police can apply reasonable regulations to the conduct of the demonstration." The future cops are advised: "The most desirable method of handling demonstrations is with reasonableness rather than confrontation."

"That's Muzak," scoffed Mary Cheh, who investigated the D.C. police. It's the kind of soothing background of platitudes that routinely accompanies harsh mobilization. "When you put people on the line, and you put them in full riot gear, shoulder to shoulder, you're not only sending a message to demonstrators," she said. "The message is being repeated to every officer on the line."

ZONING OUT FREE SPEECH

It must be satisfying to demonstrate against a president, especially if you think he might catch a glimpse of your sign as he whizzes by. But very few Americans, perhaps none at all, had the pleasure when George W. Bush was in office.

Since a president can easily slide into a comfort zone of sycophants, it can't hurt him to see a few demonstrators with rude T-shirts injecting a small dose of irreverence into a triumphant appearance. In the age of stage-managed events for television, however, White House aides don't like it. So under Bush, the Secret Service was turned into a kind of speech police. Wherever he ventured within his own country, he and the cameras covering him were shielded from uncomfortable messages. Demonstrators were penned into "protest areas" around the corner or blocks away, which came to be known sardonically as "free speech zones." Citizens wearing T-shirts with unwelcome slogans were screened or expelled from audiences. Nobody needed a manual to figure out what was going on.

But a manual existed nonetheless, a very long and detailed set of instructions to White House advance teams on how to engineer the president's appearances so that images of enthusiasm would not be tarnished by anyone exercising the First Amendment "right of the people peaceably to assemble, and to petition the Government for a redress of grievances."

Behind a cover bearing the august Seal of the President of the United States, and emblazoned with the warning "SENSITIVE—DO NOT COPY," the how-to booklet featured a section ungrammatically titled "Preventing Demonstrators." Restricting events to ticket holders was "the best method for preventing demonstrators," said the guide. "It is important to have your volunteers at a checkpoint before the Magnetometers in order to stop a demonstrator from getting into the event. Look for signs that they may be carrying, and if need be, have volunteers check for folded cloth signs that demonstrators may be bringing to the event."

The manual acknowledged that the Secret Service was responsible only for the president's physical safety, not his immunity from hecklers. But it then corrupted the security agents' role by urging planners to "work with the Secret Service and have them ask the local police department to designate a protest area where demonstrators can be placed, preferably not in view of the event site or motorcade route."

In addition, "rally squads" of "college/young republican organizations, local athletic teams, and fraternities/sororities" should be on the lookout for demonstrators. Armed with "favorable messages using large hand held signs, placards, or perhaps a long sheet banner," the teams should take up positions "in strategic areas around the site." In groups of fifteen to twenty-five, they should roam the perimeter. If protesters get inside, "the rally squad's task is to use their signs and banners as shields between the demonstrators and the main press platform. If the demonstrators are yelling, rally squads can begin and lead supportive chants to drown out the protestors (USA!, USA!, USA!). As a last resort, security should remove the demonstrators from the event site."[44]

That's just what happened to Jeffery and Nicole Rank when they tried to attend a Bush speech in West Virginia. It was the Fourth of July in 2004, a festive day on the grounds of the state capitol in Charleston. They had received tickets, entered the area, and too long before the president arrived took off their outer shirts to reveal white T-shirts with the international sign for "NO!"—a red circle with a diagonal line across the name Bush. There were other touches: a picture of Bush superimposed with the international "no" sign on the left sleeve; a John Kerry button on the right; the witty line "Regime Change Starts at Home" on the back of Jeffery's shirt; and "Love America, Hate Bush" on the back of Nicole's.

The young couple said later that they weren't shouting, making gestures, or disrupting the event, and had no plans to do so. But their timing was exquisitely premature, giving White House staffers opportunity to approach them as they stood quietly in the crowd, before Bush had a chance to see their artwork. They were told that they would have to leave if they didn't remove or cover their T-shirts. When they refused, White House officials called in local police, who handcuffed them, led them away, locked them up for an hour or two, and charged them with trespassing.

By contrast, the many audience members who wore T-shirts and buttons supporting Bush "were not arrested, asked to leave, asked to cover their political messages, or otherwise harassed by law enforcement or White House Event Staff because of their expression," the Ranks complained in a lawsuit.[45] Nicole was suspended from her job at the Federal Emergency Management Agency pending resolution of the trespassing charge, which was later dropped. In the end, the mayor and city council of Charleston issued public apologies to the couple, and the White House settled their suit before it got to trial, for $80,000 of the taxpayers' money.[46] But their message of protest was obliterated; neither the president nor the television viewers saw it.

The Ranks' lawsuit did produce a court order to pry loose that "Presidential Advance Manual," which laid out so explicitly the White House policy on silencing criticism. "Remember," the instructions warn, "avoid physical contact with demonstrators! Most often, the demonstrators want a physical confrontation. Do not fall into their trap! Also, do not do anything or say anything that might result in the physical harm to the demonstrators. Before taking action, the Advance person must decide if the solution would cause more negative publicity than if the demonstrators were simply left alone."

With "publicity" the essential test, the White House usually calculated that suppressing free speech would work better than respecting it. Fanning out through parking lots, volunteers and officials even tried to spot potential dissidents by checking bumper stickers. In Denver, two people with entry tickets from their congressman were held outside a Bush address on Social Security because their bumper sticker read "No More Blood for Oil." They were admitted after being warned not to try anything "funny," and minutes later were told to leave by a higher official, although they neither carried signs nor wore clothing with political messages. The Secret Service enforced the staff's expulsion order.[47]

Citizens with tickets to a presidential speech in La Crosse, Wisconsin, were required to unbutton their outer garments, according to an ACLU complaint, and a woman wearing a critical T-shirt "had her ticket ripped up and was ejected by security officials." Several dozen people appeared on a "do not admit list" in Fargo, North Dakota, most of them labeled as members of "a liberal organization," the ACLU noted. "Some had written letters to the editor opposing the President's policies." A student in Tucson, Arizona, was excluded from a forum on Social Security, presided over by Bush, for the offense of wearing a Young Democrats T-shirt.[48]

Again and again, as local officials candidly told protesters and judges, the Secret Service asked police departments throughout the country to restrict demonstrators to zones that were out of sight. The agency requested police in Stockton, California, to herd protesters behind a row of buses where they couldn't be seen or heard, while Bush supporters with signs were allowed in plain view as the president campaigned for a local candidate. Police in Trenton, New Jersey, were required to consult with the Secret Service about the location of a protest zone, which was created in a parking lot across a four-lane highway separated by a high wire fence from the Sovereign Bank Arena, where Bush was arriving for a fund-raiser.

Similarly, police testified in a lawsuit filed against them that they had followed Secret Service demands to locate a "designated free speech zone" on a baseball field one-third of a mile from a Bush speech in Neville Island, Pennsylvania, while supporters with signs were permitted along the motorcade route. Bill Neel, a retired steelworker, said he'd thought the whole country was a free speech zone. He learned otherwise when he was arrested for asserting his right to stand among the supporters.

A couple of years after the contested 2000 election, a sardonic sign saying "Welcome Governor Bush" got the attention of a policeman who ordered the demonstrator to a protest zone behind a building at Western Michigan University, two football fields away from the president's motorcade route. When he insisted on staying, the protester was jailed on Secret Service instructions, the police testified. Also, an environmentalist named John Blair was arrested for carrying a sign reading "Cheney—19th C. Energy Man," even though he was across the street from the Evansville, Indiana, civic center where the vice president was scheduled to speak. The sidewalk directly in front of the center remained open to unscreened pedestrians not expressing political views, meaning that security was not the concern After a summary judgment in his favor, Blair won a large, undisclosed settlement from the city.

As the trivial suppressions added up, they wounded free speech with a thousand cuts. A Secret Service agent in Washington, D.C., sent Children's Defense Fund demonstrators away from the Hilton hotel during a Bush speech, to a spot across the street. A protest zone in Missouri was placed one-quarter mile from the St. Charles Family Arena, where Bush came to campaign. In St. Louis, three months later, Andrew Wimmer was ordered to remove his sign saying "Instead of War, Invest in People" to a protest zone three blocks away and down an embankment; for refusing, he was taken into custody, while a woman was allowed to stay with her sign: "Mr. President, We Love You."[49] No matter that assassins and terrorists don't make a habit of waving signs before they strike. No matter that someone seeking to do harm could apparently get close just by holding a placard saying, "Mr. President, We Love You."

Allowing pro-Bush sign holders near and distancing anti-Bush protesters violated the "content neutral" principle that courts have required in the regulation of demonstrations—that is, to be consistent with the First Amendment, restrictions for safety and traffic flow must apply to all messages equally, not just certain viewpoints. New York City police cadets are taught the "sight and sound" rule (which the department doesn't always follow) that permits demonstrators "as near to the target of their protest as is consistent with safety and reasonable requirements of unobstructed passage."[50]

Constitutional precedent received little respect from the Bush White House, however. Typically, arrested protesters had the charges dismissed. Local officials sometimes apologized and even ended up paying monetary damages. But the vindication came too late, because the discordant speech had already been silenced—a form of prior restraint, as if a newspaper had been blocked from printing a story and won the case long after the news value had vanished. The next time, in the next city, the pattern repeated itself: exclusion, arrest, dismissal, apology, and sometimes a fat check, which the White House often left the locals to write. An attempt by the ACLU in 2003 to bring this to a halt, by seeking an injunction against the Secret Service's establishment of distant protest zones, failed when the organizations filing suit were judged to have no standing. They could not prove that they were likely to be damaged in the future.[51] Nor could an individual show ahead of time that she would be expelled for her critical T-shirt.

Only if government notifies protesters in advance that they'll be placed far from the site do they have a chance to go into court for a preemptive order. They tried and failed before the 2008 Republican convention in St. Paul, Minnesota, where authorities stayed vague about the size, rules, and location of a protest zone until it was placed on the side of the convention center opposite the main entrance.[52] Similarly, during the Democratic convention in Denver, a free speech zone was established in a parking lot seven hundred feet from the Pepsi Center, walled off on three sides by concrete barriers and chain-link fence. Afterward, the Denver police union issued a T-shirt picturing a beefy, helmeted cop looming like a giant above Denver's skyline, grinning eerily and wielding a huge club. "We Get Up Early," said the shirt, "to BEAT the Crowds: 2008 DNC."[53]

Judges don't usually interfere, because they're loath to tie the hands of an agency charged with protecting the president and presidential candidates. The law gives considerable latitude to the secretary of Homeland Security, who oversees the Secret Service, "to prescribe regulations governing ingress or egress to such buildings and grounds and to posted, cordoned off, or otherwise restricted areas where the President or other person protected by the Secret Service is or will be temporarily visiting."[54]

Oddly, the Secret Service didn't use that authority when gun-toting demonstrators turned up outside town hall meetings held by President Obama. In August 2009, a protester legally carrying a registered handgun strapped to his leg was allowed on the grounds of a church, along a road leading to a New Hampshire high school where Obama was speaking.[55] Later that month, a dozen gun-rights advocates carrying pistols, and one with an assault rifle, gathered outside an Obama speech in Phoenix.[56] Under Bush, protesters' words were dangerous; under Obama, apparently, protesters' guns were not.

Bush's "Presidential Advance Manual" was not repealed during Obama's first years in office, although citizens who disagreed seemed better able to get into Obama town meetings. Sheryl Gay Stolberg, a *New York Times* White House correspondent, observed "the political stacking of such events by the White House, which controls the flow of tickets to insure a friendly audience in the hall. In this regard Obama seems slightly more open than Bush, but only slightly," she said. "With Bush there was effectively no chance of an unfriendly questioner. With Obama the deck is stacked, but critics can at least get in the hall if they make an effort."[57] Protest zones were still established to keep demonstrators at a distance. In a report card on Obama's civil liberties record, these two items—abandoning both the manual and the "free speech zones"—were listed by the ACLU in a long series of steps not taken.[58]

On February 15, 2011, as Secretary of State Hillary Clinton called for freedom of expression on the Internet, her words struck a bizarre counterpoint to the scene just several rows in front of her. When she arrived at a small auditorium at George Washington University, members of the audience— each carefully vetted and invited by name—stood and applauded. As they took their seats, Ray McGovern remained standing and turned his back on her. He was seventy-one. For twenty-seven years he had been a Soviet analyst for the CIA, and before that an army intelligence officer. He opposed the wars now being waged. After he had entered through a metal detector, he removed a shirt covering a black T-shirt with white letters reading, "Veterans for Peace."

Egyptian protesters had just overthrown Hosni Mubarak a few days before, and Clinton combined praise for the demonstrators with a warning for oppressive regimes. "A few minutes after midnight on January twenty-eighth, the Internet went dark across Egypt," she said as McGovern stood in silence, facing the back wall. "During the previous four days, hundreds of thousands of Egyptians had marched to demand a new government. And the world, on TVs, laptops, cell phones, and smart phones, had followed every single step. Pictures and videos from Egypt flooded the Web."

McGovern kept his pose and drew no complaints, he said. "The guy I was standing in front of was politely looking around me. He didn't say anything." Clinton was trying to look around him, too. The video shows her head swinging side to side, her eyes sliding quickly past the center of her field of vision, where he stood in what he called "silent witness."

"Then the government pulled the plug," she continued. As she spoke that sentence, two men grabbed McGovern roughly, one a huge guy in a suit, the other a university guard. They did not ask him to leave or sit down, just dragged him across four women to the aisle. Clinton didn't flinch. Instead, a slight smile touched her lips. "Cell phone service was cut off," she went on evenly, "TV satellite signals jammed, and Internet access was blocked for nearly an entire country." McGovern was being wrenched and hurt in front of her.

"When I was grabbed, it was a shock," he told me. "It was such a shock I forgot the Code Pink manual, which says as soon as you're grabbed, you shout out the reason you're there." After a few seconds, as he was hauled out of camera range, he shouted, "This is America? This is America!" but Clinton continued smoothly.

"The government did not want the people to communicate with each other," she declared, as cool as ice, "and it did not want the press to communicate with the public."

"The whole thing was like out of a short story by Franz Kafka," McGovern remarked. "She didn't miss a beat. She's a real pro."

Outside in the hallway, he said, the beefy security man locked his wrists with not one but two pairs of handcuffs, clamped so tightly that he bled all over his trousers. He complained that a titanium plate, implanted after a compound fracture in his left wrist, might be dislodged. He was turned over to the D.C. police, was locked up for three and a half hours without medical treatment, and went to an emergency room after being released. Both arms, his left hand, and his left leg were badly bruised. "I'm told that NFL football players who don't make the final cut very often end up in the State Department security force or the Secret Service," he remarked, "and I can believe that."

WHEN RIGHTS CLASH

Neither end of the political spectrum can be counted on for unwavering support of First Amendment principles when emotions run high. Activists on both the left and the right have tried to stifle speech they oppose, especially when demonstrators have become personal and threatening. Then judges and legislators have stepped in. After a rash of bombings and arson attacks on abortion clinics, and following the 1998 murder of Dr. Barnett Slepian in upstate New York, government experimented with limitations on demonstrations. Operation Rescue and other aggressive anti-abortion protesters—who surrounded and blocked clinics, screamed at women entering, and waved pictures of aborted fetuses—found themselves bound by intricate, complex buffer zones imposed by courts and legislatures, and then litigated up to a divided Supreme Court.

In a series of opinions, the justices upheld modest buffers of fifteen to thirty-six feet from abortion clinic entrances but struck down zones around doctors' houses, which had become targets of protest and violence. The Court approved prohibitions against loud noise within earshot of a clinic and within three hundred feet of clinic employees' homes, but rejected bans on peaceful demonstrations within three hundred feet of clinics or residences. It overturned a moving buffer zone of fifteen feet from any patient entering or leaving, as an infringement on the speech of peaceful demonstrators lining the street or sidewalk. But the justices later left intact a Colorado statute requiring protesters to stay eight feet away from any visitor who was within one hundred feet of a clinic.[59]

The Court went back and forth on whether racketeering and extortion laws designed to fight organized crime could be used by abortion clinics to obtain injunctions against protesters, or by federal prosecutors to bring criminal charges. Two powerful statutes were invoked: RICO, the Racketeer Influenced and Corrupt Organizations Act, which carries twenty-year sentences for attempting to close down businesses (clinics, in this case), and the Hobbs Act of 1946, which punishes the obstruction of interstate commerce by force or extortion. In a clash of two rights—to abortion and to free speech—clinics and the National Organization for Women argued that Operation Rescue was trying to shut down the clinics. Free speech advocates worried that invoking such draconian laws could curb any kind of dissident protest, and on the third consideration of the case, in 2006, the justices decided unanimously that RICO and Hobbs could not be used against anti-abortion demonstrators.[60]

A more focused statute remained in effect: the 1994 Freedom of Access to Clinic Entrances Act, which provided stiff fines and a year in jail for the first offense of damaging a clinic or intimidating or interfering with anyone "obtaining or providing reproductive health services."[61] It was an attempt to draw a reasonable line between pure speech and harassing conduct.

In 2005, at the height of the Iraq war, cruel signs celebrating God's wrath began appearing outside the funerals of young Americans who had come home in flag-draped coffins. "Thank God for Dead Soldiers." "Thank God for Sept. 11." "Thank God for IEDs," a reference to the improvised explosive devices, planted at roadsides, that were causing so many casualties.

The country's principal sin was condoning homosexuality, the demonstrators preached, which brought the curse of God down upon "Sodomite America" and its people. "God Hates Fags," read the signs. "God Hates the U.S.A." "Thank God for AIDS." Every death was hailed as retribution. The protesters invaded the mourners' grief, shouting at them that every soldier was burning in hell.

Rarely if ever in American history has a fringe group's ugly speech caused such widespread fury—and such a rapid barrage of restrictions on expression. Only fifty-five people were traveling the country and picketing in small groups, but in about two years at least thirty-eight states and the federal government enacted laws creating buffer zones and time limits on demonstrations near funerals.[62] Then a federal jury in Maryland hit the protesters with a $10.9 million damage award for invading a father's privacy and causing emotional distress, and a Nebraska prosecutor reached way beyond the Constitution in charging one of the leaders with defiling the flag and endangering her child by having him stand on the Stars and Stripes. The Maryland case went to the Supreme Court.

Most of the placards were carried by members of an extended family from Kansas headed by Fred Phelps, who had founded the Westboro Baptist Church in Topeka with a mission of "opposing the fag lifestyle of soul-damning, nation-destroying filth," in the words of one of its Web sites, godhatesfags.com. Marked with an inverted American flag on its Web address, the home page declared gleefully: "God is America's enemy, dashing your soldiers to pieces."

Combining its rants against gays with slurs against Jews, blacks, and the Catholic Church ("the greatest pedophile machine in the world"), the group made sophisticated use of the Internet as a vehicle of free speech, linking its pages to self-produced music videos and flashing headlines inviting visitors into a netherworld of twisted argument.

"'God Hates Fags' is a profound theological statement," Phelps insisted in a recorded screed that oozed with scripture. To the tune of "God Bless America," an ensemble sounding like a church choir sang "God hates America, land of the fags. He abhors her, deplores her, day and night, all his might, all his ways. . . . God hates America, the filthy faggots' home."

If you clicked on an icon saying "Thank God for another tragedy that has stricken Wisconsin . . . ," you saw an exultant message about three college students who died in a housing fire in 2008.

Phelps's daughter, Shirley Phelps-Roper, was driving to the University of Wisconsin to picket one of the funerals and a memorial service when I reached her on her cell phone. "There are so many ways that God is killing these college students," she said with satisfaction. "This nation has a bunch of women, they get drunk, they put their skirts over their heads, they put it on the Web."

Video later showed huge crowds of Wisconsin students surrounding the Westboro group, yelling, "Go home! Go home!" and holding competing posters saying "God Hates No One," "God Is Love." One student raised a witty sign above her head reading "You're Not in Kansas Anymore."

Westboro's vitriol didn't generate broad outrage in the 1990s, when members targeted gays' funerals, picketing services for Randy Shilts, who died of AIDS following his book about the epidemic, *And the Band Played On*. After they demonstrated in 1998 at the funeral of Matthew Shepard, a gay student beaten to death in Wyoming, the city of Casper quickly passed an ordinance requiring funeral protesters to stay at least fifty feet away. But gays and their families didn't get a sympathetic national rush to legislation.

Nor did the church get much attention when it cheered as just punishment the destruction of New Orleans by Hurricane Katrina; the whipping of Georgia by tornadoes ("God controls the whirlwinds, and they are a tool of His judgment"); the deaths in Missouri floods ("God causes the waters to rise"); or the collapse of a construction crane in Manhattan. It was a bit like the local crazy standing on a corner with a sign saying "Doom. Repent. The End Is Near." People shrugged and walked on.

But targeting soldiers' funerals pushed a lot of buttons, patriotic and religious. Motorcycle riders—some of them Vietnam vets—quickly mobilized into the Patriot Guard, offering families an escort designed both to honor the fallen and to block the sight and sound of the protesters with shields of American flags and racing engines. Even before laws were passed, said Phelps-Roper, police often kept the pickets at a distance, so she thought a very small percentage of family members ever saw the signs. Besides, the survivors weren't the targets, she insisted. "It's not about where we're standing. It's about the words."

She remembered a soldier's mother in Minnesota, accompanied by a television crew. "She came right down there, she came down the street, she reached out and shook my hand and hung on to my hand, and she used the opportunity to say, 'I don't think you ought to be here.'"

Phelps-Roper held on to the mother's hand as well and replied without mercy. "I said, 'You raised that child for the devil. [The mother had been divorced and remarried.] You taught that child that adultery was just fine.'"

A vignette of remarkable coldness unfolded outside Arlington National Cemetery on a bright April day, where two young women held signs saying "Thank God for Dead Soldiers," "God Is Your Enemy," and "America Is Doomed." They wore inverted flags wrapped around their waists, and they sang military melodies with antigay lyrics. As federal law required, the pair was kept far enough away not to be noticed by any mourners, except perhaps as they drove briskly past. Most pedestrians reacted about the way they would to the local ranter with the "Doom" sign.

Occasionally, someone would be struck hard enough to stop, take in the scene, shake a head or make a comment, and then move on. To a trio of inquiring teenage boys, the sign-holding women brusquely refused to explain their views and referred the youngsters dismissively to a Web site. Nothing approaching conversation occurred until a woman slowed her pace along the sidewalk and announced with anger and hurt that her husband had been fighting in Afghanistan for their freedom to do what they were doing.

"If he gave us that freedom, why can't we use it?" countered Katherine Hockenbarger, who held the "Dead Soldiers" sign.

A pained look flickered across the woman's face. She walked slowly past, said calmly that she was from a military family, and mentioned that her father had fought in Vietnam.

"Shame on him!" shouted Abigail Phelps, Shirley's younger sister. "That worked out well, didn't it?"

The woman told them that in three weeks her husband was being deployed again to Afghanistan. Perhaps she was searching for a thread of compassion, but Phelps replied acidly that he should simply not go. The woman walked on, mumbled that he had no choice, then turned and shouted over her shoulder at the protesters, "Go to Canada!"

"You're never gonna win that war!" Phelps yelled back. "They're coming home in body bags!" The woman descended into the Metro.

Albert Snyder of Maryland had no such encounter near the funeral of his son Matthew, a marine who died in an accident in Iraq, but television reports of the protesters so infuriated him, and later visits to Westboro's Web sites so disgusted him, that he sued successfully for invasion of privacy and infliction of emotional distress. A jury award of $10.9 million, although reduced by a federal judge to $5 million, alarmed some lawyers who saw in the case an opening for civil suits to undermine First Amendment rights. Then a panel of the Fourth Circuit overturned the award, calling the "distasteful and offensive words" constitutionally protected.[63] The Supreme Court agreed, ruling 8–1 that the First Amendment sheltered the protesters because they had addressed "matters of public concern," not private issues, and had stood 1,000 feet away, without interfering in the funeral.

The decision appeared to leave localities with the power to regulate the time, place, and manner of such demonstrations as long as the message itself was not targeted. In forty-four states, legislators had gone into action to shield the most emotional times and places from intrusion. The majority of the laws they passed protected all funerals, but some statutes specified military services, which First Amendment scholars thought might proscribe only certain messages, undermining their "content neutrality" and thereby their constitutionality.

Like the buffer zones created around abortion clinics, the funeral laws drew lines around churches, cemeteries, and funeral homes to keep demonstrators fifty to five hundred feet away. Some allowed picketing no later than an hour before and no earlier than an hour or two after the service. Phelps-Roper had no problem with such restrictions, said that her group obeyed them after contacting local authorities in advance, and wouldn't challenge most of them in court.[64]

But a couple of the laws included floating buffer zones, requiring a certain distance from funeral processions. Those were contested, she explained, because demonstrators who stood peacefully on a street could suddenly find themselves in violation as a motorcade passed by. Missouri was such a case, as a prosecutor in McDonald County indicated by telling her in a letter that the law's prohibition of picketing "in front of or about" a funeral "will be interpreted to apply to processions to and from the cemetery."[65] As an attorney herself, Phelps-Roper understood the case law and knew that the Supreme Court had struck down a fifteen-foot traveling buffer surrounding patients going to and from abortion clinics. A federal judge in Cleveland overturned Ohio's floating buffer zone for funerals while leaving the other provisions intact.[66]

The flurry of suits brought limited results as lawmakers efficiently revised statutes to respond to judges' objections. The Missouri legislature passed a contingency backup in advance: if the vague prohibition "in front of or about" were found unconstitutional, a three-hundred-foot buffer would automatically go into effect. A federal judge granted summary judgment declaring the original restriction and the contingency section unconstitutional.[67] As soon as a federal judge overturned a Kansas law for vagueness in limiting protests to "before" and "after" services, the legislature amended it to impose precise limits of one hour before and two hours after, with a minimum distance of 150 feet. In 2008, the Kansas Supreme Court found that the law violated the separation of powers by containing a built-in injunction preventing it from taking effect until judged constitutional. Four weeks later, an agile legislature put the same statute, minus the injunction, before Democratic governor Kathleen Sebelius, who said she was signing it "to shield their families from the despicable and disgraceful displays of those seeking publicity." She thereby added to the publicity.

The Westboro cult is a classic case illustrating Oliver Wendell Holmes's observation that the Constitution guards "the principle of free thought—not free thought for those who agree with us but freedom for the thought that we hate."[68]

Widely accepted ideas don't come up in court. "The First Amendment is very much the province of ranters, provocateurs, troublemakers, lunatics," said Ronald K. L. Collins, head of the First Amendment Center. "Your average, play-it-safe kind of person doesn't tend to provoke," and so doesn't need the protection. But how much protection should grieving families receive from hateful ideas in their most vulnerable moments?

Regulating the "time, place, or manner" of demonstrations is a well-established right of the state, as long as a compelling government interest and alternative means of communication exist, and provided the restrictions are content neutral—that is, "without reference to the content of the regulated speech."[69] Some funeral laws fall short on that score. Idaho's, passed in 2007, applies to those who disturb "maliciously and willfully the dignity or reverential nature of any funeral, memorial service, funeral procession, burial ceremony, or viewing of a deceased person."[70] Pro-war demonstrators at a soldier's service would presumably pass muster. It is remarkable how often lawmakers ignore this principle and others handed down by the Supreme Court.

"If you have a funeral procession going down the street, imagine that Dr. Smith had just died," Collins explained. "Dr. Smith performed abortions for a quarter century. Along the route there are demonstrators on both sides of the streets. On one side are people yelling, 'Murderer! Baby killer!' These statutes would prohibit that. On the other side are people holding up signs saying, 'Supporter of Women's Rights.' It is curious that people on one side would be subject to these laws, the other wouldn't."

The street is a long way from the legislature and the courtroom. It's a place where police and prosecutors frequently make up rules as they go along, creating slippage between what is written by the lawmakers and the judges and what is done in the intricate, fast-paced moments of enforcement.

The Phelps clan, videotaping their demonstrations, once caught a fla-grant example of a uniformed officer (they called him "Sheriff") in Mayville, Wisconsin, trying to prohibit a particular message near a soldier's funeral. "I don't want to see that sign," the officer told the picketers. What sign? one asked, inducing him to read it aloud. "'Thank God for Dead Soldiers.' I don't want to see that sign." He added: "You will not desecrate my flag in my county."

When a couple of demonstrators challenged his attempt to suppress particular content, he reached for a security rationale: "I think some people may read those signs and be so offended that they may storm from across the street and cause harm to you. I don't want any crimes to be committed against anybody in my county." A male voice replied, "You're a Nazi, that's what you are." And the officer then said, "I'm going across the street, and if I find anybody who's making a threat toward you, I may come over here, and I may ask you to leave." The male denounced that as a "heckler's veto," an unconstitutional policy that would award, to any threatening person, power to silence speech he disliked.[71]

The rule of law seemed wholly absent when Shirley Phelps-Roper was charged with flag desecration in Nebraska. The state statute, along with all others, had effectively been ruled unconstitutional more than two decades earlier by the Supreme Court in its flag-burning case, *Texas v. Johnson*, but when she mentioned that decision, the cop who made the arrest told her, "We're not in Texas." Did he really not know that Supreme Court opinions apply nationwide?

The county attorney, Lee Polikov, displayed no more respect for the Court's ruling. "Keep in mind that was a 5–4 decision," he told me, as if the narrowness of the vote weakened its force as precedent. It was a "different time, different facts," he said, because it was "a war protest in a public place. I distinguish that from someone who inserts themselves into the private sanctity of an individual family's private funeral." Yet Phelps-Roper was also in a public place, and the content of her message was irrelevant under settled law.

She was obeying Nebraska's statute requiring a distance of at least 300 feet, Polikov conceded. She was actually about 1,200 feet away, she said, with a phalanx of bikers in between. Wherever she was, Polikov decided, it was still too close, although nothing in the law supported his view. "If Shirley Phelps-Roper were across town, I don't think it would have been a problem," he argued. "My job as county attorney is to keep the peace and to balance the interests of members of our society."

"His job isn't to be a grand balancer," Collins countered when I told him of Polikov's position. "His job is to enforce the law."

But Polikov was inventing his own law (this is called activist when applied to liberal judges), which seemed based on some down-home wisdom trying to pass as legal principle. He told me that his clerk had relayed this gem of insight: "My grandmother says your rights stop where mine begin." The prosecutor liked that and found it precisely on target in this case—although actually, in our constitutional system, rights overlap and coexist. "I think an action at someone else's burial service is provocative and is tempting to other people to breach the peace," he declared.

So he decided that Phelps-Roper, by having her son stand on the flag and by wrapping an army flag and an American flag around her waist, had in effect uttered "fighting words" that might have sparked violence and therefore could be punished. The trouble was, nothing of the sort was mentioned in Nebraska's law, which made the crime simply "mutilating, defacing, defiling, burning, or trampling" a flag, period—unrelated to its purpose or consequence.[72] The dissenters in *Texas v. Johnson,* led by Rehnquist, had argued that burning a flag constituted "fighting words," but they had been overruled by a majority noting that in Texas (as in Nebraska) another law on disturbing the peace was available. In fact, Polikov charged her under that as well.

His reasoning had Collins, the First Amendment expert, practically sputtering in distress at the prosecutor's fanciful notion that he could take an unconstitutional law and, all by himself, make it constitutional by attaching a Supreme Court doctrine, especially one that had become nearly extinct. "Flag desecration statutes are unconstitutional. You cannot take an unconstitutional statute and graft onto that 'fighting words,'" Collins

declared. Besides, he said, "if any time somebody does something provocative you can come in and charge 'fighting words,' you're not going to have
much First Amendment worth saving."

County Attorney Polikov did not seem to know that the "fighting words"
doctrine announced in *Chaplinsky* in 1942 had been narrowed severely by
the Court in 1992, made inapplicable unless there was a complete lack of
discrimination against a particular viewpoint. Fighting words were a means
of communication like a noisy sound truck, Justice Antonin Scalia had
written, and "the government may not regulate use based on hostility—or
favoritism—towards the underlying message expressed."[73] This had rendered prosecutions under the concept very rare.

Polikov also charged Phelps-Roper with negligent child abuse because
she had put her small boy into "a potentially dangerous situation." There
could have been "a bad reaction from bikers, soldiers, firemen." The prosecutor had been impressed by the absence of children in films he'd seen
of protests from the 1960s. Evidently, he didn't know about the 1963 Children's Crusade during the civil rights movement, when youngsters flooded
the streets of Birmingham, Alabama.

The prosecutor imagined danger where it hadn't occurred. He conceded
that there had been no violence. He did not know of any threats, if family members had seen the posters, how "fighting words" were defined, of
any other cases brought under the Nebraska flag law, or whether a child
negligence charge had ever been lodged for taking a youngster to a demonstration. He admitted that he'd have a tough time making the case but
wanted to see what the court would say. On the eve of the trial, however, he and Phelps-Roper reached an agreement: he dropped the charges,
and she dropped a federal lawsuit against him for malicious prosecution.
A month later, a federal judge ruled the Nebraska flag desecration law
unconstitutional.[74]

Polikov portrayed himself as devoted to free speech while noting that
the freedom was not unlimited. "You can't yell fire in a theater," he said,
getting it wrong by leaving out the "falsely" in Holmes's famous dictum. Yet
he opposed a constitutional amendment banning flag desecration. "Personally, I don't like the argument that the flag, as an entity in and of itself, is
sacred," he said. "That just becomes too difficult to prosecute. If my tie of
choice has a flag on it, is that all right? If I have underwear with a flag, am
I violating it? The issue should be how your words are used, how your acts
are used. Are they violent? Are they dangerous?"

More dangerous is the imposition of silence, as some in law enforcement understand. The point was made outside Arlington National Cem-

etery, by a plainclothes supervisor of the Park Police who was watching over the pair of Westboro demonstrators. He was an older man, seasoned by a lot of protesters, and if their speech were suppressed, he observed, the bludgeon of censorship could then be brought against your speech or ours.

The Phelps clan argues another way, that God gave the United States the First Amendment as the most beautiful garment, "the crowning jewel," as they put it, "the brightest star in the constellation." And America was now shedding God's precious gift.

But not quite. A middle-aged woman passed the picketers, then turned over her shoulder as she waited to cross the street, and said, "You wouldn't be able to do that in another country."

CHAPTER EIGHT

Inside the Schoolhouse Gate

It can hardly be argued that either students or teachers shed their constitutional rights to freedom of speech or expression at the schoolhouse gate.

—Justice Abe Fortas, for the majority in *Tinker*

The schools of this Nation have undoubtedly contributed to giving us tranquility and to making us a more law-abiding people. Uncontrolled and uncontrollable liberty is an enemy to domestic peace.

—Justice Hugo Black, for the minority in *Tinker*

TINKER'S ARMBAND

IF PUBLIC SCHOOLS were devoted to teaching children to think independently, this chapter would not have to be written. Principals would not suspend students for the mildest of political protests, school newspapers would not be censored, plays and books would not be banned, and classrooms would be sanctuaries of challenging discussion. The American roots of free speech would be nourished in a rich soil tilled by adults keen to cultivate the next generation of citizens.

In many schools, however, order is prized above invention—not everywhere and not all the time, but it's too often the case, especially at crucial moments of national stress. Conformity is valued over protest, harmony over discord, even apathy over activism. So confining is the territory of acceptable debate that students rarely have to consider their own ideas, much less the dissenting views of others.

That is the way most Americans want it. Three-quarters believe that students should not be allowed to wear T-shirts that offend others, polls show. Just over half believe that school newspapers should not be allowed to report on controversial subjects without permission from school authorities, and such censorship is supported by even more teachers and principals—61 and 75 percent, respectively.[1]

Students themselves care insufficiently about the freedoms contained in the First Amendment, according to a survey of more than 100,000 in 544 high schools. Although 83 percent say that "people should be allowed to express unpopular opinions" and 70 percent believe that offending song lyrics should be permitted, only 51 percent agree that the country's "newspapers should be allowed to publish freely without government approval of stories." Three-quarters of all students believe erroneously that flag burning is illegal.

The more actively students participate in school media, the stronger their support for First Amendment rights, yet as financially strapped schools have closed student publications and Web sites, the organized opportunities to practice free speech have dwindled: only 79 percent of schools now have any kind of student-run media.[2]

The Bill of Rights is in our culture but not in our genetic code, so it has to be relearned by every generation. Even free speech, the right Americans most actively use, is not being instilled as a compelling value by the state-required American history courses or by youngsters' daily school experience. If the right is not taught and exercised until it becomes an intuitive ingredient of being American, it gradually succumbs to peer pressure, institutional hierarchy, and apathy.

Furthermore, schools that deny rights harm the larger constitutional enterprise. The mission of "educating the young for citizenship," as Justice Robert H. Jackson wrote, "is reason for scrupulous protection of Constitutional freedoms of the individual, if we are not to strangle the free mind at its source and teach youth to discount principles of our government as mere platitudes."[3] This is a truism, yet the courts have to keep reminding school authorities to observe the First Amendment.

Jackson's words came in the Supreme Court's landmark opinion overturning a mandate that students salute the flag, the 1943 case *West Virginia State Board of Education v. Barnette*. Five years later, I began first grade, starting each day without ever being told that I could refuse to stand and dutifully recite the Pledge of Allegiance, my hand over my heart. The Supreme Court's grant of free choice never reached my classrooms, or those of most other pupils in the country, I suspect. Principals and teachers don't often advertise this particular piece of liberty.

I might have gone along even if I'd known, and not only because I never minded saluting the flag. I revere what it represents. But also, recalcitrance comes hard when your peers are all standing, and the coercive atmosphere isn't relieved unless school officials clearly announce that you're allowed to go against the flow. Several North Carolina parents complained in 2006 that their children were being forced to observe the ritual, despite a state law that required the ceremony but also declared that a public school "shall not compel any person to stand, salute the flag, or recite the Pledge of Allegiance." That's the standard escape clause, which keeps such statutes constitutional. Only after the local American Civil Liberties Union complained did the chairman of the state board of education remind principals and superintendents that students have a choice.

Other schools make the option clear. At Sammamish High in Bellevue, Washington, all the kids seemed to know their right, said Katie Piper, a teacher, so while everyone in her homeroom stood, she and a few others stayed silent, and nobody appeared bothered. Since about 30 percent of the students were children of foreigners, compulsion would have forced a charade as unjust and untrue as requiring an American in Paris to pledge allegiance to the flag of France. Foreign students, puzzled the first time the pledge suddenly crackled through the PA system at Sammamish, were let off the hook. "I explained what it was," Piper recalled, "and told them they didn't have to say it."

The country is a crazy quilt of conformity and rebellion, observance and indifference. Even at the height of nationalistic fervor following September 11, only one of twenty-five students in a class at West High in Madison, Wisconsin, "stood at attention during a tinny rendition of 'The Star-Spangled Banner,'" Mark Singer observed in *The New Yorker*. "Four boys made a point of leaving the room before the music began. Two others walked in a bit tardily, self-consciously surveyed the scene for a few seconds, and then slid into their chairs." Patriotism didn't rely on ritual, one student told Singer: "I'm probably thinking more about my country than those who stand. I'm thinking that I'm grateful to live in a nation where I have the ability to sit or stand."[4]

Nevertheless, in this and other forms of free speech, principals and boards of education routinely ignore Supreme Court precedent, usually without challenge. They set limits that most students never test, and few youngsters who hit obstacles take the trouble to sue. The visible cases are just small outcroppings, leaving a vast bedrock of enforced orthodoxy beneath the surface. Few want to go to court and sacrifice time, money, and comfort. Students who bring a tremor to the foundation of a town's unquestioned assumptions are sometimes subjected to ridicule and threats, sometimes even to the penalty of lowered grades.

John Tinker learned that lesson at age fifteen. Soon after the United States committed ground troops to Vietnam in 1965, he journeyed by bus from

Des Moines to a protest march in Washington. He came from a family distinguished in such matters—a mother, Lorena Jeanne, repelled by the raw racism she had seen as a child in segregated South Texas, who grew into a civil rights and peace activist; a father, Leonard, a Methodist minister who had been dismissed by two congregations for standing on integrationist principles that seem sturdy today but were shaky platforms half a century ago.

In Atlantic, Iowa, where the only black family in town was excluded from the municipal swimming pool, John's mother led the church youth group in an appeal to the city council to admit the family. The council refused, "and my father's church asked him to leave because they said that he was causing trouble," Tinker recalled.[5] Relocating to an all-white church in a racially mixed Des Moines neighborhood, John's mother again sparked controversy by inviting black residents to services. When some came, whites in the congregation showed the good reverend that door, too. He went to work as the peace education secretary for the American Friends Service Committee.

So young Tinker had absorbed the spirit of protest. On the bus home from the 1965 march in Washington, he and others brainstormed on how to keep the issue alive, picking up on an idea they'd heard from college students: black armbands to mourn the war deaths. After Senator Robert F. Kennedy then urged a Christmas truce, John and his friends thought the symbol could carry that call as well. They were innocently oblivious to the reaction the gesture might provoke, and never imagined that they were setting the stage for a landmark Supreme Court case that would record the name Tinker in the annals of constitutional law.

Meeting in groups with their parents, about a dozen students decided to wear simple black pieces of cloth on their sleeves, only to be dealt a preemptive blow. When one of them wrote for his school newspaper about their plans, the faculty adviser notified the principal, who mobilized the five high school principals in Des Moines to issue an advance order banning armbands under penalty of suspension.

No announcement was made to students; John learned of the ban from an article in *The Des Moines Register,* and it made him hesitate. "That morning I tried to call people and see if we should put it off a day," he said, in the hope that they could meet to discuss their plans before proceeding. But he was too late. "Several had already gone to school with armbands and got kicked out." One of them was his younger sister, Mary Beth, an eighth grader who was told to remove the armband, complied, and was then suspended anyway. Years later, Mary Beth still remembers that the girls' adviser "was real nice" as she told of her own family's Quaker background while writing out the suspension notice.

The plain gesture of protest stirred passions, mobilized friendships, and realigned allegiances. Threats of violence were made in advance, according to Christopher Eckhardt, the third student in the court case. At his school, Roosevelt High, an enraged coach decreed that instead of chanting "Beat East High! Beat North High! Beat Lincoln High!" during calisthenics, his gym classes would mark the day of protest by switching to "Beat the Vietcong!" Eckhardt said. "The coach said anyone wearing a black armband tomorrow will be considered a pinko sympathizer." So after class, a few rough boys confronted a friend who knew of Eckhardt's plans but had no intention of participating himself. "Thug elements came up to him and said, 'You better not wear a black armband tomorrow or you will find my foot up your ass and my fist in your face,'" Eckhardt remembered. "He was brave enough to not point me out." Certain moments in life are burned into memory.

The next morning, after his father dropped him at school, Eckhardt took off his coat to reveal a black band pinned to his camel jacket, "very noticeable," he said. As he walked toward the principal's office to complete his act of civil disobedience and accept the consequences, he heard threats. The football captain tried to rip the armband off, dissuaded only when a companion said, "Let him be, he's turning himself in." Nobody on school grounds took up the coach's implicit call for violence, but two students were beaten at a pizza place.[6]

In the office, Eckhardt waited forty-five minutes in full view of the hallway. A couple of passing students taunted him: "You're dead." Finally, the assistant principal appeared, asked him to remove the armband, got the expected refusal, and warned, "Do you want a busted nose? That's how the seniors are going to see it," as Eckhardt recalled the words. Then he was turned over to the girls' adviser, who "said, 'You better start looking for another high school to go to because you'll never be welcome at this high school,'" and that "I would never go to college because colleges refuse to accept protesters."

She was wrong. Eckhardt went to six colleges in three states and got his B.A. in 1994.

John Tinker left his armband off that first day, and after school met with other kids and their parents at Eckhardt's home. Trying to avoid confrontation, they called the board of education president, whose secretary told them that he wouldn't lift the order. Students who hadn't been suspended decided to go ahead anyway.

The next morning, John walked nervously to North High School, leaving his armband in his pocket out of fear of what someone driving past might do. His two youngest siblings, Hope and Paul, wore armbands to elementary school without any problems from teachers or administrators.

John eased into his protest gradually. He got to school right at the bell, "and I didn't have time to put it on. I was self-conscious about having somebody see me do it, so after homeroom I went to the restroom and tried to pin it on. I was having trouble, actually, kind of a one-handed operation, and a fellow came in, saw me working on it, and helped me put it on."

The immediate impact was nil. He had decided to look respectable, so he wore a suit and tie, making the black armband inconspicuous against his dark jacket. "I went to morning classes without any mention of it," he said. "Teachers, if they saw it, they didn't say anything. I kind of think that some of them thought it was a silly policy, and they didn't see any point in making it an issue."

After gym class he shed his jacket and accentuated the armband by pinning it to his white shirt, then went to lunch in the cafeteria. "There was discussion around the table," John remembered. "I had friends who supported me; I had friends who disagreed with me about the war but thought I should have the right to do it. Some people came over and gave me a hard time about being a communist or a coward. One guy on the football team, who I barely knew, came over and defended me, and it was really touching. I don't think he had an opinion one way or the other about the war, but it was a free speech issue."

The educational occasion for searching debate over big issues of war and speech didn't last long. The discussion was cut off when "one of the office workers saw me and reported me," John said.

Tinker's principal, "quite decent" and "somewhat patronizing but not in a bad way," tried to help him see his error, coaxed him to understand how important supporting the country was in times of war, and urged him to recognize "that I'd been influenced by people I should not be trusting. . . . I had the impression that he was trying to do the best by me. It was a long conversation, and he said, 'I'm going to ask you to take it off, but I suspect you won't take it off.' I said, 'Right.'" So the principal requested that John leave school, and the boy walked home.

Christmas break, which began a few days later, was filled with meetings among students, parents, and members of the peace community, and after

New Year's the kids returned without armbands but dressed all in black for the rest of the semester. "To me it was a wonderful example of how you can't stop communication by stopping a symbol," John said. "You just find another symbol."

Few families were willing to take up the ACLU's offer of a legal challenge, so the lawsuit bore just three names, John's, Mary Beth's, and Chris Eckhardt's. They asked for only $1 in damages and a declaration that the school policy was unconstitutional. Students at North High, at least, displayed "an amazing lack of any personal rancor," Tinker recalled, although "some of my teachers were abusive. A teacher said to the class, protesters should be hung up by the thumbs. I know I was graded down in some of the classes," a penalty that was balanced by a history grade that went from a B to an A when the teacher gave him extra credit for his constitutional exercise. "He told me he was proud of me." Eckhardt returned to Roosevelt but was denied permission to run for student council president.

By the time the case reached the Supreme Court in 1969, the public's support for the war in Vietnam had eroded, and the justices voted 7–2 for a ringing declaration of students' rights to free speech. Writing for the majority in *Tinker v. Des Moines Independent Community School District*, Abe Fortas crafted the famous line "It can hardly be argued that either students or teachers shed their constitutional rights to freedom of speech or expression at the schoolhouse gate," a principle weakened somewhat by subsequent decisions.[7]

Fortas rejected the school authorities' argument that the potential for disruption gave them the right to censor speech. Officials had worried that friends of a recent graduate killed in the war might react. Schools were no place for demonstrations. Political opinions should be expressed at the ballot box.

"In our system," Fortas ruled, "undifferentiated fear or apprehension of disturbance is not enough to overcome the right to freedom of expression. Any departure from absolute regimentation may cause trouble. Any variation from the majority's opinion may inspire fear. Any word spoken, in class, in the lunchroom, or on the campus, that deviates from the views of another person may start an argument or cause a disturbance. But our Constitution says we must take this risk, and our history says that it is this sort of hazardous freedom—this kind of openness—that is the basis of our national strength and of the independence and vigor of Americans who grow up and live in this relatively permissive, often disputatious, society."

He noted also that the ban targeted a particular symbol while other students were allowed to wear political buttons and even the Iron Cross of Nazism. "In our system, state-operated schools may not be enclaves of totalitarianism," Fortas declared for the majority. "School officials do not possess absolute authority over their students."

Yet in one sentence, the Court also listed three reasons that expression could be limited in schools: behavior that "materially disrupts classwork or involves substantial disorder or invasion of the rights of others is, of course, not immunized by the constitutional guarantee of freedom of speech."

None of those conditions existed in the armband protest, "a silent, passive expression of opinion, unaccompanied by any disorder or disturbance on the part of petitioners," the majority found, with "no evidence whatever of petitioners' interference, actual or nascent, with the schools' work or of collision with the rights of other students to be secure and to be let alone." Administrators must show "something more than a mere desire to avoid the discomfort and unpleasantness that always accompany an unpopular viewpoint."

The opinion provoked a scalding dissent from Justice Hugo Black. "I think the record overwhelmingly shows that the armbands did exactly what the elected school officials and principals foresaw they would," he wrote, "that is, took the students' minds off their classwork and diverted them to thoughts about the highly emotional subject of the Vietnam war." *Thoughts!* How disruptive for those at that cafeteria table with John Tinker to be diverting their thoughts to a war that some of them might be drafted to fight, that would cost 50,000 American lives, kill and displace millions of Vietnamese, and tear the fabric of the United States.

Black seemed intent on preserving not freedom but authority. If students "can defy and flout orders of school officials to keep their minds on their own schoolwork," he warned, "it is the beginning of a new revolutionary era of permissiveness in this country." He predicted ridiculously that the Court's decision would turn schools upside down. "It is nothing but wishful thinking to imagine that young, immature students will not soon believe it is their right to control the schools, rather than the right of the States that collect the taxes to hire the teachers for the benefit of the pupils."

Chris Eckhardt became an insurance salesman; a youth worker for government agencies in Canada, Iowa, and Florida; a consultant on energy conservation; and a stockbroker, which landed him in jail for "exploiting the elderly," he told me, after a client deeded him some real estate. Eckhardt said he'd returned it, but he was sentenced heavily by a judge who "was a Republican Vietnam veteran and knew of my black armband days." He spent more than four years in prison.[8]

Mary Beth Tinker became a nurse with a master's in public health, concentrating on children's medical issues. But the case "has defined my life in many ways," she said, propelling her to visit schools, talk about the First Amendment, and provide teenagers with a sense of empowerment by describing the big impact of a small gesture. "Look at just the little bit of courage I had, how it shook things up," she tells them, and she also lets them see the tension between bravery and fear. "I like to tell them about taking off the armband, too. I was scared, I was in trouble," she said. "I like to tell them that twenty-five years later we were invited back to the Des Moines schools, but this time we were, quote, 'visiting scholars.' So you're better off doing what you think is right rather than what you think is popular."

John Tinker became a computer specialist in constructing databases. He bought a decommissioned school with twelve rooms and a gymnasium and converted it into a home where he lives with his wife and son but no students. "I like to fix things," he told me, so he's made the rooms into "a welding shop, a woodworking shop, an electronics lab, a computer museum." He has an old printing press. And, of course, he can wear anything he wants in his school.

Justice Hugo Black may have been in the *Tinker* minority, but his anxiety over disruption has been a subtext for decades. Supreme Court opinions are rarely one-dimensional, and they're easy to misinterpret by emphasizing the restrictions rather than the rights. That is what Judith Coebly, principal of Dearborn High School in Michigan, apparently did thirty-five years later while explaining to Bretton Barber why he couldn't wear a T-shirt branding President Bush an "international terrorist." She hadn't read *Tinker* entirely but did read selectively to her student from a legal advisory by the National Association of Secondary School Principals. Ignoring the written guidance on protecting "pure or symbolic speech," she plucked out a passage on the limits, which the document said could be imposed upon "a showing of either past disruptions caused by similar speech or a showing of imminent disruption."[9]

Nearly one-third of Coebly's students were Arab, many of them from Iraq, where the war was about to begin, and she worried that the shirt might spark disorders.[10] Aside from a few unpleasant comments, however, no disruption occurred, and the federal district court judge Patrick J. Duggan seemed to have no trouble ruling in the student's favor. He chastised school authorities for assuming that an ethnic group would have a monolithic reaction to a political viewpoint.[11]

Like virtually every landmark Supreme Court opinion, *Tinker* struggles to keep its footing against stormy gusts of expedience. School authorities don't like controversy. They don't like discord. They don't like parents calling with complaints. They don't like students having arguments that could flare into fistfights or shootings. And they are increasingly under legal obligation to protect the feelings, as well as the opportunities, of minorities in their care, whether black, Muslim, or gay. So they overreact sometimes, shutting down speech because it offends their own beliefs, opposes school policy, or insults an entire group of students.

When Katie Sierra wore pro-peace T-shirts to Sissonville High School in West Virginia, she was suspended; when she asked to form a school-sponsored anarchists' club, she was denied. It was the autumn of 2001, during that spasm of national dread and anger, and a state judge found that her shirts' hand-drawn peace signs and slogans opposing the war in Afghanistan would "disrupt the educational process." She sued, and a jury half agreed with her, deciding that she could form the club but not wear the shirts. Had she appealed, precedent would have surely weighed on her side.[12] But her lawyer, Roger Forman, said the verdict was considered a victory. Katie never formed the club. She returned to her school but didn't fit in, a school board member accused her of "treason," she was taunted and threatened, so she finished her degree sitting at home on a computer and then went to Marshall University.[13]

Discomfort with homosexuality has prompted censorship in various forms. Numerous school districts have installed software blocking students' access to websites that explain or support gay and lesbian concerns, while sometimes allowing anti-gay sites to appear. In Wilson, North Carolina, administrators took down two posters of a candidate for student government president because they identified him as gay, and in Rowan County the school board denied students the right to form Gay-Straight Alliance clubs, voting unanimously "to ban all sexually oriented clubs, gay/straight or otherwise."[14] A principal at a Florida high school banned gay pride and rainbow themes on clothing as "sexually suggestive" messages that would prompt students to imagine homosexual acts and prevent them from studying; he was overruled by a federal judge who scolded the school for missing "a learning opportunity about tolerance and diversity."[15]

In contrast, administrators at Sammamish High School in Bellevue, Washington, permitted the Gay-Straight Alliance and asked teachers to honor participants who remained mute on the Day of Silence, an annual protest against the larger society's silencing of gays and lesbians. "The adviser sent out an e-mail with names of students participating, asking us to excuse them from speaking in class and suggesting other ways they could silently participate," said Katie Piper, a teacher. "Our principal then sent out an e-mail confirming their right to participate and saying there was some talk that there would be a counterprotest. All I saw in the way of that was one student who wore a 'Straight Pride' T-shirt."

In less tolerant schools, however, even the black armband legitimized in *Tinker* has been forced off students' arms when administrators don't like its being used to criticize their policies. Several cases illustrate the problem.

After the 1999 Columbine High School shootings in Littleton, Colorado, about ten students in Allen, Texas, wore black armbands to make two statements: to mourn the Columbine dead and to protest random searches and other new security measures at Allen High School. Administrators raised no objection as long as they thought the armbands were only an expression of grief; it took them three days to learn the other purpose, and when they did, they suspended the students. Once a lawsuit was filed, the school backed down.[16]

Also in 1999, Jennifer Roe and friends were suspended in Bossier City, Louisiana, for wearing black armbands to protest a new dress code. She won in federal court.[17]

In October 2006, school officials suspended about twenty students who wore them to oppose a rigid new dress code in Arkansas's Watson Chapel district. It imposed a school uniform of white shirts and khaki pants or skirts, banning all written messages on garments, except school logos. And in 2009 the Supreme Court let stand an appeals court decision upholding Texas school authorities in a similar situation: a ban on clothing with printed messages other than the school's clubs and teams.[18] The Court left the impression that as long as dress restrictions were content neutral, they would pass constitutional muster.

Dress codes have become a popular method of suppressing unwanted expression by suppressing all expression—on clothing, at least. Courts look for a specific viewpoint the school is trying to snuff out, something more consequential than a fashion statement. For example, a federal judge found that the Arkansas school, in punishing students for wearing armbands, had violated the youngsters' First Amendment rights by enforcing the code to censor a particular message.[19] But an Albuquerque student lost his argument for the right to wear sagging pants,[20] and blue hair hasn't qualified as protected expression under the First Amendment. Courts have often deferred to administrators' arguments that uniform clothing relaxes rivalries over styles, fosters school unity, eliminates gang symbols, and blurs obvious socioeconomic differences.

Nevertheless, students who want to object when expression is silenced often win struggles with their principals, if they care to try. A group at Pioneer High School in Ann Arbor, Michigan, was denied permission to form an organization opposing closed-circuit cameras, which were slated for installation throughout the building to combat thefts, fights, vandalism, and drug use. The surveillance was widely opposed by youngsters who gathered 1,100 signatures on a petition and urged the board of education, in vain, to abandon the assault on privacy.

Even after losing before the board, the student council president and others continued efforts to get the policy reversed, or at least to influence how the recordings would be used and who would be authorized to view them. They needed the school's recognition of their "club," without which they would be denied the right to communicate messages and meeting times in flyers, on bulletin boards, and through the PA system.

"Frankly, it should be embarrassing to the Ann Arbor community that the Pioneer administration is perfectly willing to recognize and give privileges to a student group like the Scooby Doo Club, but deny the same treatment to students who are organizing to advance constitutional values," said the ACLU in a letter to the school superintendent, Todd Roberts.[21]

Even more embarrassing was the ignorance by both the principal and the assistant principal, who reportedly gave two unconstitutional rationales for nonrecognition: that no "political" clubs would be allowed, and that the school would be hypocritical to take one position and permit a recognized student organization to take another. As the ACLU letter noted, both the Federal Equal Access Act and a line of court rulings prohibited schools from singling out clubs to reject "on the basis of the religious, political, philosophical, or other content of the speech at such meetings," in the statute's words. Michigan had a similar law.[22] Superintendent Roberts overruled the principal as soon as he had read the letter and announced the next day that the club would receive recognition.[23] The youngsters had pushed back and succeeded.

So American schoolchildren stand on uncertain ground. Episodes of censorship by public schools and mixed rulings by the courts have left students with an ambiguous right—to speak in some ways about some things in some circumstances. If you're a teenager traveling near the shifting, meandering boundaries between expression that is protected and expression that is unprotected by the First Amendment, you cannot be sure which side of the line you're on. What was allowed last year, in another school or by another court, may be punishable today—or vice versa. This is not the way to teach constitutional values to the next generation of citizens, but that's the way it is being done.

TOLERATING INTOLERANCE

To counter the message of a gay and lesbian awareness day in a California school, Tyler Chase Harper wore a shirt emblazoned with biblical references and the handwritten words "Homosexuality Is Shameful" and "Be Ashamed, Our School Has Embraced What God Condemned." The principal refused to let him attend class. Harper sued.

Tinker offered schools three legitimate reasons for restricting speech, and most litigation has focused on two of them combined: authorities' contention that the expression "materially disrupts classwork or involves substantial disorder." That argument has appealed to some conservative judges. But the third reason—"invasion of the rights of others"—is being cited increasingly as administrators try to protect minorities from hateful speech, a goal supported by certain liberals on the bench. It's not a neat split, since many judges of various stripes remain unwilling to subordinate the right of free speech to such concerns. Yet the First Amendment has been squeezed from both ends of the spectrum.

In 2004, two of three judges on a Ninth Circuit panel relied on the invasion-of-rights test to approve the school's prohibition against Harper's anti-gay T-shirt. Although altercations had erupted the previous year over the issue, raising concern about possible disruption, the court chose the other justification of censorship—to avoid a "collision with the rights of other students to be secure and to be let alone."

The opinion by a liberal judge, Stephen Reinhardt, emphasized the vulnerability of homosexual teenagers as a captive audience in a public school. "The demeaning of young gay and lesbian students in a school environment," he wrote, "is detrimental not only to their psychological health and well-being, but also to their educational development." Verbal abuse had led gays to cut classes or drop out, according to studies he cited. "The First Amendment does not require that young students be subjected to such a destructive and humiliating experience," he declared.

As noble as it sounded, the Reinhardt position failed to notice that suppressing a T-shirt would not silence the taunts. It might have been more beneficial—if more difficult—for the school to use the occasion as a teaching opportunity by organizing civil discussion about sexual orientation. Some believe that homosexuality is a choice or an emotional disease; others see it as a natural characteristic in the array of human variations. Across that dividing line of convictions, how many teenagers have had the chance to speak respectfully to one another? How many straight students, including those who demonstrate support, have actually heard a gay or lesbian describe the experience of self-discovery, of coming out, of negotiating through the emotions of family and friends?

The answer to hateful speech is more speech, not less. And it's not just more speech but more listening as well. Just as censorship can't eliminate the silenced slur, the pro forma demonstration won't always foster dialogue. Schools that are admirably open to T-shirt sloganeering, but don't help facilitate serious conversation, do not prepare their students adequately for the complicated debates and collisions of the larger world.

The courts have not done well at prescribing that kind of searching educational process, and educators who forfeit their responsibilities to judges invite brittle formulas for governing expression in their schools. It was probably just as well that the Supreme Court dodged this case by dismissing it as moot (because the student had graduated) and by vacating the circuit court's decision.[24]

School officials navigate between two shields: the Constitution's protection of speech and various state laws' prohibitions of harassment in public schools by race, ethnicity, religion, and—in some places such as California—sexual orientation. Walking the line so that neither right is trampled has required extraordinary equilibrium, especially in multiethnic settings of high tension.

That sense of balance eluded a superintendent in Cleveland who worried about the feelings of "Arab-American students" when Aaron Petitt, sixteen, made posters of planes bombing Afghanistan (not an Arab country) and wrote, "May God have mercy, because we will not." The boy's sister had been injured by flying debris near the World Trade Center on September 11. Petitt sued, a federal judge lifted his suspension provisionally, and the school district reversed itself, then paid compensation.[25]

The right to offensive speech also found protection from the Third Circuit, which struck down a Pennsylvania district's sweeping ban on "any unwelcome verbal, written, or physical conduct which offends, denigrates or belittles an individual" because of "clothing, physical appearance, social skills, peer group, intellect, educational program, hobbies, or values." Applying the *Tinker* test, the court ruled that such a "broad swath of student speech" could not be silenced without showing specifically why it would cause substantial disturbance. "By prohibiting disparaging speech directed at a person's 'values,'" the judges wrote, "the Policy strikes at the heart of moral and political discourse—the lifeblood of constitutional self-government (and democratic education) and the core concern of the First Amendment."[26]

Administrators sometimes step into minefields when they try to ban symbols that could cause friction. On Cinco de Mayo, the day honoring Mexican heritage, several students at Live Oak High School in Morgan Hill, California, sported T-shirts with American flags, a counterpoint meant to celebrate American heritage. They were given a choice by Miguel Rodriguez, the vice principal. The shirts posed a "safety issue," he told them, so either turn them inside out or go home. They went home, were supported by the ACLU, became heroes on right-wing radio, and were given a standing ovation at a Tea Party rally. The school superintendent reprimanded his subordinates. If the students had sued, would a court have upheld banning the American flag as disruptive? It's hard to imagine.[27]

Courts have been more willing to suppress the Confederate flag, although not universally so, in recognition of the passions it ignites as a symbol of racism and slavery. In a line of federal opinions beginning in 1972, schools that have suffered disorders over the flag's display have usually persuaded judges that the disruption test has been met.[28]

In 1969, three years after Chattanooga's Brainerd High School was integrated, racial tensions soared over the use of "Dixie" as its pep song and the Confederate flag as its emblem. Major demonstrations and counterdemonstrations erupted among the students, of whom only 170 were black and 1,224 white, prompting the school board to drop the song and the flag the following year and adopt a code of conduct banning "provocative symbols on clothing." A student who wore a flag on the sleeve of his jacket was told to remove it, refused, and was suspended. In 1972, the Sixth Circuit ruled for the school.[29]

In 1997, a South Carolina school that had suffered disorder won the right in federal court to require a student to remove a jacket bearing the flag.[30] And in 2000, two federal appeals courts upheld schools' power to act, one against a student who had taken a dare from a classmate and drawn a picture of a flag on a piece of paper,[31] the other against a student who had shown his friends a flag during a history discussion. Among a school's tasks, the court declared in the second case, was to "teach students of different races, creeds, and colors to engage each other in civil terms."[32] How they do so without examining and discussing this symbol's meanings is unclear. Suppression is not engagement.

Where schools cannot show a history of disruption, judges have leaned toward the students' First Amendment rights. In 2001, the Sixth Circuit ruled in favor of two Kentucky students suspended for wearing T-shirts celebrating a Hank Williams Jr. concert, with two Confederate flags and the words "Southern Thunder," in violation of a dress code banning clothing with "illegal, immoral, or racist implications." Although the school had experienced racial tension, including fights, there had been no evidence of clashes around the flag, and the school had permitted African-Americans to wear Malcolm X shirts as symbols of militant black power.[33]

Similarly, a teenager won in federal court after being disciplined for wearing a Confederate flag T-shirt in a West Virginia school with no history of disorders. Following *Tinker's* formula, the judge ruled that a ban was not "warranted simply because some associate it with racism," although the flag might be prohibited if used "as a tool for disruption, intimidation, or trampling upon the rights of others."[34]

The trouble with this highly practical method of judgment is that disruptive kids get to decide what speech in schools is unprotected by the First Amendment. All they have to do is demonstrate or fight whenever the unwelcome message appears, and they've given officials the evidence they need to convince a court. This presents a dilemma: it revives the "fighting words" doctrine in schools and awards a "heckler's veto," but it also provides principals with the authority to keep order, a necessary prerequisite of education.

Colleges have tried to legislate harmony by enacting speech codes. The strategy is designed to insulate minorities from hostility, but it tends to substitute discipline for education. It often permits administrators to take the easy path of suspension or expulsion when a more sophisticated, sustained effort at teaching might do better. It allows bigoted perpetrators who are punished to cast themselves as victims of censorship and wrap themselves nobly in the mantle of the First Amendment. It has given conservative students the opportunity to compete for the persecution prize on campus when they feel silenced by the doctrine of "political correctness," that old communist concept adopted sardonically by the radical right to deride the intolerance of enforced tolerance.

Since the Bill of Rights restricts only government's intrusion into individual liberties, private colleges are generally free to impose rules on expression, while state institutions are not. Even private universities that get federal grants—and practically all do—are not subject to the First Amendment, because the courts have repeatedly held that the receipt of federal funds does not convert private universities into "state actors." No federal law makes free speech a condition of such funding.[35] This stands in contrast to the Civil Rights Act, which prohibits grant recipients from discriminating on the basis of race or national origin under Title VI, and gender under Title IX.[36] So far, offensive speech has not been construed as discrimination.

Nevertheless, some private colleges, such as Harvard and Dartmouth, voluntarily adhere to First Amendment standards, and others are required to do so by state statutes such as California's, under which Stanford's speech code was declared unlawful in 1995.[37]

Where the Constitution protects individual rights against government—as at state universities—the codes have usually been struck down when challenged. That isn't enough for some right-wing organizations, which have lamented the leftward tilt of faculties, have posted public lists of "dangerous" liberal professors,[38] and have lobbied in state legislatures for a high-sounding "academic bill of rights" to preclude political orthodoxy and foster "intellectual diversity" in hiring professors, granting tenure, assigning readings, and selecting outside speakers.[39]

Promoted as a campaign to keep freedom of thought alive, the effort contains an insidious worm of state intrusion, since ensuring a range of political opinions would entail government monitoring, even inside the classroom. This would be a speech code of a different sort, not precluding certain speech but requiring it.

In state universities, speech codes create a clash between two monumental constitutional rights: the First Amendment's guarantee of freedom of speech and the Fourteenth Amendment's guarantee of equal protection under the law, which on campus means equal educational opportunity. You are not going to function well academically if you are subjected to swastikas on your dormitory door and racist slurs by e-mail, and if the college community becomes a place of unease, rejection, and hostility for members of your ethnic, religious, or racial group. Nor is the student who gets away with vilifying minorities going to learn what is needed to function well in the diverse world of adulthood. After graduation, if you try some of those hateful expressions, you'll be out the door of most workplaces in a flash.

But this conflict in college cannot be well resolved in court. A judge holds only the blunt instrument of victory or defeat; she cannot ordain a nuanced educational process. She cannot foster acceptance and mutual insight on a multiethnic campus. When administrators punish and students sue, leading and teaching fall by the wayside.

When a Dartmouth fraternity staged a "ghetto party" with Afro wigs, baggy jeans, dashikis, and gang colors in 1999, African-American students were pained, felt stereotyped, and complained. Without a speech code, though, the college could not retreat into a sanctuary of quasi-judicial hearings and punishments, and that was fortunate. Instead, black students, who are usually left to battle such slurs alone, were joined this time by many white students, and together, across racial lines, they organized a day and an evening of discussions, panels, workshops, and cathartic introspection that brought in professors and administrators to talk through the confounding issues of race and class with the hundreds who turned out. An offense became a teaching opportunity rather than a disciplinary case.

"The target of hate speech is not the only victim," observed David Tatel, a veteran civil rights lawyer who became a federal appeals court judge. "Racially offensive speech victimizes all on campus; indeed, it victimizes the entire academic institution." It is "a symptom of a deeper, underlying problem which cannot be solved through the issuance of punitive regulations." Therefore, he reasoned, both the First and the Fourteenth Amendments must be honored, not set against each other. "Imagine how successful the boycotts and marches of the civil rights movement would have been without the protective umbrella of the First Amendment," he said. Yet "the First Amendment's guarantee of free expression would have little meaning without the equal educational guarantee of the Fourteenth Amendment," he added. "Racist speech presents a real and serious threat to the educational opportunities of minority students." The solution, then, "should be educational, not disciplinary."[40]

In the wake of desegregation, as growing numbers of blacks and Hispanics moved up into the middle class, universities came to see the value of assembling diverse student bodies as a benefit not only to minorities but to whites as well, as part of their preparation for a multicolored world. Admissions officers started to recruit actively in the high schools of poor and working-class neighborhoods, and when they found talented black and Hispanic applicants, they looked past rigid test scores into capabilities less easily quantified. This was a form of affirmative action. Variegated campus communities resulted. And with the influx of minority students came hateful reactions from scattered groups of vocal whites.

During the first two months of 1987, for example, a student-run radio station at the University of Michigan broadcast racist jokes, a white Ku Klux Klan robe was hung from a dorm window, and anonymous flyers were circulated caricaturing blacks as "saucer lips, porch monkeys, and jigaboos." The leaflets declared "open season" on African-Americans.

An outcry followed in the state legislature, where a powerful committee chair threatened to delay funding if the university failed to act. A student group threatened a lawsuit against administrators "for not maintaining or creating a non-racist, non-violent atmosphere." The university president resigned nine months later.

After a dozen drafts and much discussion, the board of regents approved an intricate speech code that left expression virtually unfettered in public areas, including the university-sponsored daily newspaper and other student publications. But in dorms, recreational settings, and academic buildings, the rules punished "any behavior, verbal or physical, that stigmatizes or victimizes an individual on the basis of race, ethnicity, religion, sex, sexual orientation, creed, national origin, ancestry, age, marital status, handicap or Vietnam-era veteran status" if it conveyed a threat, interfered with academic work, or created "an intimidating, hostile, or demeaning environment."

An interpretive guide by the university's Office of Affirmative Action gave hypothetical cases of sanctionable speech and behavior; they included a flyer making racist threats, the exclusion of a suspected lesbian from a dorm party, and a demand by two men that their roommate move out and be tested for AIDS. One section began, "YOU are a harasser when . . ." and listed such examples as: "You exclude someone from a study group because that person is of a different race, sex, or ethnic origin than you are. You tell jokes about gay men and lesbians. You display a Confederate flag on the door of your room in the residence hall. You laugh at a joke about someone in your class who stutters. You make obscene telephone calls or send racist notes or computer messages."

One of the cautionary hypotheticals sparked a lawsuit: "A male student makes remarks in class like 'Women just aren't as good in this field as men,' thus creating a hostile learning atmosphere for female classmates." Reading that, a psychology graduate student, identified only as "John Doe" in court papers, worried that his right to discuss "controversial theories positing biologically-based differences between sexes and races" might be punishable as sexist and racist.

Citing *Tinker*, a federal district court judge ruled for the student and permanently enjoined the University of Michigan from enforcing its speech code.[41]

Other decisions by federal courts marked this legal landscape. In 1991, a district judge overturned the University of Wisconsin's hate speech regulation as unconstitutionally vague and overbroad. The code was unclear on whether someone had to demean the target and create a hostile atmosphere in actuality or merely intend to do so. And it was deemed overbroad because it prohibited types of speech protected by the First Amendment.[42]

In 1992, the Supreme Court in *R.A.V. v. City of St. Paul* struck down an ordinance outlawing graffiti or symbols that would "arouse anger, alarm, or resentment in others on the basis of race, color, creed, religion, or gender," which the majority found so narrow as to bar only messages with certain content.[43]

The following year, the Fourth Circuit overturned George Mason University's sanctions against a fraternity that had held an "ugly woman contest" in which a performer had put on blackface, women's clothes, and padding to create a caricature. While agreeing "wholeheartedly" with a public university's interest in "maintaining an environment free of discrimination and racism, and in providing gender-neutral education," the court cited *R.A.V.*'s ban on "selective limitations upon speech" and declared, "The University should have accomplished its goals in some fashion other than silencing speech on the basis of its viewpoint."[44]

As things stand, then, it's hard for either public schools or public universities to suppress individuals' speech merely to spare people's feelings. They keep trying, and the courts keep saying no, unless the insulting words or symbols risk igniting violence or other disruption.

EROSION

Yet the Supreme Court has begun to define those risks quite loosely, not to protect minorities, but to give school authorities license to control messages in settings that they organize. This concept of school-sponsored speech, invented and expanded by the Court, now allows principals to censor student publications, campaign speeches, and even banners just outside the schoolhouse gate.

Tinker established the foundation of speech rights in both public schools and public universities. But its scope was narrowed with the Supreme Court's rightward shift in the 1980s, especially by two significant rulings, one banning lewdness (*Bethel School District No. 403 v. Fraser*) and the other censoring student newspapers (*Hazelwood v. Kuhlmeier*). In the first case, the Court decided that vulgarity and other bad manners could be prohibited outright, and in the second, that speech seemingly sponsored by a school, as in a school publication, could be regulated to conform with an administration's policies.

If the cases had been limited to their specific circumstances, their damage to students' First Amendment rights might have been contained. But lower courts have applied their principles more broadly, allowing administrators canny enough to know the law to find ways to silence expression that they find offensive or merely inconvenient.

About an hour before nominating a friend for student government, Matthew Fraser wrote a speech full of sexual innuendo, which he delivered to his high school assembly in Bethel, Washington. "I know a man who is firm," he said. "He's firm in his pants, he's firm in his shirt, and his character is firm. But most of all, his belief in us, the students of Bethel, is firm. Jeff Kuhlman is a man who takes his point and pounds it in. . . . He doesn't attack things in spurts. He drives hard, pushing and pushing until finally he succeeds. Jeff is a man who will go to the very end—even the climax— for each and every one of you."[45] There were hoots in the assembly and congratulations afterward.

The next day Fraser was suspended. He sued, and he won in two lower courts, which found no substantial disruption as required by *Tinker*. But he lost in the Supreme Court, 7–2. While nodding respectfully to the *Tinker* standards, Chief Justice Warren Burger tempered them by declaring that "the constitutional rights of students in public school are not automatically coextensive with the rights of adults in other settings." He created a balancing test, noting that a school's functions included teaching civility. "The undoubted freedom to advocate unpopular and controversial views in schools and classrooms must be balanced against the society's countervailing interest in teaching students the boundaries of socially appropriate behavior," he wrote for the Court. "Even the most heated political discourse in a democratic society requires consideration for the personal sensibilities of the other participants and audiences. . . . A high school assembly or classroom is no place for a sexually explicit monologue directed towards an unsuspecting audience of teenage students."

That line about the assembly contained the seed of an idea that later grew and invaded students' rights: the concept that officials could stifle unwelcome words in a school-sponsored setting, in this case, because the assembly had been arranged by the school, which required students to attend or go to a study hall.[46]

Matt Fraser became a martyr of sorts, and predictably the school

couldn't shut down the sexual references. Football players made signs saying "Stand Firm for Matt," and students chose him by write-in to give the
graduation speech. He later became debate coach at Stanford University.[47]

In the old adage, bad cases make bad law. Next to the principled Tinker
kids, Matt Fraser was just an adolescent wise guy. Next to the Tinkers' serious, quiet statement on a grave issue, Fraser's was half-witty titillation, a
lightweight try. The case was nothing more than a principal's overreaction
to a sassy student's poor taste, elevated by crotchety judges to a restriction
on schoolchildren across the land—curtailing not only obscenity but other
expression that an administration deems inappropriate. Sensible principals
might draw that line reasonably, but the constitutional culture is corrupted
when battalions of autocratic principals have command authority to determine the limits of speech.

In his dissent, Justice John Paul Stevens seemed sorry that he and his
colleagues weren't teenagers themselves. Matt Fraser, he wrote, "was probably in a better position to determine whether an audience composed of
600 of his contemporaries would be offended by the use of a four-letter
word—or a sexual metaphor—than is a group of judges who are at least two
generations and 3,000 miles away from the scene of the crime."

In public, Fraser would have had much more latitude than in school,
as an appellate court judge had observed in an earlier opinion. Remembering the "Fuck the Draft" jacket that the Supreme Court had allowed Paul
Robert Cohen to wear in a Los Angeles courthouse, the judge issued a suc-
cinct appraisal of students' freedoms: "The First Amendment gives a high
school student in the classroom the right to wear Tinker's armband, but not
Cohen's jacket."[48]

So the line restricting obscenity in school was neither new nor especially
controversial. In 1992, before the vulgar meaning had been washed off the
word "suck" as it entered everyday vocabulary, a federal court backed a
middle school's suspension of a student for wearing a shirt reading "Drugs
Suck."[49] Obviously, it was not the content but the manner of speaking that
rankled administrators. Somebody should test this again to illustrate how
incessantly language evolves.

But *Fraser*'s grant of authority to determine which messages are "socially
appropriate" has been used beyond obscenity cases. It is occasionally cited
by courts upholding bans on the Confederate flag, as against the boy who
drew one on a piece of paper. The Eleventh Circuit endorsed "the more
flexible *Fraser* standard, where the speech involved intrudes upon the function of the school to inculcate manners and habits of civility."[50]

Therefore, when administrators want to censor nonpolitical, nonreligious messages that make them uncomfortable, they often win by citing *Fraser's* "boundaries of socially appropriate behavior." Such was the outcome in the Sixth Circuit after a student, Nicholas J. Boroff, donned shirts with pictures and slogans of Marilyn Manson, the Goth shock-rocker, a man who wears black lipstick, dark eye makeup, studded clothing, and tattoos as he performs bizarre music videos with allusions to sex, murder, and suicide. His stage name is taken from the suicidal Marilyn Monroe and the mass murderer Charles Manson. On one of Boroff's shirts, a three-faced Jesus was illustrated with the words "See No Truth. Hear No Truth. Speak No Truth." On the back was the word "Believe" with "LIE" highlighted.

School officials in Van Wert, Ohio, didn't like it. They said that it violated their policy banning "clothing with offensive illustrations, drug, alcohol, or tobacco slogans," and they suspended the boy. "Mocking any religious figure is contrary to our educational mission, which is to be respectful of others and others' beliefs," the principal declared in an affidavit. "Mocking this particular religious figure is particularly offensive to a significant portion of our school community, including students, teachers, staff members, and parents." He added that Marilyn Manson's promotion of drug use could influence teenagers.

The judges didn't like Manson either. Two of the panel of three described his appearance as "ghoulish and creepy," rejected Boroff's claim that his message was religious, and accepted the school's determination that "this particular rock group promotes disruptive and demoralizing values which are inconsistent with and counter-productive to education."

Even the lone dissenting judge agreed that school authorities could ban T-shirts showing rock stars identified with drug use, but here, he believed, the administration had suppressed an aspersion on a religion. The principal had conceded as much. "If the T-shirt had depicted Jesus in a positive light," the dissent said, "it would not have been considered 'offensive.'" That made the school's action "viewpoint discrimination," and thereby a violation of the First Amendment. But the school was narrowly upheld.[51]

Building on *Fraser*, the Supreme Court in 2007 confirmed a principal's right to suspend a student who refused to take down a banner, supposedly advocating drug use, at a school-sponsored event off school grounds. A major theme of the opinion in *Morse v. Frederick*, written by Chief Justice John G. Roberts Jr., was the school's right to suppress speech that contradicted its antidrug policy.

It's a good bet that the justices had no idea what a "bong hit" was before they got this case—unless they had teenage children or grandchildren candid enough to tell them. Yet those were among the words they found censorable. Several students unfurled a fourteen-foot banner reading "BONG HiTS 4 JESUS" in front of their high school in Juneau, Alaska, as the torch for the Winter Olympics passed by en route to Salt Lake City in 2002.

The principal, Deborah Morse, immediately crossed the street and ordered the students to take down the sign; all but Joseph Frederick complied, he was suspended for ten days, and he sued Morse for damages, winning in the Ninth Circuit.

A key question was whether the principal had jurisdiction. The Supreme Court found that although they were off school grounds, the students had all been let out during class hours to line the street for the torch relay, and teachers and administrators were interspersed among the youngsters, making it a school event and subject to *Fraser*'s rules allowing administrators to control the messages in such settings.

Frederick's contention "that the words were just nonsense meant to attract television cameras" was rejected by justices who accepted school officials' translation. Nor did the student define it as a religious message or a political appeal for a change in drug laws, which might have found constitutional protection.

"School principals have a difficult job, and a vitally important one," Roberts wrote for the majority. "Morse had to decide to act—or not act—on the spot," and "failing to act would send a powerful message to the students in her charge, including Frederick, about how serious the school was about the dangers of illegal drug use. The First Amendment does not require schools to tolerate at school events student expression that contributes to those dangers."

How a silly sign might contribute to those dangers the Court did not make clear. It's hard to escape the sensation, here and in certain other cases, that at least some justices begin at the end they wish to reach and work backward to find constitutional rationalizations. Here was an irreverent remark about Jesus combined with an arguably pro-drug message—a bong being a container filled with water through which a "hit" of marijuana can be smoked, as in a water pipe. If the school had a sophisticated anti-drug education program (of which there was no evidence), Justice Stevens wrote in dissent, could it really have been countered by a ludicrous, ambiguous sign "that was never meant to persuade anyone to do anything"?

It may or may not be relevant that all five Catholic justices voted as a bloc to make this a constitutional issue. If the Jesus reference was offensive, it should not have mattered in a First Amendment case, and perhaps it didn't. In fact, the student won support from a conservative Christian group founded by Pat Robertson, which worried about the trampling of speech rights as exercised by religious students elsewhere.[52] For the five justices, something else besides religion seemed to be going on. The tone of their opinion, amplified by Clarence Thomas's concurrence, suggested a strong nostalgia for the days when a strict regime prevailed in the nation's schools. Thomas, the product of a no-nonsense parochial education, reflected admiringly on the "iron hand" of schools in colonial America, declaring categorically, "As originally understood, the Constitution does not afford students a right to free speech in public schools." He termed Frederick's sign "impertinence" and recalled Black's "prophetic" dissent in *Tinker* that the landmark case would undermine teachers' authority to maintain order. Thomas wrote that he would throw out *Tinker* entirely: "We continue to distance ourselves from *Tinker,* but we neither overrule it nor offer an explanation of when it operates and when it does not. I am afraid that our jurisprudence now says that students have a right to speak in schools except when they don't—a standard continuously developed through litigation against local schools and their administrators."[53]

In judging the "BONG HiTS 4 JESUS" banner undesirable in content and censorable because it was displayed at a school event, the Court pulled together the two key exceptions it had manufactured in the 1980s—exceptions to *Tinker's* broad protection of students' freedom of speech. One was *Fraser's* test of whether the expression was socially appropriate; the other was whether it fit into a new concept—school-sponsored speech. These two rationales have since become useful tools for principals wishing to suppress uncomfortable words.

The notion that a student's speech or writing could actually be considered school sponsored grew out of innovative newspaper reporting that worried a Missouri principal. The case illustrated the famous crack by the press critic A. J. Liebling: "Freedom of the press belongs to the man who owns one." In a sense, the principal "owned" the Hazelwood East High School newspaper, the *Spectrum,* and was bothered by what he read about premarital sex and divorce in the spring of 1983, when a journalism class prepared the year's final edition.

Their new teacher edited and transmitted the articles for approval by Principal Robert Reynolds, who balked. Two features represented unusual enterprise for a high school paper but created privacy and fairness problems, he felt. The first, about teenage pregnancy, portrayed three pregnant students who were insufficiently disguised; their names had been changed, but Reynolds thought they remained identifiable, along with their boyfriends and parents. The subject also made him uncomfortable, and he worried that it might encourage unprotected sex. The second, about divorce, quoted a student as saying that her father frequently argued with her mother and "was always out of town on business or out late playing cards with the guys." Reynolds thought the story should have given the father an opportunity to comment. (The version he saw contained the student's name, which the faculty adviser had actually deleted.)

Some of the principal's concerns—identifiability, fairness, and privacy—were legitimate issues, as Martin Duggan, a former editor at the *St. Louis Globe-Democrat,* told the district court. But rather than teaching a lesson in responsible journalism and getting revisions, Reynolds simply deleted the articles—and not only those two, but the entire two pages on which they appeared, a total of six stories altogether. He did so because it was so late in the year that he believed any delay might kill the entire edition. The students didn't learn of the wholesale deletion until the paper came out and they saw what was missing.

The Supreme Court then gave them quite a different lesson. By 5–3, the justices upheld the principal's right of censorship—and not just on the narrow basis of pedagogical interests, as allowed under *Tinker.* They might have approved the refusal to publish until the stories met high standards of journalism; that would have fulfilled the curricular purpose.

Instead, the Court's majority invented a whole new category of speech—not student initiated but school sponsored, which might include statements, articles, slogans, and symbols that could be construed as an administration's views, even if not explicitly sanctioned by the school. This class of expression, the Court ruled, was susceptible to official approval or disapproval. *Tinker* had made no such distinction; *Fraser* had contained the germ of this idea. Now the Court had made it into an escape route from the First Amendment.

"Educators are entitled to exercise greater control over this second form of student expression," declared the majority opinion by Justice Byron White, "to assure that participants learn whatever lessons the activity is designed to teach, that readers or listeners are not exposed to material that may be inappropriate for their level of maturity, and that the views of the individual speaker are not erroneously attributed to the school."

The Court offered a broad array of censorable categories, including articles that were "ungrammatical, poorly written, inadequately researched, biased or prejudiced, vulgar or profane, or unsuitable for immature audiences." The "unsuitable" label could be affixed quite liberally: administrators could keep from elementary school children a discussion on the existence of Santa Claus, the opinion said, and from high school students "speech that might reasonably be perceived to advocate drug or alcohol use, irresponsible sex, or conduct otherwise inconsistent with the 'shared values of a civilized social order.'"

Officials could silence expression that would "associate the school with anything other than neutrality on matters of political controversy," the majority declared. That right to censor was limited by a vague condition: "We hold that educators do not offend the First Amendment by exercising editorial control over the style and content of student speech in school-sponsored expressive activities *so long as their actions are reasonably related to legitimate pedagogical concerns*" (emphasis added). The term "reasonably related" was legal code for a standard of review at the weak end of constitutional protection, in a zone permitting suppression if it has a "rational basis" and an incidental impact. That's not hard to prove. The tougher standard is called "strict scrutiny," which subjects a government intrusion to closer inspection to be sure that it's not vague or overly broad.

In a spirited dissent, Justice William J. Brennan Jr. branded the majority's argument as worrisome nonsense. Neither the principal nor the majority of justices honored the "pedagogical concerns," Brennan wrote acidly, "unless one believes that the purpose of the school newspaper is to teach students that the press ought never report bad news, express unpopular views, or print a thought that might upset its sponsors." Principal Reynolds had tipped his hand in meetings with students afterward, telling them that the articles were "'too sensitive' for 'our immature audience of readers'" and were "inappropriate, personal, sensitive and unsuitable for the newspaper." This led Brennan to conclude: "The case before us aptly illustrates how readily school officials (and courts) can camouflage viewpoint discrimination as the 'mere' protection of students from sensitive topics." As for erroneous attribution to the school, he added, the paper could have published a plain disclaimer reminding readers that it didn't speak for the administration.[54]

Again, a series of poor judgments in a school by both students and administrators worked their way through three levels of the federal judiciary into the stratosphere of constitutional interpretation. What might have been a reasonable delay in publication for journalistic reasons became a wrongheaded ban on uncomfortable subjects, which then grew into a significant principle of law. And the floodgate of censorship was opened.

The Student Press Law Center, which provides free legal advice, saw a 350 percent jump in calls for help from students battling censorship in the five years after the 1988 *Hazelwood* ruling, and faculty advisers increasingly reported threats that they would be fired if they didn't obey instructions to suppress unwelcome writing.[55]

Some teenage journalists pushed back. Students at Upper Arlington High School in Ohio wore black armbands to protest the ruling and adorned the next issue of their newspaper with a front-page photograph of the First Amendment on fire. But then their principal, and others elsewhere who had never tried to exercise prior restraint, began insisting on seeing articles before publication. Some demanded that papers stop defining themselves with the term "open forum" or, in legal terms, "limited public forum," which has been judged a place where speech has First Amendment protection. That label makes the publication available for students' free expression; it confers the broader rights outlined under *Tinker* and puts the content beyond the easy reach of school officials who want to censor under stricter *Hazelwood* standards.[56]

In 2007, the Thomas Jefferson Center for the Protection of Free Expression conferred three ironic Jefferson Muzzle awards—something nobody should want to win—on three schools for suppressing uncomfortable student writing: first, Ben Davis High School in Indianapolis for confiscating all copies of *Spotlight,* which ran an editorial using familiar conservative arguments to oppose illegal immigration (the principal feared "verbal confrontations"); second, Princeton High School in Cincinnati, which barred distribution of *Odin's Word,* a magazine containing a critical sports analysis attributing the football team's poor record to coaching mistakes and a weak offensive playbook (the principal insisted a publication should not "cause division within a school"); and third, Wyoming Valley West High School in Pennsylvania, which removed an artless poem from the literary journal *Interim* because it said of an unnamed teacher who suspended a student caught without a hall pass, "The beast is such a demon."[57] One of the 2009 Muzzles went to a high school principal in Horry County, South Carolina, who banned a student newspaper for editorializing in favor of same-sex marriage and running a picture of two young men holding hands.[58]

There are always crosscurrents in the law. Some lower courts have protected First Amendment rights by tight interpretations of *Hazelwood.* The New Jersey Supreme Court overturned a school's censorship of reviews of R-rated movies, finding nothing offensive and noting that the student paper had previously reviewed similar films without interference.[59] A Michigan school lost in federal court after suppressing a student newspaper's report on neighbors suing over exhaust fumes from idling school buses; the judge ruled that the article was fair, accurate, and unbiased, presenting administrators with no educational justification for action.[60] Some states have also enacted statutes that shield student publications, school boards have adopted similar regulations, and freedoms found in state constitutions sometimes exceed those in the First Amendment—at least as interpreted by state judges.

Long before the parties get to court, however, censorship and self-censorship abound. As in the wider world of authoritarian regimes, both derive from fear—fear of disruptive ideas, fear of retribution for uttering them. Principals and teachers set parameters, students obediently stay within them, and then they carry their high school miseducation into college. On campuses I've visited around the country, I've seen a worrying lack of boldness and enterprise among student editors, a flaccid style of reporting brought forward from their high school years. I find myself, in our short discussions, pushing them to dig and probe and cover the bevy of controversial issues that honeycomb their campus communities. They don't always exercise the greater freedom that most college papers enjoy over the high school press. Many are still conditioned to avoid discord. Too often, they devote their front pages to lackluster pieces regurgitating some visitor's insipid lecture: quick, safe, lazy journalism.

"My own experiences have convinced me that today, the vast majority of students are unable to practice true journalism at their high school papers," wrote Richard Just, an editor at *The New Republic,* who directed a summer program at Princeton for talented high school reporters and editors. Their newspapers "read more like school-sponsored news releases than true journalism," he said. "Many have been taught to write fluffy profiles of teachers and to celebrate the achievements of their sports teams; fewer have been encouraged to challenge, to criticize, or to investigate." This was poor preparation for work in the profession. "No high school principal would dream of telling the basketball team that it could run drills but not play games, or permit the drama club to rehearse but never to stage shows. Yet, thanks in part to *Hazelwood,* many high schools train their students in journalism without allowing them to truly practice it."[61]

Publications aren't the only forms of expression now governed by *Hazelwood*'s ruling that speech can be limited when administrators claim ownership of the statement and think it's "unsuitable." Courts have applied the standard to plays, homework assignments, team mascots, and even cheer-leading.[62] A cheerleader in Texas was kicked off the squad after she refused to cheer for a basketball player whom she had accused of sexually assaulting her at a party. (He and another boy had been arrested, but a grand jury had refused to indict them.) Her suit was thrown out by a federal district judge and a three-judge panel on the Fifth Circuit, which cited *Hazelwood* among other factors, noting, "In her capacity as cheerleader, [she] served as a mouthpiece through which [the school] could disseminate speech." The school, the judges ruled, "had no duty to promote [her] message by allowing her to cheer or not cheer, as she saw fit."[63]

In school, teachers' statements have also been subjected to these tests. Teachers generally hold the same rights as students and are circumscribed by similar restrictions. They can refuse to salute the flag under *Barnette,* the same case that preserved that right for students, and their other freedoms have been litigated into a complex checkerboard.

According to federal case law, a teacher can urge a school to observe Black History Month[64] but can't talk about the needs of special education students.[65] He cannot be fired for writing a letter to the editor accusing the school system of misallocating funds and deceiving taxpayers,[66] but she can be dismissed if her students write plays on gang violence that incorporate the profane language of the streets.[67]

A drama teacher was transferred out of a North Carolina high school, and then lost in court, after she chose a play with a lesbian character and an illegitimate child for performance by four students in her advanced acting class. It didn't matter to the school that they had won multiple awards for the production.[68] Another drama teacher, Wendy DeVore, was threatened with dismissal in Fulton, Missouri, after her students performed *Grease,* the musical set in the 1950s, even though she had bowdlerized the script by switching profanity to slang and changing "weed" to cigarettes. Complaints came from three members of a church congregation about the drinking, smoking, and kissing in the show, so the principal ducked the next possible controversy by vetoing the teacher's next choice: *The Crucible,* Arthur Miller's play about McCarthyism. Facing the possibility of being fired, DeVore resigned.[69]

Schools are constant battlegrounds over what plays and books are suitable for children. Mark Twain's *Adventures of Huckleberry Finn* has been removed from some school libraries because it contains the epithet "nigger," and Maya Angelou's *I Know Why the Caged Bird Sings* has been banned because of sexual content. In some districts, all it seems to take is a handful of complaints from a few prudish or religiously zealous parents, and banning orders go out for *The Catcher in the Rye* by J. D. Salinger, *Beloved* and *The Bluest Eye* by Toni Morrison, *Of Mice and Men* by John Steinbeck, *Slaughterhouse-Five* by Kurt Vonnegut, and other works considered classics. The Harry Potter series by J. K. Rowling, which has turned millions of children into early, avid readers, has been rejected here and there as "satanic" in its fantasy of wizardry and magic.

Narrow constituencies can easily activate school officials' impulses to avoid controversy. The Miami-Dade School Board removed a picture book, *A Visit to Cuba,* after a former political prisoner complained that it painted a rosy picture of life in the communist country.[70] Korean-Americans and South Korean consulates have mounted campaigns against *So Far from the Bamboo Grove,* a tale of persecution suffered by a Japanese family in Korea during the final months of World War II. Based on the author's experiences as a Japanese official's young daughter, it represents the other side of the better-known story of Koreans crushed under more than three decades of Japanese occupation, which is naturally the one Koreans prefer to see told. With careful teaching that fills historical gaps, the book can lead pupils into a sense of warfare's human costs.[71]

The courts have entered these struggles over books with diffidence and equivocation. In 1982, the Supreme Court was unable to muster a clear majority on the constitutional question as it ambiguously overturned the decision of a school board in New York to remove ten volumes from school libraries. The titles came from a list that several parents had obtained at a conservative conference, and the school board ultimately ruled the books "anti-American, anti-Christian, anti-Sem[i]tic, and just plain filthy." Included were Vonnegut's *Slaughterhouse-Five, Down These Mean Streets* by Piri Thomas, *Black Boy* by Richard Wright, *Soul on Ice* by Eldridge Cleaver, and *A Hero Ain't Nothin' but a Sandwich* by Alice Childress because it mentioned that George Washington had owned slaves.

Board members admitted that their decision was based on their "personal values, morals, tastes, and concepts of educational suitability" and declared it "our duty, our moral obligation, to protect the children in our schools from this moral danger as surely as from physical and medical dangers."

On this, the Court provided less than a ringing declaration. Four justices crafted a narrow ruling that while vulgarity would be a legitimate reason to remove books, administrators' personal tastes and political or social ideas were not; that while a school board could control classroom materials, it could not reach into a library and disrupt "the regime of voluntary inquiry that there holds sway"; and that this case covered only removal, not acquisition. So school librarians were free to decide not to order the books in the first place but not so free to get rid of them once they were on the shelves. The Court's fifth vote against the school board came from a hesitant Byron White, who merely sent the matter back down for more fact-finding, which he thought necessary before deciding whether to join the other four in ruling that the authorities had violated the First Amendment. Therefore, the opinion has been a weak precedent.[72]

In choosing books and films, teachers push the envelope at some risk to themselves. Kansas legislators introduced a bill levying criminal penalties on teachers for promoting obscenity, a crime that might be prosecuted because an official happens to find an assigned book too explicit sexually.[73] A teacher at Columbine High School in Colorado was fired (four years before the 1999 shooting) for showing his debate class Bernardo Bertolucci's film *1900*, which portrays two boys during the growth of fascism in Italy—and depicts violence, profanity, drug use, nudity, and masturbation. Finding that the school's action met *Hazelwood*'s standard of "legitimate pedagogical concern," the Colorado Supreme Court ruled against the teacher. But three dissenting judges affirmed a teacher's obligation to lead students into difficult terrain: "When we quell controversy for the sake of congeniality, we deprive democracy of its mentors."[74]

Efforts to quell controversy have come from both right and left. To avoid offending any conceivable viewpoint, New York State officials sanitized excerpts from great literature on the Regents English exams, which students must pass to graduate. Most passages were cleansed "of virtually any reference to race, religion, ethnicity, sex, nudity, alcohol, even the mildest profanity," *The New York Times* reported.

Every mention of Jews and Judaism was deleted from Isaac Bashevis Singer. Elie Wiesel's essay "What Really Makes Us Free?" lost references to God, so that the line "Man, who was created in God's image, wants to be free as God is free" became, simply, "Man wants to be free." Gone was Chekhov's account, in "An Upheaval," of a woman's strip search of her servants as she looks for a missing brooch, even though the exam assigned students to cite the story in writing about human dignity. A reference to America's unpaid dues to the United Nations was removed from a speech by Secretary-General Kofi Annan, along with his praise of "fine California wine and seafood," which became "fine California seafood."[75] What an insight into the minds of certain influential educators. No wonder so many kids think school is unrelated to reality.

Skittish of conflict and possible disruption, officials often try to keep the reality of strident politics outside the schoolhouse gate, as they did in Aurora, Colorado, during the 2008 presidential campaign. When the school asked students to show their patriotism one day by wearing the national colors, a fifth grader used red and blue on a white T-shirt to write "Obama—a Terrorist's Best Friend," and was given a three-day suspension.[76]

This eagerness to avoid uncomfortable disagreement can drain the electricity from a class. During the 2008 Democratic primary, sixth graders in Washington, D.C., were handed brief biographies of Barack Obama and Hillary Clinton, part of an exercise on making outlines from research material. "The students were wild about Obama," said Edie Tatel, a teacher mentor who was observing, "but the teacher said, 'Remember, we don't push politics in class,' and then stayed very evenhanded. To my taste she could have shown a lot more enthusiasm for their excitement and awareness and still been 'neutral' as she intended, and as is appropriate. I do wish educators would bring some passion and thrill to the discussion!"

That's a difficult blend in which freedom of speech and the obligations of teaching require careful mixing. Power flows down from the front of the room, where a teacher's opinions can make children who disagree feel intimidated, marginalized, or stupid. "The potential for coercion and/or groupthink is one danger," said Tatel, who also served on the advisory board of Teach for America in D.C. "Another is to discourage individual thinking, which we want to promote, not diminish." For a teacher outside school, there was "nothing wrong with displaying a bumper sticker or yard sign: no one abandons rights of expression," she believed, but not in class, where endorsing candidates would be "unprofessional and unethical."[77]

Such was the instruction to faculty at Sammamish High near Seattle. "A member of the community has raised a concern over reports of political comments made by teachers to students in our classrooms. The concern is that teachers are indicating preferences for, or negative comments about, various candidates seeking the presidency in the 2008 election," said an e-mail from Andrea Pfeifer, assistant principal. "Public school students attend school under compulsory attendance laws and they come from families with various political views, so it is important to be mindful of statements that we make regarding our own political beliefs. Of course, to the extent the content area being taught fits the topic, it is appropriate to educate students about the election process of candidates in an unbiased way. However, it is important to remember that we are employed first and foremost to educate students, not to use our public positions or work time to endorse a particular candidate, political party, or personal view."

Katie Piper took some pride in being inscrutable politically as she taught history and government at the school. Toward the end of one year, she asked students if they thought she was neutral, and "most said, 'Yes, I have no idea where you stand!'" The next year, though, her liberal views were discerned by about half of her more politically active advanced-placement class; the other half couldn't tell. "Nobody said, 'It seemed like you were conservative,'" she noted wryly. Most students thought that she should reveal her political leanings; they wanted to know.

PROFESSORS AND THEIR DISCONTENTS

College faculty can be less restrained, although some overestimate the maturity of their students, judging by the squalls stirred up by certain comments after 9/11. When professors made remarks outside the narrowed parameters of acceptable opinion, a few students on both the left and the right couldn't listen and then simply disagree. Easily offended by unwelcome ideas, they complained, sometimes generating enough outrage among alumni and politicians to drive university administrators into dubious retaliation.

The morning of September 11, Richard Berthold, a professor of classical history, had the momentary bad judgment to make this crack to one hundred brand-new freshmen in his Western Civilization class at the University of New Mexico: "Anybody who blows up the Pentagon gets my vote."

It was not meant as a joke. It reflected his "disagreement with much of our foreign policy," he later wrote, "but in an embarrassing moment of insensitivity and stupidity I made this observation when more than a hundred people had just died at the Pentagon, making those words an exercise in incredible callousness."

He was right about that, at least. He had no way of knowing whether any of his young students, most of them newly away from home, had relatives who worked there who might have been among the casualties. He did not fill the grown-up role of teacher to teenagers who, like all of us, were trapped at that moment in a well of fear.

Word of his statement rippled across the Internet, and suddenly his in-box was flooded with hundreds of hateful e-mails carrying death threats. "I was astounded," he wrote, "at how many outraged Americans reminded me how much blood was spilled to defend our freedoms and then in the next sentence denied me one of those freedoms." Yet as calls for his dismissal mushroomed, he got messages of support from many of the students who had taken his courses over thirty years, and "the week after the remark when I entered my Greek history class, the hundred plus students spontaneously applauded me, probably the finest moment in my teaching career."

Berthold insisted that he was neither "some sort of liberal or leftie" nor "an unthinking conservative." He portrayed himself as a gadfly who condemned both "liberal silliness" and "plainly silly conservatives." That failed to endear him to colleagues, apparently, for few offered their backing. In the end, the university resisted demands to fire him (for which he would probably have won in court), and he settled for a reprimand. But relations became strained. After being negatively evaluated on his teaching, removed from giving his Western Civilization course, and accused of professional misconduct for using vulgar words "anytime anywhere in the world," as he put it, he retired early, in 2002.[78]

Elsewhere, faculty members who stepped outside the unspoken limits were slapped around from both right and left. Many of the controversies turned on differences between what professors said and what students heard.

Professor Kenneth W. Hearlson, a born-again Christian and adviser to the campus Republicans, was summarily suspended for most of a semester by Orange Coast College in California after four Muslim students complained that in a political science class he seemed to blame them personally for Arab terrorism. According to an audiotape, though, his tirade, a week after the 9/11 attack, was aimed mostly at Muslim countries. He asked why they hadn't repudiated Osama bin Laden, why leading Muslim figures denied the Holocaust. He condemned "hate-filled messages" from "Muslim students on this campus," exemplified by a flyer the previous year showing a swastika over a Star of David. When he allegedly looked at the four Muslims and used the pronoun "you" as he mentioned Arab attacks on Israel, a student challenged him. "On the tape," *The New York Times* reported, "Mr. Hearlson thanks the student for the interruption and says he 'absolutely' did not mean to accuse any student personally. 'I am talking about Arab nations,' he says." He was reinstated and as of 2011 remained on the faculty.[79]

At Colorado State University, Steve Helmericks, a part-time sociology instructor, was removed from the classroom and limited to research after a student, whose husband was serving in Iraq, took offense at what he thought a "benign" comment: that American troops were dying unnecessarily in an unjust war. She quoted him as saying, more crudely, that Bush "is sending boys and girls out to die for no goddamn reason." Although many other students found him respectful and fair, the larger conservative world mobilized a campaign of vilification. He was peppered with death threats by e-mail and phone, prompting him to change his number, keep a gun, and—some students observed—shift into a guarded mode that detracted from his teaching.[80]

The list goes on: Oneida Meranto, a Navajo professor at Metropolitan State College of Denver, who began taping her own lectures when maligned and threatened after conservative students targeted her liberal take on Latin America;[81] a University of Pennsylvania physics professor who, by bashing Bush and the Iraq war, disturbed a student who had served in the air force; an English professor at California State University, Long Beach, who made one Republican freshman "very uncomfortable" by including in the suggested topics for an essay "Should Justice Sandra Day O'Connor be impeached for her partisan political actions in the *Bush v. Gore* case?"[82]

Students are not supposed to be made uncomfortable by disagreeable ideas, evidently, even if they are expressed outside of class. An assistant librarian at UCLA was punished with a week's suspension for sending e-mail declaring that American taxpayers "fund and arm an apartheid state called Israel, which is responsible for untold thousands upon thousands of deaths of Muslim Palestinian children and civilians. . . . So, who are the 'terrorists' anyway?" Alumni of the University of Texas tried but failed to get a professor fired for an op-ed piece blaming American foreign policy for 9/11. Faculty Web pages urging strong military action or denouncing homosexuality have invoked administrators' wrath.

In portraying the campus as unpatriotic, the conservative cause had no better poster boy than Ward Churchill, chairman of the University of Colorado's Department of Ethnic Studies, who wrote an essay blaming the United States for getting what it deserved when the planes plowed into the World Trade Center and the Pentagon. He saw the ghosts of American genocide returning for retribution: from perished slaves to massacred American Indians, from incinerated Japanese to the Vietnamese and Korean victims in their respective wars, and then the Iraqis dead by American hands in the 1991 Gulf War, "a performance worthy of the Nazis during the early months of their drive into Russia. . . . Good Germans gleefully cheered that butchery, too."

He gave tribute to the September 11 attackers for "their patience and restraint" in waiting so long before "they finally responded in kind to some of what this country has dispensed to their people." Then, in the lines that became infamous, he mocked the "innocence" of the dead at the World

Trade Center. "True enough, they were civilians of a sort," he wrote. "But innocent? Gimme a break. They formed a technocratic corps at the very heart of America's global financial empire—the 'mighty engine of profit' to which the military dimension of U.S. policy has always been enslaved. . . . If there was a better, more effective, or in fact any other way of visiting some penalty befitting their participation upon the little Eichmanns inhabiting the sterile sanctuary of the twin towers, I'd really be interested in hearing about it."[83]

The screed wasn't a departure for Churchill. He had long written extensively of what he saw as America's crimes. But the words seared sharply at this moment of mourning, igniting a firestorm that consumed conservative shouters on television and radio, provoked Colorado's Republican governor, Bill Owens, to call for his resignation, and triggered what the university chancellor called "a thorough examination of Professor Churchill's writings, speeches, tape recordings, and other works."[84]

He had the protection of tenure, but even if he hadn't, the university (a state institution) determined that his "offensive" and "appalling" views were insulated by the First Amendment.

So administrators went after him in another way, convening a committee that found enough academic violations to get him fired by the regents. He had committed plagiarism, the panel concluded with meticulous documentation, and had falsified and fabricated certain historical records to facilitate his assertion that smallpox had been intentionally spread among American Indians by Captain John Smith in 1614–1618 and by the U.S. Army near Fort Clark in 1837–1840.[85]

Tenure protects academic freedom, not academic misconduct. The guarantee of lifelong appointment took root after a wave of faculty dismissals in the late nineteenth and early twentieth centuries, engineered by pressure groups in business, religion, and government over concerns both ephemeral and parochial. "At universities across the country, from Stanford to Yale and Vanderbilt to Wisconsin," writes Arthur Levine, "professors were fired or threatened with discharge for taking what were judged the wrong sides of controversial issues such as Darwinism, public ownership of railroads, immigration, alcohol prohibition, bimetalism [basing currency on two metals such as silver and gold], and U.S. entry into World War I."[86]

Today, under the guise of protecting free speech, some right-wing organizations campaign vigorously for the rights of conservatives and aggressively against the same rights for liberals. They worry that the Churchills are propagandizing young people to despise their country. They yearn for a return to a curriculum centered on Western civilization; they reject the liberal academy's search beyond conventional boundaries into the cultures of foreigners and minorities. They are replaying the conflict of the 1960s and exposing their frustration that the university remains one of the few major institutions still immune to conservative domination.

One group, with the deceptively neutral name American Council of Trustees and Alumni, was co-founded by former vice president Dick Cheney's wife, Lynne, who has railed against those calling for more teaching about the Muslim world to understand the roots of 9/11, as if such thirst for knowledge represented the blaming of America.

The council publicizes the intimidation of conservative views on campus but rarely highlights the actions against liberal expression that have also occurred. It portrays classrooms as "hostile" to students who don't share the views of leftist professors, and its surveys bolster the thesis: 68 percent of students responding to one poll "reported that their professors made negative comments about President Bush."[87]

Informing on faculty even became a paid profession, briefly, when a UCLA alumni group offered to hire students to record their professors' attempts at "indoctrination." After the university's lawyer warned that this might infringe teachers' copyrights and subject students to discipline, the organization canceled the monetary arrangements, but the Web site continued to rage against "radical" professors, naming them and turning selective quotes into smears.[88]

The classroom is a place of power relationships, of course, and students in college, as well as in secondary school, should not have to tiptoe through courses afraid to give their views. They should not be subjected to derision for their politics, their sexual orientation, their religion, their race. They need to be included in the enterprise of learning how to think for themselves. Nor should they have to endure political rants in physics class. As a matter of professional ethics, the bright line between course matter and unrelated topics is long-standing, and the best teachers don't blur it.

The conservative campaign against liberalism on campus has been called a McCarthyite witch hunt akin to the 1950s, when suspected communists were hounded in faculties across the country. As then, the post-9/11 spasm of fear and jingoism has caused casualties; some professional lives have been hurt. But the First Amendment culture has survived less damaged this time, and while extremists at each end of the spectrum seem determined to shut each other up, the center of gravity has mostly held.

In fact, the thought police in the American Council of Trustees and Alumni inadvertently documented just how robust freedom of speech remained after September 11. By collecting professors' "unpatriotic" remarks critical of American policy, they put the best of American values on display—not the most admirable political opinions, perhaps, but the best principles, which include the right to self-condemnation even in time of war. As George Washington told army officers at the end of the Revolution, "If men are to be precluded from offering their sentiments on a matter which may involve the most serious and alarming consequences that can invite the consideration of mankind, reason is of no use to us; the freedom of speech may be taken away, and dumb and silent we may be led, like sheep to the slaughter."[89]

This is America's central idea: the multiplicity of ideas. It has not succumbed to enforced orthodoxy.

SECURITY AND INSECURITY

In the little farm town of Ponder, Texas, a thirteen-year-old, Christopher Beamon, was jailed for six days by a juvenile court judge for doing his homework a bit too graphically. Instructed to write a scary Halloween story, he composed a tale of drugs and guns. In the opening scene, he and a friend get high on the chemical from his air conditioner, then fire guns from his porch into the night, and finally shoot a few named classmates and his teacher "acssedently." Despite the atrocious spelling and grammar, the teacher gave him an A and had him read the story to the class. She'd called him "an outstanding student" on his report card.

His creative effort didn't score as well with other kids' parents who heard about it. They found the violent narrative alarming, and so did school authorities, who called in the police. Having previously been a discipline problem, Christopher was locked in a juvenile detention center until the prosecutor gave up trying to find a violation of law. "It looks like to me the child was doing what the teacher told him to do, which was to write a scary story," said the district attorney.[90] As for the teacher, giving a high grade for semiliterate work is not a crime—well, it is, but not one you can prosecute.

Rights are eroded by danger, and especially in schools freedom of speech is trumped by security. This happens in practice, if not in strict accordance with constitutional law, as teachers and principals watch closely for signs of incipient aggression.

"Adolescents will sometimes alert you ahead of time that they will commit violence. Don't dismiss it as idle talk," says Supervisory Special Agent Mary Ellen O'Toole of the FBI's Critical Incident Response Group. After studying fourteen school shootings and four more attacks that were planned and prevented, the unit concluded that "violent behavior develops progressively," not suddenly in a vacuum, and not always secretly. You can often spot "leakage" of a student's intentions in advance; "there are observable signs along the way."

But don't "profile" either, the team cautions in a lengthy report. Don't predict violence based only on a youngster's speech, writing, videos, or drawings without evaluating him closely in four areas of his life: his personal behavior, his family relationships, his school's dynamics, and his social interactions, where warning signs may be visible if an attack is likely.

The study includes a long list of symptoms to look for in those four dimensions, including a student's inability to cope with criticism or manage anger, the family's lack of intimacy or the child's intimidation of his parents, a school culture that tolerates bullying or disciplines unfairly, and the youngster's unmonitored Internet use or intense involvement "with a group who share a fascination with violence or extremist beliefs."[91]

Here is the most difficult intersection of safety and the First Amendment. Administrators are accountable for security and prevention, and after a string of shootings preceded by clues that were ignored, officials are easily alarmed by students who make threats or merely depict mayhem in artwork, fiction, or poetry. "In today's climate, some schools tend to adopt a one-size-fits-all approach to any mention of violence," the report observes. "The response to every threat is the same, regardless of its credibility or the likelihood that it will be carried out . . . leading to potential underestimation of serious threats, overreaction to less serious ones, and unfairly punishing or stigmatizing students who are in fact not dangerous."[92]

The FBI counsels a measured, considered evaluation of each instance, but some principals can't wait: they quickly suspend or expel, which O'Toole's unit criticizes as "kicking the problem out the door," presenting risks of its own by neglecting treatment and deepening anger. In the end, a suspended student can return with a gun.

In few of the publicized suspensions do school officials appear to have exercised the level of assessment that the FBI recommends. Detailed court records show them covering themselves by acting precipitously on the basis of speech alone.

That's hardly surprising. School shootings are mercifully rare, but those that occur cause trauma that reverberates brutally. When the sanctuary of school is invaded by its own students—children—who methodically walk from cafeteria to library to classroom gunning down teachers and class-mates, the assault has the emotional force of terrorism. Reduced to its sheer numbers, it is a limited act—at Columbine High School, twelve students and one teacher killed, the two shooters dead from suicide. But its place and manner magnify it terribly. Fears are ignited among schoolchildren and parents far beyond the crime.

And so school officials have tried to preempt danger. Even little kids get ahold of guns. In 2011, a loaded pistol fell out of a six-year-old's pocket in a Houston school cafeteria and went off, firing one bullet that fragmented and wounded three children.[93] In March 2000, two weeks after a six-year-old shot and killed a child in Flint, Michigan, the principal of a kindergarten in Sayreville, New Jersey, suspended a five-year-old for saying "I'm going to shoot you" during a game of cops and robbers at recess—and the Third Circuit ruled for the school. The principal had suspended three other little boys earlier that month for similar remarks—one who told other kids that he planned to shoot a teacher, another for saying that he would put a gun in another child's mouth, and a third for bragging (falsely) that his mother let him bring guns to school.[94]

Incidents abound. A Rhode Island high school student was interrogated by the Secret Service and suspended after fulfilling an assignment to describe "a perfect day" by writing about "doing violence to President Bush and various corporate executives," the ACLU reported.[95]

Then Enrique Ponce, a sophomore at Montwood High School in El Paso, Texas, showed a fellow student a piece of imaginative writing in the form of a "diary" in which his protagonist described forming a neo-Nazi group that attacked gays and blacks, set another student's house on fire, and planned for a "Columbine shooting." The student told a teacher, who waited a day and informed the assistant principal, who asked Enrique to show him the notebook. The young man did, protesting that it was mere fiction. His mother told the school the same thing, unpersuasively.

Even without evidence that the boy had violent tendencies, access to weapons, or any other characteristics outlined in the FBI's guidelines, the assistant principal called him a "terroristic threat" and asked the police to arrest him; the district attorney wouldn't bring a charge. So the school suspended him and transferred him to a special school for "high risk" youth, Keys Academy, although he didn't fit the profile of troubled kids that Keys was designed to help: those who had been kept back a grade, had dropped out, or were in danger of doing so. Enrique hadn't made any real threat, and his parents worried that a marred permanent record would hamper his application to college. So they put him in a private school and sued.

They lost in the Fifth Circuit, which cited Justice Samuel Alito's concurrence in the "BONG HiTS 4 JESUS" case, *Morse v. Frederick,* portraying schools as dangerous places where, in the absence of parental protection, students were forced to spend their days close to others who might do them harm. "If school administrators are permitted to prohibit student speech that advocates illegal drug use because 'illegal drug use presents a grave and in many ways unique threat to the physical safety of students,'" the federal appeals court declared, "then it defies logical extrapolation to hold school administrators to a stricter standard with respect to speech that gravely and uniquely threatens violence, including massive deaths, to the school population as a whole."[96] It was a clear example of how courts can walk step-by-step to trespass more and more deeply on the Bill of Rights. The Alaskan kid who had held the nonsensical sign had set in motion a constitutional argument that now moved well beyond his little act of defiance on that Juneau street.

A different circumstance prompted more careful consideration by a high school in Blaine, Washington, before imposing "emergency expulsion" on James LaVine after he asked a teacher for comment on his poem "Last Words." Written in 1998 after a rash of school shootings, the verse was a badly spelled, first-person sketch of a youngster yearning to feel guilt for shooting twenty-eight students, and finally—fearing that he might kill again—taking his own life.

"As I approached./the classroom door,/I drew my gun and,/threw open the door, Bang, Bang, Bang, Bang./When it was all over,/28 were/dead, and all I remember,/was not felling,/any remorce,/for I felt,/I was,/clensing my soul./ . . . I feel,/I may,/strike again./ . . . and now,/I hope,/I can feel,/remorse,/for what I did, without a shed,/of tears,/for no tear,/shall fall, from your face,/but from mine,/as I try,/to rest in peace,/Bang!"[97]

This may have been a purely artistic meditation on the inner thoughts of a fictitious boy, or it may have been "leakage," a precursor to violence. It could have reflected a fear of being killed or a fear of his own impulses. The school looked at the poem in much the same context that the FBI recommended two years later. According to court records, the teacher thought that the verses might be a call for help, that "maybe something's hurting him, maybe he's upset about something, maybe he's afraid."

She consulted with the school psychologist, who knew James well as his counselor. Two years earlier he had told her of suicidal thoughts. Earlier that fall, he had told her about conflict with his father, who had thrown a rock at James's car after the boy disobeyed instructions not to park it in a barn. James had called police, a judge had issued the father a no-contact order, and James had moved out to his sister's.

The boy had recently broken up with his girlfriend and had been stalking her, according to a complaint by the girl's mother. James's file also showed a couple of incidents in school—a fight and "insubordination" toward a teacher, as well as a run-in with the vice principal over a T-shirt he wore reading, "Eat Shit and Die."

So there was more than the poem. The vice principal called the parents, then the police, then Child Protective Services, which referred him to a mental health crisis line, which sent him to a duty psychiatrist, who suggested that the boy be brought by police for an assessment. A deputy sheriff visiting the house confirmed with James and his mother that he had no access to weapons—a key element in the FBI's checklist—and that "there were insufficient grounds for anyone to make a determination that James LaVine was in imminent danger of causing serious harm to himself and others."

Since the police wouldn't act, the principal imposed the expulsion, notifying the parents in writing that the poem "implied extreme violence to our student body." After the family hired a lawyer, the school system paid for an evaluation of the boy by a psychiatrist, who agreed that he should have been removed temporarily but believed that he was fit to return to school. The expulsion had lasted seventeen days, and he finished the school year with no problems.

Worried that the record of punishment would prevent James from enlisting in the military, his parents sued and lost. The Ninth Circuit found no First Amendment violation in the school's expulsion order, based on a loose reading of the limits under *Tinker,* which restricted student expression that would cause "substantial disruption" to the school. The Supreme Court declined to review the case, letting the decision stand.

One moral of the story might suggest banning guns rather than speech. But some colleges have done both since shootings at Virginia Tech and Northern Illinois University. Two Texas community colleges earned Muzzle awards for suppressing pro-gun speech in 2009. Tarrant County College barred students from wearing empty holsters to protest the prohibition against licensed, concealed handguns on campus, part of a nationwide demonstration. Lone Star College prevented the Young Conservatives from distributing a satirical leaflet listing "gun safety tips," which included this one: "If your gun misfires, never look down the barrel to inspect it."[98]

BEYOND THE GATE

The "schoolhouse gate" has become a permeable dividing line. While it doesn't seal off the school from the First Amendment, it does mark a setting in which authorities may limit some speech under some conditions, leaving students inside more susceptible to censorship than when they are outside in the world at large. In a digital universe, though, the boundary is easily transcended as students use home computers to circulate threatening, vulgar, bullying comments by Internet. The geographical origin of speech has less practical meaning than before, freeing students from school restrictions on the one hand, and on the other, leading some administrators to reach outside and punish expression beyond the schoolhouse gate.

Most officials who try it have been slapped down by the courts, but not always, and this area of the law is far from settled. It remains in flux because of real dangers. Eric Harris, one of the Columbine shooters, maintained a Web site describing his murderous desires and the explosives he and Dylan Klebold had assembled. Some students turn violent after being ridiculed, sometimes by way of the Internet. The suicides in Vermont and Missouri of two thirteen-year-olds, who had been tormented online, have provoked at least fourteen states to enact laws requiring school systems to report or punish "cyber-bullying."[99]

Even in the absence of danger, schools have acted against children for remarks on the Web, but without clear legal authority to do so. A Connecticut high school student was denied the right to run for senior class secretary in 2007 because, on a Web page, she called her principal and superintendent "douchebags" and urged students to "piss" them off by e-mailing complaints about the cancellation of an annual music concert. She lost both in the district court and before a unanimous panel of the Second Circuit Court of Appeals that included Sonia Sotomayor, the year before she was elevated to the Supreme Court.[100]

The long reach of censorship has cost some boards of education in settlements. A school district in Ohio had to pay $30,000 after suspending a sixteen-year-old for nasty comments online about a band instructor. In Newport, Washington, Paul Kim won $2,000 and an apology after his principal retaliated against his Web parody of the school by withdrawing his nomination for a Merit Scholarship and by sending vindictive notifications to colleges where Kim had applied. (The young man survived nicely, ending up at Columbia University with plans for law school.)[101]

Prior to the Internet, and even in the early days before its widespread use, courts tended to exempt off-campus speech from regulation. "The arm of authority does not reach beyond the schoolhouse gate," said the Second Circuit Court of Appeals in 1979, overturning administrators' efforts to close an off-campus student newspaper.[102] Similarly, a federal district judge in Maine decided in 1986 that a student could not constitutionally be suspended for giving a teacher the finger at a restaurant.[103] A federal judge in Washington state ruled against a principal who suspended a high school junior for posting vulgar criticisms of the school on his personal Web page in 1998.[104] In 2000, another federal judge in Washington labeled Internet speech "entirely outside of the school's supervision or control" after a high school student was expelled for a Web site containing mock obituaries where visitors could vote on which person should be "next to die." The judge found no intention to threaten anyone.[105]

All those cases freed students to enjoy the same First Amendment rights as adults off school grounds, including in cyberspace. Yet this is changing as courts and school officials recognize that digital expression respects no geographical boundaries. What is written at home is instantly available at school, rendering the barriers artificial. That's how the Pennsylvania Supreme Court treated a 2002 case, unanimously upholding a Bethlehem school's expulsion of Justin Swidler for posting insulting remarks about the principal and a teacher, whom he likened to Hitler and ridiculed for her appearance. "Give me $20 to help pay for the hitman," the Web site said.

The court went through a two-step analysis, first determining that the threat was not serious but rather "a sophomoric, crude, highly offensive and perhaps misguided attempt to humor or parody." Second, the judges found that while the Web site was created outside school, the speech itself occurred on campus "because the student accessed the site at school, showed it to a fellow student, and informed other students of the site."[106]

By that reasoning, the more restrictive rules on speech in school will carry over into the larger world, at least when students address school issues online. "Most courts that have examined off-campus online speech have applied the so-called *Tinker* standard," according to David L. Hudson Jr., a First Amendment specialist. That analysis allows officials to punish if the postings would substantially disrupt school activities or infringe on the rights of others, just as if the expression occurred on school grounds. Furthermore, as courts narrow *Tinker*, more and more student speech is silenced, outside as well as inside.

This may seem like a harbinger of doom for the First Amendment, especially given the role of schools in educating young Americans in constitutional democracy. What it forecasts more clearly, though, is that free speech will be preserved only by the alertness of good citizens—young citizens, in this case—willing to sound the alarm at every encroachment. Their readiness to push back is the essential ingredient of the country's resilience, its capacity for self-correction.

The Constitutional Culture

The chart is not the sea.

—Philip Booth

THE AMERICAN SYSTEM relies on a paradox. On the one hand, the Constitution restrains the whim of the official, who is supposedly shackled by the intricate web of judicial precedent enforcing the checks, the balances, and the bold restrictions on government's incursions into the people's rights. If the rule of law holds, freedom does not depend on the goodwill of those in power.

On the other hand, freedom depends on the Constitution's resonance among the citizens. The affection for liberty, animated by the written words, reaches beyond their original intent or dictionary meanings. "Liberty lies in the hearts of men and women," said Judge Learned Hand. "When it dies there, no constitution, no law, no court can even do much to help it. While it lies there it needs no constitution, no law, no court to save it."[1]

We have seen in these pages what happens when individual Americans, in high places and low, forget or abandon the elemental values enshrined in the Bill of Rights. Using legally approved tricks and lies, the detective coerces a false confession. Hiding facts that support innocence, the prosecutor forces a dubious plea of guilt. The judge sentences for acquitted conduct, as she is allowed to do. The defense attorney for the poor, overworked because of underfunding by the state, fails to summon sufficient resources to investigate and rebut. The legal immigrant is deported with no meaningful access to constitutional rights. These intrusions are woven into the statutes and enabled by the courts.

At the same time, the courts' loftier judgments protecting individual liberties sometimes slip away before reaching the everyday world of ordinary America. When a black pedestrian is stopped and frisked without reasonable suspicion, when a schoolgirl is searched invasively without probable cause, when a protester is charged for inverting a flag, when a student is suspended for his T-shirt's political slogan, it is clear that two unhealthy conditions have developed. One, the Supreme Court's rulings have not fully penetrated the culture, because they are being ignored by officials who should know better. And two, the culture has not thoroughly internalized the essence of rights that are central to the American enterprise.

Attorneys educated in the nation's finest law schools have stood ready since September 11, 2001, to rationalize torture, justify indefinite imprisonment without trial, and sanction warrantless eavesdropping on multitudes of citizens and foreigners inside the United States. Elected legislators across the country have scrambled to suppress hateful expression outside soldiers' funerals, despite long-standing prohibitions against regulating speech on the basis of its content alone. Local police have tried to enforce state laws banning flag "desecration," notwithstanding a body of judicial rulings striking down such statutes as unconstitutional. And on it goes: an unending dance between the violators and the violated, with a passive public watching, largely in silence.

Most people have an internal voice that whispers "wrong" when they do something immoral. They know instinctively that they must not cheat or steal or murder. Nobody has to spell it out for them again and again. Yet too few Americans seem to hear an internal voice speaking to them on civil liberties. Only a tiny fraction commit crimes, but many more countenance violations of the First, Fourth, Fifth, and Sixth Amendments, especially when the rights of "others" are trampled for the sake of national security, safe streets, order, and harmony. Occasionally, a feisty indignation is revived, as when privacy is shredded by a computer service such as Facebook, whose users rose up in 2010 after discovering that their personal information had been opened to general access.[2] But in schools, for example, most young citizens acquiesce as their principals and teachers suppress their First and Fourth Amendment rights. Few object to their loss of privacy or free speech. Most go along with unwarranted searches, the censorship of school newspapers, and the prohibition of controversial slogans on pins or clothing. Those who bravely resist by speaking out or filing suit are routinely vilified by many of their peers, who seem to live in a constitutional culture that has withered.

Not that a consensus ever forms on how far liberties extend and where limits can be drawn. If it did, the Supreme Court would always rule unanimously. As we have witnessed, the Bill of Rights is principled but not dogmatic, and the liberties it protects lie within a shifting horizon whose distance is always subject to debate, legislation, and jurisprudence. Not all speech is "protected" speech. Not all searches are "unreasonable." Indeed, our rights are both permanent and malleable. They transcend the moment yet yield to times of stress and danger. They are shaped by both long-standing tradition and temporary expediency. If one subscribes to natural law, as many of the framers did, then liberties exist not as creations of humankind but as transcendent features of the natural landscape—divinely given, some would say. Yet even in America, where rights are codified and shielded ingeniously, they have been anything but constant.

In practice, legal rights are expanded as the society gradually comes to recognize how vulnerable to the majority's will minorities can be, and how much protection the powerless require. Yet civil liberties are also constrained by politics, war, crime, and economic hardship, as demonstrated by Arizona's 2010 law commanding local police to stop, question, and investigate people they think might be illegal immigrants. It is evident that the fears of drug wars spilling across the Mexican border, and of a recession pitting Americans against foreigners for scarce jobs, have been enough to damage the Fourth Amendment right to be "secure" from unreasonable search and seizure.

Even as constitutional provisions are reinterpreted and adapted to evolving circumstances, citizens are entitled to count on one another to agree on a core set of rights that are indispensable to a free and pluralistic society. There is cause for worry on this point. Some provisions in the Bill of Rights do not poll well enough to guarantee that they could be easily ratified today.

Surveys show an American public full of contradictions. In the aftermath of 9/11, most said they were willing to give up civil liberties for security but also opposed stealthy, "sneak and peek" government searches of their offices as authorized by the Patriot Act, according to polls done for the American Civil Liberties Union. Respondents expressed more support for First Amendment rights than for criminal rights, probably because they couldn't picture themselves in the dock as clearly as they saw themselves practicing freedom of speech and religion.[3]

A 2003 survey of voters in Florida, Pennsylvania, Ohio, and New Mexico found significant minorities—31 to 46 percent—endorsing measures in the Patriot Act that authorize secret court orders for librarians to identify borrowers of books on certain topics; permit the government to require Internet providers to name users visiting certain Web sites; and allow law enforcement to collect average Americans' travel, credit, and medical records. About one-third thought it "appropriate" for "government to detain non-citizens secretly without charging them with a crime, giving them a hearing, or informing a judge." Nearly half were comfortable with

FBI agents keeping lists of people's attendance at religious services. Much lower numbers—only 17 percent in New Mexico to 23 percent in Florida—thought it appropriate to ease law enforcement's ability "to get a court order to secretly search someone's home and not notify them that their home had been searched." That is a key provision of the Patriot Act, but the large majorities who said it "goes too far" ranged from 74 percent in Florida to 82 percent in New Mexico.[4]

So this coin has two sides: despite the strong minorities favoring most of the intrusive mechanisms, the majorities who object to the most salient powers of the Patriot Act are rejecting a law that received overwhelming approval in both houses of Congress. Perhaps ordinary Americans are more devoted to civil liberties than their elected legislators seem to be. Yet politicians don't suffer at the ballot box after they vote to curtail rights. Almost never does the subject of civil liberties become a campaign issue. Reporters don't put the question to candidates, citizens rarely raise it at town hall meetings, and rivals usually take cover toward the right of the spectrum if the topic happens to arise. They don't want to be labeled "soft on terrorism," as in earlier periods they avoided being called "soft on crime."

In other words, much of the public feels concern but doesn't do anything about it. Except for a small elite of dedicated civil liberties advocates, the population has learned a certain helplessness. Because legislatures tend to lean with the prevailing winds, many crucial decisions are made remotely in the courts, often by judges immune to popular passions, as they should be. The interaction between politics and judicial nominations, acted out by a polarized Senate, proceeds on a superficial plane of litmus tests and ideological screening, not on the firm ground of fidelity to the constitutional heritage. The place of responsible legislating in the realm of rights has been taken by the posturing at confirmation hearings, leaving in its wake a brand of lazy lawmaking. The intricate task of protecting rights while facilitating law enforcement then passes to the courts, yielding to judges the challenge of making the brave decisions shunned by the elected representatives. This is not a new pattern: *Brown v. Board of Education* ending school segregation would not have been necessary had legislatures repealed the discriminatory laws. So the constitutional culture comes to depend excessively on the courts, and the courts are not dependable.

Furthermore, opinions in the street are honeycombed by intriguing crosscurrents that defeat most attempts at sweeping generalizations. A 2004 survey by Cornell students, for example, found that very religious

Christians were much more willing than the less religious to curtail civil liberties, especially the rights of Muslim Americans. Seventy-nine percent of those of "high religiosity" endorsed the indefinite detention of terrorists, 61 percent supported government monitoring of the Internet, and 42 percent said that all Muslim Americans should be required to register their whereabouts. The percentages of the "low religiosity" respondents approving the tough measures were 50, 35, and 15, respectively.[5]

By 2009, as the edge of danger had dulled, a survey of 1,001 adults revealed somewhat different patterns as it sought to measure knowledge about the American Revolution. In this sample, support for a fair trial was now stronger than for free speech, and the right against property searches weaker than both. But all the rights received majority support, endorsement levels that may have been boosted by the nature of the poll itself. Many of the questions reminded respondents of the nation's ideals.

People were invited to name the Revolution's central principles, then were asked, "Is it essential that Americans have [a certain right], important but not essential, or not that important?" Most of those surveyed considered the key rights essential, while substantial minorities of 15 to 38 percent thought otherwise:

RIGHT	ESSENTIAL	IMPORTANT, BUT NOT ESSENTIAL	NOT IMPORTANT
To not have property searched or seized	59	32	6
To privacy	76	22	2
To speak freely about whatever you want	70	28	2
To assemble, march, protest, or petition the government	65	29	6
To a fair trial	84	14	1
To practice your chosen religion	80	18	2
To practice no religion	66	23	10

College graduates were more likely than those with lower degrees to support these rights as essential, and so were more Republicans than Democrats, despite conservatives' inclination to favor strict anticrime and antiterrorism policies. Republicans outpolled Democrats by 87 to 81 percent on the right to a fair trial, 71 to 63 percent on the right to speak freely, 69 to 59 percent on the right to march and protest, and by wide margins on the religion questions. Republicans and Democrats came within a percentage point of each other on the search issue, and were tied at 75 percent in their endorsement of the right to privacy as essential.[6] Libertarians among Republicans probably increased the percentages.

All these surveys and statistics suggest that the glass is more than half full, but with an empty space large enough to describe a significant region of indifference to constitutional rights. Even the majority's support for civil liberties seems soft. It doesn't translate into political action, doesn't drive most voters' choices, and therefore leaves elections to lawmakers who don't put individual rights high on the agenda. The populist Tea Party movement, which has startled establishment Republicans with its grassroots outrage at "big government," has exacted no penalty from politicians who enlarge government in a most personal way through intrusions on the First, Fourth, Fifth, and Sixth Amendments. Government is evidently too big when it regulates the private sector or provides social benefits, but not when it invades the rights of defendants and dissenters.

In American culture, it should take courage to defy the principles in the Bill of Rights. Instead, it seems to take courage to uphold them. The threshold of violations at which broad criticism is triggered should be low. Instead, it seems to have risen practically beyond reach. Witness the fate of the National Security Agency's warrantless surveillance: after a spasm of protest when the secret program was revealed by *The New York Times,* Congress effectively legalized it.

Increasingly, federal judges nominated by Republican presidents have undermined the courts' modern role as defenders of individual rights. The Supreme Court, tilting toward institutional interests, is eroding some of the protective case law of the twentieth century. As one result, especially in Fourth and Fifth Amendment areas, individuals are facing a heavier responsibility to be informed about their own rights.

This might be a good thing if it spurs inventive educational programs. In a way, it is pathetic in this open system that people under arrest have to be read the Miranda warning. We should all know that we have the right to remain silent without having to be told by our interrogators. We should know that we have a right to a lawyer. We should know that we have the right to refuse a police officer's warrantless search, without probable cause, of our car and our home and our body. We should not be constitutionally illiterate. We should feel inside ourselves the power that flows to us from the Constitution.

If every American school taught the Bill of Rights in a clear and compelling way, if every child knew the fundamental rules that guide the relationships between the individual and the state, then every citizen would eventually feel the reflexive need to resist every violation. We had better begin now, for rights that are not invoked are eventually abandoned.

NOTES

INTRODUCTION: THE INSOLENCE OF OFFICE

1. This was Madison's approving summary of earlier statements by another delegate who, Madison lamented, now endorsed letting the House make its own rules on apportionment. The full sentences in the record read: "Mr. Madison was not a little surprised to hear this implicit confidence urged by a member who on all occasions, had inculcated so strongly, the political depravity of men, and the necessity of checking one vice and interest by opposing to them another vice & interest. . . . The truth was that all men having power ought to be distrusted to a certain degree." Notes, Madison Debates, Constitutional Convention, July 11, 1787, Avalon Project, Lillian Goldman Law Library, Yale Law School.

2. Among the high-income sample, the United States was ranked ahead of only Singapore and South Korea. In its peer group of Western Europe and North America, Sweden, the Netherlands, Austria, Canada, Spain, and France exceeded the United States in imposing limitations on their governmental powers. Eight factors were considered in defining those limits: the extent to which government's authority is restrained by fundamental law, by the legislature, by the judiciary, by independent auditing and review, by sanctions against officials for misconduct, by freedom of expression, by compliance with international law, and by the transitions of power in accordance with the law. World Justice Project, *Rule of Law Index: 2010* (Washington, D.C.: World Justice Project, 2010), pp. 9, 94, 105.

3. Habeas corpus ("you have the body") has ancient origins, was embedded in Anglo-Saxon common law, and was codified in the Magna Carta: "No freeman is to be taken or imprisoned or disseised of his free tenement or of his liberties or free customs, or outlawed or exiled or in any way ruined, nor will we go against such a man or send against him save by lawful judgement of his peers or by the law of the land." It appears in art. I, § 9 of the U.S. Constitution: "The Privilege of the Writ of Habeas Corpus shall not be suspended, unless when in Cases of Rebellion or Invasion the public Safety may require it." The 1689 English Bill of Rights, which placed the monarchy under the rule of parliamentary law, contained a ban on "excessive bail," "excessive fines," and "cruel and

unusual punishments." Those exact words were carried into the Eighth Amendment a century later. English common law, which took on the weight of custom and consensus in the absence of a written British constitution, was codified and explained by Sir William Blackstone, a British judge who published his *Commentaries on the Laws of England* a decade before the American Revolution. Common law remains an informing presence in American jurisprudence.

4. *McCulloch v. Maryland,* 17 U.S. 316 (1819).
5. For a fuller discussion of the five previous detours, see David K. Shipler, *The Rights of the People: How Our Search for Safety Invades Our Liberties* (New York: Knopf, 2011), pp. 9–20.
6. The Saudi-American was Yaser Esam Hamdi, raised in Saudi Arabia from the age of three, captured in Afghanistan, and transported to Guantánamo, where the military discovered his U.S. citizenship when he mentioned that he'd been born in Louisiana. He was then transferred to American soil, first to the naval brig in Norfolk, then to the brig in Charleston, South Carolina. The other U.S. citizen, Jose Padilla, was arrested in Chicago and accused in official statements of plotting to detonate a dirty nuclear bomb and to blow up apartment buildings with propane gas. He claimed to have been tortured, and neither of these charges appeared in his indictment when he was ultimately transferred to criminal court, where he was tried and convicted of membership in a cell that conspired to commit murder overseas. He was sentenced to seventeen years and four months. The third man, Ali Saleh Kahlah al-Marri, was a legal resident of the United States when arrested on American soil. He was transferred to the civilian courts after the Supreme Court agreed to hear his case.
7. First the Military Commissions Act of 2006, Public Law 109-366, then the Military Commissions Act of 2009, amending 10 U.S.C. § 47A.
8. Thomas Paine, *Common Sense* (1776).

CHAPTER ONE: TORTURE AND TORMENT

1. International Committee of the Red Cross, *ICRC Report on the Treatment of Fourteen "High Value Detainees" in CIA Custody,* Feb. 2007, p. 10.
2. The account of Andrew Wilson's torture is drawn largely from Edward J. Egan, Special State's Attorney, and Robert D. Boyle, Chief Deputy Special State's Attorney, *Report of the Special State's Attorney,* July 19, 2006, pp. 43–66, with accompanying documents, and John Conroy's reporting in the *Chicago Reader,* for example, "House of Screams," Jan. 26, 1990, http://www.chicagoreader.com/policetorture/900126/. Details on the torture of Khalid Sheikh Mohammed are based on his statement to the International Committee of the Red Cross in its Feb. 2007 report, and on corroborations by CIA and other officials cited in Jane Mayer, *The Dark Side* (New York: Doubleday, 2008), pp. 272–79. Mayer's sources include European and American intelligence experts, former CIA detainees, and their lawyers.
3. *Blackburn v. Alabama,* 361 U.S. 199, 206 (1960), summarizing its conclusion in an earlier case, *Chambers v. Florida,* 309 U.S. 227 (1940).
4. Deb Riechmann, "Bush Details 2002 al-Qaeda Plot on L.A.," AP, Feb. 9, 2006.
5. Mayer, *Dark Side,* p. 277.

6. International Committee of the Red Cross, *ICRC Report on the Treatment of Fourteen "High Value Detainees" in CIA Custody,* p. 37.

7. The truck driver was Iyman Faris. Peter Finn, Joby Warrick, and Julie Tate, "How a Detainee Became an Asset," *Washington Post,* Aug. 29, 2009. CIA Inspector General, "Special Review: Counterterrorism Detention and Interrogation Activities (September 2001–October 2003)," May 7, 2004.

8. Jane Mayer, "Bin Laden Dead, Torture Debate Lives On," News Desk blog, *The New Yorker,* May 2, 2011, "Torture," Times Topics blog, *New York Times,* May 4, 2011.

9. Based on a representative sample of 742 adults, interviewed in English and Spanish on landlines and cell phones, with a sampling error of plus or minus four percentage points. Pew Research Center for the People and the Press, "Public Remains Divided over Use of Torture," http://people-press.org/report/510/public-remains-divided-over-use-of-torture. At the Tower of London, where tourists could push a button approving or disapproving of torture, the approvals overwhelmed the disapprovals when the author visited—although nothing prevented any visitor from pushing the button as many times as he wished to register multiple votes. As unscientific as the experiment was, it made for a wry comment on the short distance humanity has traveled since Guy Fawkes was tortured there in 1605.

10. Michael Sandel, *Justice* (New York: Farrar, Straus and Giroux, 2009), p. 40.

11. He was Ali Abdul Aziz al-Fakhiri, a Libyan captured late in 2001 in Pakistan and an alleged al-Qaeda commander who used the nom de guerre Ibn al-Shaykh al-Libi. Mayer, *Dark Side,* pp. 104, 134. He was also said to have claimed falsely that Iraq was instructing al-Qaeda on using chemical and biological weapons. Douglas Jehl, "Qaeda-Iraq Link U.S. Cited Is Tied to Coercion Claim," *New York Times,* Dec. 9, 2005, p. A1.

12. Stuart Herrington, *Pittsburgh Post-Gazette,* Oct. 21, 2007. He was one of fifteen senior interrogators and intelligence officers from the military, the FBI, and the CIA who signed a statement in 2008 categorically rejecting torture: "We believe:

"1. Non-coercive, traditional, rapport-based interviewing approaches provide the best possibility for obtaining accurate and complete intelligence.

"2. Torture and other inhumane and abusive interview techniques are unlawful, ineffective, and counterproductive. We reject them unconditionally.

"3. The use of torture and other inhumane and abusive treatment results in false and misleading information, loss of critical intelligence, and has caused serious damage to the reputation and standing of the United States. The use of such techniques also facilitates enemy recruitment, misdirects or wastes scarce resources, and deprives the United States of the standing to demand humane treatment of captured Americans.

"4. There must be a single well-defined standard of conduct across all U.S. agencies to govern the detention and interrogation of people anywhere in U.S. custody, consistent with our values as a nation.

"5. There is no conflict between adhering to our nation's essential values, including respect for inherent human dignity, and our ability to obtain the information we need to protect the nation." Human Rights First, Summer 2008.

13. John Conroy, "Tools of Torture," *Chicago Reader,* Feb. 4, 2005. Burge denied torturing or witnessing torture, either in Vietnam or in the United States. Members of Burge's military police unit told Conroy that field phone interrogations had taken place at prison camps they guarded. In 1990, an investigation by the Chicago Police Department's Office of Professional Standards concluded that Burge had tortured suspects, and the Chicago Police Board then fired him. An investigation from 2002 to 2006 by a special state's attorney appointed by the chief judge of the Criminal Division of the Circuit Court of Cook County found three cases of torture provable beyond a reasonable doubt and several others with strong evidence; prosecution of Burge and other officers was impossible because the statute of limitations had run out. In 2008, Burge was indicted by a federal grand jury for perjury and obstruction of justice, for allegedly denying under oath in a civil suit that he had engaged in torture. He was convicted and sentenced to four and a half years in prison.

14. David Finkel and Christian Davenport, "Records Paint Dark Portrait of Guard," *Washington Post,* June 5, 2004.

15. John Conroy, "The Persistence of Andrew Wilson," *Chicago Reader,* Nov. 29, 2007.

16. Although the de facto finding was set aside by the Seventh Circuit, upon remand to the trial court, the district judge granted summary judgment in Wilson's favor, based on the Chicago Police Board's findings, which resulted in the dismissal of Burge and the suspension of two other officers. Of the $1 million, $100,000 went to Wilson and $900,000 to his lawyers. Egan and Boyle, *Report of the Special State's Attorney,* p. 44. Also, *Wilson v. City of Chicago,* Nos. 89-3747 and 90-2216 (7th Cir., Oct. 4, 1993).

17. Conroy, "Persistence of Andrew Wilson."

18. Arthur Koestler, *Darkness at Noon* (New York: Bantam, 1966), p. 173, originally published in 1941 by Macmillan.

19. Francine Sanders and Michael Goldston, "Special Project," Chicago Police Department, Office of Professional Standards, Nov. 2, 1990, http://humanrights.uchicago.edu/chicagotorture/torturebypolice/GoldstonSanders.pdf.

20. Indictment, *United States v. Jon Burge,* No. 08-CR-00846 (N.D. Ill., E. Div. 2008).

21. Marcus Wiggins, deposition, June 14, 1996, *Wiggins v. Burge,* at "Human Rights at Home: The Chicago Police Torture Archive," University of Chicago, http://humanrights.uchicago.edu/chicagotorture/victimsstatements.shtml.

22. Alfonzo Pinex Exhibit No. 1, Statement of Alphonso [*sic*] Pinex, June 29, 1985, Egan and Boyle, *Report of the Special State's Attorney,* p. 291.

23. Dr. John M. Raba to Richard J. Brzeczek, Feb. 17, 1982, Brzeczek Exhibit No. 2, Egan and Boyle, *Report of the Special State's Attorney,* p. 107.

24. Richard J. Brzeczek to Richard M. Daley, Feb. 25, 1982, Brzeczek Exhibit No. 3, Egan and Boyle, *Report of the Special State's Attorney,* p. 108.

25. Egan and Boyle, *Report of the Special State's Attorney,* p. 17.

26. John Conroy, "Blind Justices?" *Chicago Reader,* Dec. 1, 2006.

27. Philip Zelikow, "The OLC 'Torture Memos': Thoughts from a Dissenter," *Shadow Government* (blog), *Foreign Policy,* April 21, 2009. Also, interview, *Morning Edition,* NPR, April 23, 2009. Nearly all copies of his memo rebutting a legal

justification for torture written by John Yoo were confiscated, and it remained classified.

28. The air force officer responsible for SERE, Lieutenant Colonel Daniel J. Baumgartner, warned in a Dec. 2001 memo that "physical pressure was 'less reliable' than other interrogation methods, could backfire by increasing a prisoner's resistance, and would have an 'intolerable public and political backlash when discovered.'" Scott Shane and Mark Mazzetti, "In Adopting Harsh Tactics, No Inquiry into Past Use," *New York Times,* April 22, 2009, p. A1.

29. The CIA apparently began using the techniques before getting legal approval. In response to an ongoing lawsuit under the Freedom of Information Act by the American Civil Liberties Union, four memos were released in April 2009, from which the details of permitted abuses are drawn: "Memorandum for John Rizzo, Acting General Counsel of the Central Intelligence Agency: Interrogation of al Qaeda Operative [Abu Zubaydah]," signed by Jay S. Bybee and drafted by John Yoo, Office of Legal Counsel, Dept. of Justice, Aug. 1, 2002; "Memorandum for John A. Rizzo, Senior Deputy General Counsel, Central Intelligence Agency, Re: Application of 18 U.S.C. §§ 2340–2340A to Certain Techniques That May Be Used in the Interrogation of a High Value al Qaeda Detainee," by Stephen G. Bradbury, Office of Legal Counsel, May 10, 2005; "Memorandum for John A. Rizzo, Re: Application of 18 U.S.C. §§ 2340–2340A to the Combined Use of Certain Techniques in the Interrogation of High Value al Qaeda Detainees," by Bradbury, May 10, 2005; and "Memorandum for John A. Rizzo, Re: Application of United States Obligations Under Article 16 of the Convention Against Torture to Certain Techniques That May Be Used in the Interrogation of High Value al Qaeda Detainees," by Bradbury, May 30, 2005.

30. 18 U.S.C. § 2340. Philip Zelikow, the State Department counsel who wrote a rebuttal to Yoo's interpretation, advised against revising the law to make it more specific, noting that if banned techniques were listed, those not listed might be considered legal. Generic prohibitions were preferable, he said, and after the Bush administration's torture the rubber band had snapped back so hard and the Yoo memo had been repudiated so firmly that no lawyer would try this again. Zelikow was convinced that neither the military nor the CIA would be willing to do it. Conversation with author, March 23, 2010.

31. Vladimir Bukovsky, "Torture's Long Shadow," Outlook, *Washington Post,* Dec. 18, 2005, p. B1.

32. Douglas A. Blackmon, *Slavery by Another Name* (New York: Doubleday, 2008), pp. 71, 347.

33. Evan Wallach, "Waterboarding Used to Be a Crime," Outlook, *Washington Post,* Nov. 4, 2007, p. B1.

34. H.R. 5460 amending the Detainee Treatment Act of 2005, 42 U.S.C. § 2000dd, to include "waterboarding, which includes any form of physical treatment that simulates drowning or gives the individual who is subjected to it the sensation of drowning," in the definition of "cruel, inhuman, or degrading treatment," and in the definition of "torture" under 18 U.S.C. § 2340(1).

35. Detainee Treatment Act of 2005, 42 U.S.C. § 2000dd, and Military Commissions Act of 2006, § 948r.

36. Military Commissions Act of 2006, § 948r.

37. The standard, contained in article 16 of the Convention Against Torture, was not violated by the CIA's methods, according to Bradbury. "Application of United States Obligations Under Article 16," May 30, 2005, pp. 39–40.

38. Scott Shane, "Divisions Arose on Rough Tactics for Qaeda Figure," *New York Times,* April 18, 2009, p. A1. Initially, the CIA mistakenly identified Zubaydah as third or fourth in the al-Qaeda hierarchy.

39. Mayer, *Dark Side,* pp. 155–56; author interviews with Andrew Patel, one of Padilla's attorneys.

40. George W. Bush, "To the Secretary of Defense," June 9, 2002.

41. After Padilla petitioned for a writ of habeas corpus, the Supreme Court granted the habeas appeal of a dual Saudi-U.S. citizen, Yaser Esam Hamdi, holding that while Americans could be held as enemy combatants under the measure passed by Congress a week after Sept. 11 authorizing the president to use "all necessary and appropriate force" against "nations, organizations, or persons" associated with the attacks, Congress had not suspended habeas corpus, and the due process clause of the Fifth Amendment gave a prisoner the right "to contest the factual basis for that detention before a neutral decisionmaker." *Hamdi v. Rumsfeld,* 542 U.S. 507 (2004). Rather than try Hamdi, the government agreed to release him to Saudi Arabia in exchange for his renunciation of U.S. citizenship. The dire threat he posed suddenly evaporated. After the *Hamdi* ruling, the Bush administration transferred Padilla to the criminal justice system just before his appeal was to be heard by the Supreme Court. Earlier, the Fourth Circuit had dismissed Padilla's habeas petition, ruling that the president could hold him without factual inquiry or evidentiary hearing. *Rumsfeld v. Padilla,* 296 F.3d 278 (4th Cir. 2002). The Court had rejected Padilla's petition at first on the argument that it had been brought in the wrong jurisdiction—the Second Circuit covering New York, where he had first been jailed as a material witness, rather than the Fourth Circuit covering South Carolina, where he was currently held in the navy brig. *Rumsfeld v. Padilla,* 542 U.S. 426 (2004). The Second Circuit had found no presidential authority to hold him; the Fourth Circuit later recognized the authority. Miffed that the government was unwilling to test its ruling in the highest court, the judges of the Fourth Circuit refused to approve Padilla's transfer to civilian courts. *Padilla v. Hanft,* No. 05-6396 (4th Cir.), Order, Dec. 21, 2005. The Supreme Court then approved the transfer and vacated the Fourth Circuit's opinion without giving full consideration to the question of whether a U.S. citizen could be seized on American soil (as opposed to the battlefield) as an enemy combatant under the Sept. 11 congressional authorization.

42. Motion to Dismiss for Outrageous Government Conduct, *United States v. Padilla,* No. 04-60001 (S.D. Fla., Miami Div. 2006), Oct. 4, 2006.

43. Deputy Attorney General James Comey, testimony, Senate Judiciary Committee, June 1, 2004.

44. Declaration of Vice Admiral Lowell E. Jacoby, Director of the Defense Intelligence Agency, in *Padilla v. Bush,* No. 02 Civ. 4445 (S.D.N.Y. 2003), Jan. 9, 2003.

45. Michael Isikoff, "'We Could Have Done This the Right Way,'" *Newsweek,* April 25, 2009; Ali Soufan, "My Tortured Decision," *New York Times,* April 22, 2009. The Zubaydah interrogation reportedly took place in Thailand and was taken over by private contractors working for the CIA.

46. Michael Mobbs, "Declaration of Michael H. Mobbs," affidavit in *Padilla v. Bush*, No. 02 Civ. 4445 (S.D.N.Y. 2002), Aug. 27, 2002.

47. Judge Marcia Cooke, in Kirk Semple and Carmen Gentile, "Padilla Sentenced to More Than 17 Years in Prison," *New York Times*, Jan. 22, 2008. Lizette Alvarez, "Sentence for Terrorist Is Too Short, Court Rules," *New York Times*, Sept. 19, 2011, p. A12.

48. *Miranda v. Arizona*, 384 U.S. 436 (1966), combining four similar cases. Majority opinion by Earl Warren. The split was 5–4, with one of the dissenters, Thomas Clark, concurring only insofar as "a totality of circumstances" be used as a looser test of a confession's voluntariness and that the required advance warning be limited to the right to counsel.

49. Miranda claimed a spousal privilege with his common-law wife, the question was litigated, and Miranda lost because they were not legally married.

50. AP, "Miranda Slain: Main Figure in Landmark Suspects' Rights Case," *New York Times*, Jan. 31, 1976; RG 107 Maricopa County, SG 8 Superior Court Criminal, *Arizona v. Ernesto Miranda*, 1963–1971, Accn. No. AA-79-9, Arizona State Library, Archives and Public Records.

51. Mark 15:3–5.

52. I. F. Stone, self-interview, *New York Times Magazine*, April 8, 1979, on his work *The Trial of Socrates* (Boston: Little, Brown, 1988); reports of Socrates's silence were first made by the Greek historian Appian of Alexandria and the Greek philosopher Maximus of Tyre, according to Paul W. Gooch, *Reflections on Jesus and Socrates: Word and Silence* (New Haven, Conn.: Yale University Press, 1997), pp. 14, 82.

53. G. W. Bernard, *The King's Reformation: Henry VIII and the Remaking of the English Church* (New Haven, Conn.: Yale University Press, 2007), p. 493. See also Leonard W. Levy, *Origins of the Fifth Amendment* (New York: Oxford University Press, 1968), p. viii.

54. Phrases from lower courts and citations in *Bram v. United States*, 168 U.S. 532 (1897). See also Alan Hirsch, "Threats, Promises, and False Confessions: Lessons of Slavery," *Howard Law Journal* 49, no. 1 (Fall 2005), pp. 31–60.

55. *Brown v. Mississippi*, 297 U.S. 278 (1936).

56. *Chambers*, 309 U.S. 227. See also *Ashcraft v. Tennessee*, 322 U.S. 143 (1944), throwing out a confession given after thirty-six hours of interrogation.

57. *Blackburn*, 361 U.S. 199.

58. *Malloy v. Hogan*, 378 U.S. 1 (1964). See also *Massiah v. United States*, 377 U.S. 201 (1964), which invoked both the Fifth Amendment right against self-incrimination and the Sixth Amendment right to counsel.

59. *Dickerson v. United States*, 530 U.S. 428 (2000) (Antonin Scalia dissenting, Clarence Thomas concurring; majority opinion by Chief Justice William Rehnquist).

60. Crime Control and Safe Streets Act of 1968, 18 U.S.C. § 3501.

61. David M. O'Brien, *Constitutional Law and Politics*, vol. 2, *Civil Rights and Liberties*, 5th ed. (New York: Norton, 2003), p. 1050.

62. *Dickerson*, 530 U.S. 428.

63. *Arizona v. Fulminante*, 499 U.S. 279 (1991).

64. Miranda warnings must be given only to those in custody, that is, where a reasonable person would not think he is free to leave. Stops for traffic violations are not considered "custodial" and therefore don't require the warnings. *Pennsylvania v. Bruder*, 488 U.S. 9 (1988).

65. *Oregon v. Bradshaw,* 462 U.S. 1039 (1983), where a conversation begun by a defendant was deemed a waiver of *Miranda* rights.

66. Police chased an alleged rapist into a supermarket, arrested him, discovered an empty holster, and asked him where the gun was. "The gun is over there," he said, nodding toward some cartons. The weapon was retrieved, and only then was he Mirandized. Lower courts suppressed the pre-Miranda statement, but the Supreme Court admitted it, establishing a "public safety exception" to the *Miranda* requirement. The exception could probably be applied to battlefield interrogations of suspects later tried in criminal courts. *New York v. Quarles,* 467 U.S. 649 (1984). In a 2010 memo to agents, the FBI sought an expansive interpretation of the public safety window provided in *Quarles* by authorizing the immediate questioning of terrorism suspects without reading them their rights, in exchange for the inability to use the statements in a trial. If additional questioning without the Miranda warning "outweighs the disadvantages of proceeding with unwarned interrogation" (i.e. the possible suppression of the evidence in a criminal case), supervisory agents may give approval after consulting with FBI headquarters. Agents may also ask the suspect to waive his right to appear promptly before a judge. Such an appearance usually coincides with the assignment of an attorney, and unwarned interrogation may not continue thereafter. FBI, "Custodial Interrogation for Public Safety and Intelligence-Gathering Purposes of Operational Terrorists Inside the United States," Mar. 25, 2011, http://www.nytimes.com/2011/03/25/us/25miranda-text .html.

67. *Illinois v. Perkins,* 496 U.S. 292 (1990).

68. *Harris v. New York,* 401 U.S. 222 (1971). Also, a witness found as a result of questioning a defendant without a Miranda warning may testify, *Michigan v. Tucker,* 417 U.S. 433 (1974). Further, the wording of the warning is flexible. In *Duckworth v. Eagan,* 492 U.S. 195 (1989), the Court ruled 5–4 that it was adequate to inform a suspect that appointed counsel would be provided "if and when you go to court." The Seventh Circuit and the dissenters found that the phrase suggested that no lawyer could be made available during interrogation, although *Miranda* states that a suspect must be informed that an attorney would be appointed "prior to any questioning." The right to counsel is also offense-specific, the Court ruled in *McNeil v. Wisconsin,* 501 U.S. 171 (1991), meaning that a defendant who has a lawyer in one case can be questioned without a lawyer regarding another crime if he waives his *Miranda* rights in that separate case. Scalia wrote the opinion.

69. *Lindsey and Gayles v. United States,* Nos. 99-CF-1295, 99-CF-1670, 03-CO-1283, 03-CO-1286 (D.C. Cir. 2006).

70. *Florida v. Powell,* No. 08-1175 (2010). Liberals and conservatives joined to make a 7–2 majority, with Ruth Bader Ginsburg writing the opinion and John Paul Stevens and Stephen Breyer in dissent. Breyer wrote a split opinion, dissenting on the flexibility of the warning but agreeing with the majority that the U.S. Supreme Court had jurisdiction, in that the Florida Supreme Court, which had ruled for Powell, had not done so purely on state constitutional grounds. Stevens argued that the U.S. Supreme Court had no jurisdiction.

71. *Maryland v. Shatzer,* No. 08-680 (2010).

72. *Berghuis v. Thompkins,* No. 08-1470 (2010). Anthony Kennedy wrote for the majority, Sonia Sotomayor for the dissenters. All lower courts, both Michigan and federal, had rejected Thompkins's *Miranda* claim until the Sixth Circuit ruled for him, noting that his long, persistent silence "offered a clear and unequivocal message to the officers: Thompkins did not wish to waive his rights."

73. *North Carolina v. Butler,* 441 U.S. 369, 373 (1979).

74. *United States v. Welch,* 455 F.2d 211, 213 (2nd Cir. 1972); *United States v. Chavarria,* 443 F.2d 904, 905 (9th Cir. 1971). See also *United States v. Bin Laden,* 132 F. Supp. 2d 168, 187 (S.D.N.Y. 2001). The logic holds that the United States cannot impose its procedures on foreign police.

75. Neil MacFarquhar, "8 Tourists Slain in Uganda, Including U.S. Couple," *New York Times,* March 3, 1999.

76. Most details of the crime and the interrogations are from Judge Ellen Segal Huvelle's 150-page ruling on the suppression motion in *United States v. Francois Karake et al.,* No. 02-0256 (ESH) (D.C. D. 2006); also, author interviews with the investigator Colleen Francis, April 11, 2005, and the assistant federal public defender Shawn Moore, March 23, 2005.

77. Their transfer to the United States appears to have been "lawless," according to one of their lawyers, Shawn Moore. Rwanda's criminal code prohibits extradition of Rwandan nationals, so Rwanda proposed a joint U.S.-Rwandan prosecution in Rwanda. When the United States rejected that, the two countries "reached an agreement" on sending the three defendants to the United States, without their having an opportunity to oppose it. *Karake,* p. 68.

78. Ibid., pp. 144–45.

79. On the occasions when a State Department security officer from the embassy was the questioner, he sometimes read the standard warning used in the United States, because he didn't always have the overseas version, which states: "We are representatives of the United States government. Under our laws, you have certain rights. Before we ask you any questions, we want to be sure you understand those rights. You do not have to speak to us or answer any questions. Even if you have already spoken to [Rwandan] authorities, you do not have to speak to us now. If you do speak with us, anything that you say may be used against you in a court in the United States or elsewhere. Under U.S. law, you have the right to talk to a lawyer to get advice before we ask you any questions and you can have a lawyer with you during questioning. Were we in the United States, if you could not afford a lawyer, one would be appointed for you, if you wished, before any questioning. Because you are not in our custody and we are not in the United States, we cannot ensure that you will be permitted access to a lawyer, or have one appointed for you, before or during any questioning. If you want a lawyer, but the foreign authorities do not permit access at this time to a lawyer or will not now appoint one for you, then you still have the right not to speak to us at any time without a lawyer present. If you decide to speak with us now, without a lawyer present, you retain the right to stop answering questions at any time. You should also understand that if you decide not to speak with us, that fact cannot be used as evidence against you in a court in the United States." Ibid., pp. 27–28n.

80. "U.S. Protests to Israelis on 3 Jailed Americans," *New York Times*, Feb. 8, 1993.
81. Michael Higgins, "In Chicago Court, Israelis Deny '93 Torture of Bridgeview Man," *Chicago Tribune*, May 1, 2006. From the heavily censored transcript.
82. The jury found that he had lied in a questionnaire responding to a civil suit against him, and several Islamic charities, filed by the family of an American teenager, David Boim, who had been shot dead in the West Bank. Salah had not mentioned his ties to Hamas. A Seventh Circuit panel upheld a judgment against the charities for sending funds to Hamas but dropped Salah as a defendant. Mike Robinson, "Terror Verdict, Muhammad Salah Dropped from Suit," AP, Dec. 3, 2008; "21 Months for Man Once Accused of Funding Hamas," CBS, July 11, 2007; Libby Sander, "2 Men Cleared of Charges of Aiding Hamas Violence," *New York Times*, Feb. 2, 2007.
83. The Fourth Circuit rejected his appeal but granted a government appeal of the thirty-year sentence as too lenient. *United States v. Ali*, Nos. 06-4334 and 06-4521 (4th Cir. 2008). See also, Indictment, *Ali*, Crim. No. 1:05CR53 (E.D. Va., Alexandria Div., Feb. 3, 2005).
84. *Ali*, No. 05-53, Memorandum Opinion, Lee, J. (E.D. Va., Oct. 25, 2005).
85. The Saudis did most of the questioning and initially rejected an FBI request to interview him. When the FBI submitted thirteen questions they wanted the Saudis to pose, the Saudis agreed to ask him six, while FBI agents watched behind a one-way mirror. He was never Mirandized, even later when the FBI questioned him directly, because the purpose was said to be intelligence gathering, not criminal prosecution. Tainted by that omission, incriminating statements made during those sessions were not used in trial.
86. Jerry Markon, "Falls Church Man's Sentence in Terror Plot Is Increased to Life," *Washington Post*, July 28, 2009. Life means life, since there is no parole in the federal system. Curiously, six months later in Maryland, a young white man, Collin McKenzie-Gude, was sentenced to only five years for actually putting together the means to assassinate Obama. There was plenty of evidence: assault rifles and armor-piercing ammunition, bulletproof vests, a map of Camp David showing a motorcade route, and instructions on killing someone two hundred meters away. But he was not Muslim and had no suspected links to al-Qaeda. He was allowed to plead guilty to possessing a destructive device. Erin Donaghue, "Man Gets 5 Years for Having Explosives," *Gazette*, Jan. 20, 2010, p. 1.
87. Bukovsky, "Torture's Long Shadow."
88. David K. Shipler, *Russia: Broken Idols, Solemn Dreams*, rev. ed. (New York: Penguin, 1989), p. 438–39.
89. Bukovsky, "Torture's Long Shadow."

CHAPTER TWO: CONFESSING FALSELY

1. Arthur Koestler, *Darkness at Noon* (New York: Bantam, 1966), p. 156, originally published in 1941 by Macmillan.
2. Saul M. Kassin and Gisli H. Gudjonsson, "The Psychology of Confessions: A Review of the Literature and Issues," *Psychological Science in the Public Interest* 5, no. 2. (Nov. 2004), pp. 33–67. See also Innocence Project, "Understand

the Causes: False Confessions," http://www.innocenceproject.org/understand/ False-Confessions.php. The project lists the following factors found in cases where confessions have been proven false: duress, coercion, intoxication, diminished capacity, mental impairment, ignorance of the law, fear of violence, the actual infliction of harm, the threat of a harsh sentence, and misunderstanding the situation.

3. Cases with DNA evidence constitute only a small fraction of criminal convictions, so these represent the tip of the iceberg. Three-quarters of the first 250 DNA reversals involved eyewitnesses' misidentification. Fifty-eight percent of those who falsely confessed were under seventeen, mentally ill, or developmentally disabled. Innocence Project, "250 Exonerated: Too Many Wrongfully Convicted," 2010; and Innocence Network, "Innocence Network Exonerations 2010," for statistics through 2010. The first 2011 exoneration: Innocence Project, "Houston Man to Be Declared Innocent After Serving 30 Years for a Dallas Rape and Robbery He Didn't Commit," Jan. 4, 2011, http://www.innocenceproject .org. Data through mid-2011, http://www.innocenceproject.org/know/Browse -Profiles.php.

4. Richard A. Leo, "*Miranda*'s Revenge: Police Interrogation as a Confidence Game," *Law and Society Review* 30 (1996), pp. 259–88. See also David K. Shipler, *The Rights of the People: How Our Search for Safety Invades Our Liberties* (New York: Knopf, 2011), chaps. 2 and 3, on police officers' experience in obtaining widespread consent to search vehicles and belongings.

5. Because this case involved a minor, the records are sealed. All details come from Richard Foxall, a public defender in Alameda County, California, in interviews with the author. Felix declined to be interviewed.

6. In 2009, the Supreme Court decided that the requirement to halt questioning is not triggered unless a suspect explicitly requests a lawyer, and that if he has already been appointed counsel, he may still be questioned without his lawyer present if he is read his *Miranda* rights and waives them. The opinion related to adult suspects and did not address the questioning of minors. *Montejo v. Louisiana*, No. 07-1529 (2009). The 5–4 decision overruled *Michigan v. Jackson*, 475 U.S. 625 (1986), which invalidated any waiver of counsel during police interrogation after a defendant had asserted his right to an attorney in an earlier arraignment or other proceeding. *Montejo* made it easier for police to initiate questioning without a lawyer present but left in place the requirement, imposed by *Edwards v. Arizona*, 451 U.S. 477 (1981), that it be stopped if the suspect demanded counsel during the session. The Court loosened the rules further in 2010, ruling unanimously in *Maryland v. Shatzer*, No. 08-680 (2010), that if more than two weeks pass after a suspect requests a lawyer, he can be re-questioned and again invited to waive his rights. The case concerned a suspect who was in prison for another crime and who demanded an attorney when he was questioned about allegations that he had sexually abused his three-year-old son. The request for counsel ended the questioning. He was still in jail three years later when the police reopened the investigation, got him to sign another waiver, resumed questioning, and obtained a partial admission. Although he was still incarcerated, the Court ruled that since he had been put back with the normal prison population after the first interrogation, "a break in *Miranda*

custody" had occurred, and he had been returned to "accustomed surroundings and daily routine," giving him "the degree of control" present at the initial inquiry. By placing a time limit of two weeks on the *Edwards* presumption of involuntariness, the justices invented a time frame without citing any precedent for it. While concurring with the judgment, John Paul Stevens argued that the fourteen-day period was too brief, and Clarence Thomas argued that it could be too long and should end when custody ended.

7. *District Attorney's Office for the Third Judicial District v. Osborne,* No. 08-6 (2009), leaving the state legislatures and Congress to specify the conditions under which post-conviction DNA testing is conducted. At the time, forty-six states had laws governing such evidence. The 5–4 opinion, written by John Roberts, was joined by Anthony Kennedy, Antonin Scalia, Thomas, and Samuel Alito. Dissenters were Stevens, David Souter, Stephen Breyer, and Ruth Bader Ginsburg.

8. Jerry Markon, "Justice Dept. to Reverse Bush-Era Policy on DNA Tests," *Washington Post,* Nov. 18, 2010, p. A4.

9. "Bureau of Investigation (BOI) Policy and Procedure Manual: Interview Room Audio/Video Recording Equipment," Policy 08-04, Bureau of Investigation, Oakland Police Dept., Dec. 27, 2008. A bill passed by the California legislature requiring videotaping statewide was vetoed by Governor Arnold Schwarzenegger. Radley Balki, "Schwarzenegger Vetoes Justice," FoxNews.com, Nov. 5, 2007.

10. In March 2009, Dunakin and another motorcycle cop were shot to death after pulling over a driver who then fled and killed two other officers before dying in a shoot-out—the worst attack on policemen in Oakland's history. The shooter was Lovelle Mixon, a parole violator. Henry K. Lee, "Mark Dunakin—a Cop Committed to Oakland," *San Francisco Chronicle,* March 23, 2009, p. A8; "The Officer Down Memorial Page, Inc., Honoring All Fallen Members of the Oakland Police Department," http://www.odmp.org/agency/2872-oakland-police -department-california.

11. The actual murderer, later identified by fingerprints and DNA, was sentenced to forty years. Steven A. Drizin and Richard A. Leo, "The Problem of False Confessions in the Post-DNA World," *North Carolina Law Review* 82 (March 2004).

12. Naomi E. Sevin Goldstein, Lois Oberlander Condie, Rachel Kalbeitzer, Douglas Osman, and Jessica L. Geier, "Juvenile Offenders' *Miranda* Rights Comprehension and Self-Reported Likelihood of Offering False Confessions," *Assessment* 10, no. 4 (2003), pp. 359–69.

13. Drizin and Leo, "Problem of False Confessions."

14. Kassin and Gudjonsson, "Psychology of Confessions."

15. Drizin and Leo, "Problem of False Confessions."

16. Kassin and Gudjonsson, "Psychology of Confessions."

17. Drizin and Leo, "Problem of False Confessions."

18. Chris Smith, "Central Park Revisited," *New York,* Oct. 14, 2002. See also Drizin and Leo, "Problem of False Confessions"; and Jim Dwyer, "One Trail, Two Conclusions; Police and Prosecutors May Never Agree on Who Began Jogger Attack," *New York Times,* Feb. 2, 2003.

19. Drizin and Leo, "Problem of False Confessions."

20. Kassin and Gudjonsson, "Psychology of Confessions," citing Richard A. Leo and Richard J. Ofshe, "The Consequences of False Confessions: Deprivations of Liberty and Miscarriages of Justice in the Age of Psychological Interrogation," *Journal of Criminal Law and Criminology* 88, no. 2 (1998), pp. 429–96, and Drizin and Leo, "Problem of False Confessions."

21. Saul M. Kassin and Holly Sukel, "Coerced Confessions and the Jury: An Experimental Test of the 'Harmless Error' Rule," *Law and Human Behavior* 21, no. 1 (1997), pp. 27–46.

22. "Illinois Governor to Commute All Death Row Sentences," AP, Jan. 11, 2003.

23. Joseph Buckley, interview with author, May 11, 2006. John E. Reid & Associates Inc., Investigator Tips, http://www.reid.com/educational_info/r_tips .html?serial=11833857901642783&print=[print. The company and its methodology were developed by Reid, a Chicago police officer from 1936 to 1947, who died in 1982. Material in this and other sections on the Reid Technique is also drawn from Buckley, e-mail to author, Feb. 22, 2011.

24. Frank Horvath, J. P. Blair, and Joseph P. Buckley, "The Behavioural Analysis Interview: Clarifying the Practice, Theory, and Understanding of Its Use and Effectiveness," *International Journal of Police Science and Management* 10, no. 1 (2008), pp. 101–18.

25. Ibid., p. 107.

26. Ibid.

27. Kassin and Gudjonsson, "Psychology of Confessions."

28. Leo, "*Miranda*'s Revenge."

29. Supplementary Report, Police Department, County of Suffolk, N.Y., Sept. 14, 1988, p. 9; http://www.courttv.com/news/tankleff/docs/report1.html.

30. Saul Kassin, interview, *The Oprah Winfrey Show*, Oct. 20, 2008.

31. McCready on *Oprah* and from trial testimony.

32. Martin Tankleff, interview, *Oprah*, Oct. 20, 2008.

33. *Frazier v. Cupp*, 394 U.S. 731 (1969). The Court did not address the lie explicitly and did no analysis but relied on "the totality of the circumstances" test; other issues were considered more relevant, including whether the police had the obligation to halt questioning when the suspect wondered aloud if he should talk to a lawyer. Since the interrogation occurred before *Miranda*'s admonition that questioning must cease when an attorney is requested, the justices found no violation in this case.

34. *State v. Cayward*, 552 So. 2d 971 (Fla. App. 2 Dist. 1989).

35. Reid & Associates, "The Use of Visual Aids During an Interview or Interrogation," Investigator Tips, http://www.reid.com/educational_info/r_tips .html?serial=1215011884372476&print=[print.

36. Reid & Associates, "A Review of Legal Issues Concerning Trickery and Deceit During an Interrogation," Investigator Tips, http://www.reid.com/educational _info/r_tips.html?serial=1107286261495331&print=[print.

37. *Rochin v. California*, 342 U.S. 165 (1952). The warrantless break-in was based on "some information" about narcotics sales, and the vomited capsules were found to contain morphine. "This is conduct that shocks the conscience," Justice Felix Frankfurter wrote for a unanimous Court. "Illegally breaking into the privacy of the petitioner, the struggle to open his mouth and remove what was

there, the forcible extraction of his stomach's contents—this course of proceeding by agents of government to obtain evidence is bound to offend even hardened sensibilities. They are methods too close to the rack and the screw to permit of constitutional differentiation."

38. Kassin interview, *Oprah*.

39. Kassin and Gudjonsson, "Psychology of Confessions."

40. Gisli H. Gudjonsson and James Alexander Culpin MacKeith, "False Confessions: Psychological Effects of Interrogation," in *Reconstructing the Past: The Role of Psychologists in Criminal Trials,* edited by Arne Trankell (Deventer, Netherlands: Kluwer, 1982), pp. 253–69.

41. Hugo Münsterberg, *On the Witness Stand* (Garden City, N.Y.: Doubleday, 1908), cited in Kassin and Gudjonsson, "Psychology of Confessions."

42. A witness had heard Steuerman say that he'd murdered two people, and a teenager testified that his father, Joseph Creedon, had told him that he and Peter Kent had done the killings after Steuerman had signaled for them to enter the house. Steuerman, Creedon, and Kent all denied the accusation, but a fourth man, Glenn Harris, admitted to being the getaway driver. None was charged. Bruce Lambert, "Youth Says Father Admitted to '88 Long Island Murders," *New York Times,* Nov. 14, 2005.

43. One witness quoted in the book worked at one of Steuerman's bagel stores where his son, Todd, a convicted narcotics dealer, allegedly sold drugs and paid the police to look the other way. The witness told the author that she once saw the senior Steuerman and McCready enter the store together and go to the back room where a safe was located. A second witness, Danny Hayes, was told by Seymour Tankleff that he'd argued with Steuerman over his son's drug dealing in the store, was fearful, and that if "anything happened," he should tell the police. Hayes did, but nothing came of it. Bruce Lambert, "New Book Casts Doubt on Police Detective's Role in 1988 Long Island Killings," *New York Times,* Dec. 27, 2008; Richard Firstman and Jay Salpeter, *A Criminal Injustice: A True Crime, a False Confession, and the Fight to Free Marty Tankleff* (New York: Random House, 2008).

44. Alfonso A. Castillo, "Martin Tankleff Accuses Investigators," *Newsday,* March 24, 2009. After release, Tankleff worked as a paralegal on wrongful convictions for a Garden City, Long Island, law firm and planned to go to law school. Claude Solnik, "Q&A with Martin Tankleff, Paralegal at Quadrino Schwartz in Garden City," *Long Island Business News,* March 31, 2010.

45. Alan Hirsch, "Threats, Promises, and False Confessions: Lessons of Slavery," *Howard Law Journal* 49, no. 1 (Fall 2005), p. 37, citing *Simon v. State,* 37 Miss. 288, 293 (1859), and *Wyatt v. State,* 25 Ala. 9, 12–13 (1854).

46. Ibid., citing *Dinah v. State,* 39 Ala. 359 (1864).

47. *Bram v. United States,* 168 U.S. 532 (1897).

48. *Arizona v. Fulminante,* 499 U.S. 279 (1991). The Court cited *Bram*'s citation of the "however slight" statement, "which under current precedent does not state the standard for determining the voluntariness of a confession."

49. Hirsch, "Threats, Promises, and False Confessions," p. 48.

50. Reid & Associates, "Conducting a Custodial Behavior Analysis Interview," Investigator Tips, http://www.reid.com/educational_info/r_tips.html?serial =11987740111611314&print=[print.

51. Reid & Associates, "Use of Visual Aids During an Interview or Interrogation."
52. Ibid.
53. Davis's criminal record made him ineligible to possess a firearm. The 2008 Supreme Court decision, *District of Columbia v. Heller,* No. 07-290 (2008), confirming a Second Amendment right to keep guns in the home, did not alter the federal prohibition against gun ownership by convicted felons.
54. *Missouri v. Seibert,* No. 02-1371 (2004).
55. On the other hand, there is no duty to warn someone of his right to refuse consent to a search, as there is to warn him of his right to refuse to answer questions. *Schneckloth v. Bustamonte,* 412 U.S. 218 (1973).
56. Charles Peters, "Judge Him by His Laws," *Washington Post,* Jan. 4, 2008, p. A21.
57. *Commonwealth v. DiGiambattista,* 442 Mass. 423 (2004).
58. Camera angle is also a factor. Researchers have discovered that a confession tends to look voluntary when only the suspect is shown on the screen, but more questionable when the interrogator is pictured as well. "Videotaped Confessions Can Create Bias Against Suspect," *Science Daily,* March 15, 2007.
59. Noah Schaffer, "Tale of the Tape: Recorded Interrogations Level the Playing Field, Despite Initial Fears," *Lawyers Weekly,* April 2, 2007.
60. Dave Orrick, "Why Some Police, Prosecutors Resist Videotaping Interrogations," *Chicago Daily Herald,* May 16, 2002.
61. *DiGiambattista,* 442 Mass. 423.
62. Reid & Associates, "The Importance of Accurate Corroboration Within a Confession," Investigator Tips, http://www.reid.com/educational_info/r_tips .html?serial=1102008820455822&print=[print.

CHAPTER THREE: THE ASSISTANCE OF COUNSEL

1. *Johnson v. Zerbst,* 304 U.S. 458 (1938).
2. *Betts v. Brady,* 316 U.S. 455 (1942), rejected an appeal to require state courts to provide counsel unless exceptional circumstances existed.
3. *Gideon v. Wainwright,* 372 U.S. 335 (1963). Since Gideon had no lawyer, Chief Justice Earl Warren asked Abe Fortas, who was later elevated to the Court, to represent him. Twenty-two states' attorneys general filed an amicus curiae brief arguing on Gideon's behalf.
4. Anthony Lewis, "The Silencing of Gideon's Trumpet," *New York Times Magazine,* April 20, 2003, p. 50. See also Lewis, *Gideon's Trumpet* (New York: Random House, 1964).
5. *Strickland v. Washington,* 466 U.S. 668 (1984).
6. *Halbert v. Michigan,* No. 03-10198 (2005).
7. One exception is in a capital case, where some states, including Alabama, where Hinton was tried, require the defense attorney to have at least five years' experience.
8. *Brady v. Maryland,* 373 U.S. 83 (1963).
9. These and other factual details of the case come from *Hinton v. State of Alabama,* Nos. CC-85-3363.60 and CC-85-3364.60, Brief of the Appellant; *Hinton,* No. CR-04-0490, Opinion, Criminal Court of Appeals, 2006; and *Hinton,* No. 1051390, Opinion, Supreme Court of Alabama, 2008.
10. Bryan Stevenson, e-mail to author, Dec. 2, 2005.

11. *Hinton,* Brief of the Appellant, pp. 18–19.

12. Bryan Stevenson, interview with author, Feb. 10, 2010, e-mail to author, June 12, 2011. *Hilton v. Alabama,* CR-04-0940 (2011).

13. *Strengthening Forensic Science in the United States: A Path Forward* (Washington, D.C.: National Academies Press, 2009).

14. Out of two hundred randomly reviewed cases, nineteen were found to have serious errors. Nick Bunkley, "Detroit Police Lab Is Closed After Audit Finds Serious Errors in Many Cases," *New York Times,* Sept. 25, 2008; "Detroit Lawyers Criticize Crime Lab Probe," *Detroit Free Press,* Oct. 9, 2008.

15. *Melendez-Diaz v. Massachusetts,* No. 07-591 (2009). The decision was 5–4, the opinion by Antonin Scalia.

16. American Bar Association Standing Committee on Legal Aid and Indigent Defendants, *Gideon's Broken Promise: America's Continuing Quest for Equal Justice,* Dec. 2004. See also reports on Michigan and New York by the National Legal Aid and Defender Association, http://www.mynlada.org/michigan/michigan_report_execsum.pdf and http://www.nlada.org/DMS/Documents/1192201979.35/FINAL%20Franklin%20County%20%28October%202007%29%20version%209%200.pdf.

17. The dichotomy violates state law. *Gideon's Broken Promise,* p. 12. Texas Fair Defense Act of 2001, Tex. Code Crim. Proc. Ann. art. 26.04.

18. *Gideon's Broken Promise,* described by Chief Criminal Judge Michael Spearman of King County Superior Court in Seattle.

19. *Gideon's Broken Promise,* pp. 24–25, consultant Robert Spangenberg, Spangenberg Group.

20. Ibid., p. 25.

21. Adam Liptak, "Public Defenders Get Better Marks on Salary," *New York Times,* July 14, 2007, quoting study by Radha Iyengar of Harvard.

22. Transactional Records Access Clearinghouse, Syracuse University, "Illegal Reentry Becomes Top Criminal Charge," http://trac.syr.edu/immigration/reports/251/; "Immigration Enforcement Under Obama Returns to Highs of Bush Era," http://www.trac.syr.edu/immigration/reports/233/, and "Five Southwest Border Districts Account for Majority of DHS Immigration Criminal Enforcement" and "Prosecution Time for DHS-Immigration Cases," Tables, http://trac.syr.edu/immigration/facts/.

23. Solomon Moore, "Push on Immigration Crimes Is Said to Shift Focus," *New York Times,* Jan. 12, 2009.

24. Defenders refused to take new cases in various jurisdictions in Rhode Island, Connecticut, Maryland, Florida, Tennessee, Kentucky, Ohio, Minnesota, Arizona, Montana, and Washington State. Missouri public defenders appealed a lower court order to continue taking cases to the state supreme court. David J. Carroll, Research Director, National Legal Aid and Defender Association, interviews with author, Jan. 27, 2009, and Sept. 26, 2011.

25. Erik Eckholm, "Citing Workload, Public Lawyers Reject New Cases," *New York Times,* Nov. 8, 2008. The states where public defenders refused to take more cases were Florida, Missouri, Kentucky, Tennessee, Minnesota, Maryland, and Arizona. See also American Council of Chief Defenders, "Resolution on Caseloads and Workloads," Aug. 24, 2007. Caseload limits were recommended by the National Advisory Commission on Criminal Justice Standards.

26. Pascal F. Calogero Jr., Chief Justice, Supreme Court of Louisiana, State of Judiciary address to legislature, May 3, 2005.

27. Ken Armstrong, "Grant County Settles Defense Lawsuit," *Seattle Times,* Nov. 8, 2005. Settlement Agreement in *Best v. Grant County,* No. 04-2-00189-0, in Superior Court State of Washington for Kittitas County, Oct. 31, 2005, http://www.defender.org/files/archive/GrantCountyLitigationSettlementAgreement.pdf. The caseload is calculated as 150 "case equivalents," with more serious prosecutions, such as murder, counting as two cases, and less serious, such as probation violation, as one-third of a case.

28. Administrative Office of Courts, Alabama. The percentage rose from 66 in 2000 to 69 in 2003 and 2004. Although there is no statewide system, several local districts have public defenders.

29. Joe Curtin and Doug Mackey, consultant and staff member, Criminal Justice Coordinating Committee, Jefferson County Attorney's office, interview with author, Nov. 7, 2005.

30. "In the Matter of the Review of Issues Concerning Representation of Indigent Defendants in Criminal and Juvenile Delinquency Cases," Order, Nevada Supreme Court, Jan. 4, 2008.

31. *Lydia Diane Jones v. State,* No. CR-03-1351, Alabama Court of Criminal Appeals, Opinion, 2005. Partial transcripts of trial hearings on counsel's conflict are also contained in this opinion.

32. Results of jury form, "Mitigating Factors in the Case," *New York Times,* May 3, 2006. Nine jurors each found these factors to be mitigating: "That Zacarias Moussaoui's unstable early childhood and dysfunctional family resulted in his being placed in orphanages and having a home life without structure and emotional and financial support eventually resulting in his leaving home because of his hostile relationship with his mother," and, "That Zacarias Moussaoui's father had a violent temper and physically and emotionally abused his family." Four jurors also cited evidence that his father and two sisters were psychotic, and three mentioned that he "was subject to racism as a youngster [in France] because of his Moroccan background, which affected him deeply."

33. Sarah Elizabeth Richards, "How to Humanize a Killer," Salon.com, June 7, 2007.

34. "Admitted al-Qaida Conspirator Recants Testimony About 9/11 Involvement," AP, May 9, 2006.

35. *Rompilla v. Horn,* 355 F.3d 233, 279 (2nd Cir. 2004) (Dolores Sloviter dissenting).

36. *Rompilla v. Beard,* 545 U.S. 374 (2005).

37. "Inmate to Spend Life in Prison for 1988 Murder; U.S. Supreme Court Had Vacated Death Sentence," AP, Aug. 14, 2007.

38. *Wiggins v. Smith,* 539 U.S. 510 (2003).

39. *Rompilla v. Horn* (majority opinion).

40. Anthony Kennedy, who voted with the majority in *Wiggins,* switched sides to the dissent in *Rompilla.*

41. James Brosnahan, interview with author, June 8, 2004. The Justice Department lawyer who gave the advice, Jesselyn Radack, was stunned to discover that her e-mails on the matter had not been provided to the federal judge who had ordered all relevant documents to be turned over, and that printouts had disappeared from the case file. When they were then leaked to *Newsweek,* a

criminal investigation was opened against her for leaking, prompting a prospective employer to rescind a job offer. Jane Mayer, *The Dark Side* (New York: Doubleday, 2008), pp. 72–85, 91–97.

42. *United States v. John Lindh,* No. 02-37A (E.D. Va., Alexandria Div.), Plea Agreement.

43. Neil A. Lewis, "Official Attacks Top Law Firms over Detainees," *New York Times,* Jan. 13, 2007; Farah Stockman, "Potshot at Guantanamo Lawyers Backfires," *Boston Globe,* Jan. 29, 2007. A fresh attack was mounted in 2010 by Keep America Safe, a conservative group run by former vice president Dick Cheney's daughter Elizabeth. In a short video, the group denounced the Obama Justice Department for hiring lawyers who had represented detainees, calling the attorneys "the al-Qaeda 7." The smear drew strong denunciations from a panoply of prominent conservatives, including Charles Stimson, who evidently had a change of heart after his resignation. John Schwartz, "Attacks on Detainee Lawyers Split Conservatives," *New York Times,* March 9, 2010.

44. Larry D. Thompson, "Memorandum to Heads of Department Components, United States Attorneys: Principle of Federal Prosecution of Business Organizations," Dept. of Justice, Jan. 20, 2003.

45. Paul J. McNulty, Deputy Attorney General, "Memorandum: Principles of Federal Prosecution of Business Organizations," Dec. 12, 2006.

46. *U.S. v. Stein,* No. S1 05 Crim. 0888 (S.D.N.Y.), July 16, 2007, Judge Lewis A. Kaplan, upheld in *U.S. v. Stein,* No. 07-3042-CR (2nd Cir., Aug. 28, 2008).

47. 28 C.F.R. § 501.3(d).

48. The Court granted certiorari but ruled that the case had been brought in the wrong jurisdiction—New York, where Padilla was first held, rather than South Carolina, where he was currently held. *Rumsfeld v. Padilla,* 542 U.S. 426 (2004). His attorneys refiled, and two years later, as the case again worked its way toward the Supreme Court, the government transferred Padilla to the civilian system and prepared a criminal indictment, though on charges much less severe than its original assertion, based on a thin intelligence report, that he had planned with al-Qaeda to set off a "dirty bomb" of nuclear material. He was tried, convicted, and sentenced to seventeen years and four months.

CHAPTER FOUR: THE TILTED PLAYING FIELD

1. Bureau of Justice Statistics, "Felony Sentences in State Courts, 2006," Dec. 30, 2009, http://bjs.ojp.usdoj.gov/index.cfm?ty=pbdetail&iid=2152; Bureau of Justice Statistics, "U.S. District Courts—Criminal Defendants Disposed of . . . 12-Month Period Ending December 31, 2010," http://www.uscourts.gov/uscourts/Statistics/StatisticalTablesForTheFederalJudiciary/2010.D04Dec10.pdf.

2. Timothy Lynch, "The Case Against Plea Bargaining," *Regulation* (Fall 2003), http://www.cato.org/pubs/regulation/regv26n3/v26n3-7.pdf.

3. Benjamin Weiser, "Lawyer Who Threw a City Case Is Vindicated, Not Punished," *New York Times,* March 5, 2009, p. A23. Convicted of the murder, outside the Palladium nightclub, were Olmedo Hidalgo and David Lemus.

4. Benjamin Weiser, "A Judge's Struggle to Avoid Imposing a Penalty He Hated," *New York Times,* Jan. 13, 2004, p. A1.

5. *United States v. Angelos,* No. 2:02-CR-00708PGC (D. Utah, Nov. 16, 2004), Memorandum Opinion and Order Denying Motion to Find 18 U.S.C. § 924(c) Unconstitutional, Imposing Sentence, and Recommending Executive Clemency, Judge Paul Cassell.

6. *Blakely v. Washington,* 542 U.S. 296 (2004), which overturned sentencing guidelines in Washington and, effectively, a dozen other states, and *United States v. Booker,* 543 U.S. 220 (2005), which converted federal sentencing guidelines from mandatory to advisory. The two coalitions: Antonin Scalia, David Souter, John Paul Stevens, Clarence Thomas, and Ruth Bader Ginsburg found them unconstitutional; Ginsburg, Stephen Breyer, Anthony Kennedy, Sandra Day O'Connor, and William Rehnquist declared them constitutional if only advisory.

7. U.S. Sentencing Commission, *Final Report on the Impact of* United States v. Booker *on Federal Sentencing,* March 2006.

8. *United States v. Brown,* No. CR 04-385; *United States v. Harris,* No. CR 03-539, Judge Paul Friedman, D.C. Dist. Ct., transcript, oral opinion, March 7, 2006.

9. U.S. Sentencing Commission, *Preliminary Crack Cocaine Retroactivity Data Report,* Dec. 2008.

10. Fair Sentencing Act, S. 1789, Public Law 111-220.

11. *Kimbrough v. United States,* 552 U.S. 85 (2007).

12. U.S. Sentencing Commission, *Guidelines Manual,* § 2K1.5 (Nov. 2008).

13. U.S. Sentencing Commission, *Final Report on the Impact of* United States v. Booker *on Federal Sentencing.*

14. *Bordenkircher v. Hayes,* 434 U.S. 357 (1978). Potter Stewart wrote for the majority.

15. The one-level reduction if the plea is "timely" applies only to sentences at level 16 or higher. *Guidelines,* § 3E1.1.

16. Ibid., § 3C1.1. The judge is supposed to find by a preponderance of evidence that the defendant has suborned perjury by the witness, but in practice the two levels are often added simply because the judge thinks the witness lied.

17. *Brady v. Maryland,* 373 U.S. 83 (1963).

18. *Giglio v. United States,* 405 U.S. 150 (1972). See also Justice Department policy on disclosure for trial: Deputy Attorney General, "Memorandum to Holders of United States Attorneys Manual, Title 9, Adding New Section, § 9-5.001: Policy Regarding Disclosure of Exculpatory and Impeachment Information," Oct. 19, 2006.

19. *Boykin v. Alabama,* 395 U.S. 238 (1969).

20. *United States v. Ruiz,* 536 U.S. 622 (2002), in which the Court unanimously reversed the Ninth Circuit's finding that a guilty plea cannot be voluntary without access to impeachment information, and that a requirement to sign away the right to see such information is an unconstitutional denial of due process. The Supreme Court countered that the right goes to the trial's fairness, not the plea's voluntariness, and observed that forcing out details about informants, undercover agents, and witnesses when no trial occurs could compromise investigations and lead to burdensome pretrial preparation even for guilty pleas. Although the prosecutor had pledged to disclose exculpatory evidence during plea bargaining and the case turned on impeachment information, the Court's

language has been interpreted to preclude a right to exculpatory evidence as well.

21. U.S. Sentencing Commission, *Final Report on the Impact of* United States v. Booker *on Federal Sentencing.* A subsequent study found racial disparities increasing after *Booker.* From Dec. 2007 to Sept. 2009, sentences were 23.9 percent longer for black males than for white males, and 6.8 percent longer for Hispanic males than for white males. United States Sentencing Commission, *Demographic Differences in Federal Sentencing Practices: An Update of the* Booker Report's *Multivariate Regression Analysis,* March 2010.

22. *United States v. Mercado,* F.3d, No. 05-50624 (9th Cir. 2007).

23. *United States v. Vaughn,* 430 F.3d 518 (2nd Cir. 2005). The jury found the defendants guilty of conspiring to distribute at least 50 but not more than 100 kilograms of marijuana. The judge found a preponderance of evidence that the amount was 544 kilograms and sentenced them accordingly. Sonia Sotomayor ruled: "After *Booker,* district courts' authority to determine sentencing factors by a preponderance of the evidence endures and does not violate the Due Process Clause of the Fifth Amendment. . . . Appellants claim that the rulings in *Booker* and its predecessors preclude sentencing on the basis of acquitted conduct. We again disagree." The Supreme Court refused to hear an appeal from this decision.

24. *United States v. Gonzalez,* CA Nos. 08-10121 and 08-10144. Narrative drawn largely from Appellant Luis Alberto Gonzalez's Principal Brief and Appellant's Response and Reply Brief. "Over-shifting" allegation: Daniel Blank, Gonzalez's attorney, e-mail to author, Feb. 18, 2009.

25. 18 U.S.C. § 844(h)(1): "Whoever . . . uses fire or an explosive to commit any felony which may be prosecuted in a court of the United States."

26. *U.S. v. Settles,* No. 06-3090 (D.C. Cir. 2008), upholding acquitted conduct in enhancing sentence but questioning its fairness. Settles was sentenced to fifty-seven months for gun possession during a drug deal, even though the jury had convicted him only of the gun charge, not the drugs.

27. *Williams v. New York,* 337 U.S. 241 (1949).

28. *McMillan v. Pennsylvania,* 477 U.S. 79 (1986).

29. The Court made this clear in 1999. Two men, found guilty of carjacking, faced a fifteen-year maximum but were sentenced under a section of the law providing up to twenty-five years if someone is seriously injured. The injury hadn't been charged or proven to a jury, and the Court overturned the twenty-five-year sentences. "It is unconstitutional for a legislature to remove from the jury the assessment of facts that increase the prescribed range of penalties to which a criminal defendant is exposed," Justice John Paul Stevens wrote in a concurring opinion. "It is equally clear that such facts must be established by proof beyond a reasonable doubt." But this applies only where a sentence exceeds the statutory maximum for the convicted conduct. Below that ceiling, acquitted conduct can still enhance the sentence. *Jones v. United States,* 526 U.S. 227 (1999). See also *In re Winship,* 397 U.S. 358, 364 (1970), and *Mullaney v. Wilbur,* 421 U.S. 684 (1975).

30. *Apprendi v. New Jersey,* 530 U.S. 466 (2000). The majority opinion, by Stevens, was joined by Souter, Ginsburg, Scalia, and Thomas.

31. Under long-standing precedent, no warrant was required to search the vehicle. Police officers testified that since the car was to be towed and impounded, the search would have occurred even without consent as part of routine inventory. By contrast, premises that cannot be moved, such as houses, cannot usually be searched without warrants. Account from case file of *United States v. Zavaleta*, No. 03-10679 (9th Cir.), appeal from Calif., No. Dist., No. CR-02-40239, including Oakland Police Dept., Suspect Report, Incident 2088, May 29, 2002; transcripts of suppression and plea hearings; Jerome Matthews, interview with author, Dec. 2, 2003.

32. The federal system no longer has parole. All inmates serve their entire prison terms, with "supervisory release" often tacked onto the ends as part of their original sentence. By contrast, most states permit early release by parole boards.

33. Account of the Jenkins case comes from *United States v. Neale L. Jenkins,* Crim. No. 99-0337 (D. D.C. 2005), Report and Recommendation, U.S. magistrate judge John M. Facciola, Aug. 25, 2005; Order, Judge Paul L. Friedman, Sept. 12, 2005; Transcript, Hearing on Violation of Supervised Release, March 23, 2005; Statement of Patrice Kerry to Public Defender Service Investigator, Oct. 6, 2005; Appeal of Neale L. Jenkins to U.S. Parole Commission, Oct. 6, 2005; Tony Miles, multiple interviews with author; Thomas L. Dybdahl, interview with author, April 26, 2006.

34. Transcript, Hearing, March 23, 2005. Elana Tyrangiel later became associate counsel to President Obama.

35. The D.C. crime was possession with intent to distribute heroin, the federal was unlawful possession of a firearm by a convicted felon. His prior felony was distribution of cocaine.

36. Indigent, Jenkins had free investigators and lawyers from the Federal Public Defenders (Tony Miles) and, for his D.C. case, the Public Defender Service (Thomas L. Dybdahl).

37. John Burnett, "Deputy Has Midas Touch in Asset Seizures," *All Things Considered,* NPR, June 17, 2008.

38. John Burnett, "Seized Drug Assets Pad Police Budgets," *Morning Edition,* NPR, June 16, 2008.

39. Ibid.

40. *Bennis v. Michigan,* No. 94-8729 (1996).

41. A bank or brokerage account can be emptied on a judge's order equivalent to a search warrant issued on probable cause, and a piece of real estate can be frozen with a *lis pendens,* which is attached to the land record on a judge's order. The owner may continue to reside there, however; actual forfeiture of real property isn't effected, if it's contested, until the case is resolved in court.

42. The case was referred by the local police to the federal authorities. The cash, forwarded to the Drug Enforcement Administration, was returned by the assistant U.S. attorney who was assigned as prosecutor and who conceded the error.

43. John Burnett, *Reporter's Notebook,* NPR, June 21, 2008; DEA, "Money Laundering," http://www.usdoj.gov/dea/programs/money.htm.

44. Avery Gilbert, *What the Nose Knows: The Science of Scent in Everyday Life* (New York: Crown, 2008), p. 32.

45. Jay Poupko, Toxicology Consultants Inc., cited in *United States v. U.S. Currency, $30,060,* 39 F.3d 1039 63 USLW 2351 (9th Cir. 1984).
46. Arthur S. Hayes, "Cocaine-Tainted Cash Faulted as Evidence," *Wall Street Journal,* June 2, 1993.
47. Jonathan Oyler, William D. Darwin, and Edward J. Cone, "Cocaine Contamination of United States Paper Currency," *Journal of Analytical Toxicology* 20, no. 4 (1996), pp. 213–16.
48. *United States v. $506,231,* No. 96-3308 (7th Cir. 1997), citing "Courts Reject Drug-Tainted Evidence," *American Bar Association Journal* 79 (Aug. 1993).
49. Theodore W. Pope et al., "Bacterial Contamination of Paper Currency," *South Medical Journal* 95, no. 12 (Dec. 2002), pp. 1408–10, http://www.ncbi.nlm.nih .gov/pubmed/12597308.
50. "Who Really Knows What a Dog's Nose Knows?" *Criminal Practice Report* 12, no. 23 (Nov. 18, 1998), p. 462.
51. *Illinois v. Caballes,* 543 U.S. 405, 410–12 (2005) (Souter dissenting).
52. Under the Daubert standard, after *Daubert v. Merrell Dow Pharmaceuticals,* 509 U.S. 579 (1993), calculations of error rates and other scientific checks are required for such evidence to be admissible.
53. Civil Asset Forfeiture Reform Act, 18 U.S.C. § 983(b).
54. "FEAR's Gideon Project," http://www.fear.org/.
55. *United States v. $30,060,* No. 92-55919 (9th Cir. 1994).
56. *United States v. $242,484,* No. 01-16485 (11th Cir. 2003), in which no probable cause was found justifying the civil forfeiture of cash from a woman flying from New York to Miami.
57. Colloton's credentials make his opinion even more startling. He graduated from Princeton and then Yale Law School, clerked for Chief Justice William H. Rehnquist, served as an associate independent counsel with Kenneth W. Starr during the investigation of President Clinton, and was U.S. Attorney for the Southern District of Iowa.
58. *United States v. $124,700 in U.S. Currency,* No. 05-3295 (8th Cir. 2005) (opinion by Morris Sheppard Arnold and Steven M. Colloton; dissent by Donald P. Lay).
59. John Burnett, *All Things Considered,* NPR, June 16, 2008. Under CAFRA, legal fees are supposed to be reimbursed by the government, but not all judges will order the award.
60. David B. Smith, e-mails to author, Jan. 12, 2010.
61. *All Things Considered,* June 16, 2008.
62. Ibid.

CHAPTER FIVE: BELOW THE LAW

1. Immigration and Nationality Act, 8 U.S.C. § 1101.
2. Debi Sanders, e-mail to author, June 10, 2005. She has since become staff attorney for Catholic Charities' Immigration Legal Services program in Washington, D.C.
3. In 2009, the Obama administration announced a plan to alleviate these abuses by assigning twenty-three federal agents to twenty-three local prisons housing 40 percent of the immigration detainees, and within three to five years by building enough federal facilities for most detainees, thereby reducing reliance

on local or private penal institutions. However, the ACLU complained that the plan contained no standards for the conditions of incarceration, no due process to prevent unjustified detention, and no method to prevent deaths in detention resulting from inadequate medical care. ACLU, "DHS Plan to Improve Immigration Detention an Encouraging Step," Oct. 6, 2009, http://www.aclu.org/immigrants-rights_prisoners-rights/dhs-plan improve-immigration-detention -encouraging-step; and U.S. Immigration and Customs Enforcement, "2009 Immigration Detention Reforms," Aug. 6, 2009, http://www.ice.gov/pi/news/factsheets/2009_immigration_detention_reforms.htm.

4. Immigration and Nationality Act, § 292. Those without lawyers fare less well in deportation proceedings. See Donald Kerwin, "Revisiting the Need for Appointed Counsel," *Insight,* Migration Policy Institute, April 2005.

5. Toward the end of the Bush administration, Attorney General Michael Mukasey ruled that there was no constitutional right to effective counsel in a removal proceeding. His successor in the Obama administration, Eric Holder, withdrew the decision and pledged to issue new rules on the issue. Spencer S. Hsu, "Precedent Reinstated in Deportation Cases," *Washington Post,* June 4, 2009.

6. The Illegal Immigration Reform and Immigrant Responsibility Act (IIRAIRA) of 1996. Under *Immigration and Naturalization Service v. St. Cyr,* 533 U.S. 289 (2001), the Supreme Court restored the waiver for someone who pleaded guilty prior to 1996 to a crime not listed then as an aggravated felony, but left intact the law's elimination of the waiver for someone convicted in a trial for that crime.

7. *Zadvydas v. Davis,* 533 U.S. 678 (2001). The Court, 5–4, interpreted the statute to limit detention to approximately six months, finding that indefinite detention would violate the due process clause, which applies to everyone within the United States, whether citizens or aliens. Using the technique of "constitutional avoidance," the justices actively interpreted the law rather than strike it down as unconstitutional.

8. Jodi Wilgoren, "Refugees in Limbo: Ordered out of U.S., but with Nowhere to Go," *New York Times,* June 4, 2005, p. A1. He was released in July 2005. Cost estimate from Elizabeth Stawicki, "U.S. Immigration Spent $200K on Keyse Jama Deportation," Minnesota Public Radio, June 23, 2006, http://minnesota .publicradio.org/display/web/2006/06/23/jamaflight/. At any given time, more than a thousand long-term deportees are behind bars with no country willing to take them. The GAO found that ICE tracking systems were inadequate to make sure the six-month rule was followed. See Government Accountability Office, "Immigration Enforcement: Better Data and Controls Are Needed to Assure Consistency with the Supreme Court Decision on Long-Term Alien Detention," May 2004. See also *Jama v. ICE,* Civil No. 01-1172, Order on Motion and Release (U.S. Dist. Ct., Minn., May 20, 2005), which ordered his release after he lost 5–4 in the Supreme Court, which ruled that aliens can be deported even to countries that have not agreed to accept them. *Jama v. ICE,* 543 U.S. 335 (2005).

9. Transactional Records Access Clearinghouse, Syracuse University, July 2009, http://trac.syr.edu.

10. Transactional Records Access Clearinghouse, "Immigration Courts: Still a Troubled Institution," July 2009.

11. Office of Inspector General, Dept. of Justice, "An Investigation of Allegations of Politicized Hiring by Monica Goodling and Other Staff in the Office of the Attorney General," July 2008, http://www.justice.gov/oig/special/s0807/. The leading official in the political hiring, Monica M. Goodling, was subjected to a criminal investigation but received limited immunity in exchange for testifying before Congress. Eric Lipton, "Colleagues Cite Partisan Focus by Justice Official," *New York Times,* May 12, 2007.

12. Mary Holper, "Immigration Consequences of Criminal Convictions," Capital Area Immigrants' Rights Coalition, Jan. 19, 2005. Aggravated felonies are listed in 8 U.S.C. § 1101(a)(43).

13. Bryan Lonegan, "The Court of Appeals Sends the Wrong Message Regarding the Obligations of Defense Counsel to Non-citizens," draft of paper, citing *People v. McDonald,* 2003 WL 22764237, N.Y.2d (2003), and *People v. Ford,* 86 N.Y.2d 397 (1995).

14. *Padilla v. Kentucky,* No. 08-651. The petitioner, Jose Padilla (no relation to the convicted terrorist), won part of his argument—ineffective assistance of counsel—but the Court sent the case back down to Kentucky courts to determine whether the ineffective assistance had actually prejudiced him, a second prong required for a reversal. The majority of 7–2 (Justices Antonin Scalia and Clarence Thomas dissenting) also limited the ruling to clear-cut immigration situations such as this one, adding that in more nebulous circumstances, a defense attorney had only the obligation to warn that there might be adverse consequences, not to research and determine precisely what they would be. Justice Samuel Alito, joined by Chief Justice John Roberts, concurred narrowly, only insofar as a lawyer gives incorrect advice, not when he refrains from giving any advice, and not when he fails to explain the immigration consequences, even where they are clear-cut.

15. Case No. GC97011965-00, Virginia Beach General District, July 1, 1997.

16. Obituary, *Virginian-Pilot,* Aug. 15, 2009.

17. A violent sexual crime triggers deportation as an aggravated felony if the sentence, suspended or not, is for at least one year. If nonviolent, it is classified as a crime involving moral turpitude. One such crime committed within five years of getting a green card, or two convictions at any time after receiving a green card, can result in deportation.

18. As long as the marijuana is not for sale, possession of thirty grams or less is also the sole exception to designating an arriving alien with a drug conviction as inadmissible. There is no possibility of a waiver. Otherwise, cancellation of removal for a drug crime that is not a felony is available only to immigrants already in the country, in narrow circumstances. The reasons for excluding foreigners are much broader than for deporting them, requiring only a "reason to believe" that the person falls into any of a long list of categories that include "habitual drunkard," drug addict, prostitute, illegal exporter, or the spouse or child of a drug trafficker. In general, a legal immigrant gets caught by the reason-to-believe standard when he has left the United States and is stopped upon his return. 8 U.S.C. § 1182(a)(2).

19. To make an arrest, ICE has the authority to issue an administrative warrant based on probable cause, without a judge's approval. Immigration and Nationality Act, § 287(a).

20. 8 U.S.C. § 1357(a)(1), (3).
21. Explanation from Mary Holper, e-mail to author, July 23, 2009. In fact, courts have held that a Miranda warning in immigration matters might work to the detainee's disadvantage: "A principal purpose of the *Miranda* warnings is to permit the suspect to make an intelligent decision as to whether to answer the government agent's questions. In deportation proceedings, however—in light of the alien's burden of proof, the requirement that the alien answer nonincriminating questions, the potential adverse consequences to the alien of remaining silent, and the fact that an alien's statement is admissible in the deportation hearing despite his lack of counsel at the preliminary interrogation—*Miranda* warnings would be not only inappropriate but could also serve to mislead the alien." *Chavez-Raya v. INS,* 519 F.2d 397, 402 (7th Cir. 1975).
22. In their brief, Conteh's lawyers cited *Matter of Davis,* 20 I.&N. Dec. 536 (BIA 1992), and *Matter of Barrett,* 20 I.&N. Dec. 171 (BIA 1990), which held that the offense must be punishable under the Controlled Substances Act (21 U.S.C. §§ 801 et seq.). Also, federal court rulings that giving drugs without remuneration is not trafficking: *Steele v. Blackman,* 236 F.3d 130, 137 (3rd Cir. 2001); *United States v. Rivera-Sanchez,* 247 F.3d 905, 908 (9th Cir. 2001).
23. Virginia Code § 18.2-248.2(a)(1), a Class 1 misdemeanor, maximum punishment, twelve months. At the time, it was enough for the detainee to show that he could theoretically have been convicted under that statute even without having dealt drugs for remuneration. Since then, however, the Board of Immigration Appeals has ruled that the detainee has the burden to prove that in actuality he had not been involved in dealing of a "business or merchant nature." Conteh's lawyer, Mary Holper, believes he would lose his case under the new standard.
24. Deportable Aliens, 8 U.S.C. § 1227(a)(2)(B), Controlled Substances.
25. Mary Holper, Conteh's attorney, interview with author, Oct. 12, 2005.
26. Because he had been caught at the airport returning to the United States, Abel was declared "inadmissible" and therefore had to apply for a waiver, even though fewer than thirty grams of marijuana would not have made him deportable if he had remained in the country. Because his pre-1996 conviction resulted from a guilty plea, not a trial, he fit into the narrow category of people deemed eligible for waivers when the Supreme Court, in *St. Cyr,* struck down that retroactive provision of the 1996 law.
27. Larry G. Hansen, Dept. of Veterinary Biosciences, University of Illinois at Urbana-Champaign, letter to federal judge Gerald Bruce Lee, July 30, 2004.
28. In Lahore, Taliban squads attacked crowds of Ahmadi worshippers in two mosques with grenades, suicide vests, and AK-47s, killing ninety-five in 2010. Banyan, "We Decide Whether You're Muslim or Not," *Economist,* June 10, 2010. Her husband's visits to Pakistan were cited by Special Agent Ramon Oyegbola, of the Bureau of Immigration and Customs Enforcement, to suggest that the family had nothing to fear, implying deceit in his asylum application. Criminal Complaint, *United States v. Waheeda M. Tehseen,* No. 04-108-M (E.D. Va. 2004).
29. Dr. Ajmal Khan, Neurology Dept., National Institute for Handicapped, to Whom It May Concern, re: Manahil Chohan, July 29, 2004; Dr. Khalida Perveen, National Commission for Human Development, Islamabad, to Judge Gerald Bruce Lee, July 16, 2004; Special Education Eligibility Form, Fairfax

County Public Schools, re: Warda Chohan, with attached WJ III Compuscore and Profiles Program Version 1.1b test results, Oct. 29, 2003.

30. If she had honestly checked "Yes" to the question of whether she had claimed citizenship, she probably would have had her green card revoked and been deported, according to Debi Sanders, an immigration attorney. Immigrants in that situation are often advised by advocates not to apply for naturalization and simply to live in the United States on their green cards, as permanent residents. Debi Sanders, interview with author, Feb. 3, 2011. Mani's two oldest children did their own applications. Lisa Faeth, e-mail to author, Feb. 18, 2011. Also, Form N-400, Application for Naturalization, Waheeda Mani Tehseen, signed Sept. 15, 2001, sworn in personal interview, Aug. 6, 2002.

31. Certificate, "Unsung Hero Award," U.S. Environmental Protection Agency, Christine Todd Whitman, June 6, 2002.

32. This is known because tapes and transcripts of the tapped conversations were turned over to Mubarak Hamed's defense team after his indictment.

33. Second Superseding Indictment, *United States v. Islamic American Relief Agency et al.*, No. 07-00087-01/07-CR-W-NKL (W.D. Mo., W. Div.), filed Oct. 21, 2008.

34. 18 U.S.C. § 1425(a). If the fraud is committed to facilitate drug trafficking or terrorism, the maximums are twenty or twenty-five years, respectively.

35. John T. Morton to Danny Onorato (Tehseen's lawyer), June 23, 2004. See also Criminal Complaint, *United States v. Waheeda M. Tehseen,* No. 04-108-M (E.D. Va. 2004).

36. Morton to Onorato, June 23, 2004.

37. Judgment in a Criminal Case, *United States v. Waheeda M. Tehseen,* No. 1:04CR00092-001 (E.D. Va., Alexandria Div.), Aug. 9, 2004.

38. Dr. Riffat A. Chaudhary to Whom It May Concern, National Institute for Handicapped, Lahore, Pakistan, July 27, 2004.

39. Office of Foreign Assets Control, Dept. of the Treasury, "Recent OFAC Actions," Oct. 13, 2004. The previous Jan., IARA had been listed by the Senate Finance Committee as being suspected of supporting international terrorism.

40. Second Superseding Indictment, *Islamic American Relief Agency et al.,* No. 07-00087-01/07-CR-W-NKL; and Plea Agreement, *United States v. Mubarak Hamed,* No. 07-CR-00087-02-W-NKL (W.D. Mo., W. Div.), filed June 25, 2010. Ahmed Ghappour, Hamed's attorney, e-mail to author, Feb. 22, 2011.

41. *Detroit Free Press v. Ashcroft,* 303 F.3d 681, 683 (6th Cir. 2002). The Supreme Court let stand an opposite decision in the Third Circuit, *North Jersey Media Group v. Ashcroft,* 205 F. Supp. 2d 288, 300 (3rd Cir. 2002). The Court also declined to hear the appeal in *Center for National Security Studies et al. v. U.S. Department of Justice,* Nos. 02-5254 and 02-5300 (D.C. Cir. 2003), which endorsed the government's decision to keep secret the names of detainees.

42. Office of Inspector General, U.S. Dept. of Justice, "The September 11 Detainees: A Review of the Treatment of Aliens Held on Immigration Charges in Connection with the Investigation of the September 11 Attacks," April 2003.

43. Rachel Meeropol, e-mail to author, July 20, 2009.

44. *Ashcroft v. Iqbal,* No. 07-1015 (2009). The complaint was sent back down to lower courts for revision and refiling, yet it seemed to have little chance of succeeding. The opinion "now requires plaintiffs to come forward with concrete

facts at the outset, and it instructs lower court judges to dismiss lawsuits that strike them as implausible." Adam Liptak, "Sidebar: Case About 9/11 Could Lead to a Broad Shift on Civil Lawsuits," *New York Times,* July 21, 2009. A companion case, *Turkmen v. Ashcroft,* No. 02 CV 2307 (JG), was equally handicapped by the Supreme Court's decision, but both continued to work their way through the courts. The government paid six of the plaintiffs in *Turkmen* a $1.26 million settlement, and six new plaintiffs were added to the suit in 2010. Center for Constitutional Rights, "*Turkmen v. Ashcroft,*" http://ccrjustice.org/ourcases/ current-cases/turkmen-v.-ashcroft.

45. James Ziglar, interviews with author, March 17, 2005, and Nov. 12, 2009. In the first interview, Ziglar described the planned sweeps as aimed at "Arabs and Muslims" but in the second interview revised his statement to include Arabs only; he could not be certain that Muslims had been explicitly mentioned. He may have been right the first time, at least in describing intent, since the more restricted sweeps that were actually conducted targeted communities of Pakistanis, who are Muslim but not Arab. He declined to allow publication of the names of the two participants in the meeting who later commended him. He still faulted them for not speaking up during the meeting itself but did not want to criticize them publicly.

46. By contrast, in April 2010, Obama invited immigrants serving in the military to hold their naturalization ceremony in the White House Rose Garden, where he praised them for being "willing to risk their lives to defend our country even before they could call it their own." Barack Obama, remarks, Rose Garden, White House, April 23, 2010, http://www.whitehouse.gov/the-press-office/ remarks-president-naturalization-ceremony-active-duty-service-members.

47. Rachel L. Swarns, "More Than 13,000 May Face Deportation," *New York Times,* June 7, 2003, p. A9, and "Program's Value in Dispute as a Tool to Fight Terrorism," *New York Times,* Dec. 21, 2004, p. A26. Homeland Security and Justice Department officials claimed to have arrested six suspected terrorists among the registrants, but the 9/11 Commission found the assertion unsupported. A modified registration requirement—the National Security Entry-Exit Registration System (NSEERS)—was later instituted for nonimmigrant, nondiplomatic citizens from certain Muslim countries, who were directed to special passport booths upon arrival in the United States and were required to appear at Customs and Border Protection offices periodically during their stay and again upon departure. The system was scrapped in May 2011. Customs and Border Protection, "Important NSEERS Information," May 5, 2011, http://www.cbp .gov/xp/cgov/travel/id_visa/nseers/imp_nseers_info.xml.

48. Patrick J. McDonnell, "Pakistanis Fleeing U.S. Seek Refuge in Canada," *Los Angeles Times,* March 15, 2003, p. 1.

49. Michael Powell, "An Exodus Grows in Brooklyn," *Washington Post,* May 29, 2003, p. A1.

50. American Civil Liberties Union Blog of Rights, "Local Enforcement Tactics Lead to Racial Profiling, Human Rights Abuses," Mar. 29, 2011, http://www .aclu.org/blog/human-rights-immigrants-rights/local-enforcement-tactics-lead -racial-profiling-human-rights-abu. Emergency Petition for Writ of Habeas Corpus, *Rita Cote v. Lubins et al.* (U.S. D.C. Middle D. Fla., Ocala Div.).

51. Andrea Elliott, "In Brooklyn, 9/11 Damage Continues," *New York Times,* June 7, 2003, p. A9.

52. Nina Bernstein, "A Mother Deported, and a Child Left Behind," *New York Times,* Nov. 24, 2004, p. A1.

53. Greg St. Martin, "MBTA Police Will Release Advisory to Officers That Immigration Law 'Is Generally Best Left to' Federal Agencies," *Boston Metro,* Dec. 7, 2005. Detective Andrea Purcell failed to respond to several phone messages requesting comment.

54. Immigration and Customs Enforcement, "Fact Sheet: Delegation of Immigration Authority Section 287(g) Immigration and Nationality Act," http://www.ice.gov/news/library/factsheets/287g.htm#signed-moa. Authorization under the Illegal Immigration Reform and Immigrant Responsibility Act (IIRAIRA) of 1996, § 287(g). See also ACLU's criticism at http://www.aclu.org/immigrants-rights/ice-should-end-not-expand-agreements-local-and-state-law-enforcement-says-aclu. Dept. of Homeland Security, "Secure Communities," fact sheet, Aug. 13, 2009, http://www.ice.gov/pi/news/factsheets/secure_communities.htm; Dept. of Homeland Security, "ICE Secure Communities Criminal Alien Initiative Expanded to Sacramento, Solano Counties," Jan. 12, 2010; "Secure Communities: IDENT/IAFIS Interoperability, Monthly Statistics Through July 31, 2011," http://www.ice.gov/doclib/foia/sc-stats/nationwide_interoperability_stats-fy2011-to-date.pdf.

55. Mary Beth Sheridan, "Va. Police Back Off Immigration Enforcement," *Washington Post,* June 6, 2005, p. B1.

56. Migration Policy Institute, "Blurring the Lines: A Profile of State and Local Police Enforcement of Immigration Law Using the National Crime Information Center Database, 2002–2004," Dec. 2005.

57. Senate Bill 1070, amending Arizona Revised Statutes, Title 11, chap. 7, adding art. 8 (B): "For any lawful contact made by a law enforcement official or agency of this state or a county, city, town or other political subdivision of this state where reasonable suspicion exists that the person is an alien who is unlawfully present in the United States, a reasonable attempt shall be made, when practicable, to determine the immigration status of the person. The person's immigration status shall be verified with the federal government pursuant to 8 United States Code Section 1373(c)." Undocumented immigrants are to be turned over to federal authorities, but they are also "guilty of trespassing" if "present on any public or private land in this state," and can be charged with a misdemeanor for applying for or performing work, or entering a vehicle that impedes traffic while picking up day laborers. The law also permits a warrantless arrest based on probable cause to believe that a person has committed a crime making him deportable. In addition, the statute enables citizens to sue local authorities that are not enforcing federal immigration laws.

58. *Terry v. Ohio,* 392 U.S. 1 (1968).

59. Center for Constitutional Rights, "Advocates Issue Statement Condemning Obama Administration's Expansion of DHS' Failed 287(g) Program," http://ccrjustice.org/newsroom/press-releases/advocates-issue-statement-condemning-obama-administration%E2%80%99s-expansion-dhs%E2%80%99-f.

60. Sheridan, "Va. Police Back Off Immigration Enforcement."

61. *United States v. Brignoni-Ponce,* 422 U.S. 873 (1975).
62. *Abdul Ameer Yousef Habeeb v. Thomas Castloo et al.,* No. CVO5-24-GF-CSO, First Amended Complaint (D. Mon. 2006). Government agents enjoy "qualified immunity" from lawsuits if they are faithfully executing their duties according to the Constitution, established law, and regulation, but under *Bivens v. Six Unknown Named Agents of Federal Bureau of Narcotics,* 403 U.S. 388 (1971), federal officials can be held liable for punitive damages if they violate the law or the Constitution and deprive persons of their civil liberties. In that case, federal agents entered a suspect's apartment without a warrant, searched and then arrested him, thereby violating the Fourth Amendment, the Court held. *Bivens* has since been the main basis of such lawsuits against federal officials, and it was so in Habeeb's suit.
63. Jeffrey G. Sullivan, U.S. Attorney, Western District of Washington, to Abdulameer Habeeb, June 13, 2007.

CHAPTER SIX: SILENCE AND ITS OPPOSITE

1. Jerry Markon, "Terrorism Case Puts Words of Muslim Leader on Trial in Va.," *Washington Post,* April 4, 2005, p. B01.
2. Milton Viorst, "The Education of Ali al-Timimi," *Atlantic,* June 2006. Viorst recounts that at his son's 1977 bar mitzvah, with Ali present among the friends, the rabbi delivered an "anti-Arab diatribe" in his sermon, alleging that Arabs would strive to kill Jewish boys. Al-Timimi told an interviewer years later: "I was offended that I would be associated with seeking to murder my Jewish classmate and one of my closest friends."
3. Jeffrey Rosen, "Say What You Will," review of *Freedom for the Thought That We Hate,* by Anthony Lewis, *New York Times Book Review,* Jan. 13, 2008, p. 10.
4. Espionage Act of June 15, 1917, 40 Stat. 217.
5. *Schenck v. United States,* 249 U.S. 47 (1919).
6. *Pierce v. United States,* 252 U.S. 239 (1920). See also *Debs v. United States,* 249 U.S. 211 (1919); and *Frohwerk v. United States,* 249 U.S. 204 (1919).
7. *Abrams v. United States,* 250 U.S. 616 (1919). Oliver Wendell Holmes was joined in dissent by Louis Brandeis.
8. *Whitney v. California,* 274 U.S. 357 (1927).
9. *Gitlow v. People of the State of New York,* 268 U.S. 652 (1925). The appeal was brought on the basis of the Fourteenth Amendment. The majority opinion by Edward Sanford said, "For present purposes we may and do assume that freedom of speech and of the press—which are protected by the First Amendment from abridgment by Congress—are among the fundamental personal rights and 'liberties' protected by the due process clause of the Fourteenth Amendment from impairment by the States." Holmes and Brandeis endorsed the extension of the First Amendment and thought the conviction should be overturned.
10. *Chaplinsky v. New Hampshire,* 315 U.S. 568 (1942).
11. In *R.A.V. v. City of St. Paul,* 505 U.S. 377 (1992), a unanimous Court struck down a city ordinance prohibiting cross burning or other symbols likely to spark "anger, alarm, or resentment in others on the basis of race, color, creed, religion,

or gender." Justice Antonin Scalia wrote that in proscribing fighting words, "the government may not regulate use based on hostility—or favoritism—towards the underlying message expressed."

12. *Dennis v. United States*, 341 U.S. 494 (1951), 6–2 upholding convictions under the Smith Act, with Hugo Black and William O. Douglas dissenting.

13. The Smith Act, formally entitled the Alien Registration Act, prohibits advocating the overthrow of the government "by force or violence." It was stretched to cover simple membership in communist or fascist organizations and also required all noncitizens to register with the government. 54 Stat. 670, 671, title I, §§ 2–3 (June 28, 1940), current version at 18 U.S.C. § 2385.

14. Geoffrey R. Stone, *Perilous Times: Free Speech in Wartime* (New York: Norton, 2004), pp. 396–97.

15. Muhammed Aatique, sentenced Dec. 12, 2003, to ten years, two months, released March 31, 2006, and Khwaja Mahmood Hasan, sentenced Nov. 7, 2003, to eleven years, three months, released March 24, 2006. Paul J. McNulty, U.S. Attorney, E.D. of Va., Dept. of Justice, News Release, April 26, 2005; Inmate Locator, U.S. Bureau of Prisons, http://www.bop.gov/iloc2/LocateInmate.jsp.

16. Jerry Markon, "Views of Va. Muslim Leader Differ as Terror Trial Opens," *Washington Post,* April 5, 2005, p. B04.

17. Ibid., quoting opening trial statement by Assistant U.S. Attorney Gordon Kromberg.

18. Superseding Indictment, *United States v. Timimi*, No. 1:04CR385 (E.D. Va., Alexandria Div.), Feb. 2005.

19. Markon, "Views of Va. Muslim Leader Differ as Terror Trial Opens."

20. *Dennis,* 341 U.S. 494. In subsequent cases, the Court also upheld contempt citations by the trial judge against all five defense attorneys, who served thirty days to six months in prison and were barred from practicing law. Stone, *Perilous Times,* p. 398n.

21. Stone, *Perilous Times,* p. 411. The Supreme Court also ruled that cities could require employees to swear that they had not belonged to organizations advocating the violent overthrow of the government. *Garner v. Board of Public Works,* 341 U.S. 716 (1951); *Adler v. Board of Education,* 342 U.S. 485 (1952). In addition, the Court ruled that long-term immigrants in the country for more than thirty years could be deported for having once joined the Communist Party. *Harisiades v. Shaughnessy,* 342 U.S. 580 (1952).

22. *Yates v. United States,* 354 U.S. 298 (1957). The vote was 6–1, with Thomas Clark dissenting.

23. Stone, *Perilous Times,* p. 416.

24. *Brandenburg v. Ohio,* 395 U.S. 444 (1969).

25. As quoted in Viorst, "Education of Ali al-Timimi."

26. It is also encoded in federal law: "The flag should never be displayed with the union down, except as a signal of dire distress in instances of extreme danger to life or property." 4 U.S.C. § 8(a).

27. *Stromberg v. California,* 283 U.S. 359 (1931). Section 403a of the California Penal Code read: "Any person who displays a red flag, banner or badge or any flag, badge, banner, or device of any color or form whatever in any public place or in any meeting place or public assembly, or from or on any house, building or window as a sign, symbol or emblem of opposition to organized government or

as an invitation or stimulus to anarchistic action or as an aid to propaganda that is of a seditious character is guilty of a felony." Of the three clauses, only the first was ruled unconstitutional; the second two involving anarchistic action and seditious propaganda were upheld.

28. *Street v. New York,* 394 U.S. 576 (1969). After the civil rights activist James Meredith was shot in 1966, Sidney Street took his neatly folded flag, which he had hung on holidays, to a street corner near his Brooklyn apartment, lit it with a match, dropped it on the sidewalk while it burned, and told about thirty people there, "We don't need no damn flag," and, "If they let that happen to Meredith, we don't need an American flag." Since Street was punished for his words as well as the burning, the two being entangled, the Court ruled on the words only, finding them not severe enough to incite, and therefore protected speech. It did not rule on the burning. John Marshall Harlan wrote for the majority; Earl Warren, Byron R. White, Abe Fortas, and Black dissented.

29. *Spence v. Washington,* 418 U.S. 405 (1974). A Seattle college student was convicted under a state statute for hanging an inverted flag, half covered with a peace sign made from removable black tape, from his apartment window to protest the 1970 invasion of Cambodia and the shooting of student demonstrators at Kent State. He was charged under Wash. Rev. Code 9.86.020: "No person shall, in any manner, for exhibition or display: (1) Place or cause to be placed any word, figure, mark, picture, design, drawing or advertisement of any nature upon any flag, standard, color, ensign or shield of the United States or of this state." The peace sign, he said at his trial, represented his belief that the United States stood for peace, not for killing. The Supreme Court vacated his conviction.

30. *Smith v. Goguen,* 415 U.S. 566 (1974). Goguen was sentenced to six months in jail for wearing a four-by-six-inch flag sewn to the seat of his jeans. The Court, 6–3, declared void for vagueness under the due process clause of the Fourteenth Amendment a Massachusetts statute punishing anyone who "treats contemptuously the flag of the United States." Lewis Powell wrote the opinion, with Harry A. Blackmun, William Rehnquist, and Warren Burger in dissent.

31. Before the 2004 Republican National Convention in New York City, police officers were advised in a legal handbook that while "New York State General Business Law § 136, which prohibits burning, defacing, defiling, or trampling on the American flag, may not be enforced," the Administrative Code prohibits an open fire in the city. "A summons for this offense, made returnable to Criminal Court, will be issued only when the fire created by the burning flag poses an imminent danger to persons or property." "New York City Police Department: Legal Guidelines for the Republican National Convention," March 10, 2004, p. 13.

32. *Texas v. Johnson,* 491 U.S. 397 (1989), finding Texas Penal Code Ann. 42.09 (1989) unconstitutional. This was followed by a 5–4 decision in *United States v. Eichman,* 496 U.S. 310 (1990), striking down the 1989 federal Flag Protection Act, which provided up to a year in prison for anyone who "knowingly mutilates, defaces, physically defiles, burns, maintains on the floor or ground, or tramples upon" a flag. The government's brief arguing the law's constitutionality was co-written by John G. Roberts Jr., the future chief justice. Text of the brief at http://www.usdoj.gov/osg/briefs/1989/sg890147.txt.

33. Norman Thomas, speech to National Student Association, New York, 1969, recounted in letter from his son, Evan W. Thomas II, *New York Times,* July 19, 1989.
34. ACLU press release, April 15, 2003, http://www.aclu.org/freespeech/flag/11177prs20030415.html; Matthew Rothschild, "An Upside Down Flag and a Dead Coyote," *Progressive,* June 4, 2003, http://www.progressive.org/mag_mc coyote2.
35. *United States v. O'Brien,* 391 U.S. 367 (1968). The vote was 7–1, with Thurgood Marshall not participating and Douglas dissenting.
36. 50 U.S.C. § 462(b).
37. *O'Brien,* Appendix.
38. *Virginia v. Black,* No. 01-1107 (2003). The 6–3 opinion (with dissenters David Souter, Anthony Kennedy, and Ruth Bader Ginsburg, who held the law entirely unconstitutional) refined *R.A.V.,* 505 U.S. 377, in which the same justices had unanimously struck down a city ordinance prohibiting the display of a burning cross or Nazi swastika that arouses "anger, alarm, or resentment in others on the basis of race, color, creed, religion, or gender." That law fell because it was aimed at disfavored topics in an attempt to regulate the political or social content of speech. By contrast, the Virginia statute made no mention of race and the like, thereby making its focus the intimidation, a majority found. The Virginia Supreme Court had ruled it unconstitutional because of its discrimination by content, in that it made only cross burning illegal.
39. "Indiana Man Sentenced for Role in Cross Burning," Justice Dept. release, PR Newswire, Jan. 4, 2008; "Michigan Man Sentenced to 36 Months for Cross-Burning," Justice Dept. release, PR Newswire, Dec. 14, 2007; "Defendant Convicted in 2000 of Cross Burning Returns to Prison," States News Service, July 12, 2006.
40. Daniel J. Sharfstein, *The Invisible Line: Three American Families and the Secret Journey from Black to White* (New York: Penguin, 2011), p. 110.
41. John Leo, "Don't Tread on Free-Speakers," *U.S. News & World Report,* Nov. 5, 2001.
42. The authorities capitulated by settling out of court. The students, Juan Díaz and John Bohman, who were represented by the Iowa chapter of the ACLU, agreed to take no money damages, just attorney's fees, and decided not to pursue the case to get a constitutional ruling, according to their lawyer, Randall C. Wilson. Bohman later became Grinnell's student government president.
43. Andrew and Melanie Black, Livingston, Mont., "Inverted Flag Shows National Distress," blog, *Billings Gazette,* Jan. 30, 2010, http://billingsgazette.com/news/opinion/mailbag/article_3e14346e-0d54-11df-a0a5-001cc4c03286.html.
44. Mike McWilliams, "Flag-Defiling Charge Ends in Fight, Arrests," *Asheville Citizen-Times,* July 26, 2007; ACLU of North Carolina, Legal Docket: Recently Settled and Ongoing Cases, http://www.acluofnorthcarolina.org/legal/docket.html#speech.
45. Iowa Code §§ 723.4(6) prohibiting "disorderly display of a flag" and 718A.1 on "desecration of flag or insignia." The latter read: "Any person who in any manner, for exhibition or display, shall place or cause to be placed, any word, figure, mark, picture, design, drawing, or any advertisement of any nature, upon any flag, standard, color, ensign, shield, or other insignia of the United States, or

upon any flag, ensign, great seal, or other insignia of this state, or shall expose or cause to be exposed to public view, any such flag, standard, color, ensign, shield, or other insignia of the United States, or any such flag, ensign, great seal, or other insignia of this state, upon which shall have been printed, painted, or otherwise placed, or to which shall be attached, appended, affixed, or annexed, any word, figure, mark, picture, design, or drawing, or any advertisement of any nature, or who shall expose to public view, manufacture, sell, expose for sale, give away, or have in possession for sale, or to give away, or for use for any purpose any article or substance, being an article of merchandise or a receptacle of merchandise or article or thing for carrying or transporting merchandise, upon which shall have been printed, painted, attached or otherwise placed, a representation of any such flag, standard, color, ensign, shield, or other insignia of the United States, or any such flag, ensign, great seal, or other insignia of this state, to advertise, call attention to, decorate, mark, or distinguish the article or substance on which so placed, or who shall publicly mutilate, deface, defile or defy, trample upon, cast contempt upon, satirize, deride or burlesque, either by words or act, such flag, standard, color, ensign, shield, or other insignia of the United States, or flag, ensign, great seal, or other insignia of this state, or who shall, for any purpose, place such flag, standard, color, ensign, shield, or other insignia of the United States, or flag, ensign, great seal, or other insignia of this state, upon the ground or where the same may be trod upon, shall be deemed guilty of a simple misdemeanor."

46. Summary judgment, Judge Robert Pratt, *Roe v. Milligan,* 479 F. Supp. 2d 995 (S.D. Iowa 2007). The court did not rule on the First Amendment issue. In a settlement, Roe received $12,500 in damages and $5,000 in attorney's fees, Klyn $7,000 and $3,000. Klyn's protest had also been motivated by what he considered a wrongful decision against him as a creditor in a bankruptcy case.

47. Jason Clayworth, "House Approves Revision to Flag Laws," *Des Moines Register,* April 4, 2007, p. 5B.

48. The judge was Wayne Sturtevant in Hamilton County. "Flag-Burning Suspect Ordered Not to Touch, Handle, or Possess Any U.S. Flag," AP, Oct. 9, 2001; http://www.firstamendmentcenter.org//news.aspx?id=4561&SearchString =eichman.

49. *New York Times,* March 3, 1917. For state laws, see First Amendment Center Web site at http://www.firstamendmentcenter.org/speech/flagburning/topic .aspx?topic=flag_statelaws.

50. Earlier attempts at a constitutional amendment included a close call in 1995, when it lost in the Senate by three votes, and in 1997, when it passed in the House and failed to come to a vote in the Senate. Legislatures in forty-nine states were prepared to ratify. David M. O'Brien, *Constitutional Law and Politics,* vol. 2, *Civil Rights and Liberties,* 5th ed. (New York: Norton, 2003), p. 90.

51. *Minersville School District v. Gobitis,* 310 U.S. 586 (1940), opinion by Felix Frankfurter.

52. *West Virginia State Board of Education v. Barnette,* 319 U.S. 624 (1943). Robert Jackson noted that the Court had never held that a symbol could be used for one message but not another. See also *Schacht v. United States,* 398 U.S. 58 (1970), overturning federal law prohibiting an actor from wearing a military uniform to "discredit" the armed forces. The Court muddied the issue in 2009 by

refusing to hear an appeal from a circuit court opinion upholding Florida's law requiring students to recite the pledge unless parents exempted them in writing. This left the suggestion that the First Amendment right in school belongs not to the children but to their parents.

53. *Cohen v. California*, 403 U.S. 15 (1971). Harlan wrote for the majority. Blackmun, in dissent with Burger, Black, and White, wrote: "Cohen's absurd and immature antic, in my view, was mainly conduct and little speech."

54. Garfield Harris, Answer to Complaint and Jury Demand, *Raed Jarrar v. Harris et al.*, No. CV-07-3299 (E.D.N.Y. 2007).

55. A reference to the hundreds picked up in the weeks after 9/11, mostly on minor immigration violations, jailed, and then deported to their home countries, where some were tortured. See Chapter 5.

56. "White Rose," *Holocaust Encyclopedia*, http://www.ushmm.org/wlc/article.php?lang=en&ModuleId=10007188.

57. Raed Jarrar, Complaint and Jury Demand, *Raed Jarrar v. Harris et al.*, No. CV-07-3299 (E.D.N.Y. 2007).

58. In his court filing, the agent denied this account without offering a competing narrative. He conceded that Jarrar had asked if there were any laws or regulations banning clothing with Arabic writing from airports, but Harris did not tell the court his answer. Jarrar remembered that he gave no reply. Harris, Answer to Complaint.

59. JetBlue Airways Corporation, Answer, *Raed Jarrar v. Harris et al.*, No. CV-07-3299 (E.D.N.Y 2007). A JetBlue spokeswoman, Alison Croyle, repeated the denial but presented no other version of what had happened. Spencer S. Hsu and Sholnn Freeman, "JetBlue, TSA Workers Settle in T-Shirt Case," *Washington Post,* Jan. 6, 2009, p. A2. She did not return a telephoned inquiry seeking the airline's account.

60. The DOT finding stated: "The fact that other passengers or crew have a feeling of discomfort or uneasiness that can be attributed to an individual's skin color, race, ethnicity or clothing that may be indicative of an individual's race, ethnicity or religion (e.g., t-shirt with Arabic writing, turban) is not a justifiable reason to deny boarding to that individual or to require that individual to accept restrictions such as sitting in the rear of the aircraft in order to be allowed to fly." ACLU, "Department of Transportation Completes Investigation of Jet-Blue," March 19, 2008.

61. Jarrar, Complaint, citing 42 U.S.C. § 1981 and 42 U.S.C. § 2000d. In its answer, JetBlue claimed immunity under the Aviation and Transportation Security Act of 2001, Airport Security Improvement Act of 2000, Air Transportation Security Act of 1974, Federal Aviation Act, and Airline Deregulation Act.

62. Niki had immigrated to the United States as a child in the 1980s, had become a citizen in the 1990s, and had chosen to study Arabic in Jordan on her way to a Ph.D. There she met Jarrar, who had fled to Jordan from Iraq during the maelstrom following the 2003 American invasion. They married and decided to escape from Jordan's difficult economy. As her husband, he sailed through the U.S. immigration process and arrived in 2005.

63. ACLU, "ACLU Sues over Unconstitutional Airport Detention and Interrogation of College Student Carrying Arabic Flashcards," Feb. 10, 2010, with links to

court documents at http://www.aclu.org/national-security/aclu-sues-over-uncon
stitutional-airport-detention-and-interrogation-college-studen.

64. ACLU, *Freedom Under Fire: Dissent in Post-9/11 America,* May 2003, pp. 5–6.

65. Kris Axtman, "Political Dissent Can Bring Federal Agents to Door," *Christian Science Monitor,* Jan. 8, 2002; ACLU, "Caught in the Backlash: Stories from Northern California," p. 14.

66. Axtman, "Political Dissent Can Bring Federal Agents to Door."

67. Charlie Brennan, "Arrest over Cheney Barb Triggers Lawsuit," *Rocky Mountain News,* Oct. 3, 2006; *Howards v. Reichle,* complaint, Civil Action No. 06-CV-01964-WYD-CBS (D. Colo. 2006).

68. Mike Stallings to Marcia Perez, Oct. 4, 2001. Stallings, reached by phone and contacted by e-mail, declined to answer questions.

69. Bill Carter and Felicity Barringer, "In Patriotic Time, Dissent Is Muted," *New York Times,* Sept. 28, 2001, p. A1; Barry Didcock, "The Man Who Fell to Earth— Madman or Genius," *Sunday Herald* (Glasgow), March 27, 2005.

70. Howard O. Stier, "Bush Portrait Draws Criticism for Its Details, Not Its Subject," *New York Times,* Dec. 13, 2004, p. A25.

71. ACLU, *Freedom Under Fire,* p. 5.

72. Letter and news release from ACLU, July 16, 2003. The case overturning the sodomy law was *Lawrence v. Texas,* 539 U.S. 558 (2003).

73. ACLU, *Freedom Under Fire,* p. 7

74. In *PruneYard Shopping Center v. Robins,* 447 U.S. 74 (1980), the Court ruled unanimously that despite its earlier opinions granting shopping centers authority to curb picketing and pamphleteering, California could interpret its state constitution to define a mall as a public forum where freedom of expression was guaranteed. See also Samuel H. Weissbard and Camellia K. Schuk, "States Speak Out on Free Speech in Malls," *Commercial Investment Real Estate,* Nov.–Dec. 1999.

75. Slightly revised, the policy as of Feb. 12, 2010, stated: "The wearing of apparel which tends to provoke a disturbance, negatively impact the interest of merchants, or engage shoppers or other legal invitees in conflict is prohibited." No official of Crossgates or the mall would elaborate on the current policy toward political messages. The guard who signed the trespassing complaint, Robert Williams, said he was fired, even though he claimed to be following the orders of the assistant director of security. Bruce Scruton, "Guard Says He Lost Job in T-Shirt Flap," *Albany* (N.Y.) *Times-Union,* March 8, 2003.

76. Dixie Chicks publicity background paper at http://www.frontpagepublicity .com/dxc/bio.html.

CHAPTER SEVEN: A REDRESS OF GRIEVANCES

1. Order Denying Defendant's Motion to Lift or Modify Stay-Away Order, Judge John Ramsey Johnson, Superior Court of D.C., 2007 CMD 10758, Dec. 14, 2007. Johnson was a former prosecutor and Clinton appointee.

2. The stay-away order addresses a modern expansion of the conditions under which a defendant can be jailed pending trial. Traditionally, the sole reason was to guarantee her appearance in court; someone deemed a flight risk would be

either held or released on high enough bail that the penalty for fleeing would outweigh the possible consequences of appearing. Gradually, many state legislatures and Congress added a second reason for denying release: the likelihood that the crime would be repeated. The stay-away order is designed to reduce that possibility.

3. "He's Back with His Impeachment Message," *News & Observer*, Oct. 20, 2007.

4. D.C. Code § 22-405(b): "Whoever without justifiable and excusable cause, assaults, resists, opposes, impedes, intimidates, or interferes with a law enforcement officer on account of, or while that law enforcement officer is engaged in the performance of his or her official duties shall be guilty of a misdemeanor and, upon conviction, shall be imprisoned not more than 180 days or fined not more than $1,000, or both." Defendant has a right to a jury trial only where the maximum sentence is over 180 days, so a judge alone can hear such a case.

5. Karen Matthews, "Peace Activists Denied Entry to Canada Will Try Again Thursday," AP, Oct. 24, 2007. They were denied again.

6. Murphy was never able to mount a challenge, because on the eve of her trial she was arrested while driving on Second Street, the boundary of her stay-away zone, and charged with contempt of court for violating the exclusion order. Facing jail time, she agreed to the prosecutor's offer to lift the order in exchange for a guilty plea to unlawful conduct and a $100 fine.

7. *Jeannette Rankin Brigade v. Chief of Capitol Police*, 409 U.S. 972 (1972), summarily affirmed, and *United States v. Grace*, 461 U.S. 171 (1983), respectively.

8. *Lederman v. United States*, Nos. 01-5157 and 01-5158 (D.C. Cir. 2002).

9. *Hague v. Committee for Industrial Organization*, 307 U.S. 496 (1939), overruling Jersey City's denial of a public hall for a labor rally. See David M. O'Brien, *Constitutional Law and Politics*: Vol. 2, Civil Rights and Liberties, Fifth Ed. (New York: Norton, 2003), pp. 633–40.

10. *Edwards v. South Carolina*, 372 U.S. 229 (1963).

11. *Cox v. Louisiana*, 379 U.S. 536 (1965).

12. *Police Department of City of Chicago v. Mosley*, 408 U.S. 92 (1972).

13. *Boos v. Barry*, 485 U.S. 312 (1988), which overturned a law barring demonstrations within five hundred feet of an embassy.

14. *Lehman v. City of Shaker Heights*, 418 U.S. 298 (1974), regarding placards in buses.

15. *Adderley v. Florida*, 385 U.S. 39 (1966).

16. *Flower v. United States*, 407 U.S. 197 (1972), and *Greer v. Spock*, 424 U.S. 828 (1976).

17. *United States v. Kokinda*, 497 U.S. 720 (1990).

18. *International Society for Krishna Consciousness v. Lee*, 505 U.S. 672 (1992), upholding a ban on solicitation at New York Port Authority airports. An earlier opinion, in *Board of Airport Commissioners of Los Angeles v. Jews for Jesus Inc.*, 482 U.S. 569 (1987), found a complete ban on First Amendment activities at Los Angeles International Airport unconstitutional but did not reach the question of whether terminals were public forums.

19. "Man's Anti-Bush Bumper Stickers Prompt Visit by Secret Service," AP, Sept. 1, 2001, http://www.firstamendmentcenter.org/news.aspx?id=4666.

20. *Cox v. New Hampshire,* 312 U.S. 569 (1941). In *Ward v. Rock Against Racism,* 491 U.S. 781 (1989), the justices also ruled in favor of New York City's requirement that performers in Central Park use a city sound system and engineer.

21. *Walker v. City of Birmingham,* 388 U.S. 307 (1967). Opinion by Potter Stewart, with Earl Warren, William J. Brennan Jr., and Abe Fortas in dissent.

22. Monica Davey, "Subpoenas on Antiwar Protest Are Dropped," *New York Times,* Feb. 11, 2004. Statement by American Association of University Professors, Feb. 11, 2004, http://www.aaup.org/AAUP/comm/rep/DrakeSubs.htm.

23. Stone, *Perilous Times,* p. 556. The Supreme Court ruled nonjudiciable the contention that speech was chilled by military surveillance of lawful domestic activity. *Laird v. Tatum,* 408 U.S. 1 (1972).

24. Nick Madigan, "Documents Show State Police Monitored Peace and Anti–Death Penalty Groups," *Baltimore Sun,* July 18, 2008. Documents were released by the state's attorney general in response to a request by the ACLU of Maryland under the Maryland Public Information Act. See http://www.aclu-md.org/Index%20content/NoSpying/NoSpying.html.

25. Office of the Inspector General, Justice Dept., "A Review of the FBI's Investigations of Certain Domestic Advocacy Groups," Sept. 2010.

26. "Pennsylvania Intelligence Bulletin No. 131, Aug. 30, 2010," *ProPublica,* http://www.propublica.org/documents/item/pennsylvania-intelligence-bulletin-no.-131-aug.-30-2010. The complaint about false leads was made by Major George Bivens, head of the Bureau of Criminal Investigations, about the Institute of Terrorism Research and Response. Brad Bumsted, "State Police: Terror Bulletins Sent Them on Wild Good Chases," *Pittsburgh Tribune-Review,* Sept. 27, 2010, http://www.pittsburghlive.com/x/pittsburghtrib/news/breaking/s_701509.html.

27. Documents obtained through a lawsuit by the ACLU of Colorado, http://aclu-co.org/spyfiles/samplefiles.htm.

28. Larry Valencia, Statement, Denver Police Dept., May 12, 2000, http://aclu-co.org/spyfiles/Documents/Valencia_undercover.pdf.

29. Stone, *Perilous Times,* p. 493. See also displays and reports in the National Civil Rights Museum, Memphis.

30. "Information on 'Rukus' and Catholic Workers Group," FBI Memo 266D-LA-226745, May 23, 2001. "Catholic Workers Group" may refer to the Los Angeles Catholic Worker, an organization that often demonstrates at the base.

31. In 2007, two years after the revelations, the Pentagon announced plans to shut down the database of TALON (Threat and Local Observation Notices). "ACLU Applauds Decision to Shut Down Pentagon Database of Secret Information on Peaceful Groups," Aug. 21, 2007.

32. ACLU, "No Real Threat: The Pentagon's Secret Database on Peaceful Protest," Jan. 17, 2007, http://www.aclu.org/safefree/spyfiles/27988pub20070117.html. The full report, with original documents, is at http://www.aclu.org/pdfs/safefree/spyfiles_norealthreat_20070117.pdf.

33. The cleric was Anwar al-Awlaki, described by the terrorism specialist Bruce Hoffman at Georgetown University as "a vessel for the message of al-Qaeda whose goal is radicalizing others." Scott Shane and David Johnston, "Accused Gunman's Exchanges with Cleric Raised Questions, Not Alarms," *New York Times,* Nov. 12, 2009, p. A22.

34. Marianne Kyriakos, "Roosevelt Bridge Blocked in Protest of D.C. Budget," *Washington Post*, Sept. 21, 1995.

35. Mary Cheh, "Legislative Oversight of Police: Lessons Learned from an Investigation of Police Handling of Demonstrations in Washington, D.C.," *Journal of Legislation* 32 (2005), p. 10.

36. *Killmon et al. v. City of Miami et al.*, described by the Center for Constitutional Rights at http://ccrjustice.org/ourcases/current-cases/killmon%2C -et-al.-v.-city-miami%2C-et-al. A filmmaker, Carl Kesser, was shot in the head with a beanbag rifle, and the right side of his face was left permanently paralyzed by a ball that lodged in his temple. He won a settlement of $180,000 from the city. City of Miami Civilian Investigative Panel, *Report on the Free Trade Area of the Americas Summit*, July 20, 2006, http://www.miamigov.com/ cip/Downloads/FTAAReport.pdf. The panel found that the Miami police "did not adequately protect the First Amendment rights of demonstrators." It also found that "more time and attention were devoted to training personnel to protect property rather than persons, and even less training time was spent addressing the constitutional protections guaranteed to all." The police refused to give the panel its operational plan, and a court refused to order it disclosed.

37. *In Re the City of New York*, on a petition in *Hacer Dinler et al. v. The City of New York*, No. 10-0237-op (2nd Cir. 2010). The district court, which ordered the field reports' release during the discovery phase of a civil suit, was reversed on a writ of mandamus issued by a unanimous three-judge panel of the Second Circuit. In an opinion written by Judge José Cabranes, the panel ruled that the law enforcement privilege, akin to executive privilege, prevailed in this case. Otherwise, "we would risk discouraging law enforcement agencies from conducting undercover investigations (or from keeping records of those investigations)," and "other police officers may be less willing to become undercover agents if they fear that their identities may be disclosed in court proceedings." Ongoing "law enforcement techniques and procedures" would be compromised, the judges decided. Those arrested wanted to prove that the city's "mass arrest policy" was unjustified by the intelligence gathered through undercover work. The appeals court found, after reviewing the field documents, that they did not undermine the end user reports, which had already been provided to the parties, but reinforced the city's contention that "a substantial threat of disruption and violence" existed. The field reports would therefore not be of "compelling need" to those suing the city.

38. *Handschu v. Special Services Division*, S.D.N.Y. 71 Civ. 2203 (CSH). The consent decree initially required approval of surveillance by a three-member panel, the Handschu Authority, made up of the first deputy police commissioner, the deputy commissioner for legal matters, and a civilian appointed by the mayor. The decree was eviscerated in 2007 when a judge required that any plaintiffs show a pattern of abuse beyond a specific instance. See ACLU fact sheet at http://www.nyclu.org/node/1084 and Tom Perotta, "New York Police Request Broader Surveillance Rights," *New York Law Journal*, Sept. 27, 2002.

39. NYPD intelligence documents, memos, and manuals are at http://www.nyclu .org/rncdocs. See N.Y. City Police Dept., "Police Student's Guide: Maintaining

Public Order," July 2004, and "Legal Guidelines for the Republican National Convention," March 10, 2004.

40. "RNC Intelligence Update," Oct. 9, 2003, p. 38, http://www.nyclu.org/files/Pre -RNC%20Surveillance%20Documents%20Section%201.pdf. See also http:// www.criticalresistance.org/.

41. Report CJB No. 156-2004-0016 memo of May 4, 2004, from Commanding Officer, Criminal Justice Bureau, to RNC Coordinator.

42. "Cops Put Brakes on Bike Protest," *Wired*, Aug. 31, 2004; Geeta Dayal, "Bikes Against Bush Gets a Flat," *Village Voice*, Aug. 24, 2004; See also Legal Guidelines, pp. 13–14, 16, and N.Y.C. Admin. Code 10-117, N.Y.C. Traffic Rules 4-07(c)(3)(i).

43. *Police Student's Guide: Maintaining Public Order*, July 2004, http://www.nyclu .org/rncdocs.

44. White House, "Presidential Advance Manual," Oct. 2002. Most of the 103 pages were blanked out, or "redacted."

45. *Rank et al. v. Jenkins*, No. 07-CV-01157, D.C. District, Complaint, pp. 3–5.

46. "ACLU Calls Government Settlement in Anti-Bush T-Shirt Case a Victory for Free Speech," Aug. 16, 2007, http://www.aclu.org/freespeech/protest/ 31331prs20070816.html.

47. Their suit was dismissed by federal district court judge Wiley Y. Daniel, a Clinton appointee, who ruled that their constitutional rights were not violated. ACLU, "Federal Court Upholds Exclusion of Denver Residents from Bush Speech Based on Political Expression," Nov. 7, 2008, http://www.aclu .org/freespeech/protest/37727prs20081107.html. A Tenth Circuit panel upheld the dismissal, 2–1. "2 Thrown Out of Bush Event Can't Revive Lawsuit," AP, Jan. 29, 2010, http://www.firstamendmentcenter.org/news.aspx?id=22557. The Supreme Court refused to review the case.

48. *Rank*, Complaint, pp. 5–9. The Wisconsin incident involved Leslie Weise and Alex Young, who joined the Ranks in their lawsuit as complainants.

49. ACLU, "Free Speech Under Fire: The ACLU Challenge to 'Protest Zones,'" Sept. 23, 2003.

50. *Police Student's Guide*.

51. *Acorn et al. v. City of Philadelphia et al.*, No. 03-CV-4312 (E.D. Pa. 2003).

52. A lawsuit on the issue by protest groups failed in federal court. "District Court Denies Motion for Temporary Injunction in Demonstration Zone Lawsuit," ACLU of Minnesota release, Aug. 26, 2008.

53. See ACLU of Colorado, http://www.aclu-co.org/news/2008news.htm, and ACLU of Minnesota, http://www.aclu-mn.org/issues/freedomofspeechpress .htm. Also, 2009 Jefferson Muzzles to both the Republican and the Democratic Parties, Thomas Jefferson Center for the Protection of Free Expression, http:// www.tjcenter.org/muzzles/muzzle-archive-2009/#item01.

54. Since 9/11, the Department of Homeland Security has designated each convention as a "National Special Security Event." Secret Service authority is contained in 18 U.S.C. § 1752(d)(2).

55. Rachel Weiner, "Protester with Gun Outside Obama Town Hall," *Huffington Post*, Aug. 11, 2009.

56. "Gun-Toting Protesters, Including One with Assault Weapon, Mill Outside Obama Speech in Arizona," AP, Aug. 18, 2009.

57. Sheryl Gay Stolberg, e-mail to author, Feb. 1, 2010.
58. ACLU, "America Unrestored: An Assessment of the Obama Administration's Fulfillment of ACLU Recommended 'Actions for Restoring America,'" Jan. 2010, p. 57.
59. *Madsen v. Women's Health Center*, 512 U.S. 753 (1994); *Schenck v. Pro-Choice Network of Western New York*, 519 U.S. 357 (1997); and *Hill v. Colorado*, 530 U.S. 703 (2000).
60. *Scheidler v. National Organization for Women*, No. 04-1224, and *Operation Rescue v. National Organization for Women*, No. 04-1352. Opinion by Stephen Breyer. The vote was 8–0. Samuel Alito did not participate.
61. 18 U.S.C. § 248.
62. The federal Respect for America's Fallen Heroes Act restricts demonstrations during funerals to no closer than 300 feet from a military cemetery, 150 feet from a road leading to the cemetery, and no nearer in time than one hour before and after a service.
63. The trial judge dismissed the claims of defamation and "publicity given to private life," leaving for the jury: intrusion upon seclusion, infliction of emotional distress, and civil conspiracy. But he also erred in empowering the jury to decide a purely legal question: whether or not the speech enjoyed First Amendment protection, a constitutional question reserved to the courts. Two of the three judges on the appeals panel overturned the award as a First Amendment violation, noting that the words were obviously opinion and not provable or disprovable facts about the Snyders. The third judge concurred, but on the basis of insufficient evidence, without reaching a decision on the free speech issue. *Snyder v. Phelps*, No. 08-1026 (4th Cir.), Sept. 24, 2009. Once the Supreme Court agreed to hear the case, Snyder was supported in amicus curiae briefs by the attorneys general of forty-eight states and by forty-two senators led by the majority and minority leaders. Nevertheless, by an unusual liberal-conservative consensus of 8–1, the Supreme Court ruled that the First Amendment protected the Westboro demonstrators. The majority, with Justice Alito dissenting, found that the case turned "largely on whether that speech is of public or private concern." Snyder had argued that the context—his son's funeral—rendered the protests private, a position the Court rejected. "While these messages may fall short of refined social or political commentary," wrote Chief Justice John Roberts, "the issues they highlight—the political and moral conduct of the United States and its citizens, the fate of our Nation, homosexuality in the military, and scandals involving the Catholic clergy—are matters of public import." The justices noted that the protesters had coordinated with the police, had remained at a distance, and had not been noisy or violent. Thus, the Court left First Amendment case law intact. *Snyder v. Phelps*, No. 09-751 (2011).
64. For example, in a letter the day before a funeral demonstration, Mark A. Goodwin, prosecuting attorney of Carroll County, Missouri, wrote to the Westboro group: "Dobson Street from Main Street to Virginia will be blocked off for your protest. This is public property that is approximately Four Hundred Twenty (420) feet from the front doors of the First Baptist Church where the memorial service is to be held. There is a clear line of sight to the church and you will be able to reach your target audience. The protest must be over by no later than

9:00 a.m., as the funeral begins at 10:00 a.m. Anyone continuing to protest after 9:00 a.m. will be arrested, photographed, fingerprinted, booked and placed on a Twenty-Four (24) hour hold pending charges." Mark A. Goodwin to Margie J. Phelps, May 16, 2006. Other Missouri prosecutors warned the group that violations of the statute would be vigorously prosecuted.

65. W. Stephen Geeding, Prosecuting Attorney, McDonald County, Pineville, Mo., to Whom It May Concern, March 2, 2006.

66. AP, March 26, 2007. The Sixth Circuit upheld the lower court's decision. *Phelps-Roper v. Strickland,* No. 07-3600, Aug. 22, 2008.

67. Missouri Revised Statutes, Miscellaneous Offenses, § 578.03.

68. *United States v. Schwimmer,* 279 U.S. 644 (1929). The Court ruled 6–3 against a Quaker woman from Hungary denied citizenship for her pacifist refusal to state that she would take up arms to defend the United States, despite her eloquent regard for the American system and Constitution. Oliver Wendell Holmes wrote the dissent. The policy remains in effect, denying citizenship to a Jehovah's Witness in North Carolina who asked to take a modified oath. ACLU of North Carolina, http://www.acluofnorthcarolina.org/legal/docket.html.

69. *Ward,* 491 U.S. 781.

70. AP, March 15, 2007.

71. The funeral of Michael Wendling. The clip can be viewed at http://www .youtube.com/watch?v=Wzbo1eE8pFo&NR=1.

72. Laws 1977, 28, § 928, Mutilating a Flag.

73. *R.A.V. v. City of St. Paul,* 505 U.S. 377 (1992).

74. The trial judge ruled that the prosecution could proceed, and Phelps-Roper filed a constitutional challenge in federal court, which she won. "Neb. Prosecutors, Funeral Protester Reach Deal," AP, Aug. 24, 2010; "Federal Court Overturns Neb. Law on Flag Desecration," AP, Sept. 3, 2010.

CHAPTER EIGHT: INSIDE THE SCHOOLHOUSE GATE

1. First Amendment Center, "The State of the First Amendment 2007," national telephone survey of 1,003 respondents conducted Aug. 16–26 by New England Survey Research Associates. Sampling error plus or minus 3.2 percent. Data on teachers and principals from John S. and James L. Knight Foundation, "Future of the First Amendment," Jan. 2005, based on responses to written questionnaires by over 100,000 students, 8,000 teachers, and 500 principals and administrators in 544 high schools. Conducted by the Department of Public Policy at the University of Connecticut, http://firstamendment.jideas.org/findings/findings.php.

2. Among active student participants, 61 percent endorse the right to publish without government approval, as opposed to 51 percent of all students. As the degree of involvement in school media declines, so does approval of the right "to burn or deface the American flag as a political statement," from 39 percent of those most active down to 15 percent of students with no participation whatever. Knight Foundation, "Future of the First Amendment," Key Findings 2, 4, and 8.

3. *West Virginia State Board of Education v. Barnette,* 319 U.S. 624 (1943).

4. Mark Singer, "I Pledge Allegiance," *New Yorker,* Nov. 26, 2001.
5. Quotations from Tinker's Web site, schema-root.org, and interview with the author, April 21, 2008.
6. Notes by Lorena Jeanne Tinker, Dec. 16, 1965, http://schema-root.org/region/americas/north_america/usa/government/branches/judicial_branch/supreme_court/decisions/schools/tinker_v._des_moines/~jft/ljt.notes.1965.html.
7. *Tinker v. Des Moines Independent Community School District,* 393 U.S. 503 (1969). Hugo Black and John Marshall Harlan dissented.
8. Division for Public Education, American Bar Association, Biography of Christopher Eckhardt, http://www.abanet.org/publiced/lawday/tinker/chrisbio.html.
9. *Barber v. Dearborn Public Schools and Judith Coebly,* Supplemental Memorandum in Support of Preliminary Injunction, No. 03-71222 (E.D. Mich. 2003).
10. "Michigan School Bans Student's Anti-Bush T-Shirt," AP, Feb. 19, 2003.
11. *Barber,* Sept. 30, 2003.
12. "Teen Barred from Forming Anarchy Club, Wearing Anti-war T-Shirt," AP, Nov. 2, 2001; "Teen Anarchist Sues School Principal: The Verdict," Court TV News, Aug. 27, 2002; Emily Was, "The Consequences of Objection," *Washington Post,* Dec. 9, 2001, p. C1.
13. Kevin Canfield, "Emblems of a Nation of Discontent and Dissent," *San Francisco Chronicle,* Aug. 8, 2004.
14. ACLU of North Carolina, "Gay-Straight Alliance Clubs in Rowan County High Schools," http://www.acluofnorthcarolina.org/?q=student-youth-rights.
15. "Federal Judge Rules That Students Can't Be Barred from Expressing Support for Gay People," ACLU release, May 13, 2008, http://www.aclu.org/lgbt/youth/35265prs20080513.html. Transcript in *Gillman v. Holmes County School District,* Judge Richard Smoak, http://www.aclu.org/images/asset_upload_file971_35264.pdf. Damages of $1 plus legal fees awarded to Heather Gillman. The offending principal was David Davis at Ponce de Leon High School, Ponce de Leon, Florida.
16. David L. Hudson Jr., *The Silencing of Student Voices: Preserving Free Speech in America's Schools* (Nashville: First Amendment Center, 2003), p. 19.
17. Ibid., p. 17.
18. A student, sent home for a T-shirt saying "San Diego," submitted for review two T-shirts supporting John Edwards for president and one reading "Freedom of Speech." The school district rejected them. *Palmer v. Waxahachie Independent School District,* No. 08-10903 (5th Cir. 2009).
19. *Lowry v. Watson Chapel School District,* 508 F. Supp. 2d 713 (E.D. Ark. 2007), and Amended Complaint, Feb. 6, 2007; 2007 Jefferson Muzzles, Thomas Jefferson Center for the Protection of Free Expression, http://www.tjcenter.org/muzzles/muzzle-archive-2007/#item08; "Watson Chapel School District Student Handbook," pp. 27–29, http://watson2.arsc.k12.ar.us/District%20website%20material/Board%20Policies/StudentHandbook.doc.
20. Hudson, *Silencing of Student Voices,* p. 65.
21. Michael J. Steinberg to Todd Roberts, Superintendent, Ann Arbor Public Schools, March 25, 2008, http://www.aclumich.org/pdf/psasletter.pdf.
22. Federal Equal Access Act, 20 U.S.C. §4071. See also *Board of Education of the Westside Community Schools et al. v. Mergens,* 496 U.S. 226 (1990), and Mich. Comp. Laws § 380.1299(1).

23. David Jesse, "Anti–School Camera Group Gets Official Status," *Ann Arbor News*, March 26, 2008. Michael J. Steinberg, e-mail to author, April 27, 2008.

24. *Harper v. Poway Unified School District et al.*, No. 04-57037 (9th Cir. 2006).

25. "Student, School District Settle Lawsuit over War Posters," AP, Nov. 30, 2001. The school district agreed to pay $21,000 in legal fees, $2,000 compensation to the student, and $1,000 for his parents' lost wages.

26. Hudson, *Silencing of Student Voices*, pp. 89–90; *Saxe v. State College Area School District*, 240 F.3d 200 (3rd Cir. 2001).

27. ACLU, "Students' American Flag T-Shirts Are Protected Speech," May 11, 2010, http://www.aclu.org/blog/free-speech/students-american-flag-t-shirts-are -protected-speech; Lindsay Bryant, "Live Oak High School Flag Feud Entices Tea Party Rally," *Morgan Hill Times*, May 10, 2010, http://www.morganhilltimes .com/news/265549-live-oak-high-school-flag-feud-entices-tea-party-rally#.

28. For an overview of Confederate flag cases, see Michael J. Henry, "Student Display of the Confederate Flag in Public Schools," *Journal of Law and Education*, Oct. 2004.

29. *Melton v. Young*, 465 F.2d 1332 (6th Cir. 1972). The panel was divided, 2–1.

30. *Phillips v. Anderson County School District*, 987 F. Supp. 488 (D. S.C. 1997).

31. *West v. Derby Unified School District*, 206 F.3d 1358 (10th Cir. 2000). The Supreme Court denied cert.

32. *Denno v. School Board of Volusia County*, 218 F.3d 1267 (11th Cir. 2000).

33. *Castorina v. Madison County School Board*, 246 F.3d 536 (6th Cir. 2001). The appeals court overturned a district court judge's summary dismissal of the students' complaint and sent it back for trial. The school board then settled.

34. ACLU of West Virginia, "Charleston School Officials Violated Student's Rights by Punishing Him over a T-Shirt, Court Rules," June 1, 2005, http://www.acluwv .org/Newsroom/PressReleases/06_08_05.htm.

35. Some see government violating free speech on campuses in the 1995 Solomon Amendment, 10 U.S.C.A. § 983 (Supp. 2005), which cuts off federal funding to universities that deny equal access to military recruiters. The Supreme Court unanimously upheld the law against arguments that it restricted a law school's First Amendment rights to free speech and association, noting that debate and demonstrations over the recruiting were not impeded. The Court did not interpret the law as requiring schools to observe the First Amendment as a condition of funding. *Rumsfeld v. Forum for Academic and Institutional Rights*, No. 04-1152 (2006). The vote was 8–0, with Samuel Alito, who joined the Court after oral argument, not participating.

36. Title VI, 42 U.S.C. § 2000d, enacted in 1964, and Title IX of Education Amendments, enacted in 1972, 20 U.S.C. § 1681.

37. *Robert J. Corry et al. v. Leland Stanford Junior University et al.*, No. 740309 (Superior Ct., Santa Clara County, Calif., Feb. 27, 1995).

38. David Horowitz, *The Professors: The 101 Most Dangerous Academics in America* (Washington, D.C.: Regnery, 2006).

39. Barry Latzer and Jerry L. Martin, *Intellectual Diversity: Time for Action* (Washington, D.C.: American Council of Trustees and Alumni, 2005); Students for Academic Freedom, "Academic Bill of Rights," http://www .studentsforacademicfreedom.org/documents/1925/abor.html.

40. David Tatel, "Racist Speech on Campus and the Protection of First and Fourteenth Amendment Values," address, Southern University Conference, Boca Raton, Fla., March 23, 1991.
41. *John Doe v. University of Michigan,* 721 F. Supp. 852 (E.D. Mich. 1989).
42. *UWM Post Inc. v. Board of Regents of the University of Wisconsin System,* 774 F. Supp. 1163 (E.D. Wis. 1991).
43. *R.A.V. v. City of St. Paul,* 505 U.S. 377 (1992). A juvenile was convicted of a misdemeanor for burning a cross in the yard of a black family. Antonin Scalia found the law too narrow in its ban on a particular viewpoint.
44. *Iota Xi Chapter of Sigma Chi Fraternity v. George Mason University,* 993 F.2d 386 (4th Cir. 1993). George Mason is part of the Virginia state university system.
45. Matthew Fraser reads an excerpt on NPR that is slightly different from the quotation in the court record, http://www.npr.org/templates/story/story.php?storyId =8993111.
46. *Bethel School District No. 403 v. Fraser,* 478 U.S. 675 (1986). Thurgood Marshall and John Paul Stevens dissented.
47. Hudson, *Silencing of Student Voices,* p. 26.
48. *Thomas v. Board of Education, Granville Central School District,* 607 F.2d 1043 (2nd Cir. 1979). Jon O. Newman concurring, quoted approvingly by the majority in *Fraser.*
49. *Broussard v. School Board of the City of Norfolk,* 801 F. Supp. 1526 (E.D. Va. 1992).
50. Hudson, *Silencing of Student Voices,* pp. 73, 76.
51. *Boroff v. Van Wert City Board of Education,* 220 F.3d 465 (6th Cir. 2000) (Ronald Lee Gilman dissenting).
52. The American Center for Law and Justice filed an amicus brief, explaining in a statement: "School districts must not be entrusted with the authority to arbitrarily determine what student speech is offensive and off limits. In the future, that could put all student speech at risk—including speech that advocates Christian beliefs on any issue." David Masci, "Strange Bedfellows: Why Are Some Religious Groups Defending 'Bong Hits 4 Jesus'?" Pew Forum on Religion and Public Life, March 26, 2007, http://pewresearch.org/pubs/436/ bong-hits-4-jesus.
53. *Morse et al. v. Frederick,* No. 06-278 (2007) (Clarence Thomas concurring; Stevens, David Souter, and Ruth Bader Ginsburg dissenting). The five who carved out an exception to First Amendment protection—John Roberts, Scalia, Thomas, Anthony Kennedy, and Alito—were joined by Stephen Breyer only to find the principal immune from damages. Breyer would not have made it a constitutional question. The question of the justices' Catholicism has been addressed by Geoffrey R. Stone in compiling data showing huge disparities in abortion cases. Among ten justices appointed since *Roe v. Wade* in 1973, he notes, the non-Catholics have "cast twenty-one votes in support of abortion rights (75%), and seven votes to constrict those rights (25%)," while the Catholics have "cast only one vote in support of abortion rights (6%), and sixteen votes to contract abortion rights (94%)." (Scalia was so infuriated by Stone's article that he pledged never to speak at the University of Chicago as long as Stone remained on the faculty there.) The arrival on the Court of a sixth Catholic,

Sonia Sotomayor, who is regarded as liberal, may change this pattern. Stone, "Justice Sotomayor, Justice Scalia, and Our Six Catholic Justices," *Huffington Post,* Aug. 28, 2009. For Scalia's remark, made to the biographer Joan Biskupic, see Adam Liptak, "Stevens, the Only Protestant on the Supreme Court," Week in Review, *New York Times,* April 9, 2010. After the confirmation of Elena Kagan, who is Jewish, the Court had no Protestant justices for the first time in its history.

54. *Hazelwood School District v. Kuhlmeier,* 484 U.S. 260 (1988). There were only eight sitting justices following Lewis Powell Jr.'s retirement.

55. Mike Hiestand, "*Hazelwood School District v. Kuhlmeier:* The Supreme Court Decision, Its Aftermath, and What It Means for Student Media 20 Years Later," *SPLC Report* 29, no. 1 (Winter 2007–2008), p. 32, http://www.splc.org/report _detail.asp?id=1406&edition=44#end34.

56. Maggie Beckwith, "Twenty Years of *Hazelwood,*" *SPLC Report* 29, no. 1 (Winter 2007–2008), p. 19, http://www.splc.org/report_detail.asp?id=1399&edition =44. Judges do "forum analysis" to determine the extent of First Amendment protection. A "public forum," such as a town square, a street, or a sidewalk, is open to any speaker. A "limited" or "designated" public forum is opened by a government agency to particular people, such as students in a school paper and citizens at a town meeting. A student publication with this status has more protection than offered in *Hazelwood.* A "non-public forum," which may include a courtroom, or a newspaper under strict school control, affords the least protection for speech. School intent and historical practice are critical. The Hazelwood paper had never been labeled a forum, and the adviser exercised ultimate control, allowing the Court to find for the first time that a student publication was not necessarily a forum. Lower courts have subsequently overturned the censorship of school publications that are considered forums because administrators have historically taken a hands-off approach to their content. Hiestand, "20 Years Later," p. 32.

57. 2007 Jefferson Muzzles, Jefferson Center, http://www.tjcenter.org/muzzles/ muzzle-archive-2007/.

58. 2009 Jefferson Muzzles, Jefferson Center, http://www.tjcenter.org/muzzles/ muzzle-archive-2009/#item07.

59. *Desilets v. Clearview Regional Board of Education,* 137 N.J. 585, 593; 647 A.2d 150 (N.J. 1994).

60. *Dean v. Utica,* 345 F. Supp. 2d 799 (E.D. Mich. 2004).

61. Richard Just, "Unmuzzling High School Journalists," *Washington Post,* Jan. 27, 2008.

62. David L. Hudson Jr., "Hazelwood Still Extends Far Beyond Student Press," First Amendment Center, April 21, 2008, http://www.firstamendmentcenter .org/commentary.aspx?id=19943.

63. The district attorney, who was also named in the girl's suit, reportedly said that there was sufficient evidence, but that because the two boys were African-American, the blacks on the grand jury would not vote to indict them. *John Doe et al. v. Silsbee Independent School District et al.,* No. 09-41075 (5th Cir. 2010).

64. *Belyeu v. Coosa County Board of Education,* 998 F.2d 925 (11th Cir. 1993).

65. *Fales v. Garst,* 235 F.3d 1122 (8th Cir. 2001).

66. *Pickering v. Board of Education,* 391 U.S. 563 (1968).

67. *Lacks v. Ferguson,* 154 F.3d 904 (8th Cir. 1998). The teacher, Cecilia Lacks, won a jury verdict in federal district court, which was overturned by the Eighth Circuit. The Supreme Court denied cert. Hudson, *Silencing of Student Voices,* p. 82.

68. The teacher, Margaret Boring, at Charles D. Owen High School in Buncombe County, North Carolina, chose *Independence,* which "powerfully depicts the dynamics within a dysfunctional, single-parent family—a divorced mother and three daughters; one a lesbian, another pregnant with an illegitimate child," according to her lawsuit. She argued that the play was about "love, compassion, communication, and forgiveness—all family values." She lost 7–6 in a decision by the full membership of the Fourth Circuit in 1998. (Federal appeals courts usually hear cases in panels of three judges; thereafter, the losing side may petition the court to rehear the case en banc, "in the bench," or "full bench," that is, with all the judges in a circuit participating.) Hudson, *Silencing of Student Voices,* pp. 83–84; *Boring v. Buncombe Board of Education,* 136 F.3d 364 (4th Cir. 1998).

69. Diana Jean Schemo, "In Small Town, 'Grease' Ignites a Culture War," *New York Times,* Feb. 11, 2006; "Play Canceled; Mo. High School Drama Teacher Quits," AP, March 20, 2006.

70. 2007 Jefferson Muzzles, Jefferson Center, http://www.tjcenter.org/muzzles/muzzle-archive-2007/#item11.

71. Lisa Kocian, "Author Defends Memoir on Korea, Apologizes for Furor," *Boston Globe,* Feb. 16, 2007; Yoko Kawashima Watkins, *So Far from the Bamboo Grove* (New York: HarperCollins, 1986).

72. *Board of Education, Island Trees Union Free School District No. 26 v. Pico et al.,* 457 U.S. 853 (1982). Plurality opinion by William J. Brennan Jr., dissent by William H. Rehnquist.

73. The bill, championed by Republican state representative Lance Kinzer, chairman of the House Judiciary Committee, had not passed as of 2010.

74. Hudson, *Silencing of Student Voices,* p. 86; *Board of Education of Jefferson County School District R-1 v. Wilder,* 960 P.2d 715 (Colo. 1998) (Gregory Hobbs dissenting).

75. N. R. Kleinfield, "The Elderly Man and the Sea? Test Sanitizes Literary Texts," *New York Times,* June 2, 2002, pp. A1, A30. The discovery was made by Jeanne Heifetz, the mother of a Brooklyn high school student.

76. 2009 Jefferson Muzzles, Jefferson Center, http://www.tjcenter.org/muzzles/muzzle-archive-2009/#item05.

77. In 2010, a federal judge upheld a New York City school district's ban on teachers wearing political buttons. David L. Hudson Jr., "Hazelwood Limits Teacher Speech, Too," First Amendment Center, Jan. 30, 2010, http://www.firstamendmentcenter.org/commentary.aspx?id=22559.

78. Richard M. Berthold, "My Five Minutes of Infamy," *History News Network,* Nov. 25, 2002.

79. Diana Jean Schemo, "New Battles in Old War over Freedom of Speech," *New York Times,* Nov. 25, 2001; William Lobdell, "Academics and Muslims Await Results of Probe," *Los Angeles Times,* Nov. 26, 2001.

80. Amy Resseguie, "CSU Prof Withdraws from Teaching over Political State-ments," *Rocky Mountain Collegian,* Sept. 28, 2004. The complaining student, Heather Schmidt, approached him after class and claimed that he told her to switch courses. He quoted himself as saying, "If you are having trouble with what you've heard in today's lecture, I think you're going to have trouble with lots of things we're going to talk about in this class, and there may be other sociology classes that might better suit your needs." She took his advice. The college president later exonerated him entirely.

81. Jennifer Jacobson, "A Liberal Professor Fights a Label," *Chronicle of Higher Education,* Nov. 26, 2004.

82. Michael Janofsky, "Professors' Politics Draw Lawmakers into the Fray," *New York Times,* Dec. 25, 2005.

83. Ward Churchill, "Some People Push Back: On the Justice of Roosting Chick-ens," http://www.kersplebedeb.com/mystuff/s11/churchill.html.

84. Remarks by Chancellor Phil DiStefano at the CU Board of Regents special meeting, Feb. 3, 2005.

85. *Report of the Investigative Committee of the Standing Committee on Research Misconduct at the University of Colorado at Boulder Concerning Allegations of Academic Misconduct Against Professor Ward Churchill,* May 9, 2006. He won a jury verdict in state court, but the judge threw it out based on the univer-sity's quasi-judicial immunity and found that the plagiarism and fabrication were sufficient grounds for dismissal. *Churchill v. University of Colorado,* No. 06CV11473 (Dist. Ct., City and County of Denver), Judge Larry J. Naves, July 7, 2009. The judge's ruling was upheld by the Colorado Court of Appeals.

86. Quoted in Vartan Gregorian, "The Relevance of Academic Freedom," Herbert Gutman Memorial Lecture, City University of New York, Oct. 15, 2002.

87. Anne D. Neal, President, American Council of Trustees and Alumni, fund-raising letter, Dec. 1, 2004. Co-founders with Lynne Cheney included Senator Joseph Lieberman, former governor Richard Lamm of Colorado, the social sci-entist David Riesman, and the author Saul Bellow.

88. Bruin Alumni Association, http://www.uclaprofs.com/letter.html.

89. George Washington, address to officers of the army, March 15, 1783.

90. "Texas Boy Earns 'A,' Six Days in Jail for Halloween Tale," AP, Nov. 3, 1999. The district attorney was Bruce Isaacks.

91. Federal Bureau of Investigation, "School Shootings: What You Should Know," Oct. 6, 2006, http://www.fbi.gov/page2/oct2006/schoolshootings100606.htm.

92. Mary Ellen O'Toole, "The School Shooter: A Threat Assessment Perspective," edited by Arnold R. Isaacs, Critical Incident Response Group, FBI Academy, Quantico, Va., 2000, http://www.fbi.gov/publications/school/school2.pdf.

93. James C. McKinley Jr., "Students Hurt as 6-Year-Old Drops Pistol," *New York Times,* Apr. 20, 2011, p. A15.

94. *S.G. v. Sayreville Board of Education,* No. 02-2384 (3rd Cir. 2003), citing *Bethel v. Fraser* in allowing schools "to prohibit the use of vulgar and offensive terms in public discourse."

95. ACLU of Rhode Island, "Investigation Is 'Inappropriate Intrusion' on First Amendment, ACLU Says," Feb. 2, 2006.

96. *Ponce v. Socorro,* No. 06-50709 (5th Cir. 2007).

97. James LaVine, "Last Words," *LaVine v. Blaine School District*, 257 F.3d 981 (9th Cir. 2001) (appendix, Andrew J. Kleinfeld dissenting).

98. 2009 Jefferson Muzzles, Jefferson Center, http://www.tjcenter.org/muzzles/muzzle-archive-2009/#item05.

99. The two suicides were Ryan Patrick Halligan in 2003, who was called gay online and ridiculed by a girl who distributed sections of their personal instant messages, and Megan Meier in 2006, who hanged herself after being manipulated on Myspace by a neighborhood mother, Lori Drew, posing as an adolescent boy who first befriended her and then posted such remarks as "Megan Meier is a slut. Megan Meier is fat." A jury convicted Drew of violating Myspace's terms of service, but the conviction was overturned by a federal judge who ruled the law unconstitutionally vague. *United States v. Lori Drew*, No. CR 08-0582-GW (D.C. C. D. Ca. 2009), Decision on Defendant's F. R. Crim. P. 20(c) Motion. See http://www.ryanpatrickhalligan.org/ and "Parents: Cyber Bullying Led to Teen's Suicide," ABC News, Nov. 19, 2007; Student Press Law Center, "Md. Legislators Approve Bill Aimed at Curbing Cyber-bullying," April 9, 2008, http://www.splc.org/newsflash.asp?id=1734&year=; Rebecca Cathcart, "Judge Throws Out Conviction in Cyberbullying Case," *New York Times*, July 2, 2009.

100. 2008 Jefferson Muzzles, Jefferson Center, http://www.tjcenter.org/muzzles/muzzle-archive-2008/#item09. The student was Avery Doninger of Lewis S. Mills High School in Burlington, Connecticut. Neither the district court nor the Second Circuit would grant her motion for a preliminary injunction to rerun the election or appoint her class secretary. "Avery's blog post created a foreseeable risk of substantial disruption" at the school, the appeals court ruled. *Doninger v. Niehoff*, 527 F.3d 41 (2nd Cir. 2008).

101. Hudson, *Silencing of Student Voices*, pp. 54–55.

102. *Thomas*, 607 F.2d 1043. See David L. Hudson Jr.'s overview on cyber-speech at http://www.firstamendmentcenter.org/speech/studentexpression/topic.aspx?topic=cyberspeech.

103. *Klein v. Smith*, 635 F. Supp. 1440 (D. Me. 1986).

104. *Beussink v. Woodland R-IV School District*, 30 F. Supp. 2d 1175 (E.D. Mo. 1998).

105. *Emmett v. Kent School District Number 415*, 92 F. Supp. 2d 1088 (W.D. Wash. 2000). The site, named the "Unofficial Kentlake High Home Page," carried a disclaimer, saying it was independent and for entertainment. The expulsion was later converted to a suspension, which was erased from school records after the judge's ruling. The school board reimbursed the student for $6,000 in legal fees and paid $1 in damages.

106. *J.S. v. Bethlehem Area School District*, 807 A.2d 803 (Pa. 2002).

EPILOGUE: THE CONSTITUTIONAL CULTURE

1. Judge Learned Hand, address in Central Park, New York City, on "I Am an American Day," May 21, 1944.

2. Facebook did not violate the Fourth Amendment, however, because constitutional protections apply only to government actions, not to private entities. Nick Bilton, "Price of Facebook Privacy? Start Clicking," *New York Times*, May 12, 2010.

3. Survey descriptions from Ann Becson, ACLU associate legal director, interview with author, April 3, 2003. The ACLU refused to make detailed results of these polls public: Emily Whitfield, ACLU spokesperson.

4. The majorities in the four states who thought various provisions went "too far" were: 60–65 percent for secret indefinite detention, 51–55 percent for government collection of travel and medical records, 50–59 percent for FBI tracking of religious attendance, 51–58 percent for requiring librarians to reveal names, 53–61 percent for requiring Internet providers to reveal names. Belden Russonello & Stewart for ACLU, polling Nov. 20–25, 2003, sampling error plus or minus 4.9 percentage points.

5. A sample of 715, interviewed from Oct. 25 to Nov. 23, 2004. Margin of error plus or minus 3.6 percentage points. The Media and Society Research Group, Cornell University, "Restrictions on Civil Liberties, Views of Islam, & Muslim Americans," Dec. 2004.

6. The American Revolution Center, *The American Revolution: Who Cares?* 2009, pp. 16–17. The survey had a margin of error of plus or minus four percentage points. The right to own firearms was supported as "essential" by 45 percent, "important but not essential" by 35 percent, and "not important" by 19 percent.

INDEX

Page numbers beginning with 313 refer to notes.

A NOTE ABOUT THE AUTHOR

David K. Shipler worked for *The New York Times* from 1966 to 1988, reporting from New York, Saigon, Moscow, and Jerusalem before serving as chief diplomatic correspondent in Washington. He shared a George Polk Award for his coverage of the 1982 war in Lebanon and was executive producer, writer, and narrator of two PBS documentaries on the Israeli-Palestinian conflict, one of which won an Alfred I. duPont–Columbia University Award for excellence in broadcast journalism. He is the author of five other books: *Russia: Broken Idols, Solemn Dreams; Arab and Jew: Wounded Spirits in a Promised Land* (which won a Pulitzer Prize); *A Country of Strangers: Blacks and Whites in America; The Working Poor: Invisible in America;* and *The Rights of the People: How Our Search for Safety Invades Our Liberties.* He has been a guest scholar at the Brookings Institution, a senior associate at the Carnegie Endowment for International Peace, a trustee of Dartmouth College, chair of the Pulitzer jury on general nonfiction, a writer in residence at the University of Southern California, and a Woodrow Wilson Visiting Fellow. He has taught at Princeton University, at American University in Washington, D.C., and at Dartmouth College. He writes online at The Shipler Report.

A NOTE ON THE TYPE

This book was set in Fairfield, the first typeface from the hand of the distinguished American artist and engraver Rudolph Ruzicka (1883–1978). In its structure Fairfield displays the sober and sane qualities of the master craftsman whose talent has long been dedicated to clarity. It is this trait that accounts for the trim grace and vigor, the spirited design and sensitive balance, of this original typeface.

Rudolph Ruzicka was born in Bohemia and came to America in 1894. He set up his own shop, devoted to wood engraving and printing, in New York in 1913 after a varied career working as a wood engraver, in photo-engraving and banknote printing plants, and as an art director and freelance artist. He designed and illustrated many books, and was the creator of a considerable list of individual prints—wood engravings, line engravings on copper, and aquatints.

Typeset by Scribe, Philadelphia, Pennsylvania
Printed and bound by Berryville Graphics, Berryville, Virginia
Book design by Robert C. Olsson